Context as Other Minds

Context as Other Minds

The Pragmatics of Sociality,
Cognition and Communication

T. Givón

University of Oregon

John Benjamins Publishing Company

Amsterdam / Philadelphia

Library of Congress Cataloging-in-Publication Data

Givón, T.
    Context as Other Minds : The Pragmatics of Sociality, Cognition and
        Communication / T. Givón.
        p. cm.
    Includes bibliographical references and index.
        1. Pragmatics. I. Title.

    B831.5.G57 2005
306.44--dc22   2004058557
ISBN 90 272 3226 1 (Eur.) / 1 58811 592 5 (US) (Hb; alk. paper)
ISBN 90 272 3227 X (Eur.) / 1 58811 593 3 (US) (Pb; alk. paper)

John Benjamins Publishing Co. · P.O. Box 36224 · 1020 ME Amsterdam · The Netherlands
John Benjamins North America · P.O. Box 27519 · Philadelphia PA 19118-0519 · USA

For Linda and Nathaniel

Contents

Preface   **xiii**

CHAPTER 1: PERSPECTIVE   1
1.1. The conundrum of context   1
1.2. Russell's paradox   2
1.3. Objectivism   3
1.4. Relativism   6
1.5. Other minds   6
1.6. Recurrent themes   8
    1.6.1. Relevance and importance   8
    1.6.2. Similarity, analogy and metaphor   8
    1.6.3. Kind vs. degree: Categories and classification   9
    1.6.4. Abductive inference and analogical reasoning   11
    1.6.5. Explanation and understanding   11
    1.6.6. Teleology, purpose and function   11
    1.6.7. Figure/ground: Saliency, frequency and markedness   11
    1.6.8. Gradation, continuum and non-discreteness   12
    1.6.9. The semiotic relation   12
1.7. Early roots   15
    1.7.1. The mystics   15
    1.7.2. Plato/Socrates   17
    1.7.3. Aristotle   17
    1.7.4. Immanuel Kant   22
    1.7.5. Charles Sanders Peirce   26
    1.7.6. Ludwig Wittgenstein   28
1.8. Modern strands   29
    1.8.1. Cultural relativism   29
    1.8.2. Early functionalism   31
    1.8.3. Speech-acts   32
    1.8.4. Logical presupposition   32
    1.8.5. Modal logic and possible worlds   33
    1.8.6. Ethnography of Speech   34
    1.8.7. Developmental pragmatics   34
    1.8.8. Pragmatics and the machine   34
    1.8.9. Cognitive Psychology   35
    1.8.10. Evolutionary biology   35
1.9. Toward an integrated pragmatics of life, mind and language   35
    Notes   36

CHAPTER 2: CATEGORIES AS PROTOTYPES:
              THE ADAPTIVE MIDDLE   39
2.1. Preamble   39
2.2. Philosophical roots   41
        2.2.1. Platonic ('logical') categories   41
        2.2.2. Wittgensteinean ('flat') categories   42
2.3. Linguistic roots   43
        2.3.1. Generativity   43
        2.3.2. Emergence   44
        2.3.3. Psychological roots   45
2.4. Prototypes: The adaptive middle   46
2.5. The adaptive underpinnings of prototype-like categories   47
2.6. Some social consequences of natural categorization   51
        2.6.1. Essentialism and stereotyping   51
        2.6.2. Reasoning by feature association   52
        2.6.3. Over-generalization as an adaptive strategy   53
        2.6.4. Logically-faulty but adaptively-sound conditional reasoning   53
        2.6.5. Perspective effects on construed adaptive context   54
        2.6.6. Are social categories *not* natural kinds?   55
2.7. The cultural context of social decision-making   56
        2.7.1. The society of intimates   56
        2.7.2. Is the society of intimates still relevant?   60
        Notes   36

CHAPTER 3: SEMANTIC NETWORKS
              AND METAPHORIC LANGUAGE   65
3.1. Culturally shared generic mental maps   65
3.2. General design of the human communication system   65
        3.2.1. The cognitive representation system   65
        3.2.2. The sensory-motor codes   69
        3.2.3. The grammar code   69
3.3. The generic lexicon as a network of nodes and connections   69
3.4. Metaphoric or non-literal meaning   72
        3.4.1. The Aristotelian tradition   72
        3.4.2. Lakoff *et al.'s* "conceptual metaphors"   75
        3.4.3. The cognitive evidence   79
        3.4.4. The diachronic evidence   81
3.5. Figurative language and semantic networks   84
3.6. Adaptive motivation and frequency distribution of figurative language   86
3.7. Final reflections   88
        Notes   89

CHAPTER 4: GRAMMAR AND OTHER MINDS:
              AN EVOLUTIONARY PERSPECTIVE   91
4.1. Sociality, communication and other minds   91
4.2. Mental models   92
       4.2.1. Semantic ('procedural') memory   92
       4.2.2. Episodic ('declarative') memory   93
       4.2.3. Working memory and/or attention   93
       4.2.4. Interaction between memory systems   94
4.3. Grammar   95
       4.3.1. Developmental-evolutionary perspective   95
       4.3.2. Grammar as structure   95
       4.3.3. Grammar as adaptive function   96
       4.3.4. Communication without grammar   97
4.4. Grammar and other minds   100
       4.4.1. The mental representation of context   100
       4.4.2. Access to definite referents   101
       4.4.3. Access to the interlocutor's epistemic and deontic states   104
4.5. The selectivity of mental models   106
4.6. Other minds in an evolutionary perspective   108
       4.6.1. Overview   108
       4.6.2. 'Reasoning' by feature association: The wrong metaphor?   111
       4.6.3. Neurological incrementation: From old-brain to limbus
               to neo-cortex   112
       4.6.4. Transformations of the referent   113
       4.6.5. The puzzle of consciousness   116
       4.6.6. The adaptive context of representing other minds   120
       Notes   123

CHAPTER 5: REFERENTIAL COHERENCE   125
5.1. Coherence as mental operations   125
5.2. Coherence as grounding   126
       5.2.1. Grounding in episodic representation   126
       5.2.2. Cataphoric grounding   126
       5.2.3 Anaphoric grounding   134
5.3. Use frequency, markedness and cognitive status   139
5.4. Cognitive model   141
       5.4.1. Preamble   143
       5.4.2. Cognitive operations   143
5.5. Discussion   145
       Notes   147

CHAPTER 6: PROPOSITIONAL MODALITIES   149
6.1. Propositions vs. speakers   149
6.2. Epistemic modalities   150
  6.2.1. Recapitulation   150
  6.2.2. Presupposition vs. assertion   151
6.3. Tense   153
6.4. Aspect   156
  6.4.1. Perfectivity   156
  6.4.2. Preterit, perfect and deferred relevance   158
  6.4.3. Immediacy and affect: Remote vs. vivid   159
  6.4.4. Correlation between modality, tense and aspect   161
6.5. Deontic sub-modes of irrealis   161
  6.5.1. Preamble   161
  6.5.2. The subjunctive mood   162
6.6. The pragmatics of NEG-assertions   166
6.7. Evidentiality   168
6.8. Knowledge and power: The interaction between epistemics
     and deontics   171
  6.8.1. Epistemic vs. deontic speech-acts   171
  6.8.2. The social deontics of knowledge   173
6.9. Summary: Propositional modalities and other minds   177
  Notes   177

CHAPTER 7: DISCOURSE COHERENCE   179
7.1. Reorientation   179
7.2. Clause chaining   180
  7.2.1. Clauses, chains, and paragraphs   180
  7.2.2. Major clause-types in the chain   180
7.3. Chain-initial clauses ('coherence bridges')   182
  7.3.1. Pre-posed adverbial clauses   182
  7.3.2. Pre-posed adverbial phrases   184
  7.3.3. Left-dislocation clauses   185
7.4. Chain-initial vs. chain-medial clauses   186
7.5. Clause-level vs. chain-level conjunction   188
7.6. Chain-medial cataphoric switch-reference (DS) devices   191
7.7. Recapitulation: clause chaining and other minds   193
  Notes   194

CHAPTER 8: COMMUNITY AS OTHER MINDS: THE PRAGMATICS
            OF ORGANIZED SCIENCE   195
8.1. The scientist vs. the organism   195
8.2. Reductionist extremes in the philosophy of science   196
      8.2.1. Preamble   196
      8.2.2. Deductivist accounts   196
      8.2.3. Inductivist accounts   200
8.3. The pragmatics of empirical science   203
      8.3.1. Preamble   203
      8.3.2. Theory-laden facts   203
      8.3.3. Abductive inference   205
      8.3.4. Explanation   208
8.4. Multiple loci of pragmatic inference in the empirical cycle   214
8.5. The social pragmatics of science: Community as other minds   216
      Notes   219

CHAPTER 9: THE ADAPTIVE PRAGMATICS OF 'SELF'   221
9.1. Preamble   221
9.2. The essentialist self   222
9.3. The multiple self   224
      9.3.1. Henrik Ibsen and Erving Goffman   224
      9.3.2. Faust, Freud and the multiple self   227
9.4. The impaired self   228
      9.4.1. Schizophrenia: The unconstrained multiple   229
      9.4.2. Autism: The unyielding essence   231
9.5. The complex self as an adaptive strategy   234
      9.5.1. Evolutionary incrementation in framing complexity   234
      9.5.2. Between intimates and strangers   235
      9.5.3. Other minds and the ontology of 'self'   236
      9.5.4. Internalized other minds as a social-restraint mechanism   236
      Notes   237

CHAPTER 10: THE PRAGMATICS OF THE MARTIAL ARTS   239
10.1. Preamble   239
10.2. Adaptive realism: There shall be weeping and wailing
       and gnashing of teeth   239
10.3. The paradox of Karma   241
10.4. Tao and Wu-Wei   242
10.5. Wu-Wei as paradox   243
10.6. Wu-Wei as strategy   243
10.7. The paradox of the invisible leader   245
10.8. The yoga of form   246
10.9. The ritualization of form   247

10.10. Complexity: Seven paradoxes   248
    10.10.1. The paradox of *Yin* and *Yang*   249
    10.10.2. The paradox of discreteness and continuity   250
    10.10.3. The paradox or rootedness and lightness   250
    10.10.4. The paradox of speed and consciousness   251
    10.10.5. The paradox of attention and automaticity   251
    10.10.6. The paradox of diffuse attention   253
    10.10.7. The paradox of out-of-context practice   253
10.11. Closure   254

References   255
Index   275

Preface

In the forty-odd years since the publication of Austin's *How to Do Things with Words* (1962), pragmatics has proven itself to be in equal measures indispensable and frustrating. Indispensable because almost every facet of our construction of reality, most conspicuously in matters of culture, sociality and communication, turns out to hinge upon some contextual pragmatics. Frustrating because almost every encounter one has with context opens up to the slippery slope of relativity, thus sooner or later to the triumphant crowing of the absolutists, who insist that because nothing is 100 percent context-free, everything is 100 percent context-dependent; and that a systematic, analytic investigation of mind, culture and language is therefore hopeless, indeed misguided.

One task pragmatics is yet to measure up to, it seems, is how to account, in a principled way, for the organism's amazing propensity for stabilizing its frames, so that the appearance — or illusion — of firmament, of a stable reality, always emerges in spite of the ubiquity of contextual flux. This is indeed an evolutionary issue of the highest order, sitting as it is at the very crux of adaptation and survival.

The non-objective nature of "context", the fact that the frame around the picture is construed for the occasion through a ubiquitous if still mysterious judgement of "relevance", has been conceded by pragmatists from Lao Tse to Aristotle to Kant to, more recently, Sperber and Wilson (1986). But affirming that "context is a mental construct" only opens up a vast research agenda — how to describe the organism's adaptively-successful framing of reality. That is, how to account for the fact that those organisms who select particular frames thrive, but those who insist on viewing reality via other frames — in principle just as "legitimate" or "valid" — perish. To this day, the challenge of elaborating the neuro-cognitive — thus ultimately evolutionary — mechanisms via which contextual framing exerts its ubiquitous control over what is, to paraphrase Kant, "real to us", remains largely unanswered.

Almost from the moment my *Mind, Code and Context* (1989) came out, indeed even before, I knew — to my sorrow — that the book fell woefully short of my own expectations. Something was missing, something vital and pivotal, whose absence made it impossible to generalize from the pragmatics of individual cognition to the pragmatics of sociality and communication. The bridging principle was not there, the one that would connect first-order framing of 'external' reality, second-order framing of one's own mind, and third-order framing of other minds. That bridge, I believe, can be found in the work of the last two and a half decades — beginning with Premack and Woodruff (1978) — on so-called "Theories of Mind". With the bridge in place, the pragmatics of sociality and communication can now be re-formulated in terms of one's mental models of the mind of one's interlocutor or collaborator, a reformulation that is surely implicit in Grice's "maxims" (1968).

What I have attempted to do here is re-position pragmatics, and most conspicuously the pragmatics of culture, sociality, and communication, in a neuro-cognitive, bio-adaptive, evolutionary context. This is indeed a tall order, and the book is thus, inevitably, only an opening sketch. It begins with a compressed intellectual history of pragmatics (ch. 1). The next two chapters deal with the construction of generic — lexical–semantic — mental categories, primarily thus with 1st-order framing of "external" reality. Chapter 2 treats the formation of generic mental categories, that is with what cognitive psychologists know as "Semantic Memory". It outlines the prototype-like nature of mental categories, showing them to be an adaptive compromise between conflicting but equally valid imperatives: rapid uniform processing of the bulk, and contextual flexibility in special cases that are highly relevant. Chapter 3 elaborates on the network — nodes-and-connections — structure of semantic memory. Within this framework, the metaphoric extension of meaning is revisited, and the contextual-adaptive basis for metaphoric language is reaffirmed.

Chapter 4 outlines the core of the book, the interpretation of "communicative context" as a systematic on-line construction of mental models of the interlocutor's belief and intention states. Within this context, grammar is shown to be a pivotal instrument for automated, high-speed information processing. It is argued that mental models of the interlocutor's epistemic and deontic states are constructed rapidly on-line during grammar-coded human communication. The theoretical underpinnings of this approach to grammar, the so-called "Theories of Mind" tradition, is surveyed from an evolutionary perspective. Three subsequent chapters flesh out this adaptive approach to grammar, ranging over the three main foci of grammatical structure: The grammar of referential coherence (ch. 5), the grammar of verbal modalities (ch. 6), and the grammar of clause-chaining (ch. 7).

The last three chapters extend pragmatics somewhat beyond its traditional bounds. Chapter 8 sketches out the close parallels between the pragmatics of individual cognition (epistemology) and the pragmatics of organized science (philosophy of science). In the latter, the 'relevant interlocutor' whose mind is to be anticipated turns out to be the community of scholars. Chapter 9 contrasts two extreme theories of the "self" — one contextual-pragmatic wherein the self is an illusory, unstable multiple; the other of an invariant, centralized, controller self. Two well-known mental disturbances — schizophrenia and autism — are identified as the respective clinical expressions of these two extreme "selves". The neurological basis for the two disturbances, it turns out, is to be found at two distinct loci of the attentional network. An unimpaired self, it is suggested, must accommodate both extremes, and is thus — much like mental categories — a classical pragmatic-adaptive compromise. Chapter 10, lastly, deals with the contextual pragmatics of the martial arts, whereby one's every move is enacted in the context of the opponent's putative current states of belief and intention. The grammar of social interaction thus turns out to recapitulate the grammar of inter-personal communication; or is it the other way around?

In writing this book I have benefitted enormously from the vast knowledge and generous comments offered by many correspondents, colleagues and friends. Their help is acknowledged at the appropriate junctures throughout. Whether they approve of the final product or not, I couldn't have done it without them. Nor could I have done any of it without the tireless efforts of my long-time editor, Kees Vaes. And none of it would have been done without the two people who light up my life, Linda and Nathaniel, to whom this book is dedicated.

White Cloud Ranch
Ignacio, Colorado
August 2004

CHAPTER 1

Perspective

1.1. The conundrum of context*

> A context is a psychological construct.
>
> (D. Sperber and D. Wilson 1986: 15)

The de-stabilizing effect of context on the mental construction of reality has be-deviled biological organisms ever since the dawn of evolution, much as it has con-founded philosophers and scientists ever since the advent of the study of mind. The relativity inherent in contextual framing can play havoc with the organism's attempt to construct a stable, coherent account of experience. For atomic chunks of reality are but artifacts of their framing, arbitrary time-slices of the experiential continuum. If their frames render them utterly unique, how do we relate them? Or relate to them?

Yes, *that* one there-and-then was 'a snake'. It bit my now-defunct compadre, after which I killed it. Now, *this* one here-and-now — different in color, size and shape — is surely not the same one. Yet it is tantalizingly similar, along the very same dimen-sions that render it so different. Well, is it or is it not "a snake"? Will it or will it not bite? Will its bite be lethal? Should I kill it?

But the very same aspect of context, its maddening elasticity, has also made it possible to relate unique time slices of experience to each other by tagging some as tokens of the *same type*. Soon, relatively firm islands of similarity are extracted from their ever-fluxing context, gradually assembled into a body of seemingly sta-ble knowledge.

So, this one here-and-now is not the same one as that one then-and-there. In some absolute sense, therefore, it is neither a proven "snake" nor a sure-fire killer. Yet it is my construed contextual differences between the two would-be "snakes" — color, size, shape, space–time coordinates — that let me to extract their similarities. Likewise, the very same cylinder when observed from one perspective looks like a rectangle, from another like a circle. How do we know to ignore such radical differ-ences and decide that the two observations represent the very same object?

This feat of extraction, or abstraction — ascribing the variance to the frame, con-struing the similarities as an invariant picture — is what makes contextual framing biologically indispensable. For what is extracted is not any good old invariance or similarity, but only those similarities that have proven *adaptively relevant*.

But the core gambit of pragmatics — selecting the relevant frame — is also the source of its ancient conundrum. For it is the act of framing that accounts for both the flux and the invariance of our mental constructs. The challenge facing sentient organisms is how to, somehow, cobble the *right* frame around the picture, set the fig-ure in its *proper* ground, choose an *apt* point-of-view for a description, zoom onto the *relevant* perspective. Such contextual judgements may be logically arbitrary, but they are adaptively indispensable. The survival of myriad extant species attests to the adaptive validity of old framing choices made by their ancestors; as does the increasing level of stability, automaticity and genetic encoding conferred upon repeatedly-validated framing choices by one's evolutionary forebears.

Likewise, the seeming relativity entailed by that context-dependence of mental constructs is not a matter of principle, to be determined by logic, but an empirical issue to be resolved through the study of the frequency and stability of successful adaptive choices. A reductionist insistence on a forced either/or choice between 'objective' and 'relative' reality is a false framing manoeuver.

1.2. Russell's paradox

> There was only one catch and that was Catch-22, which specified that a concern for one's own safety in the face of danger [...] was the process of a rational mind. Orr was crazy and could be grounded. All he had to do was ask; and as soon as he did, he would no longer be crazy and would have to fly more missions. Orr would be crazy to fly more missions and sane if he didn't, but if he was sane he had to fly them. If he flew them he was crazy and didn't have to; but if he didn't want to he was sane and had to.
>
> (J. Heller, *Catch-22*, 1962: 54)

A picture is not fully specified until it has been framed, but the frame itself remains outside the picture. A figure only stands out vis-à-vis its ground, but the ground is not part of the figure. A map is useless without its scale and coordinates, i.e. without the point-of-view from which it was drawn; but the point-of-view is outside the map. An expression is only meaningful from a given communicative perspective, but the perspective ('I hereby say to you that . . .') is not part of the expression. These four metaphors of pragmatics are but special cases of the more general — if inadvertent — definition of pragmatics given by Bertrand Russell in his attempt to insulate formal logic from the ravages of recursive framing.

In his *Theory of Types*, Russell (1908) outlined a set-theoretical approach to description, his unintended stand-in for mental representation, that would skirt the contradictory effect of self-inclusion paradoxes, such as the celebrated *Epimenides*:

> Epimenides the Cretan said that all Cretans were liars [. . .] Was this a lie? (1908: 59).

Referring to similar paradoxes, Russell observes:

> In all the above contradictions [...] there is a common characteristic, which we may describe as self-reference or reflexiveness. The remark of Epimenides includes itself within its scope. If *all* classes, provided they are not members of themselves, are members of *w*, this also must apply to *w*.   (*ibid.*: 61)

The offending culprit, Russell goes on, are statements about *all* propositions, which must perforce exclude the next statement in the hierarchy of types, the one that affirms the last proposition:

> This, however, makes it clear that the notion 'all propositions' is illegitimate; for otherwise, there must be propositions [...] which are about all propositions, and yet cannot, without contradiction, be included among the propositions they are about.   (*ibid.*: 62)

Russell then outlines his — somewhat ungainly — set-theoretical template of all self-inclusion paradoxes:

> In this case, the class *w* is defined by reference to 'all classes', and then turns out to be one among classes. If we seek help by deciding that no class is a member of itself, then *w* becomes the class of all classes, and we have to decide that this is not a member of itself, i.e. is not a class. This is only possible if there is no such thing as the class of all classes in the sense required by the paradox. That there is no such a class results from the fact that, if we suppose there is, the supposition immediately gives rise [...] to new classes lying outside the supposed total of all classes.   (*ibid.*: 62)

Put another way (T. K. Bikson, in personal communication):

> The set of all sets that don't include themselves, does it or does it not include itself?

What Russell has given us is another version of Goedel's theorem: A system may be either complete or consistent, but never both. For an entity to be described finitely without succumbing to logical contradiction, a contextual upper bound must be imposed. One must frame the picture and then ignore the frame. One must insist on an arbitrary *closure*.

A system — and thus its description, as Russell's formal logic purported to be — is by definition a hierarchic entity, made out of a progression of levels each acting as a *meta-level* to the one embedded directly within it. Each meta-level frames some lower level. Within such a system, logical consistency can only be maintained if one disallows switching meta-levels (points-of-view, perspectives) in mid-description. In other words, a logically-consistent, and thus in principle incomplete, description can only operate within a fixed perspective, context, meta-level.

But human mental representation, and language as its most celebrated example, is notoriously replete with constant switching of perspective, with zooming in and out, with repeated acts of re-framing; as is the 'mental' representation of all biological organisms. Is human cognition — and natural language, as Russell was inclined to suspect — illogical, contradictory, unequal to the task of representing reality? Have biological organisms since the amoeba been sadly deluded? And how have a billion years of natural selection allowed them to get away with such a monumental folly?

1.3. Objectivism

> Now spoken sounds ['words'] are symbols of affections of the soul['thoughts'], and written marks are symbols of spoken sounds. And just as written marks are not the same for all men ['are language specific'], neither are spoken sounds. But what

these are in the first place signs of — affections of the soul — are the same for all ['are universal']; and what are these affections are likenesses of — actual things — are also the same for all men.

Aristotle, *De Interpretatione*

Russell's fellow logical positivist Rudolph Carnap shared Russell's low regard for natural language as means of knowledge representation, most emphatically of scientific knowledge. As a self-described *physicalist* (a latter-day species of Aristotelian empiricism), Carnap was only interested in a language that could be defined in terms of observables:

> The thesis of physicalism, as originally accepted in the Vienna Circle, says roughly: Every concept of the language of science can be explicitly defined in terms of observables; therefore every sentence of the language of science is translating into a sentence concerning observable properties.   (1963: 59)

Carnap's very definition of pragmatics — and by inference of context — thus relegates it to the domain of empirical observation, i.e. the objective context:

> According to present terminology, we divide the theory of language (semiotics) into three parts: pragmatics, semantics and logical syntax. The descriptive concepts mentioned belong to pragmatics; logical analysis belongs either to semantics (if referring to meaning or interpretation) or to syntax (if formalized).   (1950: 432)

Though the 'objective' frame may also be *language use*:

> If in an investigation an explicit reference is made to the speaker, or, to put it in more general terms, to the user of the language, then we assign it to the field of pragmatics.   (*ibid.*; cited from Morris 1963: 88).

In his later reflections, Carnap rued the split in 20th century analytic philosophy between philosophy of language and formal logic:

> Only slowly did I recognize how large the divergence is between the views of the two wings of analytic philosophy in the question of natural language versus constructed languages: the view which I share with my friends in the Vienna Circle and later with many philosophers in the United States, and the view of those philosophers chiefly influenced by G. E. Moore and Wittgenstein [...] In the Vienna Circle mathematics and empirical science were taken as models representing knowledge in its best, most systematized form, towards which all philosophical work on problems of knowledge should be oriented. By contrast, Wittgenstein's indifferent and sometime negative attitude towards mathematics and science was accepted by many of his followers, impairing the fruitfulness of their philosophical work.   (1963: 68–9)

And in an observation reminiscent of the idealization common to Plato, Saussure and Chomsky, Carnap consigns pragmatics to the domain of empirical investigation:

> The analysis of meanings of expressions occurs in two fundamentally different forms. The first belongs to *pragmatics*, that is, the empirical investigation of historically given *natural languages*. This kind of analysis has long been carried out by

> linguists and philosophers, especially analytic philosophers [...] The second form
> was developed only recently in the field of symbolic logic; this form belongs to *se-*
> *mantics* (here understood in the sense of pure semantics, while descriptive seman-
> tics may be regarded as part of pragmatics), that is, the study of constructed *lan-*
> *guage systems* given by their rules.   (1956: 233)

Pragmatics is grudgingly conceded a useful role:

> Nobody doubts that the pragmatic investigation of natural languages is of great-
> est importance for an understanding both of the behavior of individuals and of the
> character and development of whole cultures.   (1956: 234)

But for Carnap pragmatics remains a means to and end, subservient to the goals of
formal semantics:

> Many of the concepts used today in pure semantics were indeed suggested by cor-
> responding pragmatical concepts which had been used for natural languages by
> philosophers or linguists, though usually without exact definitions.   (1956: 234)

It is perhaps ironic that in imposing his constraint on formal descriptions — no
perspective-shifting in mid-description — Russell, in a wave of his magical wand,
exorcized the specter of pragmatics out of deductive logic. This intellectual gambit
yielded two results, the first intended, the second perhaps not:
- Deductive logic was rescued as a closed, internally-consistent system.
- Deductive logic was removed, once and for all, as serious contender for modeling,
  describing or explaining language and mind.

Put another way, Russell saved the instrument by giving up on its historic purpose.
His (and Carnap's) nemesis, Ludwig Wittgenstein, accomplished much the same in
his *Tractatus* (1918), pointing out that the propositions of logic can be all reduced
to either tautologies or contradictions. That is, they are purely analytic and thus in
principle not capable of representing human knowledge, scientific or otherwise:

> The propositions of logic are tautologies. Therefore the propositions of logic say
> nothing.   (1918: 121)

> This throws some light on the question of why logical propositions cannot be con-
> firmed by experience any more than they can be refuted by it. Not only must a
> proposition of logic be irrefutable by any possible experience, but it must also be
> unconfirmable by any possible experience.   (*ibid.*: 127)

> Hence there can *never* be surprises in logic.   (*ibid.*: 129)

Given Carnap's program of making formal logic the proper instrument for representing scientific knowledge, neither Russell nor Wittgenstein should have rendered
him much comfort. For where there is no surprise, there's no information (Shannon
and Weaver 1949; Attneave 1959). Closed systems are just that, immune to the accretion of knowledge. The open-ended pragmatics of framing and re-framing is the
only venue through which organisms can increase their knowledge base. As we shall
see further below (ch. 8), the same turns out to be true of organized science.

1.4. Relativism

It is easy to see now why pragmatics could be, and often has been, taken as license for unbridled relativism. If mental representation is but a process of framing and re-framing, objective reality ceases to be an issue. Since context is a subjective construct, constrained neither by logic nor by reality, in principle then anything goes. For reality is but a whim of the observer–framer, an artifact of arbitrarily chosen perspective. The spread of relativism in the 20th century into various academic disciplines presumed direct descent from the pragmatic philosophy of Kant, Peirce and Wittgenstein.

As elsewhere, the rejection of one brand of extreme reductionism often spawns its equally extreme and just as reductive converse. This is a sad fact in the history of philosophy and science, as well as an ancient logical trap, the notorious mis-construal of the one-way conditional:

$B \supset A$
therefore
$A \supset B$

But of course, A could just as well entail C, D or Z. One needs to remind oneself that logical necessity and/or objectivity are not necessarily the overriding issue. A perspective that is logically arbitrary may still be *adaptively unimpeachable*. And it is this adaptive motivation that has stabilized — objectivized — our Newtonian universe of time and space, sizes and colors, boundaries and shapes, gravity and inertia, motion and action.

If there is anything Relativity and Quantum Mechanics have taught us, it is that the Newtonian universe is objective only from a given perspective. But this perspective just happens to be the one most relevant to the adaptive needs of biological organisms. Logically, this perspective may be a mirage. But it is a stable mirage within which reliable, consistent survival bets can be made — and on the whole won — by large populations of countless species.

The reality, solidity, velocity and weight of the bus coming down the street is not a question of logic but a matter of survival. And, it just so happens, the relativistic organisms that refused to construe the bus as real did not live to tell the tale, nor have they left any descendants to perpetuate their relativism-prone genome. Natural selection has been, since the dawn of evolution, the ultimate arbiter of 'reality'. It testifies, vividly and conclusively, to the adaptive validity of some theories of 'reality' and the adaptive bankruptcy of others.

1.5. Other minds

> While Bill, if he is in pain, has every right to say that Bill is in pain, Arabella has not, because she is in pain[,] the right to say [that] Bill is in pain.
>
> (J. Wisdom, *Other Minds*, 1956: 227; brackets added)

> [...] we contrasted two cases of doubt as to whether a certain man, Smith, say, believes that flowers feel, namely (1) a case of *natural* doubt arising because the doubter knows only that Smith had once at a party said, "I believe flowers feel", and thinks Smith might have been saying this for the sake of something to say; and (2) a case of *philosophical* doubt arising because the doubter knows only *outward* signs of Smith's *inward* state, and feels that from these he can never be sure what that state is.
>
> (J. Wisdom, *ibid.* 1956: 1)

In an earlier foray into pragmatics as a meta-discipline (*Mind, Code and Context*, 1989), I took it for granted that two related features stood at the core of pragmatics, and thus at the core of the evolutionary adaptation called 'cognition':

- the construal of logically-arbitrary but adaptively-relevant frames;
- the consequent context-dependence of all framed 'reality'.

Taken together, the two certainly characterized the successful behavioral gambits of individual organism in their struggle to adapt to their inanimate physical environment. Out of the myriad random stimuli emanating from the 'real' environment, evolution has taught biological organisms — gradually, painstakingly, through numerous detours, cul-de-sacs and oft-lethal trials and errors — to selectively attend to, internally represent, and then respond to only a minuscule sub-set of stimuli, those that were deemed adaptively relevant in specific contexts.

While my old assumptions are, strictly speaking, still valid, they leave a major component of the evolutionary rise of human cognition, culture and communication outside the scope of the discussion — *context as the construal of other minds*. For the survival of social species is, by definition, predicated on cooperation and communication, and both of those are immensely dependent on access to — or at least the successful construal off — the interlocutor's mental states of belief ('knowledge') and intention ('predisposition to act').

The mental construal of the mind of the other has, of course, been implicit in all works on communicative pragmatics. Even the most logic-bound treatments of 'intensional logic' (Carnap 1956), 'definite description' (Geach 1962; Strawson 1964; Donellan 1966), 'presupposition' (Keenan 1969, 1972; Gazdar 1979), 'conversational implicatures' (Grice 1968/1975; Levinson 1983) or 'presumptive meaning' (Levinson 2000) are suffused with assumptions about the mind of the other.

Likewise, although my own earlier explorations of grammar-coded human communication (e.g. Givón 1989, 2001a) has often been couched, oft implicitly, in terms of other minds, I have often failed to acknowledge explicitly the absolute centrality of mental models of other minds to a realistic account of human cognition and communication. For the mental representation of other minds turns out to be the most ubiquitous and systematically-exploited facet of context in social interaction and communication. I hope this book goes some distance in redressing the balance.

The quotes from John Wisdom, above, are of course entertaining. But their profound, indeed endearing, empiricist reticence continues to haunt the discussion of mental models of other minds. In the burgeoning literature on so-called *Theories of Mind* (see ch. 4), what cannot be demonstrated by external means, or accessed through conscious introspection or verbal testimony, often remains taboo. A major re-orientation of the discussion of context — from the construal of physical reality to the construal of mental reality — is surely in order. Even more than external reality, social reality is not an objective phenomenon, but rather an intentional, purposive, framed construct.

The study of communication in its social setting has often fallen prey to a like empiricist reticence, whereby only the transcribed text or the recorded video — the reified speech situation — are conceded the status of 'context'; and where asymmetrical ('narrative') communication is deemed lacking in social context — since the 'objective' record shows only a single interlocutor. This throw-back to objectivism obscures the fact that the relevant social context during communication are neither the audible words nor the visible gestures, but rather the mental states of beliefs and intention of one's interlocutor — whether present or presumed. The text and the video are of course part of the empirical evidence. But the evidence should never be confused with what can be inferred from it (see ch. 8).

1.6. Recurrent themes

A number of recurrent themes have been traditionally associated with pragmatics. Without exception, they harken back to the central core of pragmatics — the dependence of mental representation on its selected frame, chosen perspective, construed context. In this section I will briefly survey some of the more durable *leitmotifs* of pragmatics.

1.6.1. Relevance and importance

These two partly overlapping notions, *relevance* and *importance*, are indispensable to the pragmatic program. They are both contextual subjective judgements that can be captured by neither deduction nor induction, but only by the third mode of inference, *abduction* (see 1.6.4 below as well as ch. 8). They are, much like context itself non-discrete, thus a matter of degree.

1.6.2. Similarity, analogy and metaphor

Much like relevance and importance, similarity and analogy are in principle impervious to deductive or inductive reasoning, dependent as they are on contextual judgement. Like relevance again, they are non-discrete, graded notions. In principle, anything can be similar to anything, and anything may be the analog of anything — if construed in the right context.

Closely related is the phenomenon of the non-literal — figurative, metaphoric — meaning. Metaphors are based on contextual judgement of similarity and analogy, and thus have no objective sense. They are constructed for the occasion, in specific contexts, on the fly. Or, as Lakoff and Johnson (1980) put it:

> These similarities do not exist independently of the metaphor. The concept of swallowing food is independent of the metaphor, but the concept of swallowing ideas arises only by virtue of the metaphor.   (1980: 148).

The same point may be found at the intersection of Aristotle's treatment of metaphor in the *Rhetoric*, and his context-dependent approach to similarity in the *Metaphysics*. Aristotle's dismissal of literal ('ordinary') usage as source of new information is indeed reminiscent of Wittgenstein's view of deductive logic in the *Tractatus*:

> Ordinary words convey only what we know already; it is from metaphor that we can best get hold of something new.   (*Rhetoric*, 1410b: 2250)

For Aristotle, metaphors are founded on similarity:

> The simile also is a metaphor [...] All these ideas may be expressed either as similes or as metaphors; those which succeed as metaphors will obviously do well also as similes, and similes, with the explanation omitted, will appear as metaphors.   (*Ibid.*, 1407a1: 2243–4)

But similarity is in turn dependent on the choice of relevant context. Thus, in discussing Socrates' question "Is gold more like silver than tin is, or is gold more like fire?", Aristotle (*Metaphysics*) observes that the answer will depend on whether the relevant context for similarity is 'precious metal' or 'color':

> [. . .] tin is like silver in color, and gold is like fire in so far as it is yellow or red.   (*Metaphysics*: 206).

Essentially the same point was made in Plato's *Hippias Major*:

> And didn't Heraclitus, who you yourself bring in, say the same thing too, that 'the wisest of men is seen to be but a monkey when compared to God in wisdom and fineness and everything else'?   (*Hippias Major*: 10–11)

1.6.3. Kind vs. degree: Categories and classification

Somewhat dependent on similarity and analogy is the issue of differences in *kind*, which set boundaries between types, vs. differences in *degree*, which set apart tokens within a type. This distinction, again wholly dependent on contextual judgement, goes to the heart of *categorization, taxonomy* and *hierarchies of types* (ch. 2). In spite of strenuous efforts by the logical positivists (e.g. Russell 1911, 1918), categorization and thus taxonomy are in principle impervious to deductive or inductive logic. As both Plato (*Hippias Major*) and Aristotle (*Metaphysics*) observed, all taxonomies are in principle dependent on our ability to tell 'major' traits, those that characterize differences in kind, from 'minor' ones, those that characterize differences in degree. But such a distinction is in turn dependent on contextual judgements of relevance, thus ultimately on the construed *purpose* of the taxonomy. As Ernst Mayr (1976) has observed in a more down-to-earth context (and, incidentally, in a stunning rejection of the Logical Positivists purported distinction between descriptive and theoretical statements; see ch. 8):

> Every biological classification is a *scientific theory*. Classifications have the same properties as all theories in science. A given classification is *explanatory* [. . .] A good classification, like a good scientific theory, has a high *predictive power* with respect to the assignment of newly-discovered species and the pattern of variation of previously unused characters.   (Mayr 1976: 427; italics added).

In Aristotle's classification of *scala naturae* one finds hedges that reveal the taxonomist's pre-empirical theoretical bias; that is, his/hers contextual judgement about central vs. less-central criteria, thus important vs. less important taxonomic boundaries. In distinguishing between the three *major* taxa — plants, animals and humans — Aristotle first considers the criterial properties (nutritive soul, sensory soul, or rational soul, respectively) to be absolute and discrete, arranged in a formal hierarchy of types:

> The power of self nutrition can be separated from all other powers [of the soul], but not they from it — in mortal beings, at least. The fact is obvious in plants; for it is the only psychic power they possess. This is the originative power the possession of which leads us to speaks of things as *living* at all; but it is the possession of *sensation* that leads us for the first time to speak of living things as *animals*.   (*De Anima*; J. Barnes, ed. 1984: 658; italics and brackets added)

> Plants have none but the first, while another order of living things has this *plus* the sensory.   (*ibid.*: 659)

> [...] and still others, i.e. man and possibly another order like man or superior to him, [have] the power of thinking and thought.   (*ibid.*: 660; brackets added)

That is:

> Humans possess reason, animals (including humans) possess perception, plants the nutritive/reproductive faculty, *threptike*, alone.   (Lloyd 1996: 67).

But even here, at the apex of nature's classificatory hierarchy, the first two criteria, nutritive and sensory soul, are eventually conceded to be a matter of degree, given the complex facts of biology:

> Nature proceeds little by little from things lifeless to animal life in such a way that it is impossible to determine the exact line of demarcation, nor of which side thereof an intermediate form should lie. Thus, next after lifeless things come the plant, and of plants one will differ fron another as to its amount of apparent vitality [...] In regard to sensibility, some animals give no indication whatsoever of it, while others indicate it but indistinctly [...] And so throughout the entire animal scale there is graduated differentiation in amount of vitality and in capacity for motion.   (*De Partibus Animalium*; Barnes ed. 1984: 922)

Only the criterion that sets humanity apart from all other living beings, possession of the rational soul (*nous*), remains absolute and discrete. And in treating lower sub-

taxa in all three major divisions, Aristotle allows as a matter of course for gradation, as well as for classification by similarity, analogy and metaphor (Lloyd 1996:
150–1).

1.6.4. Abductive inference and analogical reasoning

Logicians and philosophers of science ever since Aristotle speak primarily of two
modes of inference — *deduction* and *induction*. The first proceeds from the general
rule to its specific instances, the second presumably from specific instances to the
general rule.[1] But there exists a third mode of distinctly pragmatic inference, recognized first by Aristotle (see 1.7.3.5. below, as well as ch. 8) and re-christened *abduction* by C.S. Peirce. This is the mode of inference used in reasoning about relevance
and importance, similarity and analogy, hypothesis and explanation. In reasoning
abductively, one argues neither that something is necessarily the case, nor that it is
most likely the case, but rather that it *must* be the case — if the seemingly-chaotic
facts are to be interpreted coherently. The 'must' of abduction is but a promissory
note, a low-odds bet on one's intuition. It is thus also a bet on one's successful construal of the right context. Hypotheses are only validated *post hoc*, by the accumula-
tion of further evidence as well as by deductive and inductive reasoning about the
validity of the evidence (see ch. 8).

1.6.5. Explanation and understanding

Explanation and theoretical understanding are also, in principle, pragmatic notions;
first because they are the product of abductive reasoning; second because they always involve placing the phenomenon in a wider context; and third because the ap-
propriateness of the wider context can only be construed (or abduced) but never
deductively or inductively supported (see ch. 8).

1.6.6. Teleology, purpose and function

Intent and *purpose* are crypto-pragmatic notions, whereby the mind of some in-
tender is the construed context for a communication or an action. In much the
same way, the more subtle teleological notions of *function* and *adaptative motivation* are pragmatic — abductive, theoretical — constructs; they are hypotheses that
do not necessarily attribute self-consciousness to purposeful behavior. Such teleological notions often form the context within which behavior, cognition, communication — and biological evolution — are to be understood or explained (see ch. 8).

1.6.7. Figure/ground: Saliency, frequency and markedness

The notion of *saliency* is fundamentally pragmatic, since the saliency of a *figure* depends on how it stands out vis-à-vis some *ground*, i.e. its context. All other things

being equal, the figure/ground contrast is distributional, whereby the less-frequent, surprising figure stands out vis-à-vis the more frequent, predictable ground. This statistical skewing is the most fundamental link between cognitive psychology and information theory (Attneave 1959).

Likewise, the linguistic contrast of *marked* vs. *unmarked* is fundamentally a frequency-dependent figure/ground contrast, albeit with well-known structural consequences — that sooner or later the less frequent marked form also becomes the perceptually more salient one (Zipf 1935; Givón 1995, ch. 2).

1.6.8. Gradation, continuum and non-discreteness

Non-pragmatic approaches to description, thus to multi-level hierarchic systems, have always taken it for granted that categories are discrete. That is, that their membership criteria are governed by the strict laws of *non-contradiction* and *the excluded middle*. This approach is usually attributed to both Plato and Aristotle, in spite of the fact that both of them, as noted above, succumbed, at least on some occasions, to non-discrete categories and analogical criteria of classification.

In contrast, pragmatics has always been associated, whether explicitly or implicitly, with a non-discrete, graded approach to categories. While not all exponents of non-discreteness explicitly relate it to the core pragmatic notion of context, I would like to suggest that context is the real arbiter of non-discreteness. The argument runs roughly as follows:

- The contextual frame, being itself outside the picture, cannot be constrained by the frame-internal system of discrete categories. Whatever the outermost meta-level may be, it remains outside the classificatory schema.
- In principle, therefore, adjustments to the ultimate frame are made without regard to discrete categorial boundaries.
- If the frame can be adjusted gradually and non-discretely, the figure within it will perforce also adjust gradually and non-discretely.
- In principle, then, non-discreteness inside the frame is but the consequence of the non-discreteness of the contextual frame itself.

The necessary connection between contextual framing and non-discreteness can only be broken by 'discretizing' context; that is, by integrating the frame into the categorial schema inside it. But, as Russell would have surely protested, the minute such a manoeuver is accomplished, the erstwhile frame cedes its context status to a yet-wider, non-discrete meta-frame on the outside.

1.6.9. The semiotic relation

Any cogent discussion of semiotics should begin with the opening salvo of Aristotle's *De Interpretatione*, the paragraph that also launched philosophical empiricism and linguistic structuralism:

> Now spoken sounds ['words'] are symbols of affections of the soul ['thoughts'], and written marks are symbols of spoken sounds. And just as written marks are not the same for all men ['are language specific'], neither are spoken sounds. But what these are in the first place signs of — affections of the soul — are the same for all ['are universal']; and what are these affections are likenesses of — actual things — are also the same for all men.   (*De Interpretatione*, tr. by J.L. Ackrill; in Barnes, ed. 1984: 25)

At first glance, Aristotle seems to incorporates the language-user's mind into his semiotic equation. This impression is illusory, however, since Aristotle considered our mental constructs to be perfect isomorphic reflections of objective reality. No active construal, let alone subjective contextual effects, were contemplated.

C.S. Peirce's use of the third term *interpretant* in his semiotics is taken by some scholars (e.g. Morris 1938) to have transcended Artistotle's objectivist program, with the interpretant standing in for the contextualizing, framing, intending mind. But the validity of this claim is not all that transparent in Morris's rendition of Peirce, a rendition that merely recapitulates Aristotle's *De Interpretatione*:

> The interpretant of the sign is the mind; the interpretant is a thought or a concept. These thoughts or concepts are common to all men and arise from the apprehension by the mind of objects and their properties; uttered words are then given by the mind the function of directly representing these concepts, and indirectly the corresponding things; the sounds chosen for this purpose are arbitrary and vary from social group to social group; the relations between the sounds are not arbitrary but correspond to the relations of concepts and so of things.   (1938: 30)

That Peirce's 'interpretant' has spawned a cottage industry of baffling and oft-conflicting interpretations is not surprising, given Peirce's penchant for metaphysical turn of phrase. Morris (1938) goes on to assert that Peirce's semiotics "...prepared the way for the contemporary emphasis on rules of usage ... (1938: 31). Similar claims are made by Short (1981) and Shapiro (1983). While Peirce's general pragmatics program may have indeed had such an impact, it remains unclear whether the 'interpretant' itself ever transcended Aristotle's 'affectations of the soul'.

The semiotic relation itself, between a sign and it *designatum*, has been taken by structuralists (e.g. Saussure) and positivists (e.g. Carnap) alike to involve no framing mind. Indeed, Carnap's entire program in *The Logical Syntax of Language* (1937/1959) rests on the strict segregation of rule-governed syntax-semantics-logic from messy pragmatics (see 1.3 above). The same distinction is echoed in the work of more recent formal pragmatists, such as Gazdar (1979):

> Pragmatics has as its topic those aspects of the meaning of utterances which cannot be accounted for by straightforward reference to the *truth conditions* of the sentence uttered.   (1979: 2; italics added)

Even more cognitively oriented pragmatists seem to take the structuralist/positivist notion of 'code' for granted. Thus, for example, Sperber and Wilson (1986) argue, at times rather ingenuously, that there exist two distinct modes of communication:

(i) rule-governed *coding-decoding* communication; and (ii) context-dependent *ostensive-inferential* communication, suggesting, at least implicitly, that some natural — biologiocally-based — communication modes can somehow function without any pragmatics:

> We maintain, then, that there are at least two different modes of communication: the coding-decoding mode and the inferential mode [...] [though] complex forms of communication can combine both modes.   (1986: 27; brackets added)

This distinction, between the 'code itself' and the pragmatic inferences that govern its use, is a somewhat inelegant way of dragging the *contextualizing mind* back into the communicative transaction through the back door and without proper admission. Sperber and Wilson insist that the inferencing mind be conceptually segregated from the 'strictly-linguistic' code itself, even when in actual practice the two can never be too far apart.

The intellectual program of segregating an idealized linguistic code, on the one hand, from the context-sensitive pragmatic conventions that govern its use, on the other, is of course reminiscent of Chomsky's distinction between the idealized, invariant *competence* and the messy, context-dependent *performance*, itself indebted to both Saussure and Plato. A similar segregation is conceded by Katz (1977):

> [Grammars] are theories about the structure of sentence types [...] Pragmatic theories, in contrast [...] explicate the reasoning of speakers and hearers in working out the correlation in a context of sentence token of a proposition. In this respect, pragmatic theory is part of *performance*.   (1977: 19; italics added)

The most sensible comments on the intellectual program of segregating the rule-governed *code* ('logical' syntax and semantics) from the more messy, context-bound pragmatics of *usage*, are found in Levinson (1983):

> The fact remains that there are clear interactions between the organization of syntactic elements in a clause and pragmatic constraints of various sorts.   (1983: xi)

Levinson entertains various segregationist definitions of pragmatics, the most prominent being:

> Pragmatics is the study of those relations between language and context that are **grammaticalized**, or encoded in the structure of the language.   (*ibid.*: 9)

> Pragmatics is the study of the relations between language and context that are basic to an account of language understanding.   (*ibid.*: 21)

> Pragmatics is the study of the ability of language users to pair sentences with the context in which they would be appropriate.   (*ibid.*: 24)

He then goes on to conceded the empirical inadequacy of all segregationist programs:

> This amounts to a concise argument that semantics is not autonomous with respect to pragmatics, and that pragmatics provides part of the necessary input to a seman-

tic theory. But if pragmatics is, on occasion, logically prior to semantics, a general linguistic theory simply must incorporate pragmatics as a component or level in the overall integrated theory.   (*ibid.*: 35)

1.7. Early roots

Any philosophical doctrine that should be completely new could hardly fail to prove completely false; but the rivulets at the head of the river of pragmatism are easily tracked back to almost any desired antiquity. Socrates bathed in these waters. Aristotle rejoiced when he could find them. They run, where one would least suspect them, beneath the dry rubbish-heaps of Spinoza. Those clean definitions that strew the pages of *Essay Concerning Humane Understanding* (I refuse to reform the spelling) had been washed out in these same pure springs. It was this medium, and not tar-water, that gave health and strength to Berkeley's earlier work [...] From it the general views of Kant derive such clearness as they have.

(C. S. Peirce, "Pragmatism in Retrospect: The Last Formulation", in Buchler ed. 1939: 269)

1.7.1. The mystics

In the somewhat catty but still generous words quoted above, the founder of modern Pragmatism pays homage to his illustrious antecedents. These antecedents, however, go further back within Western tradition, to the pre-Socratic *dialecticians*. The dialecticians' program involved first the observation that reality was unstable, forever in flux and changing from one context to the next. This is rendered most vividly in the celebrated two fragments from Heraclitus of Ephesos:

The river where you set your foot just now is gone — those waters giving way to this, now this.   (*Fragments*, 41: 27)

Just as the river where I step is not the same, and is, so I am as I am not.   (*ibid.*, 81: 51)

What renders the river different is thus not only that time has elapsed and the water is never the same, but also, perhaps primarily, that the experiencing mind keeps changing its perspective.

A recurrent grand theme among the early pragmatists, East and West, is the mutual dependence of opposites, presumably because they furnish the context — *ground, frame* — for each other:

The poet was a fool who wanted no conflict among us, gods or people. Harmony needs low and high, as progeny needs man and woman.   (*ibid.*, 43: 29)

[...] from the strain of binding opposites comes harmony.   (*ibid.*, 46: 31)

The beginning is the end.   (*ibid.*, 70: 45)

The epistemological intent of the dialectician's unity-in-opposition thesis is even clearer in:

> Without injustices, the name of justice would mean what?.   (*ibid.*, 60: 39)

The dependence of truth on the speaker's perspective, a *leitmotif* of modern pragmatics, is well articulated in the anonymous manuscript *Divided Logic*, attributed to the Protagoran tradition:

> If we [all] sat in a row and said 'I am an initiate', we would all say the same thing, but only I speak the truth, since I really am one.   (Diels 1969, vol. II; cited from Haberland 1985; brackets added)

The pragmatic agenda of the early mystics is just as clear in the writings of Lao Tsu, the 6th century BC Chinese mystic, founder of philosophical Taoism and reputed author of the *Tao Teh Ching*. The first tenet of Taoist epistemology is the existence of two modes of understanding, one bound to the discrete categories of percepts, concepts, and words, the other transcendent and undifferentiated:[2]

> The Tao that can be told of is not the real Tao,
> Names that can be given are not real names.   [TTC, 1]

The contrast between these two parallel trends of reality — the one perceived, cognized, and verbalized, the other holistic, uncategorized and non-verbal — is drawn perhaps most succinctly in the *Tao The Ching*'s sutra 11. Unlike other Eastern mystics, Lao Tse concede the usefulness of mundane reality in a language reminiscent of the adaptationist argument noted above (1.3.; see also ch. 8). It is not the absolute reality of the perceived universe that is at issue, but rather its utility:

> Thirteen spokes unite at the hub,
> But the wheel hinges on its empty hole.
> One molds clay into a cup,
> But the emptiness within is what is used.
> Walls and a roof make a house,
> But the hollow inside is where you live.
> Thus, while the tangibles have their place,
> It is the intangible that is used.   (TTC, 11)

The second grand pragmatic themes of philosophical Taoism is the context-dependence of mental categories, illustrated, as in Heraclitus, with paired antonyms. Lao Tse considers all perceptual and conceptual pair-wise oppositions to be more concrete manifestations of the underlying universal *Yin-Yang* — female-male, respectively — opposition:

> Yin is the back of all
> And Yang its face.
> From the union of the two
> The world attains its balance.   (TTC, 42)

The mutual context-dependence of opposites is given first in terms of temporal framing:

What shrinks must first be large,
What weakens must first be strong,
What falls must first be high,
What loses must first possess.   (TTC, 36)

And, in words reminiscent of Heraclitus', the figure-ground nature of paired opposites is asserted:

When the world sees beauty, it knows ugliness,
When the world perceive good, it recognizes evil.
Thus,
The dark and the light reflect each other,
The hard and the soft explain each other,
The long and the short reveal each other,
The high and the low define each other,
The loud and the silent expose each other,
The front and the back outline each other.   (TTC, 2)

Anybody who has ever puzzled over the semantics of antonymic pairs could only
applaud.

1.7.2. Plato/Socrates

The inclusion of Plato/Socrates in the line of descent of Pragmatism is at first
surprising, given other facets of both Plato and Platonism (see ch. 2). Still, we noted
that in *Hippias Major* Plato/Socrates concedes the pragmatic, context-dependent
nature of the antonymic concepts such as 'fine' and 'foul', invoking Heraclitus:

> Don't you know that what Heraclitus said holds good: The finest of monkeys is
> foul when put together with another class, and the finest of pots is foul put together
> with the class of girls […] If you put the class of girls together with the class of gods,
> won't the same thing happen as happened when the class of pots was put together
> with that of girls? Won't the finest girl be seen to be foul? And didn't Heraclitus
> (whom you bring in) say the same thing too, that 'the wisest of men is seen to be a
> monkey compared to god in wisdom and fineness and everything else'?.   (*Hippias
> Major*; in Woodruff, tr. and ed. 1982: 10–11)

1.7.3. Aristotle

Despite his celebrated objectivism and his preoccupation with discrete categories,
strict classification and logic, Aristotle turns out to have been the most prolific classical pragmatist, touching, over the course of his far-flung intellectual agenda, upon
most of the major themes of pragmatics.

1.7.3.1. *Similarity, analogy and metaphor*

We have already noted above (1.6.2, 1.6.3) Aristotle's inherently pragmatic approach to similarity and analogy, expressed in both his epistemology (*Metaphysics*) and his biological writings (*De Partibus Animalium, De Generationem Animalium, Historia Animalium*).

1.7.3.2. *Non-discreteness and gradual change*

Likewise, we have noted above (1.6.3.) that Aristotle's confrontation with graduality in biology — in terms of both ontogenetic change (growth) and classification — led him to make major concessions to non-discreteness, as well as to analogical and metaphoric criteria for classification. Thus recall:

> Nature proceeds little by little from things lifeless to animal life in such a way that it is impossible to determine the exact line of demarcation, nor of which side thereof an intermediate form should lie.   (*De Partibus Animalium*; Barnes ed. 1984: 922)

Aristotle was never able to resolve the contradiction between the truth-conditional requirements of logical categorization laid down in the *Posterior Analytic* (non-contradiction, the excluded middle) and the rampant flux and gradations he observed in nature. At one point, he resorted the somewhat ungainly notion of the *synolon* ('undifferentiated whole'), which when associated with underlying essences is well defined, but when associated with real, growing, changing matter is undefined:

> The *synolon* is Aristotle's concession to the Heraclitean flux. It manages an existence of sorts even while it is coming-to-be or passing away. This is because it contains matter, the *sine qua non* for anything that undergoes a process of change. (Tweedale 1986: 5)

But as Lloyd (1996) points out, Aristotle's *synolon* remained a problematic, elusive, metaphysical concept:

> There is no definition (indeed no *logos*) of [...] the *synolon*, composite whole, in one sense, even though there is in another. There is definition of the essence [*eidos*], of what is called in these chapters of *Metaphysics Z* the *prote ousia*, the primary substance, of the *eidos to enon*, the inherent ['essential'] form [...] But there is no definition of the composite whole, the *synolon*, taken with matter, since precisely, it — the matter — is indeterminate.   (1996: 68–9; brackets added).

1.7.3.3. *The doctrine of The Mean*

Aristotle's doctrine of the mean ('the intermediate') in *Nichomachean Ethics* may be interpreted as the pragmatist's *Golden Mean*, whereby the extreme, pure cases are to be eschewed in favor of the delicately balanced, hard to grasp middle:

> In everything that is continuous and divisible it is possible to take more, less or an equal amount, and that either in terms of the thing itself or relative to us; and the equal is an intermediate between excess and defect. By the intermediate *in the object* I mean that which is equidistant from each of the extremes, which is one and

the same for all men; by intermediate *relative to us*, that which is neither too much nor too little — and this is not one, nor the same for all. For instance, if ten is many and two is few, six is the intermediate, taken in terms of the object [...] But the intermediate relative to us is not to be taken so; if ten pounds is too much for a particular person to eat and two too little, it does not follow that the trainer will order six pounds.   (*Nichomachean Ehics*; in McKeon, ed., 1941: 957–8; italics added)

Aristotle is once again confronted with the graded continuum, thus implicitly perhaps also with the problem of context, especially in making the intermediate 'relative to us' a contingent notion. This is even clearer in:

[...] both fear and confidence and appetite and anger and pity and in general pleasure and pain may be felt both too much and too little, and in both cases not well; but to feel them at the right time, with reference to the right objects, toward the right people, with the right motive, and in the right way, is what is both intermediate and best.   (*ibid.*: 958)

1.7.3.4. *Aristotle's functionalism*

While Aristotle's *De Interpretatione* (see above) indeed launched structuralism in linguistics, he is the intellectual progenitor of functionalist, adaptive biology, having single handedly disposed of the two dominant structuralistschools of Greek biology. The *materialist* school of Empedocles sought to describe and explain living organisms the same way as inorganic physical objects — by reference to their component elements ('atoms'). But Aristotle notes that chemical composition by itself won't do:

But if men and animals are natural phenomena, then natural philosophers must take into consideration not merely the ultimate substances of which they are made, but also flesh, bone, blood and all the other homogeneous parts; not only these but also the heterogenous parts, such as face, hand, foot.   (*De Partibus Animalium*; McKeon, ed., 1941: 647)

The *structuralist-proper* school of Democritus, in turn, sought to describe and explain living organisms by reference only to their component parts — tissues and organs. This, Aristotle argues, won't do either:

Does, then, configuration and color constitute the essence of the various animals and their several parts? For if so, what Democritus says will be strictly correct [...] no hand of bronze or wood or constituted in any but the appropriate way can possibly be a hand in more than name. For like a physician in a painting, or like a flute in a sculpture, it will be unable to do *the office* which that name implies.   (*ibid.*: 647; italics added)

Aristotle then outlines a teleological, functional-adaptive approach to biology, using the analogy of usable artifacts:

What, however, I would ask, are the forces by which the hand or the body was fashioned into its shape? The woodcarver will perhaps say, by the axe or the auger; the physiologist, by air and by earth. Of these two answers the artrificer's is the better, but it is nevertheless insufficient. For it is not enough for him to say that by the stroke of his tool this part was formed into a concavity, that into a flat surface; but he must state *the reasons* why he struck his blow in such a way as to affect this, and what *his final object* was.   (*ibid.*: 647–8; italics added)

And the need for form-function correlations is driven home again with the analogy of tools:

[…] if a piece of wood is to be split with an axe, the axe must of necessity be hard; and, if hard, must of necessity be made of bronze or iron. Now exactly in the same way the body, which like the axe is an instrument — for both the body as a whole and its several parts individually have definite *operations* for which they are made; just in the same way, I say, the body if it is to do its work, must of necessity be of such and such character.   (*ibid.*: 650; italics added)

In an altogether different context, trying to decide whether the soul of living organisms could be separate from their body, Aristotle observes that with the possible-but-still-doubtful exception of the faculty of thinking, all mental activities require that the soul always be *embodied*:

Thinking seems to be the most probable exception; but if this too proves to be a form of imagination or to be impossible without imagination [i.e. visual representation], it too requires a body as a condition for its existence […] It seems that all affections of the soul involve a body — passion, gentleness, fear, pity, courage, joy, loving and hating; in all these there is a concurrent affection of the body.   (*De Anima*, in J. Barnes ed. 1984: 642; brackets added)

The soul, site of will and purpose, thus becomes part of the functional-adaptive mechanism that accounts for the consistent pairing of bodily forms with their respective functions in bio-organisms:

That is precisely why the study of the soul — either every soul or souls of this sort — must fall within the science of nature [*physis*]. Hence a physicist [naturalist] would define an affection of the soul differently from a dialectician; the latter would define e.g. anger as the appetite for returning pain for pain, or something like that, while the former would define it as a boiling of the blood or warm substance surrounding the heart. The one assigns the material condition, the other the *form* or *account*; for what he [the dialectician] states is the account of the fact, though for its actual existence there must be embodiment of it in a material such as described by the other [the naturalist]. Thus the *essence* of a house is assigned [by the dialectician] in such an account as 'a shelter against destruction by wind, rain, and heat'; the physicist [naturalist] would describe it as 'stones, bricks and timber'; but there is a third possible description that would say that it was that form in that material with that *purpose* or *end*.   (*ibid.*: 643; italics and brackets added)

Aristotle argues repeatedly, indeed exhaustively, that what divides biological organism from inorganic matter is the possession of the soul (see also 1.6.3 above):

If now the form ['essence', 'definition'] of the living being is the soul, or part [aspect] of the soul, or something that without the soul cannot exist, as would seem to be the case, seeing at any rate that when the soul departs, what is left is no longer an animal, and that none of the parts remain what they were before, excepting in mere configuration.   (*De Partibus Animalium*, in J. Barnes ed. 1984: 997; brackets added)

The knowledge of the soul admittedly contributes greatly to the advance of truth in general, and, above all, to our understanding of Nature, for the soul is in some sense the principle of animal life.   (*De Anima.*, in J. Barnes ed.: 641)

In rejecting both extreme dualism and extreme monism, Aristotle seeks a third, admittedly hard to put across, alternative, whereby the soul is a necessary, inseparable *property* of the living organism, part of its *essence* or definition (see also 1.6.3 above):

[...] the soul is an actuality of the first kind of a natural body having life potentially in it. The body so described is a body which is organized. The parts of plants in spite of their extreme simplicity are organs; e.g. the leaf serves to shelter the pericarp, the pericarp to shelter the fruit, while the roots of plants are analogous to the mouth of animals, both serving for the absorption of food. If then we have to give a general formula applicable to all kinds of soul, we must describe it as an actuality of the first kind of a natural organized body. That is why we need to dismiss as unnecessary the question of whether the soul and the body are one: it is as though we were to ask whether the wax and its shape are one, or generally the matter of a thing and that of which it is the matter [...] As the pupil *plus* the power of sight constitute the eye, so the soul plus the body constitute the animal [...] the soul is inseparable from its body.   (*ibid.*: 656–7)

1.7.3.5. *Abductive inference*
As Hanson (1958) notes, Peirce attributed his third mode of inference, abduction, to Aristotle:

Aristotle lists the types of inferences. These are deductive, inductive and one other called *apagoge*. This is translated as 'reduction'. Peirce translates it as 'abduction' or 'retroduction'. What distinguishes this kind of argument for Aristotle is that the relation of the middle to the last term is uncertain, though equally or more probable than the conclusion; or again an argument in which the terms intermediate between the last term and the middle are few. For in any of these cases it turns out that we approach more nearly to knowledge [...] since we have taken a new term.   (1958: 85)

Still, it is not easy to decide whether the Perceian notion of abduction is really what Aristotle had in mind in the *Prior Analytic*:

By reduction we mean an argument in which the first term clearly belongs to the middle, but the relation of the middle to the last term is uncertain though equally or more convincing than the conclusion; or again an argument in which the terms intermediate between the last term and the middle are few; For in any of these cases it turns out that we approach more nearly to knowledge. For example, let A stand

> for *what can be taught*, B for *knowledge*, C for *justice*. Now it is clear that *knowledge can be taught*; but it is uncertain whether *virtue is knowledge*. If now BC ['justice is knowledge'] is equally or more convincing than AC ['justice can be taught'] we have a reduction; for we are nearer to knowledge, since we have made an extra assumption, being before without knowledge that A belongs to C ['justice can be taught'].   (*Prior Analytic* II, 25; J. Barnes ed.: 110)[3]

Put another way, the conclusion 'justice can be taught' cannot be proven by clean deduction, given the uncertainty of 'virtue is knowledge'. But since the hypothesized 'justice is knowledge' is somewhat plausible, and since it may yet be proven true, one has — potentially — gained some, albeit tentative, knowledge through the 'reduction'. We will return to this issue later on (ch. 8).

1.7.4. Immanuel Kant

1.7.4.1. *Extreme reductionism in Western Epistemology*
The source of our mental categories and what exactly they stand for is a question that had dogged Western epistemology since its inception, with two post-Socratic schools dominating the discussion in a sea-saw fashion for the first two millennia. *Rationalists*, following Plato/Socrates, took mental categories to be *innate* and the primal cause for why we perceive the world the way we do. Thus, in his knowledge-as-prior-memory argument in *Phaedo*, Socrates concludes:

> Then we must have had some previous knowledge of equality before the time when we first saw equal things and realized that they were striving after equality, but fell short of it [. . .] So before we began to see and hear and use our other senses we must somewhere have acquired the knowledge that there is such a thing as absolute equality.   (*Phaedo*, in E. Hamilton and H. Cairns, eds 1961: 58)

In *Meno*, Socrates asks Meno for a definition of 'virtue'. All Meno has to offer in return are multiple descriptions of virtue in different contexts, i.e. instances:

> If it is a manly virtue you are after, it is easy to see that the virtue of a man consists of managing the city's affairs capably, and so that he will help his friends and injure his foes [. . .] If you want a woman's virtue, that is easily described. She must be a good housewife, careful with her stores and obedient to her husband. Then there is another virtue for a child, male or female, and another for an old man, free or slave.   (*Meno*; in E. Hamilton and H. Cairns, eds 1961: 355)

To which Socrates retorts:

> I wanted one virtue and I find that you have a whole swarm of virtues to offer [. . .] Even if they are many and various, at least they have *some common character* which makes them virtues.   (*ibid.*: 355; italics added).

That common character is of course Plato's *essence (eidon)*, and what Socrates has just purported to demonstrate is that essences can not be extracted from our experience of mundane exemplars; by inference, therefore, we must know essences prior to experiencing reality.[4] Socrates' argument is further buttressed later on in *Meno* (*ibid.*: 370–1), where he invokes his fateful encounters with experts, who all seemed unable to verbalize on their habituated skills; so that one could not extract the essence of skilled knowledge by repeatedly observing instances of its mundane practice.

Empiricists, taking their cue from Aristotle's opening paragraph of *De Interpretatione* (see above), asserted the exact opposite — that our concepts of the world, including our knowledge of universals, arise through induction and generalization from perceived mundane exemplars. This is driven home in the conclusion to the *Posterior Analytic*, one of the earliest systematic treatments of scientific inquiry:

> Thus the states [of knowledge] neither belong in us in a determinate form, nor come about from other states that are more cognitive; but they come about from perception — as in a battle when a rout occurs, if one man makes a stand another does and then another, until a position of strength is reached. And the soul is such to be undergoing this […] When one of the undifferentiated things makes a stand, there is a primitive universal in the mind (for though one perceives the particulars, perception is of the universal — e.g. of man but not of Callias the man […] Thus it is clear that it is necessary for us to become familiar with [mental universals] by induction; for perception too instills universals this way.   (*Posterior Analytic* II; in J. Barnes ed. 1984: 166).

While at opposite ends of the epistemological chasm, rationalist and empiricist philosophers have nonetheless tended to share two fundamental assumptions about mental categories, assumptions that set them apart from the pre-Socratic (and Eastern) mystics:

- **Separateness of mind from world**: The mind and the world — internal and external — are distinct and separate entities brooking *no direct access* from one to the other.
- **Stability of mental categories**: Categories of the mind — be they Plato's innate essences or Aristotle's perceived forms — are universal, discrete, and absolute, with membership adjudicated by rigid — necessary and sufficient — criteria which members either do or do not abide by; with contradiction barred and the middle excluded.

With the stage thus set, rationalists and empiricists did battle for two millennia. An obscure early skirmish took place in 3rd century AD medicine, in the context of a nascent philosophy of science (see Walzer and Frede, tr. and ed., 1985).[5] Within the confines of the Church, rationalism gained the upper hand in the early Middle Ages with St. Augustine, then empiricism in the 12th century with St. Thomas Aquinas.

Rationalism rebounded in the 17th century with Descartes and then Leibnitz,[6] but empiricism regained grounds in the 18th century with Hume and Locke. Rationalism rose again in the 19th century with the German Romantics, to be slapped back rudely in the early 20th century by the Logical Positivists (Russell, Carnap), Behaviorists (Watson, Skinner) and Structuralists (Bloomfield). Whereby extreme rationalism countered at the latter half of the century with Chomsky and Katz.

Between the two ever-oscillating extremes, Kant's is the first and most conspicuous attempt at a non-reductive middle-ground resolution, thus the opening to modern pragmatics.[7]

1.7.4.2. *The source of mental categories*

Kant pointed out that neither sensory experience nor innate ideas could by themselves account for how we come to know. Thus, following Kemp's (1968) interpretation of the *Critique of Pure Knowledge*:

> Human knowledge arises through the *joint functioning* of intuition (the product of sensibility) ['perception'][8] and concept (the product of understanding). Sensibility is a passive receptivity, the power of receiving representations of the objects by which it is affected; understanding is an active spontaneity, the power of exercising thought over objects given us in sensible intuition. Neither by itself gives us knowledge: 'Thoughts without ['perceptual'] contents are empty', says Kant in a famous phrase (KRV A51 B75), 'intuitions without concepts are blind' [...] (Kemp 1968: 16; italics and brackets added)

That is,

> Concepts without percepts are empty, percepts without concepts are blind.[9]

Kant's middle-ground epistemology stresses the interactive, mutually-dependent ('dialectic') relation between percepts and concepts; they form the respective *contexts* for each other, within which each receives its relevant interpretation. None is by itself a viable prime. Kant's contribution thus lies in his attempt to do away with the artificial mind-vs.-world dichotomy and, instead, suggests a *constructivist* view of 'reality':

> We do not find them [our sense impressions of the worlds] already organized [...] but rather organize them ourselves [...] [*ibid.*: 23]

> [...]'the order and regularity in the appearance, which we entitle *nature*, we introduce ourselves. We could never find them in appearance, had not we ourselves, or the nature of our mind, originally set them there' (A125) [...] [*ibid.*: 32]

> Our empirical knowledge has two sources, sensibility and understanding. If our mind consisted of nothing but the passive ability to receive sensations, we should have a manifold multiplicity of intuitions, but no knowledge of what the manifold contained [...] [*ibid.*: 23]

1.7.4.3. *Kant's apriori-synthetic as context-dependent perspective*

Following in Aristotle's footsteps, Kant discusses *analytic* knowledge, which comes to us by knowing the definitions of terms or the rules of logic or games. Such knowledge is in principle tautological (viz. Wittgenstein's *Tractatus*), thus contrasting with factual or *synthetic* knowledge. He then introduces the notion of *apriori-synthetic* knowledge of facts that are always true of this world, but not logically necessary. The latter is Kant's *transcendental schema* of space and time, the underpinnings of our perceptual/conceptual apparatus, and thus the pre-condition to all possible experience of this world. Possible experience *presupposes* such a schema, rather than comprises it. The schema is not logically necessary, but is rather a fact of this particular world. It is thus the *context* within which all mundane experience is possible. The a-priori — thus presumably innate — nature of the transcendental schema makes Kant's argument in the *Critique of Pure Reason* seem like a recapitulation of Platonism:

> the representation of space must be presupposed. The representation of space cannot, therefore, be empirically obtained from the relations of outer appearance. On the contrary, this outer experience is itself possible at all only through that representation.   (Smith 1929/1973: 68)

It is possible to interpret Kant's transcendental schema as the innate product of evolution, born of the species' adaptive experience of this rather than any other world. At least in principle, this is not an objectivist view:

> It is, therefore, only from the human standpoint that we can speak of space, of extended things etc. If we depart from the *subjective condition* under which we alone can have outer intuition [...] the representation of space stands for nothing whatsoever.   (*ibid.*, p. 71; italics added)

Our perspective on the outside world is thus relative and context-dependent:

> we cannot judge in regard to the intuitions of other thinking beings, whether they are bound by the same conditions as those which limit our intuition and which *for us* are universally valid. If we add to the concept of the *subject* of a judgement the *limitation* under which the judgement is made, the judgement is then unconditionally valid.   (*ibid.*: 72)

In other words, a judgement — knowledge, description — is only valid ('fully characterized') if the subject making it, and his/her point of view (context) are taken into account. This is certainly a clear articulation of a pragmatic, context-dependent theory of knowledge.

Kant's caution about the low likelihood of our ever coming to know *the thing for itself* — as distinct from *the thing for us* — may thus be viewed not as just an instance of healthy Lockean skepticism, but as an early precursor of pragmatics. Kant is willing to concede the empiricists the existence of something out there that stimulates our sensory perception. For a constructivist, this is a safe bet, an abduction from the mere existence of experience. The thing for itself, however, remains unavailable to our limited perspective:

> the most the understanding can achieve *a priori* is to anticipate the form of a possible experience in general' (A246 B303). It does not give us knowledge of things as they are in themselves, but only of things as they appear to us.   (Kemp 1968: 38)

1.7.5. Charles Sanders Peirce

Charles Sanders Peirce is generally acknowledged as the Godfather of modern pragmatism, with insights ranging all over the pragmatic agenda. What follows is but a brief enumeration of his main contributions.

1.7.5.1. *Abductive inference*

Ever since Plato and Aristotle, empiricists have tended to emphasize *induction* as the prime mode of obtaining knowledge, while rationalists have tended to emphasize *deduction*. Echoing Kant's rejection of both reductionist extremes, Peirce resuscitated Aristotle's third mode, *apagoge* ('reduction'), which he rechristened *abduction*. This is the mode of arguing by hypothesis, often by analogy. It is thus a pragmatic mode *par excellence*, dependent as it is on notions of similarity and/or relevance (Hanson 1958; see ch. 8).

1.7.5.2. *The interpretant as a third term in semiotics*

As noted earlier above (1.6.9.), to the extent that Peirce's notion of *interpretant* as the third term in the semiotic equation is distinct from Aristotle's perfect-mirror mind, it may be interpreted as a stand in for the *construed context*.

1.7.5.3. *Non-discrete, context-dependent categories*

Peirce's well documented penchant for discrete trichotomies leaves off a distinctly Platonic odor. Nonetheless, in his treatment of a number of sub-areas of pragmatics, he comes down — in the final analysis — on the side of non-discrete, context-dependent categorization. His treatment of iconic signs, for example, hinges on similarity, which both Plato and Aristotle conceded was a pragmatic, non-discrete, context dependent notion (see 1.6.2. above).

Peirce's divided icons into three main types — picture, diagram, metaphor, with the difference explained in his somewhat lugubrious terminology:

> Hypoicons may be roughly divided according to the mode of Firstness of which they partake. Those which partake of simple qualities, or first firstness, are *images*; those which represent [only] the relations, mainly dyadic, or so regarded, of the parts of one thing by analogous relations in their own parts, are *diagrams*; those that represent the representative character of a representamen by representing a parallelism in something else, are *metaphors*.   (Buchler 1939: 105).

The three types of icons are implicitly just three points along a continuum of generality (i.e. of concreteness-abstractness; Givón 1989, ch. 3). Whether Peirce intended such an interpretation explicitly remains a matter of conjecture. Buchler (1939) seems to suggest context-mediate meaning:

> A term has meaning, in other words, if it is definable by other terms describing sensible properties. The way in which, generally speaking, these other terms, which may not be in turn thus defined, acquire meaning, is by being associated or correlated in their *usage*, according to empirical conventions.   (1939: 113; italics added)

And further:

> Peirce's emphasis on 'percept' and 'operation' is in effect an emphasis that meaning
> is something *public*. We properly explain the meaning of a term to someone not by
> eloquently attempting to evoke familiar images in his mind, but by prescribing how
> he can gain perceptual acquaintance with the word denoted. The appeal is not pri-
> marily to imagination but to tests that can be undertaken by everybody.   (*ibid.*:
> 115).

With sufficient leniency, one may detect an echo of post-Wittgenstein Philosophy
of Ordinary Language (see further below). Peirce may have indeed considered categorial space to be scalar, a suggestion implicit in two key components upon which,
he believed, meaning was founded — circumstances and habits. Both are graded,
non-discrete:

> Mill says that it means that if in all circumstances attending two phenomena are the
> same, they will be alike. But taken strictly this means absolutely nothing, since no
> two phenomena ever can happen in circumstances precisely alike, nor are two phe-
> nomena precisely alike.   (*ibid.*: 221)

> Habits have grades of strength varying for complete dissociation to inseparable
> association. These grades are mixtures of promptitudes of action, say excitability
> and other ingredients [...] Habits change often consists of raising or lowering the
> strength of habit.   (*ibid.*: 277–8).

Of similar import is Peirce's discussion of vagueness:

> Logicians have too much neglected the study of *vagueness*, not suspecting the im-
> portant part it plays in mathematical thought [...] Wherever degree or any other
> possibility of continuous variation subsists, absolute precision is impossible. Much
> else must be vague, because no man's interpretation of words is based on exactly
> the same experience as any other man's.   (*ibid.*: 294–5)

Finally, in his discussion of natural categories, such as biological classification,
Peirce anticipates the modern theory of *prototypes* (Rosch 1973a, b; see ch. 2). The
crucial ingredient is his observation on the role of *frequency distribution* and the
clustering of token populations around the categorial mean:

> It may be quite impossible to draw a sharp line of demarcation between two classes,
> although they are real and natural classes in strict truth. Namely, this will happen
> when the form about which the individuals of one class cluster is not so unlike
> the form about which the individuals of another class cluster, but the variations
> from each middling form may not precisely agree. In such a case, we may know in
> regard to any intermediate form what proportion of the objects of that form has
> one *purpose* and what proportion the other; but unless we have some supplemen-
> tary information we cannot tell which one had one *purpose* and which one the
> other.   (Peirce 1931: 87–8; italics added)

1.7.6. Ludwig Wittgenstein

Wittgenstein is the last and most celebrated, if controversial, figure in the intellectual upheaval that ushered in modern pragmatics. His specific contributions to a pragmatic theory of mental categories will be discussed later on (ch. 2). His meteoric burst onto the scene with *Tractatus Logico Philosophicus* (1918) effectively derailed Russell's Logical Positivist program. His 'late' reincarnation with *Philosophical Investigations* (1953) was a frontal attack on Platonism and had an enormous impact on the cognitive sciences, particularly psychology, anthropology and linguistics (as well as, in a less salutary way, on a wide swath of the humanities and social sciences). In the space below I will confine myself to summarizing only two major points that constitute, in my judgement, the core of Wittgenstein's contribution to the modern pragmatic agenda.

1.7.6.1. *The rejection of deductive logic as a means for transacting new information*

In his *Tractatus* (1918), a book that is often — mistakenly — subsumed under Logical Positivism, Wittgenstein observed in passing that the propositions of deductive logic could be reduced to either *tautologies* or *contradictions* (see sec. 1.3. above). Neither, he points out, could serve to transact new knowledge. This was not a novel idea. The closing pages of Aristotle's *Posterior Analytic* make very much the same point, albeit in a different context.

Now, since the Positivist agenda of Russell and Carnap hinged, in large measure, on the contention that truth-conditional logic was the proper language for characterizing knowledge and science, Wittgenstein, probably unintentionally, came tantalizingly close to defining the main tenet of the pragmatics of communication: that new information, the 'figure', can only be understood vis-à-vis what is already known, presupposed, or taken for granted as 'ground' (Shannon and Weaver 1949). Neither Russell nor Carnap had deigned to incorporate the presupposed 'ground' into their logical framework. They both relegated it to the neverland of pragmatics, explicitly in Carnap's *Logical Syntax*, implicitly in Russell's *Theory of Types* (see sec. 1.2. above).

1.7.6.2. The attack on Platonic categories

Wittgenstein's contribution to pragmatics is of course more explicitly associated with the *Investigations* (1953), which can be factored out into three interlocking pragmatic themes:

- The contextual, intentional, frame-dependent nature of meaning.
- The non-discreteness and scalarity of semantic features.
- The 'family resemblance' metaphor for mental categories.

All three will be discussed in some detail later on (Ch. 2).

1.8. Modern strands

In retrospect, the pragmatic agenda of the last half-century may be likened to a dam burst. Many of the streams feeding into the now-swollen river, to borrow Peirce's metaphor, had been meandering, sluggish and unobtrusive, for a long time, cumulating leisurely behind the high dam of Platonic essentialism and deductive logic. Somewhere along the way, the flow began to thicken, the tempo to pick up. Soon the dam bursts. Quantity into quality?

In this section I will recount, alas only briefly, some of the more conspicuous rivulets that fed into the modern pragmatic explosion. The account is not meant to be comprehensive, a task I do not feel equal too. For by the latter half of the 20th century, pragmatics had acquired the somewhat unenviable status of a *zeitgeist*. As in the case of other ghosts, it is not easy to tell the inspired vision from the deluded mirage.

1.8.1. Cultural relativism

The balance between universality and diversity of the human mind easily translates into the question of how universal — as against group-specific — human culture is. As noted above (sec. 1.3.), Aristotle in *De Interpretatione* had opted for the universality of mind but the group-specificity of language, given the manifest cross-cultural variability of lexical coding.

But the question can just as easily translate into that of naturalness vs. arbitrariness, respectively. Here modern structuralism — cleaving to Saussure's dogma of arbitrariness of the linguistic sign — harkens back to *De Interpretatione*. In Plato's *Cratylus*, the eponymous character himself argues, with Aristotle, for the arbitrariness (*nomos*) — thus non-universality — thesis; while Socrates, perhaps in jest, argues for naturalness (*physis*) and universality, an argument that fed back into the doctrine of innate essences.

When the serious empirical study of cross-cultural and cross-linguistic diversity commenced in the 19th century, early pioneers such as von Humboldt and Whitney were still under the sway of Platonic (Cartesian, German Romantic) mentalism and universalism, a position wholly compatible with the *Cratylus* argument for naturalness. Their interpretation of cross-linguistic diversity often translated into the assumption that if language structure varied from one culture to the next, so must the construal of reality. And with the advent of Darwin, a natural framework now presented itself for explaining human linguistic-cultural diversity — environmental adaptation.

Some of the towering figures of 19th century linguistics, such as W. von Humboldt (1838) and Paul (1890), wound up holding onto the somewhat contradictory belief in *both* universality and environmental determinism. But toward the end of the century, the growing impact of newly-discovered linguistic and cultural diversity led to the re-emergence — after two millennia of slumber — of Aristotle's structuralist dogma of *arbitrariness*. As Leonard Bloomfield, the patriarch of American structuralism, put it:

> North of Mexico alone there are dozens of totally unrelated groups of languages, presenting the most varied types of structure. In the stress of recording utterly strange forms of speech, one soon learns that philosophical presuppositions were only a hindrance [...] The only useful generalizations about language are inductive generalizations.   (Bloomfield 1933: 19–20)

The so-called Sapir-Whorf *linguistic relativity* hypothesis (Whorf 1950, 1956), a direct outgrowth of Bloomfield's anti-universalism, is somewhat of an inelegant chimera, taking 19th century mentalism — but shorn of its Platonic universalism — and grafting it into Aristotelian arbitrariness — but now refurbished with Platonic naturalness. Language diversity, goes this thesis, must surely imply cultural-cognitive diversity, an argument that could only be true if arbitrariness is rejected. Cultural perspectives are relative, and so is reality, since it is always framed through language-culture's lense.

Its internal contradictions notwithstanding, the Sapir-Whorf hypothesis turned out to be a highly influential contextual theory of mind and reality, albeit one largely bereft of methodological constraints or empirical substance. It is perhaps useful to observe a more current — if somewhat baffling — version of cultural relativism, one that perhaps could but never did bloom into cultural pragmatics. It may be found in C. Geertz's *The Interpretation of Culture* (1973). Geertz opens with a vehement rejection of both epistemological extremes, beginning with cognitive subjectivism:

> To quote Ward Goodenough, perhaps its leading proponent, "culture [is located] in the minds and hearts of men". Variously called ethnoscience, componential analysis, or cognitive anthropology [...] this school of thought holds that culture is composed of psychological structures by means of which individuals or groups of individuals guide their behavior. "A society's culture", to quote Goodenough again [...] "Consists of whatever it is one has to know or believe in order to operate in a manner acceptable to its members"   (1973: 11)

Extreme objectivism is then rejected just as vehemently:

> To play the violin it is necessary to possess certain skills, habits, knowledge and talent, to be in a mood to play, and [...] to have a violin. But violin playing is neither the habits, skills, knowledge, and so on, nor the mood, nor [...] the violin [...] To make a trade pact in Morocco you have to do certain things in a certain way (among others cut, while chanting Quranic Arabic, the throat of a lamb [...]) and to be possessed of certain psychological characteristics (among others the desire for distant things). But the trade pact is neither the throat cutting nor the desire.   (*ibid.*: 12)

One is now primed, indeed pining, for the pragmatic denouement, a context-dependent Kantian synthesis: cultural reality as mediated by the framing, intending mind. But instead one finds a most unfortunate quote from Wittgenstein at his empiricist worst — the denial of private meaning:

> Culture is public because meaning is.   (*ibid.*: 12)

It is, so it turns out, the *methodological* difficulties of accessing the mind of the other that license the *theoretical* denial that a description (theory, interpretation) could ever penetrate its purported 'subject', the mind of members of a culture, anthropology's proverbial holy grail, "what the natives *really* think":

> Anthropologists don't study villages, they study *in* villages.   (*ibid.*: 22)

And quoting from Ricoeur at his metaphysical, obfuscatory worst hardly improves matters:

> What does one fix in writing ['description']? [...] Not the event of speaking, but the "said" of speaking, where we understand by the "said" of speaking that intentional exteriorization constitutive of the aim of discourse thanks to which the *sagen* — the saying — wants to become *Aus-sagen* — the enunciation. In short, what we write is the *noema* ["thought", "contents", "gist"] of the speaking. It is the meaning of the speech event, not the event as event.   (*ibid.*: 19)[10]

1.8.2. Early functionalism: The communicating mind

As noted earlier, a functional approach to biology, cognition and communication is inherently pragmatic, since it defines the phenomenon — be it biological design, mental representation or communication — with reference to some purposive, intentional context. Thus, the towering 19th century linguists, from the early Indo-Europeanists through von Humboldt and Paul, were confirmed functionalists. Consider, for example, the following passage from Paul's *Principles of the Development of Language* (1890):

> The real reason for the variability of usage is to be sought in regular linguistic activity [...] No other purpose plays in this save that which is directed to the immediate needs of the moment — rendering the intention of rendering one's wishes and thoughts intelligible to others. For the rest, purpose plays in the [historical] development of language no other part than that assigned to it by Darwin in the [evolutionary] development of organic nature — the greater or lesser fitness of the forms which arise is decisive for their survival or disappearance.   (1890, vol. I: 13; brackets added).

Likewise in his approach to grammar, Paul is firmly cognitive and intentional:

> Every grammatical category is produced on the basis of a psychological one [...] The grammatical category is a petrification of the psychological. It adheres to a fixed tradition. The psychological, on the other hand remains always a free, living agent.   (*ibid.*: 288)

> The psychological subject [...] is that one [of] which the speaker wishes to make the hearer think, and to which he would direct his observation; the psychological predicate [,] that which he wishes him to think about it.   (*ibid.*: 113; brackets added).

The so-called 'traditional grammarians' of the early 20th century took Paul's adaptive-cognitive approach for granted. Thus in his *Philosophy of Grammar* (1924/1965), Jespersen notes:

> The essence of language is human activity — activity on the part of one individual to make himself understood by another, and activity on the part of that other to understand what was in the mind of the first.   (1924/1965: 17)

And likewise:

> Grammar thus becomes a part of linguistic psychology or psychological linguistics. (*ibid.*: 29)

And, in an echo of Aristotle:

> The principles and rules of grammar are the means by which the forms of language are made to correspond with the universal forms of thought.   (*ibid.*: 47)

The subsequent functionalism of Bolinger (1977), Dik (1978), Halliday (1967) and the discourse pragmatics of Chafe (1970, 1994), among many others, arose out of this tradition, whether directly or indirectly.

1.8.3. Speech-acts

Wittgenstein's *Philosophical Investigations* (1953) left in its wake a distinctly British school of *Ordinary Language Philosophy*. Within this school, a sub-tradition occupied itself with the analysis of the intentional states ('illocutionary force') associated with speech-acts ('performatives': declarative, interrogative, imperative, etc; see Austin 1962; Searle 1970; Grice 1968/1975; *inter alia*). This pragmatic tradition, together with that of logical presupposition (see directly below), fed into the burgeoning pragmatics renaissance of the 1970s (Cole and Morgan eds 1975; Cole ed. 1978, 1981; *inter alia*).

1.8.4. Logical presupposition

There is a strong interaction, and historical connections, between the speech-act tradition, the discourse-pragmatic tradition and the logical presupposition tradition. The ontology of presupposition goes back, in one sense, to Russell's *On Denoting* (1905), which did not differentiate between indefinite-referring nouns, introduced into the discourse for the first time, and definite nouns, introduced under a supposition of prior *identifiability to the hearer* (see ch. 5). Formal logicians attempted a rectification of sorts, beginning with Strawson (1950), by proposing a "three valued logic" (true, not-true, presupposed), not always noticing that the 'third value' — presupposed — was but a species of Aristotle's truth by *deduction* or *definition*, or of Kant's *analytic* (see ch. 8).

True to the Positivist program, presupposition was taken to be a logical property of proposition rather than a pragmatic property associated with the communicating mind. As such, the tradition spilled over into linguistics with Keenan (1969, 1972), where presupposition was now discovered to be associated with grammatical constructions or lexical items (Kiparski and Kiparski 1968; Fillmore 1971; Horn 1972; Givón 1973a; Karttunen 1974; Oh and Dinneen eds 1979; *inter alia*).

Unfortunately, much of the presuppositional literature soon bogged down in attempts to sub-divide context into neat, discrete sub-categories that needed to be rigorously segregated from truth-conditional logic (e.g. Katz 1977; Gazdar 1979; Sperber and Wilson 1984b; *inter alia*). What had begun as a potential opening to pragmatics and the study of language in its wider communicative context thus turned, at least implicitly, into a rear-guard attempt to salvage Carnap's and Russell's intellectual program.

1.8.5. Modal logic and possible worlds

Somewhat the same fate befell the parallel tradition of modal logic, initially an attempt to formalize non-fact propositional modalities such as *possible* and *future*, as well as other *intentional modalities*, including tense; and most particularly, to deal with problems of reference under the scope of such modalities. Soon, a *possible worlds logic* was pressed into service to deal with intensional contexts (Kripke 1963, 1972; Cocchiarella 1965; Hinttika 1967; Purtill 1968; Scott 1970; *inter alia*). The pragmatic nature of the enterprise, given the reference to *intention*, was soon recognized, e.g. by Montague (1970):

> To interpret a pragmatic language L we must specify several things. In the first place, we must determine the set of all possible contexts of *use* — or rather, of all complexes of *relevant aspects* of possible contexts of use; we may call such complexes indices, or to borrow Dana Scott's term, *points of reference*.   (1970: 144; italics added)

As possible candidates for 'indices' only the indexical 'I' was explicitly mentioned, although in outlining the problem of context earlier, Montague refers to indexical expressions in general (i.e. person, time, place), an opening soon exploited by Lewis (1972):

> any octuple of which the first coordinate is *a possible world*, the second coordinate is *a moment of time*, the third coordinate is *a place*, the fourth coordinate is a set of persons (or other creatures capable of being *a speaker*), the fifth coordinate is a set of person (or other creatures capable of being *an audience*), the sixth coordinate is a set (possible empty) of concrete things *capable of being pointed at*, the seventh coordinate is *a segment of discourse*, and the eighth coordinate an infinite sequence of things.   (1972: 176; italics added)

Later on, Lewis (1979) acknowledged the problem with detailed illustrations from a more realistic sample of quasi-natural conversation. Similar misgivings were expressed earlier by Creswell (1972):

> Writers who, like David Lewis [. . .], do try to give a bit more body to these no-
> tions, talk about time, place, speakers, hearers, [. . .] etc. and then go through
> agonies of conscience in trying to decide whether they have taken account of
> enough.   (Creswell 1972: 8)

The program soon collapsed into the by-now-familiar attempt to squeeze pragmatics — or whatever portions of it could be made to fit — into a strict truth-conditional mold.[11]

1.8.6. Ethnography of Speech: Social interaction as context

Another strand in the tapestry of modern pragmatics comes from the interface of
sociology, anthropology and linguistics, via the works of Labov (1972a, b); Basso
(1972); Garfinkel (1972); Geertz (1972); Goffman (1974, 1976); Gumperz (1977,
1982); Gumperz and Hymes (eds 1972); Sachs *et al.* (1974); Brown and Levinson
(1978, 1979); Ochs (1979); among many others. Coming variably under the label of 'Ethnolinguistics', 'Ethnomethodology', 'Sociolinguistics' or 'Conversational
Analysis', these works purport to describe the way the social or cultural context
shapes language use, language change, and thus, at least to some extent, language
structure.

1.8.7. Developmental pragmatics

An important addition to the pragmatic agenda came with the communicatively
oriented studies of child language acquisition, as in e.g. Ervin-Tripp (1970), Limber (1973), Scollon (1976), Bates (1976,1979), Bates *et al.* (1975, 1979), Bates and
MacWhinney (1979), Ochs and Schieffelin (eds, 1979), among many others. A
strong modern Platonist dogma holds that human language capacity is largely innate, and that therefore the role of linguistic input — and the communicative context — in language acquisition is trivial (Chomsky 1965,1966,1968; Pinker 1989).
Developmental pragmatics has emerged as an empirical reaction to this dogma, en-
deavoring to examine the acquisition of language in its natural adaptive context.

1.8.8. Pragmatics and the machine

Within the briefly-ascendant agenda of *Artificial Intelligence* (AI), a largely dis-
credited attempt to implement in 'thinking machines' the Positivist program of
truth-conditional logic, there emerged a small but persistent pragmatic strand. It
began with Winograd's (1970) attempt, later disavowed, to incorporate speech-
act notions into the computer's algorithm. Later on, Schank and Abelson (1977)
and Levy (1979), *inter alia*, attempted to absorb discourse-context entities such as
'scripts', 'plans' and 'goals' into a computerized framework. Since in principle pragmatics cannot be constrained inside a closed algorithm without ceasing to be prag-

matics (or without busting the algorithm; cf. Russell's *Theory of Types*), the various pragmatic moves within AI have tended to self-destruct. In a way, though, they have served a useful purpose, that of reiterating both the theoretical and practical limit of the entire *Mind-as-a-Computer* intellectual program (cf. Turing 1950); thus indirectly vindicating Russell's and Carnap's reticence (Dreyfus 1972; Simon and Kaplan 1989).

1.8.9. Cognitive Psychology

One may as well note that pragmatics has had a vigorous if not always explicit presence in post-Behaviorist cognitive psychology: in the study of *figure-ground* phenomena ('gestalt'; Koffka 1935); in contextual *semantic priming* (Swinney 1979) and *selective attention* (Posner 1978; *inter alia*; see ch. 4); in the psychology of perception (Attneave 1959) and *perceptual priming* (Epstein and Rock 1960); in the priming by expectation of *selective episodic memory* (Loftus 1980) and *selective visual memory* (Treisman and DeSchepper 1996). Rosch's (1973a, b) work on natural categories and prototypes is at least implicitly pragmatic (see ch. 2), as is much of the empirical work on metaphors and figurative language (Ortonyi ed. 1979; Gibbs 1994; Cacciari and Glucksberg 1994; *inter alia*; see ch. 4). Likewise, analogical reasoning (cf. Glenberg *et al.* 1994b) is at least in principle a contextual-pragmatic domain, albeit not always in practice; as is the effect of discourse context on language comprehension (Anderson *et al.* 1983; Garrod and Sanford 1994; Sanford and Garrod 1994).

1.8.10. Evolutionary biology

As noted earlier, adaptive-functionalist biology ever since Aristotle has been squarely pragmatic, in that it introduces intentionality, purpose of function into the interpretation of what biological structures 'mean' and how they come about. Within such a framework, Darwinian evolutionary biology is but a reaffirmation of an old, vigorous contextual-pragmatic perspective. However revolutionary the Darwinian amplification of Aristotle still seems, its main contribution was the suggested *developmental mechanism* by which structures come to 'fit' or perform their respective functions.

The adaptive-selectional mechanism proposed by Darwin is itself just as inherently pragmatic, in that it is founded upon the interaction of organisms with their *environment*; that is, their context. What is more, the environment to which organisms adapt or 'fit' is not a purely objective entity, but rather the *relevant* environment as *construed*, selectively, by the behaving-cognizing organism during adaptive interaction. This relevant environment is often social, and thus includes both the construed 'objective' behavior and construed *mental states* of others, be they cooperative or hostile.

1.9. Toward an integrated pragmatics of life, mind and language

This book is, alas, likely to fall short of the definitive, a failing that is due in part to the inherent contradictions of pragmatics itself. For the 'same' phenomenon can always be re-framed more insightfully, once one has gained added perspective. And the ultimate perspective is, as Russell's paradox ought to remind us, never at hand, forever receding. This tantalizing elusiveness of perspective is both the glory and heartbreak of science. But, if this be comfort, this is a predicament we share with all cognizing organisms.

It is nonetheless my firm conviction that pragmatics — as a natural phenomenon, as a theoretical perspective, and as an empirical method — holds the key to an integrated understanding of life, behavior, cognition and communication, and thus ultimately to an understanding of the biological constraints on the evolution of sentient social beings.

The integration of non-mechanistic evolutionary biology — not just the 'wet' brain — into the study of mental representation furnishes the necessary framework for a comprehensive theory of mind, behavior, culture and communication. It is perhaps not an accident that Aristotle's audacious program for biology was predicated, from the very start, upon the organism's possession of a soul, the *anima*, agent of both intentionality and knowledge.

To the extent that Cognitive Science, or its more recent inheritor, Cognitive Neuroscience, are ever to transcend the status of political catch-phrases, or the domain of mechanistic reductionism, pragmatics holds the key to a yet-to-be-integrated field. The intent of such integration is, while perhaps broader, reminiscent of Levinson's (1983) program:

> if pragmatics is, on occasions, logically prior to semantics, a general linguistic theory simply must incorporate pragmatics as a component or level in the overall integrated theory.   (1983: 35).

This vision is surprisingly orthogonal, in its structure if not in its ultimate goals, to Carnap's program of pragmatics as the empirical advance scout to logical syntax. It is fully in line with Paul's view of grammar as 'petrified cognition'. It is also consonant with Jespersen's vision of grammar as the language-specific mapping onto cognitive universals.

Notes

* I am indebted to Marcelo Dascal, Esa Itkonen, Brian MacWhinney and Mike Posner for helpful comments on an earlier version of this chapter. They are hereby absolved of any responsibility for the final product.

1. As we shall see further below (ch. 8), the contention that generalization may be arrived at via induction alone is controversial.

2. All the following quotations from the *Tao The Ching* are from my own unpublished translation. See also Givón (1989: ch. 11).

3. See also discussion of hypothetical deduction in *Prior Analytic* I, 44, in J. Barnes (ed. 1984: 80). In the *Posterior Analytic*, Aristotle likens abductive inference to a string of pearls: "The particular facts are not merely brought together but there is a new element added to the combination by the very act of thought by which they are combined . . . The pearls are there, but they will not hang together till someone provides the string." (*Posterior Analytic* II)

4. The very same facts could have been used, of course, to argue for the context-dependent construction of meaning.

5. The labels 'rationalist' and 'empiricist' were first used in this early context, in the debate about how to deal with hitherto unknown medical conditions — by similarity to prior instances (empiricist), or by general principles (rationalist). Only later did the terms migrate into epistemology.

6. Marcelo Dascal (in personal communication, but see also Dascal 2004) suggests that Leibnitz was not the pure case of a rationalist that seems so conspicuous in his epistemology (*Scientia Generalis*); and that in Leibnitz' late writing (*Topics, Rhetoric*) more pragmatic elements can be found.

7. Leaving aside the medieval mystics, who in all likelihood entertained more holistic, perhaps pragmatic, theories of knowledge.

8. Kemp notes that Kant's *Anschauung* means 'immediate apprehension' and is often translated as 'perception'. However, it subsumes not only 'sensory perception' but also 'pure intuition'. For this reason, Kemp prefers to render *Anschauung* as 'intuition'. I suspect that such a rendition is bound to be even more confusing, in that it suggests the exclusion of sensory perception.

9. Due to T. K. Bikson, in personal communication.

10. Especially that Ricoeur has violated here, most flagrantly, Geertz's own cogent, indeed celebrated, injunction against hermetic interpretive theories:

> The besetting sin of interpretive approaches to anything — literature, dreams, symptoms, culture — is that they tend to resist, or to be permitted to resist, conceptual articulation, and thus to escape systematic modes of assessment. You either grasp an interpretation or you do not, see the point of it or you do not, accept it or you do not. Imprisoned in the immediacy of its own detail, it is presented as self validating, or, worse, as validated by the supposed developed sensitivities of the person who presents it; any attempt to cast what it says in terms other than its own is regarded as a travesty — as the anthropologist's severest term of abuse, ethnocentric.   (1973: 24).

I could have never, in a lifetime, said it better. Tho I would have been sorely tempted to substitute, as an infinitely worse form of abuse, validation by the supposed developed sensitivities of the *interlocutor*.

11. The impulse of formal pragmatics is somewhat schizophrenic. Russell and Carnap had recognized clearly the detrimental effect on their program of contextual pragmatics, and had labored to keep it out of bounds. Formal pragmatics, be it presuppositional or modal, attempted to draw pragmatics in. One wonders whether pragmatics' destructive potential went unrecognized.

CHAPTER 2

Categories as prototypes:
The adaptive middle

2.1. Preamble*

Categorization — the mental representation of individual tokens of experience as members of recognizable recurrent types — is one of the most profound adaptive moves in the annals of biological evolution. This is as true of the amoeba's rudimentary somatic representation of heat, light, touch and salt concentration as it is of our own seemingly open-ended Oxford English Dictionary. The discussion of mental categories in the preceding chapter dealt primarily with their *source* — innate (Plato) vs. acquired by experience (Aristotle). Between these two extremes, it was noted, Kant represented the pragmatic — interactive, constructivist — middle.

In this chapter we deal with a related but still distinct question: How are mental categories organized as a *system*, and what are that system's *formal properties*? This question can be broken down into four related issues:

- **Boundaries: Discrete vs. fuzzy**: Are mental categories discrete, or do they admit gradation? Are their boundaries sharp, or fuzzy? Do they abide by necessary & sufficient criteria as well as by the laws of non-contradiction and the excluded middle?
- **Stability: Invariant vs. context-dependent**: Are mental category invariant in all contexts, or are they elastic and adjust to their context?
- **Criteria: Single vs. multiple**: Can a single necessary-and-sufficient criterion — a definition — govern categorial membership, or are there multiple membership criteria?
- **Distribution: Clustered vs. dispersed**: Do the members of a category cluster meaningfully around the mean, or are they so dispersed as to render the mean meaningless?

We will begin by outlining the two extreme traditional approaches to categorization, tracing their descent in philosophy, linguistics and psychology. We will then sketch out a pragmatic middle-ground position that, like all pragmatic middles, mimics the salient properties of both extremes. This middle turns out to be an *adaptive compromise* designed to satisfy two conflicting but equally valid adaptive requirements:

- The need to represent *most* tokens of the same type the same way, in order to trigger, in the majority of instances, the *same* adaptive response.
- The need to recognize as deviant *some* tokens, in order to trigger, in a minority of instances, *exceptional*, context-sensitive adaptive responses.

Each of the two extreme approaches to categorization can, by itself, take care of only one of these requirements. Only the hybrid, middle-ground pragmatic approach can take care of both. This mode of resolution of adaptive conflicts is well known in biology, where it accounts for many of the paradoxical properties of complex systems in the living organism.

Given the dual task undertaken by biologically-based representation — to take care of both central tendencies and exceptional outliers — it is easy to see why *analogy* and *metaphor* are such prominent venues of categorial change, be it individual learning or historical-cultural innovation: Analogical-abductive reasoning is the most natural means we have for construing contexts in a novel way, and thus for reinterpreting erstwhile *outlier* members of an entrenched category as *central* members of a new category. For this reason, a discussion of metaphoric, non-literal meaning is essential to a comprehensive account of mental categories. This discussion will be undertaken in the next chapter.

Gradual change and restructuring of mental categories may also be viewed as a process of revising the figure-ground relation between *contexts*. Through small analogical steps, an erstwhile marginal, infrequent context is reinterpreted as the *central, frequent norm* of the restructured category.

This model of change in mental categories, by incremental steps of similarity and analogy, is fully consonant with evolutionary change in biology, where early stages of innovation most commonly involve the sharing of one structure by two *similar but non-identical* functions, one old, the other new. And it is *outlier* members, at the margins of biological populations, that drift away in unpredictable directions toward innovation and, on occasion, *speciation*.

While conceding the overwhelming role of analogy and metaphor in categorial change, one need not cede them timeless rigidity. To begin with, today's literal usage is littered with yesterday's live metaphors now dearly departed. What is more, live metaphoric usage springs out serendipitously in specific adaptive contexts, most commonly:

- for obtaining a strong 'extra-semantic' perceptual or affective impact; and
- for connecting old to new usage at early stages of change and learning.

Equally valid adaptive pressures, however, impel metaphoric meanings toward petrification, re-conventionalization and reversion to literality, a counter-process that is driven by changes in usage frequency. What is more, the balance between literal and figurative meaning in a usage population — say a coherent text or a conversation — is in some fundamental way the very same adaptive compromise noted above, between central and outlying members of a category. The majority of usage tokens tend to be literal, insuring a measure of stability, predictability and streamlined processing. The figurative minority guarantees contextual adjustment, flexibility and adaptive change.

2.2. Philosophical roots

2.2.1. Platonic ('logical') categories

While often ascribed to Plato, this extreme approach to categories could have just as easily been ascribed to Aristotle the logician. And both Plato and Aristotle departed from this approach in many contexts. Still, Plato's doctrine of innate essences, as depicted in the *Cratylus*, *Meno* and *Phaedo* dialogues (Everson 1994; Bostock 1994; Williams 1994), is a good point of departure.

As noted earlier, Socrates' argued, in *Meno* and elsewhere, that natural usage is disorderly, ambiguous, graduated and context-dependent. For this reason, he suggested, reliable *essences* of meaning could not be extracted from our experience with everyday usage. But since we must make discrete categorial judgements (Is this a token of type x or of type y?), the mental entities that licence such decisions must be discrete. Thus, Meno enumerates the multiple context-specific instances of 'virtue':

> If it is a manly virtue you are after, it is easy to see that the virtue of a man consists of managing the city's affairs capably, and so that he will help his friends and injure his foes [...] If you want a woman's virtue, that is easily described. She must be a good housewife, careful with her stores and obedient to her husband. Then there is another virtue for a child, male or female, and another for an old man, free or slave.   (*Meno*; in E. Hamilton and H. Cairns, eds 1961: 355)

To which Socrates retorts:

> I wanted one virtue and I find that you have a whole swarm of virtues to offer [...] Even if they are many and various, at least they have *some common character* which makes them virtues.   (*ibid.*; italics added).

Mental categories in the Platonic tradition are discrete and well bounded, no fuzzy edges, no intermediates, no ambiguity or gradation. A single necessary-and-sufficient criterion decides membership. This idealized perspective was passed down through an illustrious logic-oriented chain of transmission, from Aristotle via Descartes, Leibnitz and Frege and on to Russell and Carnap.[1]

The Platonic approach to categories may be illustrated with the ven diagram (1) below, whereby individual tokens are either members or non-members, but never part-members.

(1)

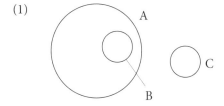

In terms of frequency distribution of members ('tokens') of two different categories ('types') along the categorial space, all members of a Platonic/logical category cluster equally at the mean, displaying no variability or *degree of membership*. The memberships of two contrasting categories thus never overlap.

(2)

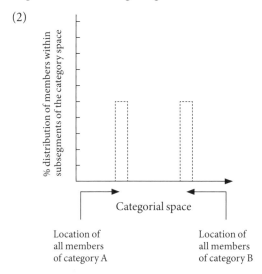

2.2.2. Wittgensteinean ('flat') categories

The other extreme approach to categorization is often attributed to Ludwig Wittgenstein, whose untimely demise may have made it impractical for him to disavow such imputations had he been so inclined. In his 'late' work (*Philosophical Investigations*, 1953), Wittgenstein suggests that meaning is profoundly context-dependent and usage-driven:

> A move in chess doesn't consist simply in moving a piece in such-and-such way on the board — nor yet in one's thoughts and feelings as one makes the move; but in the *circumstances* that we call "playing a game of chess", "solving a chess problem", and so on.   (1953: 33, 17; italics added).

> For a large class of cases — though not for all — in which we employ the word "meaning" it can be defined as thus: the meaning of a word is its *use* in language.   (*ibid.*: 43, 20; italics added).

What is more, meaning is non-discrete and replete with gradation. This gradation is due, in large measure, to the use of *multiple membership criteria*, none of which is by itself necessary or sufficient. Wittgenstein's celebrated metaphor of semantic relatedness as *family resemblance* runs as follows:

> (we) can see how similarities crop up and disappear. And the result of this examination is this: we see a complicated network of similarities overlapping and criss-

crossing, sometimes overall similarities, sometimes similarities of detail. I can
think of no better expression to characterize these similarities than *"family resemblances"*; for the various resemblances between members of a family: build, features,
colour of eyes, gait, temperament etc. etc. overlap and criss-cross in the same way.
— And I shall say: 'games' form a family.   (*ibid.*, 66, 67, 32.; italics added)[2]

Lastly, Wittgenstein argues that natural language abounds in inexact concepts with
ill-defined boundaries:

Frege compares a concept to an area and says that an area with vague boundaries
cannot be called an area at all. This presumably means that we cannot do anything
with it. — But is it senseless to say: "Stand roughly here"?.   (*ibid.*, 71: 34)

Expressed as a ven diagram, the Wittgensteinian 'family resemblance' approach to
mental categories may be given as:

(3)

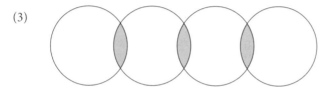

In terms of frequency distribution of members ('tokens') of two different categories ('types') along the categorial space, the extreme Wittgensteinean approach to
categorization may be illustrated by finely-graduated curves, with the categorial
means either arbitrary or meaningless:

(4)

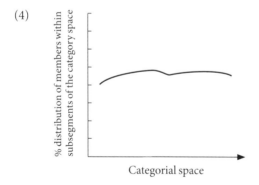

2.3. Linguistic roots

2.3.1. Generativity

The most conspicuous and certainly most celebrated representative of the Platonic
approach to categories in Linguistics is of course Noam Chomsky, whose logical-
computational — generative — approach to language has haunted linguistics since
1957. In *On the Notion 'rule of Grammar'* (1961), Chomsky writes:

By "grammar of the language L" I will mean a device of some sort (that is, a set of rules) that provides, at least, a complete specification of an infinite set of grammatical sentences of L and their structural description. In addition to making precise the notion "structural description", the theory of grammar should meet requirements of the following kind. It should make available:

a. a class of possible grammars $G1, G2$ [...]
b. a class of possible sentences $S1, S2$ [...]
c. a function $\underline{f}$ such that $f(i,j)$ is a set of structural descriptions of the sentence Si that are provided by the grammar Gj,
d. a function $m(i)$ which evaluates Gi,
e. a function g such that $g(i,n)$ is the description of a finite automaton that takes sentences of (b) as input and gives structural descriptions assigned to these sentences by Gi.   (1961:6)

Chomsky's vision of grammar as an algorithm, the core axiom of Generative Grammar, likens grammatical regularities to the rules of logic and mathematics. Like the exceptionless laws of physics, the rules — and thus categories — of grammar are viewed here as inviolable, governed by necessary-and-sufficient criteria and the laws of Non-Contradiction and the Excluded Middle. The same Platonic vision is reiterated by Katz and Fodor (1963).[3]

2.3.2. Emergence

A seemingly Wittgensteinean account of linguistic categories has been offered by Paul Hopper (1987), most conspicuously in his work on *emergent grammar*:

The notion of emergence is a pregnant one. It is not intended to be a standard sense of origins or genealogy, not a historical question of "how" the grammar came to be the way it "is", but instead it takes the adjective emergent seriously as a *continual movement toward structure*, a postponement or "deferral" of structure, a view of *structure as always provisional, always negotiable*, and in fact as *epiphenomenal* [...] Structure, then, in this view is not an overarching set of abstract principles, but more a question of *a spreading of systematicity* from individual words, phrases and small sets.   (1987: 142; italics added)

This passage seems to assert that grammar is totally flexible and *always* negotiated for the occasion, and is thus 100% dependent on its communicative context. Whatever systematicity, rigidity or generality that can be detected in grammar are but an artifact of the linguist's analytic habits.

In a subsequent paper, Hopper (1991) further elaborates his position by suggesting that since the boundaries between grammatical, semantic and phonological change are not absolute, they therefore do not exist. This proposition is supported by the early contention that grammar does not 'really' exist, in the traditional sense of relatively stable relationships between structures and their paired semantic or pragmatic correlates:

> The more extensive definition of grammaticalization implicit in this work raises the question of whether, when grammaticalization has done its work, there would in the end be any room left for the notion of grammar in a sense of static structural relationships [...] If grammar is not a discrete, modular set of relationships, it would seem to follow that no set of changes can be identified which distinctively characterise grammaticalization as opposed to, say, lexical change of phonological change in general.   (1991: 18–19)

Both extreme positions, I think, are founded on the same illicit application of reasoning by *modus ponens*. In Chomsky's case, the implicit inference is:

- rules of grammar are *not 100% flexible*
- therefore rules of grammar must be *100% rigid*

In Hopper's case, it is:

- rules of grammar are *not 100% rigid*
- therefore rules of grammar must be *100% flexible*

It is perhaps worth noting that a pragmatic middle-ground position on this issue has existed in linguistics for a long time. This alternative readily concedes that both Chomsky and Hopper are right — but only to a point. Consider, for example, Sapir's (1921) celebrated adage:

> Were a language ever completely "grammatical", it would be a perfect engine of conceptual expression. Unfortunately, or luckily, no language is tyrannically consistent. *All grammars leak.*   (1921: 38; italics added)

Unless I am wide off the mark, Sapir did not mean to assert here that *all* rules of grammars *always* leak, but rather that no grammar is 100% leak-proof.

The partial fallibility of grammatical categories (or 'rules') has also been noted by Jespersen (1924):

> Most of the definitions given in even recent books are little better than sham definitions in which it is extremely easy to pick holes [...] [...] Not a single one of these definitions is either exhaustive or cogent.   (1924: 58–9)

Again, it seems, Jespersen did not object here to the existence of considerable rigidity in grammatical generalizations ('rules'), but only to the tyrannical assumption that rules of grammar are *always* exceptionless.

2.3.3. Psychological roots

The very same dichotomy between extreme discreteness and extreme graduality of mental categories has also cropped up in cognitive psychology. A close analog of Platonic categorization may be seen in Smith *et al.* (1974), where lexical-semantic concepts are characterized in terms of lists of discrete, atomic features. The similarity between concepts is then expressed in terms of the precise number of shared features.

A close analogue of the Wittgensteinean approach to categories may be seen in the *semantic networks* cum *spreading activation* model of Quillian (1968), Collins and Quillian (1972) and Collins and Loftus (1975). In this model, concepts are like nodes in a connected network. A node is activated by an adjacent node, a 'spreading' that can, in principle, go on for a considerable distance. Semantic similarity within such a system is presumably expressed in terms of the distance — number of intervening connections — between two nodes.

2.4. Prototypes: The adaptive middle

The articulation of the pragmatic middle-ground in both psychology and linguistics is due to the work of Eleanor Rosch (1973a, b, 1975), building on the semantic network model of Collins and Quillian (1972) as well as on earlier work on abstract concepts by Posner and Keel (1968). Four salient features characterize prototype-like categories:

a. **Multiple criterial features**:
   Membership in a natural category, unlike a logical category, is not determined by a single criterial feature that is either present or absent, but rather by a large basket of features. Some of those features may be more central to the category, in the sense that more — or nearly all — members display them. Others may be more peripheral. Thus, for example, shape is much more central to the category 'horse' than size, and size is yet more central than color.

b. **Graded membership**:
   The most prototypical member of a category is the one displaying the largest number of criterial features. It is, presumably, the one that comes to mind most readily when the categorial name is invoked. That is, 'horse' > 'quarter-horse'; 'apple' > 'red delicious'; 'flower' > 'rose'; 'bird' > 'sparrow'; etc. But less prototypical members, those that display fewer features, are still members of the category.

c. **Strong feature association**:
   The criterial features of a natural category tend to be strongly associated, so that in the majority of cases, having one feature implies having many of the others. Thus, a miniature horse may still have most of the other salient horse features, such as shape, color, behavior, etc.

d. **Strong clustering around the mean**:
   As a logical consequence of (c), the vast majority of members of a natural category will tend to cluster around the categorial mean. That is, they tend to resemble the prototype (and thus each other). Outliers, odd and ambiguous members are a relatively small minority.

Prototype-based categories are a hybrid system, a quintessential adaptive compromise (Posner 1986). Their features (a) and (b) represent the dynamic — Wittgensteinean — aspect of natural types, providing for variation, graded membership and change. Features (c) and (d) represent the static — Platonic — aspect of natural types, providing for a high level of uniformity, discreteness, stability and cognitive coherence. Features (c) and (d) thus let the vast majority of members of one category be easily distinguished from the vast majority of members of contrasting categories.

A ven-diagram representation of prototype-based categories may be given as:

(5)

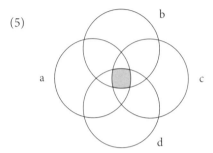

The frequency distribution of token-members of such categories along the categorial continuum in such a system may be given as:

(6)

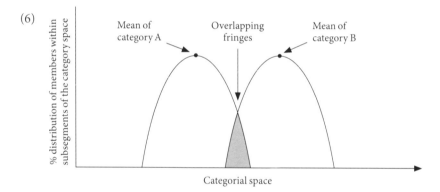

2.5. The adaptive underpinnings of prototype-like categories

As noted earlier (ch. 1), all taxonomies — categorization schemata — are in principle arbitrary. In making them, we draw heavily on contextual-pragmatic judgements of similarity, saliency and relevance. But categorization and mental representation as practiced by biological organisms — or, for that matter, by empirical scientists — is not an idle exercise in parsing. It is, rather, a profound adaptive move (or, in the case of the scientist, a profoundly theoretical move).

Sorting tokens of experience into separate categories is the foundation upon which biological organisms structure their adaptive behavior. One's mental categories determine how one responds — with decision and action — to one's physical, biological, mental and social environment. The hybrid nature of mental categories — partly Platonic, partly Wittgensteinean — is not a philosophical caprice but an adaptive strategy, a compromise designed to accommodate two conflicting demands on biologically-based information processing:

- Relatively rapid and error-free processing of the bulk;
- Fine contextual discrimination of small but relevant minorities.

Biologically based information-processing systems tend to process rapidly and with low error rates information that is:

- repetitive, frequent and highly predictable; and/or
- of great adaptive urgency or relevance.

Most commonly, the processing of such information becomes *automated* (Posner and Boies 1971; Posner and Klein 1971; Posner and Warren 1972; Posner and Snyder 1974; Posner 1978; Schneider and Shiffrin 1977; Schneider 1985; Schneider and Chein 2003; Kahneman 1973; Kahneman and Treisman 1984; *inter alia*).

The same is true in the domain of motor performance, where repetition leads to habituation, skill and automaticity (Denier, van der Gon and Thuring 1965; Grillner 1975; Schmidt 1975, 1980; Herman *et al*. eds 1976; Shapiro and Schmidt 1980; Shapiro *et al*. 1980; Whiting *et al*. 1980; *inter alia*).

Automated processing is heavily dependent on discrete, hierarchic, categorial structures. That is, it depends on information *chunking* (Chase and Simon 1973; Chase and Ericsson 1981, 1982), whereby a long sequence of nodes of equal rank becomes sub-divided into shorter sequences, each dominated by a hierarchically-higher more abstract node. That is, schematically:

(7)   **Chunking and rhythmic-hierarchic structure:**
  a.   **Before chunking:**

  b.   **After chunking:**

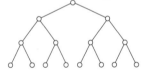

The unique identification of, or 'access to', a terminal node in the un-chunked serial structure (7a) may require the scanning of up to 7 nodes. Unique identification in the chunked structure (7b) can be accomplished by scanning only 3 nodes in a top-down order. Such chunking and rhythmic-hierarchic structure is typical of, among others, the *syntax* of human languages.

In sharp contrast, the processing of less frequent, less typical, uncertain or ambiguous information proceeds, typically, in a slower and more error-prone fashion.

Such processing must allow fine-grained discrimination of shades and gradations, contextual scanning, and pragmatic judgements of relevance. Irrelevant information is ignored. Relevant information is sifted more finely before filing and action decisions are made.

Understandably, the processing of 'outlier' information remains un-automated and heavily dependent on the more powerful, energy consuming but slower *attentional system* (Posner and Warren 1972; Posner and Snyder 1974; Posner 1978; Schneider and Shiffrin 1977; *inter alia*).

The contrast between attended and automated processing may be summarized as follows:

(8)   **Mode of processing**

Property	Attended	Automated
speed:	slow	fast
error rates:	error prone	error-free
information:	uncertain, rare	certain, repetitive
inference:	pragmatic	deductive
context:	context-scanning	context-free
consciousness:	conscious	sub-conscious
categoriality:	Wittgensteinean	Platonic
structure:	non-hierarchic	chunked/hierarchic

The strong adaptive pressure toward automated processing arises from the need to draw rapid conclusions about — and fashion a rapid response to — the category membership of tokens of experience, all based on a relatively quick scan of a few — or even one — highly observable features. In a nut shell, *stereotyping*. This is where the Platonic features (c) and (d) of prototype-based categories furnish a crucial advantage. Strong feature association (c) guarantees that stereotyping is, in the main, valid and reliable. Clustering around the mean (d) insures that stereotyping snap decisions be relevant to the bulk of the population.

As a simple-minded example, consider the task of deciding, when walking in the thick bush, whether an animal with characteristic tiger-like stripes, viewed only briefly, is a dangerous predator. While encounters with tigers may be rare, there is a strong association between the innocuous visual feature 'tiger-like stripes' and the lethal behavioral feature 'dangerous predator'. What is more, making the wrong decision here would have rather costly adaptive consequences. The high predictability of the feature association 'stripes' ⊃ 'tiger', coupled with the high adaptive relevance of avoiding tigers, is at the root of our automatic reaction to the mere perception of the telltale stripes, from which we instantly extract "tiger, danger!" We do so with little regard to the fine gradation of the specific context (How close is it? Does it look hungry? Has it seen me? Is it an untested juvenile? Does this particular one really bite?)

From the discussion thus far, it may appear that non-prototypical members of a category impose an adaptive burden on the organism's cognitive system, a necessary but lamentable concession to the imperfection of either the world or cognition, or both. For the existence of such outliers, so it seems, forces the organism to expend precious attentional resources on the processing of a relatively small minority of tokens.

In fact, however, this is only half of the story. The other half has to do with the central role that variation plays in the evolution and adaptive health of natural populations, be they biological species or mental categories. For in natural categories, variation is the very guarantor of *adaptation* and *change*. Ever since Darwin, it has been recognized that the core explanatory concept of theoretical biology — evolution — is wholly dependent on intra-group variation. Or, as Douglas Futuyma (1986) puts it:

> [...] variation is at the heart of the scientific study of the living world. As long as *essentialism*, the outlook that ignores variation in its focus on fixed essences, held sway, the possibility of evolutionary change could hardly be conceived, for variation is both the product and the foundation of evolution. Few other sciences take variation as a primary focus of study as does evolutionary biology.   (1986: 82)

In the same vein, Mayr's (1976) contrasts physics-chemistry and biology:

> Until a few years ago, when an evolutionist or a systematist opened the book on the philosophy of science, and read about the basic concepts, methods and objectives of science, he was bound to be distressed to discover how little all this had to do with his own particular endeavor. The reason for this incongruity is that these books were written either by logicians or physicists. These authors did not realize that the physical sciences are a very specialized branch of science. Its ideal is to explain everything under a few general laws and to subordinate all diversity under a limited number of broadly-based generalizations [...] Perhaps the outstanding aspect of the physical sciences is the identity of the entities with which it deals. A sodium atom is a sodium atom no matter where you encounter it and what its chemical history might have been. It always has exactly the same properties. The same is true for the elementary particles, the protons, electrons, mesons, etc., or for the aggregates of atoms, the molecules. It is the sameness of these entities that permits the determination of extremely precise constants for all the properties of these constituents as well as their inclusion in general laws.

> How different is the material of the systematist and evolutionist! Its outstanding characteristic is uniqueness. No two individuals in a sexually reproducing population are the same (not even identical twins), no two populations of the same species, no two species, no two higher taxa [...] Such uniqueness does not mean that generalizations are impossible, but it does mean that generalizations and predictions are achieved in a rather different way. Some time they are formulated by determining mean values, and by proceeding afterwards as if these mean values correspond to the true constants of the identical entities of physical science. A more valid, and usually far more interesting, approach is to study diversity spectra of classes composed of unique entities.   (1976: 408–9)

In biological populations, the price of excessive homogeneity is a decrease in adaptive experimentation, and thus paucity of novel solutions to unpredictable environmental challenges. But the adaptive price of excessive diversity is equally steep — speciation, and with it the loss of new adaptive solutions to the general population (Bonner 1988). Or, as Mayr (1969) puts it:

> [. . .] the obvious advantage to a population of storing genetic variability [is] to serve as material for evolutionary responses to changing conditions [. . .] Yet too much genetic variability will inevitably result in the wasteful production of many locally inferior genotypes [. . .] Extreme genetic variability is as undesirable as extreme genetic uniformity. How does the population avoid either extreme? As so often in the realm of evolution, the solution is a *dynamic equilibrium* between the two opposing forces.   (1969: 95–6; italics and brackets added)

Let us turn back briefly to the first core property of prototype-based categories — (a) multiple membership criterial. Unlike logical and abstract objects, natural concrete objects tend to be multi-featured. Most typically, they possess inherent, durable perceptible characteristics such as color, shape, size, sound, smell, taste, consistency etc. But to the cognizing organism they may also possess socially construed, perceptually inaccessible but adaptively significant properties, such as behavior, use, kinship or spirituality.

When biological organisms contrast natural objects with each other for the purpose of classification, decision and action, more than one salient feature is thus available for the task. Some of those features are easier to perceive under some conditions (light, distance, clear path), others are easier to perceive under others (dark, silence). Some are more relevant in some contexts, others more relevant in others. The multiple-criteria feature (a), is thus by itself a great adaptive boon. It allows organisms the freedom to make snap categorial judgements in an expanded range of contexts. But such freedom of contextual adjustment is only possible because of feature (c) — strong feature association.

2.6. Some social consequences of natural categorization

2.6.1. Essentialism and stereotyping

In the pantheon of contemporary social ills, *stereotyping* — this ungainly progeny of Platonic *essentialism* — has been elevated to the status of bogeyman. A considerable amount of philosophical revisionism and empirical license has gone into exorcizing this unaccountably resilient scourge of human habit. My interest in the academic rite of casting out this demon harkens back to a paper by Rothbart and Taylor (1992), where one finds the observation:

> The idea of essentialism, while counter to contemporary thinking about category structure, persists in people's perception of both natural kinds and social categories.

> We have argued that the characteristics of natural kinds have been implicitly used as a model for thinking about social categories, which seems to us particularly inappropriate given the degree to which a given social category can vary in its perceived alternability and centrality. A number of interesting predictions follow from the essentialist principle, as applied to social category. First, it suggests that stereotypes based on physical differences may be particularly pernicious, given the strong inferences that are based on surface similarities.   (1992: 32–3)

In biology too, essentialism has been singled out by no other than the eminent evolutionary theorist Ernst Mayr, as a bad habit in the taxonomy of natural types:

> Plato's concept of the *eidos* ['essence'] is the philosophical codification of this form of thinking. According to this concept the vast observed variability of the world has no more reality than the shadow of an object on a cave wall [...] Fixed, unchangeable "ideas" underlying the observed variability are the only things that are permanent and real. Owing to its belief in essences this philosophy is also referred to as *essentialism* [...] [which] dominated the natural sciences until well into the nineteenth century. The concept of unchanging essence and of complete discontinuity between every *eidos* ['type'] and all others make genuine evolutionary thinking neigh-well impossible.   (Mayr 1969: 4; brackets added)

In the space below, I will try to evaluate the core assertions made by Rothbart and Taylor (1992), in the process also dispensing, albeit more implicitly, with Mayr's (1969) observations. Earlier above, we traced back the intellectual roots of essentialism in philosophy, linguistics and psychology. We have also pointed out the evolutionary-adaptive underpinning of the hybrid pragmatic middle-ground approach to natural categories. In this section we extend the discussion into the notoriously slippery grounds of culture and society.

2.6.2. Reasoning by feature association

The adaptive decision-making strategy associated with prototype-based categories may be called *reasoning by feature association*. It is one of the most profound early adaptive moves in the evolution of biological organisms. Reasoning by feature association is the centerpiece of all biologically-based categorization. It is the very essence of cognition and internal representation — mental and otherwise. This marvelous adaptive invention is captured by an old maxim:

> If it looks like a duck, walks like a duck and quacks like a duck,
> then — by golly — it *must be* a duck.

The type of reasoning embodied in this trite maxim allows bio-organisms to draw quick inferences from visible-but-innocuous features to invisible-but-adaptively-urgent features. The mode of inference involved here is not deductive, but rather probabilistic-pragmatic, ('psychological', cf. Popper 1934/1959). It has roughly the same logical status as *hypothetical-abductive* reasoning (cf. Peirce 1940, Hanson 1958). That is, roughly:

(9)   a.   All members of category *A* possess property *b*.
     b.   Hitherto unsorted individual *x* displays property *b*.
     c.   If *x* is not a member of *A*, then the fact it possesses property *b*
        would be a strange accident.
     d.   But if I assume, by hypothesis, that *x* is a member of *A*, then
        the hitherto strange fact (b) is a logical consequence of (a).

     e.   Therefore *x* must be a member of category *A*

Again, what makes the abductive reasoning in (9) a relatively safe bet is feature (c) of prototype-like categories — strong feature association.

2.6.3. Over-generalization as an adaptive strategy

The amoeba, a single-cell organism with a semi-permeable external membrane, categorizes like an old-fashioned Platonist — when its survival is at stake. In the process, the amoeba indulges in rank over-generalization. The adaptively-vital dimension of salt concentration in the surrounding substrate is in reality a graded continuum. Somewhere above 0.9% saline concentration in the substrate, the amoeba faces the rising threat of excessive water-loss and (eventually) catastrophic dehydration. Somewhere below 0.9 %, it faces the converse threat of excessive water absorption and (eventually) catastrophic bursting. But the amoeba does not wait till the exact point of real threat is at hand in order to react. Nor does it merely calibrate its reaction gradually to the gradual changes in substrate salt concentration (although it may do that to some extent). Rather, the amoeba reacts categorically, in a trip-wire fashion. At a level of substrate salt concentration well below or well above the actual danger point, it begins to furiously expel or absorb water, respectively.

Why hasn't the amoeba developed a more finely-calibrated strategy, a greater context sensitivity, a more subtle decision procedure? Why does it over-react? Why does it stereotype so brazenly? Because the adaptive consequences of waiting too long and missing the cutoff point by a hair are too dire to contemplate. Whatever early kin the amoeba may have had who opted for a more subtle and fine-grained strategy did not live to tell the tale.

2.6.4. Logically-faulty but adaptively-sound conditional reasoning

As Tversky and Kahneman (1974) were fond of reminding us, humans appear notoriously bad at reasoning about one-way conditional associations, often succumbing to the strong temptation to run a faulty inference from one-way conditional to bi-conditional; that is, the faulty *modus ponens*, as in:

(10) $(A \supset B) \supset (B \supset A)$

There are two distinct reasons why the faulty deductive inference (10) may be a perfectly rational adaptive strategy. The first has to do with the logic itself, i.e. the relation of *set inclusion*. In pure deductive logic, inference (10) above is equally illicit in both inclusion relations (11a) and (11b) below:

(11)   a.   b.

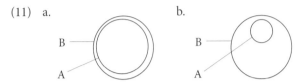

But in terms of probability, inference (10) is a reasonable, high-probability bet in set-inclusion situations such as (11a), where the population of "member of *B* but not of *A*" is a small minority of *B*. In contrast, inference (10) is a miserable low-probability bet in set-inclusion situations such as (11b), where that population is the overwhelming majority of *B*. As noted above, natural types display strong feature association, thus a strong overlap between populations that display one feature and those at display another.

   Logic aside, humans seem to be rather selective as to the contexts in which they do or don't practice the logically-fallacious inference (10). As a brief illustration, compare the two adaptive inferences (12) below:

(12)   **Visible features   Inferred adaptive value**

a.	apple-like ⊃	desirable food
b.	snake-like ⊃	lethal bite

The one-way conditional association between 'apple-like' and 'desirable food' (12a) is, in real-world terms, much stronger than between 'snake-like' and 'lethal bite' (12b). In both cases, the real-world probability of the logically-faulty bi-conditional interpretation ('if desirable food, then apple'; 'if lethal bite, then snake') is rather low. Nevertheless, categorial over-generalization of the one-way conditional is much more likely in (12b), as is a logically-faulty bi-conditional interpretation. Again, this is so presumably because the adaptive consequences of betting wrong are much more devastating in (12b) than in (12a). The aptness of an inference — whether logically correct or faulty, and however low the probability — is thus heavily dependent on the relevant adaptive context.

2.6.5. Perspective effects on construed adaptive context

As noted earlier (ch. 1), the notion *adaptive context* within which categorial snap judgements are made is not an objective entity, but rather a perspective-dependent mental construct. As an illustration, consider the matrix of possible adaptive reasoning in a small primate or early-human society in (13):

(13)

Category	Perspective	Adaptive consequences
Large male conspecific	male	dangerous foe or desirable ally
	female	desirable mate or dangerous rapist
Good-looking female conspecific	male	desirable mate or forbidden kin
	female	desirable ally or dangerous competitor

The adaptive perspective of male and female are different. And what is more, both males and females are capable of construing the same 'objective' context from multiple perspectives.

Lastly and uncomfortably closer to home, consider a current and most egregious example of stereotyping — *profiling*:

(14)

Conditional association	Probability
a. Dangerous terrorist ⊃ young Islamic male	Extremely high
b. Young Islamic male ⊃ dangerous terrorist	Extremely low

The conditional association of features in one direction (14a) is extremely high, while in the other direction (14b) it is extremely low. But it is in fact our knowledge of (14a) that seems to license the logically fallacious inference (14b). For while illogical, the *profiling* inference (14b) is adaptively unimpeachable, given the dire costs to be incurred if the statistically marginal association (14b) just turns out, for once, to be the case here and now.

2.6.6. Are social categories *not* natural kinds?

We are now in the position to take a closer look at the two central assertions made by Rothbart and Taylor (1992):

(a) essentialism [...] [is] counter to contemporary thinking about category structure

(b) the characteristics of natural kinds have been implicitly used as a model for thinking about social categories, which seems to us particularly inappropriate given the degree to which a given social category can vary in its perceived alternability and centrality

Assertion (a) is of course strictly-speaking true if by 'essentialism' one means the radical, extreme Platonic–logical approach to categories, an approach that does not recognize frequency distributions. But as noted above, the prototype approach, while mimicking two important aspects of Platonic categorization (strong feature association, robust clustering around the mean), does not indulge in the idealizing excesses of Platonism. So that while members of a natural population don't share an invariant 'essence', they do, statistically, exhibit a strong similarity to either an abstract prototype or a representative exemplar, and thus also to each other. We have noted that this allows biological organisms to reason like good essentialists *in the main*, in dealing with the bulk of members of a category, while reserving the more subtle context-scanning strategy for dealing with the small body of exceptional or ambiguous tokens — when those are adaptively relevant.

In order to evaluate assertion (b), we must first examine the evolutionary ontology of social categories, beginning with the early *society of intimates* prevalent among all social primates, including humans till ca. 8,000 BC. We may then ask — are social categories in our contemporary *society of strangers* really all that different? Have they lost their adaptive value? Are they but another atavistic bad habit, once perhaps adaptive but now a cognitive fossil?

2.7. The cultural context of social decision-making

2.7.1. The society of intimates[4]

Humans and their primate relatives evolved as a small-group adaptation, the *society of intimates*. This social organization prevailed in foraging societies (hunters-and-gatherers) exclusively till ca. 8,000 BC (Diamond 1999). With plant and animal domestication and the rise of sedentary village life, the pattern of social cooperation that had evolved during millions of years of hunting-and-gathering persisted in the early societies of cultivators and pastoral nomads.

As increasingly complex social units and institutions emerged, rather than disappear altogether, the society of intimates persisted, co-existing with as well as within the larger social units of cities, states and empires, the large-scale, complex *societies of strangers*. Even within present-day industrialized Western societies, substantial vestiges of the society of intimates persist, most notably in small isolated rural communities and cohesive urban neighborhoods. Likewise, in less developed countries, substantial populations of small-scale indigenous societies of intimates exist as enclaves within the nation-state, only partially integrated into the large national grid. Such enclaves retain many of their peculiar cultural norms, including patterns of trust and cooperation.

The salient characteristics of societies of intimates are:

(a) **Small size of social group**: The size of small hunter-and-gatherer societies seldom exceeds 100. For foraging social primates, including early hominids, the size range of 50–150 has remained extremely stable over the last several million years

(Dunbar 1992). And the relevant social unit of subsistence cultivators and pastoral nomads seldom exceeds 200 individuals. Such small size is conducive to familiarity and high frequency of daily personal contact among all members.

(b) **Foraging economy**: The society of intimates evolved in the context of hunting and gathering (foraging), supporting flexible omnivorous feeding. The technological simplicity of such an economy most commonly also involved a feast-or-famine cycle, since little could be stored for later feeding. Within-group sharing of both food and foraging activities in such a context mitigates the feast-or-famine cycle, and thus has a great adaptive value for both the individual's and the group's survival.

(c) **Restricted territory**: The effective range of hunting-and-gathering groups was traditionally within a 10–20 miles radius. Such societies thus occupied a relatively stable native terrain whose features were intimately familiar to all members. Individuals developed a strong emotional attachment to the group's territory (Schieffelin 1976). The overall population density of foraging societies was low, and social groups live, effectively, in *communicative isolation*, except for rare and primarily hostile contact at group boundaries.

(d) **Restricted gene pool**: Social grouping in foraging societies was invariably kinship- or descent-based, binding together individuals who acknowledge shared ancestry. Various provisions are made for exogamy, usually with a highly restricted set of other groups, as well as for splitting the group when its size exceeds the optimal range. The social group is thus the product of a much more restricted gene pool than is the case in complex societies of strangers.

(e) **Cultural uniformity**: Status and role differentiation within the society of intimates is relatively restricted, and is based primarily on biologically defined parameters — gender, age, descent line and personality. There is no full-time, rigid occupational specialization, and little social stratification. While perhaps not egalitarian in the absolute sense of Power (1991), societies of intimates — both human and pre-human — are notoriously non-hierarchic, with the well-known exception of personal *dominance hierarchies*. Such hierarchies are, paradoxically, both rigid and fluid: rigid at any given moment, so that group members always know their exact position vis-à-vis all other members; but fluid in the sense of being largely dependent on personality (culturally desired personal abilities; charisma) and thus essentially open to readjustment and change (de Waal 1982; Power 1991). But the fluidity and possible readjustment are themselves governed by relatively rigid *cultural norms* that are known to all members.

(f) **Informational homogeneity and stability**: The world-view of group members is relatively uniform and universally shared. With the absence of occupational differentiation, the small size of the descent-based group, the small and stable terrain and the relatively low rate of physical and cultural change, most *generic cultural knowledge* is shared, more or less equally, by all members. New information spreads rapidly and quickly becomes universal, due to proximity, intensive daily contact and small group size. The idiosyncratic behavior, motivation, propensities or caprices of all members are relatively well-known in the social unit, for the same reasons. The society of intimates is thus a society of high *informational predictability* in the three major categories that comprise the context upon which social communication is founded:

- culturally-shared generic knowledge of the world;
- situationally-shared knowledge of the communicative moment; and
- individually-shared knowledge of past action or communication.

(g) **Consensual leadership structure**: The society of intimates has always been profoundly consensual in the organization of action, cooperation and leadership. The latter is seldom formalized by either volunteering or election. Leadership in the society of intimates remains contingent, undertaken for the occasion, and quick to dissolved. While age and kinship are important factors in the emergence of leaders, their role is mediated by charisma and attested competence (Power 1991):

> The immediate-return foraging group is a consensus polity (Turnbull 1968; Silberbauer 1981). Nowhere in these societies do we find a secular authority backed by power (Turnbull 1968a). There is no permanent leader. Indeed, the constant change of leaders gives the appearance of there being none (Woodburn 1982).   (1991: 46)

(h) **Kinship-based social cooperation**: The social organization of the society of intimates is either *descent-based* (in a biological sense), as in the case of all social primates, or *kin based*, as in the case of humans. The latter is a more elaborate transformation emerging from the former, and may also include association by marriage, adoption, or various ritual associations. But whatever the exact basis of the kinship, virtually all social cooperation is predicted from it. For, as Stiles (1994) has noted:

> the principal objective is the survival of the group, not the individual.   (Stiles 1994: 438)

All interaction in societies of intimates, if not based explicitly on ties of consanguinity or affinity, is modeled after them. That is, friendly relations among non-kinsmen are functional analogues — or metaphors — of kin relations. The society of intimates leaves its members relatively few open choices in matters of social cooperation. As Stiles (1994) puts it:

> people in traditional societies are constrained in their decisions by cultural rules.   (Stiles 1994: 438)

Every member of the social unit knows, by virtue of membership and for each social context — procreation, child-rearing, subsistence, warfare, construction, ceremonies — who owes what whom under what conditions. This knowledge is shared by all members, is an indispensable part of socialization of the young, and is largely taken for granted. This is part of the paradox of consensual egalitarian societies: Their structure is quite rigid, available choices are limited and well circumscribed.

This rigidity of social structure and the limits on available choices is an important ingredient of the high predictability of the social behavior of group members. And this predictability is in turn a major factor in promoting trust and cooperation among members, each of whom can almost automatically rely on cooperation and reciprocation in each culturally-defined social context. This rigid social calculus is, in turn, the main guarantor of a reliable *reasoning by feature association* about members of various social categories in the society of intimates.

(i) **Non-cooperation with strangers**: There are few provisions in the kin-based society of intimates for knowing, meeting, communicating or cooperating with strangers. Almost by definition, lack of a well-defined position within the rigid social grid renders non-hostile interaction with strangers unlikely. From the perspective of network organization, a *floating node* without clear connections to other nodes cannot be part of a viable network. Aside from hostility, the only consistent provisions made for dealing with strangers are those of *incorporation*, by either marriage, adoption or kidnap/slavery. Such provisions may be viewed as mechanisms for *de-alienation*.

The two most important rules in the rigid social calculus of the society of intimates are:

- No cooperation without trust.
- No trust without intimacy.

The most important social-categorial contrast in the society of intimates is, therefore, between *member* and *stranger*. Within the group, most social interaction is governed by the rigid calculus of the kinship system. This system is, in turn, made up of (most commonly) the social categories of *gender*, *age*, *descent* and *marriage*. Social categories in the society of intimates are thus incredibly predictive. They exhibit strong feature association.

Was the society of intimates deluded in setting up social categories whose behavior closely resemble that of 'natural types'? The question is indeed bizarre, for why should any organism set up any categorial schema, social or otherwise, unless it was predictive enough to serve as the basis for reliable adaptive decision-making? If no feature association is found through protracted experience, why bother setting up a category? As has been noted since Aristotle, all taxonomies are logically arbitrary but pragmatically, contextually determined. That is, in the context of both biological and cultural evolution, categorization is adaptively driven. It is an adaptive gambit by the organism, much like scientific taxonomies are theoretical gambits by the scientist (Mayr 1976):

> Every biological classification is a *scientific theory*. Classifications have the same properties as all theories in science. A given classification is *explanatory* [. . .] A good classification, like a good scientific theory, has a high *predictive power* with respect to the assignment of newly-discovered species and the pattern of variation of previously unused characters.   (1976: 427; italics added).

2.7.2. Is the society of intimates still relevant?

2.7.2.1. *The society of strangers*

As far as can be ascertained, the society of intimates remained a remarkably stable pattern of social organization from the dawn of social primates 10 million years ago until the late neolithic era ca. 8,000 BC. Complex *societies of strangers* began to appear around that time, invariably associated with technological advances such as plant and animal domestication, metallurgy, pottery, and literacy (Diamond 1999). Almost invariably, the larger social units that sprang up beginning with early Bronze Age were associated with two profound departures from foraging economy. The forager's hunting adaptation converted its expert knowledge of the fauna into animal domestication and pastoralism. The forager's gathering adaptation converted its equally expert knowledge of the flora into plant domestication and cultivation. Both changes precipitated (or made possible) more sedentary settlements, the creation of surplus foodstuff and its storage (whether on the hoof or in the granary), higher population densities and larger social units. With durable land improvements, cultivation, irrigation and shelter, unambiguous private ownership of 'real' property, henceforth held in common by the foraging group, became an entrenched cultural feature.

With the increase of relevant group size came the classical problems of management, coordination, and hierarchic organization. As a result, the flat, relatively amorphous and typically leaderless governance structure of the society of intimates was converted into well-defined hierarchic structures. That is, schematically:

(15)

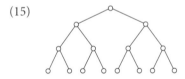

The social and communicative consequences of hierarchic social organization are profound, and may be expressed in terms of the interaction between vertically-adjacent or horizontally-adjacent nodes in schema (15) above:

- **Vertically**, a node interacts, as either governor or governed, only with vertically-adjacent nodes.
- **Horizontally**, a node interacts, as cohort, only with horizontally-adjacent nodes that are governed directly by the same node.

Complex hierarchic organization, once it has attained the scope of cities, states, kingdoms and empires, harbors a vast potential for alienation and *loss of intimacy*. Leaders ('governing nodes') of relevant units are alienated from all but a relatively small portion of their governed community — their immediate subordinates. Subordinates ('governed nodes') can maintain intimacy only within small commonly-governed units (clan, village, urban neighborhood), but otherwise are alienated from daily contact with other, similarly-isolated *nuclei of intimacy*. Social fragmentation and lack of intimacy guarantees mistrust. Invariably, wherever complex societies arose in human history, non-consensual coercive governance arose with them.

It is truly remarkable how little experimentation in consensual government has been recorded over the protracted history of complex societies of strangers, be they in Mesopotamia, Egypt, China, India, or the Americas. The few experiments in consensual governance in complex societies of strangers that have taken place, all within the Western tradition, amount to a frail 200 years in Greece, 100 years in Rome, and the relatively precarious last 200 years of Western Europe and North America — out of the roughly 10,000 year lifetime of the society of strangers.

2.7.2.2. *The persistence of the society of intimates*

The society of intimates, and the mechanisms through which social cooperation within it were made possible, is not a dead relic of our stone-age past. Rather, it is an amazingly persistent evolutionary adaptation that, through many metamorphoses in new contexts, has retained its adaptive motivation. It has made it possible for complex societies of strangers to exist and function as — admittedly somewhat pale imitations of — consensual societies.

To the extent that governance in complex societies of strangers can be non-coercive, it invariably depends on — or falls back to — the deeply ingrained cultural calculus of the society of intimates. So far as can be ascertained, non-coercive societies of strangers have remained viable only when they succeeded in recapturing some of the intimacy and solidarity of the society of intimates. In this section we will note four adaptive mechanisms that provide for at least a measure of *de-alienation*.

(a) **Islands of intimacy**
     Within complex societies of strangers, intimacy, trust and cooperation have of course never died out, but rather have become confined to small-size *islands of intimacy* whose members remain in frequent face-to-face contact — families, friends, schools/classes, congregations, work-places, sports teams, clubs, neighborhood bars, musical bands, theatrical casts, etc. Almost any frequent association based on common interests seems to reproduce — and depend on — the old evolutionary pattern of intimacy, personal loyalty, trust and cooperation. Within the complex society of strangers, these islands of intimacy are created, maintained, and re-created for the occasion. They make social cooperation possible, they furnish the considerable emotional support that all social beings apparently expect from their intimates. The fundamental assumptions and cultural calculus of such social islands are remarkably like those of the traditional society of intimates.

(b) **Mass communication**
     Mass intimacy may sound like an oxymoron, and yet it is a major adaptive mechanism in complex societies of strangers. Until the advent of universal media, geographic separation sooner or later led to the linguistic-cultural

equivalent of biological *speciation*, and thus the loss of the most important prerequisite for a community — common language and shared cultural perspective. In the absence of spatial intimacy, complex societies have, almost invariably, resorted to mass media of communication — national language, literacy, standardized education. What used to be daily face-to-face contact is replaced by other forms of public, universally-accessible discourse. The national media do not only re-homogenize linguistic and cultural perspective, they also contributes — via the universal consumer culture — to the maintenance of external manifestations of shared cultural identity: food, dwelling, dress, hairstyle, art, sports, humor. Such devices may be viewed as a move to outflank spatial separation and recapture the major precondition for intimacy and trust — shared values.

(c) **Rituals of de-alienation**

In the complex society of strangers, one does not talk to a stranger without first going through standard rituals of de-alienation: Greetings, introductions, small talk, the sharing of 'meaningless' confidences, comparison of backgrounds, of shared knowledge and common interests, of common friends or acquaintances. Such innocent social maneuvers (Goffman 1963, 1967, 1971), seemingly of self definition, constitute a systematic search for *common grounds*, for the *threshold of commonality* without which cooperation is inadvisable. Many of the innocuous games of urban living can be understood as rituals of de-alienation, as tactical moves through which one may decide, progressively and with the option to disengage at any point along the route, whether to become more intimate, develop trust, and eventually proceed to transacting the business at hand. And many of these mechanisms have been honed to fine edge in traditional societies of intimates (see e.g. Basso 1972).

(d) **Shared cultural perspective**

Probably the most fundamental universal condition for social cooperation has always been the existence of a shared cultural perspective. Granted, 'shared' like 'similar' is a relative notion, a matter of degree. No culture, however small and traditional, is ever 100% homogeneous. In this, cultures resemble biological species, where a fine balance — Mayr's *dynamic equilibrium* — is maintained between genetic/phenotypic homogeneity and diversity (see discussion earlier above). A minimal level of common perspective, most conspicuously coded in the categories of a common lexicon, is an absolute prerequisite not only for communication but also for trust and cooperation in a consensual society.[5]

The construction of highly predictive prototype-based cognitive and linguistic categories, with their partial mimicry of Platonic essentialism, is thus not only the individual organism's adaptive strategy for dealing with the physical environment. It is also the prime adaptive strategy of social species. For the most profound adaptive strategy of a social species is the ability of members to predict — i.e. construct — the mental representations held by other members. That is, *knowing other minds*.

This provision may, in turn, be broken down into two distinct sub-parts:

(i)   Communication and cooperation about the world requires a considerable overlap in individual members' mental representation of that world.
(ii) Cooperation and communication about anything whatever requires some minimal access to the interlocutor's current states belief and intention.

Provision (i) requires a shared *conceptual map* of the wold, as represented in the group's commonly held lexical-semantic categories (see ch. 4). Provision (ii) is the adaptive substratum over which the rise of grammar — be it in evolution, ontogeny or diachrony — takes place (see ch. 4).

2.7.2.3. *Maladaptive features of the society of intimates*
As noted above, the cultural mechanisms that make possible trust and cooperation in the society of intimates have proved themselves remarkably resilient and adaptive in the protracted evolutionary history of not only that society, but also the current consensual society of strangers. But the very same adaptive features may on occasion prove maladaptive in complex modern contexts. And this is where, I suspect, one may find the legitimate core of Rothbart and Taylor's (1992) concerns.

A long lineup of familiar scourges — the Old Boys' Network, nepotism, favoritism, clannishness, discrimination, racism, sexism, gay-bashing, social condescension, over-stereotyping and erroneous profiling — may all be viewed as regrettable but nonetheless natural consequences of the highly adaptive social calculus of the society of intimates.

The entrenched cultural mechanisms suggested above — shared meaning, common cultural perspective, extended public intimacy, rituals of de-alienation — remain the only natural means we have for extending nuclei of trust and cooperation in the complex society of strangers, to the point where erstwhile strangers may become, however provisionally, intimates and then cooperators. Indeed, Rothbart and Taylor's (1992) study suggests just this: Once we become familiar with individuals of an over-stereotyped category, we are more receptive to re-evaluating our erstwhile categorial judgements. But lamenting the persistence of deeply-ingrained — automated, genetically selected — adaptive strategies is not a coherent recipe for engineered social change.

In the next chapter we will survey some of the consequences of the nodes-and-connections — network — cognitive design of lexical memory, most specifically those that pertain to semantic change and metaphoric extension.

Notes

* I am indebted to Sam Glucksberg, Bernd Heine, Mike Posner and Mick Rothbart for helpful comments on an earlier version of this chapter. They are, needless to say, absoved from responsibility for the final product.

1. It is of course obvious that only because of idealization — the dismissal of real instances of language use — is it possible to attribute such clean properties to naturally-evolved categorization schema to an underlying logic (see 2.2.2. below). Chomsky' *competence* is what licenses his *generativity*.

2. In another — perhaps prescient — passage of the *Investigations*, Wittgenstein observes:

> I want to say: we have here a *normal* case and abnormal cases. It is only in normal cases that the use of a word is clearly prescribed; we know, we are in no doubt, what to say in this or that case. The more abnormal a case, the more doubtful it becomes what we are to say ... if there were for instance no characteristic expressions of pain, of fear, of joy; if rule became exception and exception became rule; or if both became phenomena of roughly equal frequency — this would make our normal language-games lose their point.   [1953; 141, 142; 56].

This is, to my mind, the strongest suggestion that Wittgenstein considered frequency distribution and thus figure-ground relations an important ingredient of natural categories. In other words, the membership of natural categories, in the main, clusters around their mean. That is, they are prototypes-like categories (see below). This passage is logically incompatible with some interpretation of the 'family-resemblance' metaphor, such as Lakoff's (1987) notion of 'radial category'.

3. Katz and Fodor's semantic categories are discrete and binary. Ambiguity — polysemy — is 'handled' by 'projection rules' whose input is (i) the semantic categories as listed in the dictionary; and (ii) the grammatical description of sentences. Such a treatment only accounts for the explicit linguistic context — sentences and/or their structure. But since that context abides by Generative rules, it is just as discrete and Platonic as the semantic categories themselves.

4. The discussion in this section owes much to Phil Young (in personal communication; see also Givón and Young 2002).

5. From this perspective, the current intellectual and political infatuation with so-called 'multi-culturalism' and 'diversity' is indeed bizarre. Truly multi-cultural societies have always been either ruthlessly coercive (old Persia, ancient Egypt, Rome, the Holy Roman Empire, the Third Reich, the Soviet Union) or murderously violent (Lebanon, Ruanda, Congo, Afghanistan, Yugoslavia) or, most often, both.

Chapter 3

Semantic networks and metaphoric language

3.1. Culturally shared generic mental maps*

In this chapter we return to take a closer look at the cognitive design of culturally shared lexical-semantic categories; that is, at the mental map of the external, internal and/or social universe we must assume we hold in common with members of our relevant social group. We will begin by a brief outline of the general design of the human communication system, and where the generic categorial map fits in.

3.2. General design of the human communication system

Well-coded human communication may be divided, broadly, into two sub-systems:

- The cognitive representation system
- The communicative codes

The human cognitive representation system comprises of three concentric levels:

- The conceptual lexicon
- Propositional information
- Multi-propositional discourse

The communicative codes comprise of two distinct coding instruments:

- The sensory-motor codes
- The grammatical code

3.2.1. The cognitive representation system

a. **The conceptual lexicon**

The human conceptual lexicon is a repository of relatively time-stable, socially-shared, well-coded concepts which, taken together, constitute the cognitive map of our experiential universe:

- the external-physical universe
- the social-cultural universe
- the internal-mental universe.

By *time-stable* one means knowledge that is not in rapid flux. That is, the meaning of 'horse' today will probably remain the same tomorrow. Though gradual change of meaning in not precluded.

By *socially shared* one means that when launching into communication, speakers take it for granted that words have roughly the same meanings for all members of their speech community. Though membership is conceded to be a matter of degree.

By *well-coded* one means that each chunk of lexically-stored knowledge is more-or-less uniquely, or at least strongly, associated with its own perceptual code-label. Though again, well-codedness may be a matter of degree.

Lexical concepts are conventionalized types of experience rather than individual tokens of experience. That is, they are *generic*. Such conventionalization presumably involves the development of a prototypical activation pattern of a cluster of connected nodes (see below).

A lexical concept may represent a relatively time-stable entity — physical object, landmark, location, plant, animal, person, cultural institution or abstract concept — thus typically a *noun*. It may be represent a more temporary action, event, process or relation, thus typically a *verb*. It may represent a time-stable quality or temporary state, thus typically an *adjective*. Cognitive psychologists have long recognized the conceptual lexicon under the label of *permanent semantic memory* (Atkinson and Shiffrin 1968; Quillian 1968).

b. Propositional information

One can combine concepts ('words') into propositional information ('clauses') about states or events in which entities partake. Such states or events may pertain to the external world, the internal mental world, the culturally-mediated world, or to various combinations thereof. Cognitive psychologists have long recognized our capacity to process and store propositional information as *episodic-declarative memory* (Atkinson and Shiffrin 1968; Squire 1987).

c. Multi-propositional discourse

Individual state or event clauses may be combined into coherent discourse. Human discourse is predominantly multi-propositional. That is, its *coherence* transcends the bounds of its component clauses. Multi-propositional discourse is also processed and stored in *episodic-declarative memory* (Kintsch 1977, 1988, 1994; Kintsch and van Dijk 1978; Loftus 1980; Gernsbacher 1990; Givón 1995; Ericsson and Kintsch 1995).

d. Interaction between words, propositions and discourse

As an illustration of the combinatorial relation between lexical concepts, propositional information and discourse coherence, consider the simple-minded examples in (1), (2) and (3) below:

(1) **Concepts = words**:
  a. drive   b. insane
  c. constant   d. abuse
  e. maid   f. kill
  g. butler   h. knife
  i. hide   j. fridge

(2) **Clauses = propositions**:
  a. The maid was driven insane.
  b. The butler constantly abused the maid.
  c. The maid killed the butler with a knife.
  d. The maid hid the knife in the fridge last night.

(3) **Multi-propositional discourse**:
  Having been driven insane
  by constant abuse,
  the maid killed the butler with the knife
  that she had hidden in the fridge the night before.

Taken by themselves, outside any propositional context, the words in (1a–j) convey only conceptual meaning. That is, you may only ask about them questions such as:

(4) a. What does *drive* mean?
  b. Does *drive* mean the same as *abuse*?
  c. If someone is a *maid*, can she also a *butler*, or a *woman*?
  d. Is *kill* related in meaning to *die, slaughter* or *murder*, and if so how?

Combined into clauses, as in (2a–d), the very same words now partake in the coding of *propositional information*. In addition to questions of conceptual meaning as in (4), the individual clauses in (2) may now prompt questions of information, such as in (5) below:

(5) a. Was the maid driven insane?
  b. Who abused the maid?
  c. Who killed the butler?
  d. Who did the maid kill?
  e. What did the maid kill the butler with?
  f. Did the maid kill the butler?
  g. Where did the maid hide the knife?
  h. When did the maid hide the knife in the fridge?

Finally, the multi-propositional text in (3), in which the very same propositions of (2) are now combined, has *discourse coherence*. In addition to questions of conceptual meaning such as (4) and propositional information such as (5), one may now ask questions that pertain to that coherence, such as:

(6)   a.   Why did she kill him?
     b.   How come she had a knife?
     c.   Why had the maid hidden the knife in the fridge?
     d.   Could she perhaps have talked to him first before taking such a dras-
        tic step?
     e.   Was her action reasonable? Was it defensible in a court of law?

The questions in (6) may appear deceptively akin to those in (5). However, each question in (5) can be answered on the basis of knowing only one atomic proposition in (2). In contrast, none of the questions in (6) can be answered on the basis of such atomic propositional knowledge. Rather, the knowledge of several propositions in the connected discourse (3), or even of the entire coherent text, is required in order to answer such questions.

The partial dissociation between conceptual meaning and propositional information is easy to demonstrate by constructing grammatically well-formed sentences that make no sense; that is, sentences whose words are perfectly meaningful, each taken by itself, but still do not combine into a cogent proposition; as in Chomsky's ubiquitous example:

(7)   Colorless green ideas sleep furiously

The meaning incongruities that make proposition (7) bizarre — 'colorless green', 'green ideas', 'ideas sleep', 'sleep furiously' — are all due to the semantic specificity of individual words. The relation between lexical meaning and propositional information is thus one of *inclusion*, or a one-way conditional. That is:

- One can understand the meaning of words independent of the proposition in which they are embedded; but one cannot understand a proposition without understanding the meaning of the words that make it up.

The partial dissociation between propositional information and discourse coherence can be just as easily demonstrated, by stringing together perfectly informative but incoherently combined propositions. Thus for example, re-scrambling the coherent discourse in (3) yields the incoherent (8) below:

(8)   a.   Having killed the butler with the knife
     b.   by constant abuse,
     c.   the maid had been driven insane
     d.   and had hidden it in the fridge the night before.

No propositional-semantic anomaly is discernible in any of the individual clauses (8a–d). The bizarreness of (8) as a connected discourse is due to two factors:

- the lack of cross-propositional coherence; and
- the use of grammatical forms designed to code another coherent order, that of (3).

One could indeed conceive of ways by which the sequence of clauses in (8) can be made coherent. But this would require adjusting their grammatical structure to the new order, as in (9) below:

(9)   a.   Having failed to kill the butler
       b.   despite the constant abused,
       c.   the maid was finally driven insane
            [upon realizing that]
       d.   she had hidden the knife in the fridge the night before.

The relation between propositional information and discourse coherence is thus also an *inclusion* relation, or a one-way conditional. That is:

- One can understand the meaning of clauses independent of the discourse in which they are embedded; but one cannot understand the discourse without understanding the propositions that make it up.

3.2.2. The sensory-motor codes

The peripheral sensory-motor codes of human language are the subject matter of three fields — phonetics, phonology and cognitive neuroscience — which jointly investigate speech production (coding), speech perception (decoding), and the mental representation of code units. The perceptual and productive modality of these peripheral codes may vary (auditory-oral, visual-gestural, writing, etc.). Its primary use is to code the conceptual lexicon (words), but it also codes an important part of grammar (morphology).

3.2.3. The grammar code

At this point, I will simply assert that grammar is used primarily[1] to code *discourse coherence*. This, in turn, translates into the coding of *communicative intent*. And this, in the framework outlined in this book, translates into mental models of *the interlocutor's current states of belief and intention*. Not any good old belief and intention states, but those that are relevant to the current communication. Within this framework, communication is but a sub-species of cooperative transaction. Several subsequent chapters (chs 4, 5, 6 and 7) will develop this perspective more fully.

3.3. The generic lexicon as a network of nodes and connections

The most plausible assumption one can make, given the facts of language, cognition and neurology, is that conceptual/semantic meaning is represented in the mind/brain as a *network of nodes and connections* (Quillian 1968; Collins and Quillian 1972; Collins and Loftus 1975; Spitzer 1999). This model was chosen by Rosch (1973a, b, 1975) to accommodate the dual aspects of prototype-like phenomena — a stable core of frequent, conventional uses vs. a periphery of infrequent, variants. This is also the model that best accounts for *spreading activation* (Quillian and Collins 1972), *semantic priming* (Meyer and Schwaneveldt 1975), automatic vs. context-primed activation (Swinney 1979; Neeley 1990), *word association* effects (Spitzer 1999), as well as the facts of neural basis of lexical categories (Spitzer 1999). Lastly, this model also accommodates *metaphoric* (non-literal) meaning and thus semantic change and learning.

The network model of lexical semantics assumes that when a conceptual node ('word') is activated, be it by an internal impulse or by its perceptual label (phonological form), a cluster of adjacent nodes — a local sub-network — is automatically also activated by it. This sub-network is never exactly the same across usages of the same word, but only approximately so. In this fashion, a group of 'core nodes' tends to be automatically activated in most contexts. This automatic activation pattern represents the stable, conventionalized, high-frequency *prototype* of the lexical category.

In infrequent, less conventional, peripheral contexts, other nodes may also be activated, nodes that are specific only to particular off-prototype contexts. The activation of these nodes is *primed* by such contexts (Meyer and Schwaneveldt 1975, Swinney 1979; Neeley 1990).

As an illustration, consider the conceptual node 'house', which in our culture most commonly — thus automatically — activates the closely-linked nodes 'roof', 'walls', 'floor', 'living room', 'bedroom(s)', 'bathroom(s)', 'kitchen', 'basement' etc. Presumably because of such automatic activation, when 'house' is introduced into the discourse for the first time, each of its closely-linked nodes are automatically activated or 'primed', and are thus mentally accessible to the interlocutor even without explicit mention. This is the so-called *frame* or *script* effect. For this reason, presumably, we can mark each of the concepts activated by the frame 'house' in (10) below as *definite* — even when they are introduced into the discourse for the first time (Linde 1974):

(10)   We stayed in **this house**, and boy, ... *the livingroom* was too small, *the kitchen* too far from *the dining-room*, *the bathrooms* were too dark, *the roof* leaked and *the walls* had cracks, plus *the bedrooms* were upstairs and *the floors* were tiled with cheap stuff ...

Other conceptual nodes may be connected to 'house' indirectly, more distantly, or only in special, infrequent, non-prototypical contexts. Thus consider:

(11)   a.   We saw **this house** there,
              ?but then *the electricians* went on strike.
        b.   My brother-in-law promised to **build** us **this house** by December,
              but then *the electricians* went on strike.
        c.   We saw **this house** there,
              ?but *the escrow company* was closed.
        d.   There was **this house** we wanted to **close the deal** on,
              but *the escrow company* was closed.

In (11) above, the conceptual node 'house' by itself does not license the automatic activation — thus the assumption of accessibility and definiteness — of 'electricians'

(11a) and 'escrow company' (11c). It is the special context of 'build' in (11b) or 'close the deal' in (11d) that, in combination with 'house', licenses the activation of 'electricians' or 'escrow company', respectively.

Schematically, one may describe the effect of contextual priming, and thus the activation pattern of the same word in less-habituated contexts, as slight shifts or adjustment in the most common activation pattern. The activation pattern of the same word in different contexts thus tends to include the core of *prototype nodes*, those that tend to be activated automatically in all contexts. These core nodes may be viewed operationally as the intersection of the majority of uses of the word. But in addition each context also activates other, less central, more context-specific nodes.

(12) **Prototypical vs. less prototypical node-activation patterns:**

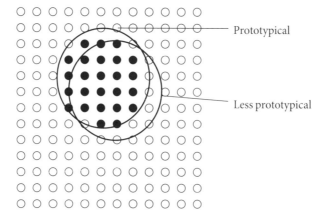

The more distant a context — or usage — is from the prototype of the category, the more likely it is to involve the activation of non-prototypical nodes and/or fewer prototype-core nodes. This relatively innocuous context-induced shifting of activation pattern during on-line communication also characterizes metaphoric meaning, the proliferation of multiple senses (polysemy) and semantic change. It is the *relative frequency* of contexts that determines what is the prototype core and what is the periphery in semantic networks. *Use frequency* thus drives both the establishment and the dis-establishment of automatic activation patterns in the semantic network.

One may as well note that the very same network model of lexical-semantic representation can also account for *cross-cultural differences* in the cognitive mapping of the world. Thus, for example, 'house' is likely to involve, in most if not all cultures, the cluster of semantic nodes 'dwell', 'shelter', 'construct', or 'family'. This cluster may be considered a human universal 'core'. But the conceptual nodes 'living room', 'bathroom', 'kitchen', 'bedroom' or 'basement' are neither connected to nor activated by 'house' in many cultures, where the prototype dwelling is a single room. Just as the concepts 'walls', 'ceiling', 'roof', 'floor' or 'window' are meaningless in cultures where the prototypical dwelling is a tipi.

In describing the cross-cultural variation of semantic networks, one can thus, tentatively, talk of the *relatively* universal 'core' of concepts — thus contexts — that most human societies have found adaptively relevant. This core can be then contrasted with more culture-specific 'peripheral' contexts, those that not all cultures deem adaptively relevant.

3.4. Metaphoric or non-literal meaning

3.4.1. The Aristotelian tradition

The view of metaphor I will pursue here harkens back to Aristotle, where the relation between literal senses and their metaphoric or metonymic usage is viewed as a species of *similarity* or *analogy*. What this approach focuses on is metaphoric behavior, the *process* of abductive-analogical reasoning by which senses are extended, first during live communication and ultimately over historical time. In thinking and speaking metaphorically, one *re-construes* the established, conventional, habituated, literal sense of a word, re-interpreting it as similar or analogical but not identical. And one does this in specific less-conventional usage contexts, thus for specific less-conventional communicative ends.

The key element in this approach to metaphor is, not surprisingly, *context*. It is contextual snap-judgements during live communication that drive the inventive flight of metaphoric language. And it is the serendipitous discovery — and instant exploitation — of novel expressive opportunities that motivates it.

While admitting similarity and analogy as the foundations of metaphoric behavior, the Aristotelian approach is not to be confused with an objectivist, 'feature-counting' *comparison model*, as implied in both Cacciari and Glucksberg (1994) and Lakoff and Johnson (1980). For Aristotle's notion of similarity (cf. *Metaphysics*) was emphatically not objective or discrete, but rather pragmatic and context-driven.

Like all contextual judgements, the on-line use of metaphoric senses is marked by a certain measure of *serendipity*. For a context is not there objectively, waiting to be noticed. A context is construed on the fly, for the occasion. It is a *synthesis di novo*. This serendipitous, ephemeral, context-dependent nature of metaphoric language is put aptly by Gibbs (1987):

> Which properties of the metaphor are the salient ones depends precisely on what knowledge is shared by the speaker and the hearer on any given occasion. The properties of any given term in a metaphor may be *ephemerally* rather than eternally salient.   (1987: 40)

This approach to metaphor is thus transparently pragmatic. It view metaphoric behavior as an instance of the more general process of learning, innovation and cognitive or linguistic change, where a construed novel sense is understood in terms of what is already known, familiar, conventional.

The Aristotelian view of metaphor is thus deeply embedded in the pragmatic approach to learning and change. It is part and parcel of the pragmatic middle-ground in epistemology (see ch. 1). It is an approach that views abduction, analogical reasoning and fresh construal of context as the very core of discovery and accretion of knowledge.

In the same vein, this approach view the analogical, metaphoric re-casting of older senses of words as the prime mechanism that drives both semantic change (Nunberg 1979; MacCormack 1985; Lee 1990; Lehrer 1990; Sweetser 1991; Cacciari and Glucksberg 1994) and syntactic innovation (Givón 1989). The latter includes, prominently, *grammaticalization* — the diachronic rise of grammatical morphemes out of lexical words (Heine 1993, 1997; Heine and Reh 1984; Givón 1973a, 1989; Sweetser 1990; Heine *et al.* 1991; Bybee *et al.* 1994; *inter alia*). Because diachronic change in both lexicon and grammar is gradual, it is not surprising to find a fine gradient between live metaphors and fully conventionalized literal usage (Gibbs 1984; Dascal 1987; Cacciari 1993; Glucksberg 1991; Cacciari and Glucksberg 1994;).

While the construal of context *di novo* is logically unconstrained, the pragmatic approach to metaphor does not reject linguistic or cognitive universals. This is so because some analogies or similarities are more likely to be construed during live communication than others. They may be more *cognitively transparent* and thus, ultimately, more *adaptively valid*. They may have been systematically selected for during the course of neuro-cognitive evolution.

The brain/mind is chock-ful of such innate biases. But however rigidly biased the system may seem, a certain level of cross-cultural diversity in metaphoric behavior can always be found. So that the balance between universal and culture-specific metaphoric processes may mimic, in obvious ways and for obvious reasons, the relation between the prototype/core and outlier/periphery of mental categories.

Let us consider some examples of metaphoric usage in two fiction texts. In both, I have tried to identify the two extreme points on the diachronic continuum between fully conventionalized literal meaning and live metaphoric usage. The diachronically younger, relatively non-conventionalized fresh metaphoric uses are bold faced in the two texts. In the main, such expressions have not yet become fixed collocations or idioms, and their use remains highly context-dependent.

The diachronically older, fully conventionalized usages are italicized in the text below. Such usages have become fixed and indexed to conventional semantic contexts, have become fully-conventionalized *idioms*, or are *dead metaphors*. Since we are dealing with a finely-shaded continuum, the distinction between the two extremes is not always easy to make, and intermediate cases abound.

Consider first a passage from a novel by Walker Percy (1960):

> Down I *plunk* myself with a *liberal* weekly at one of the *massive* tables, read it from cover to cover, nodding to myself whenever the writer **scores a point**. *Damn right*, old son, I say, jerking my chair in approval. **Pour it on them**. Then up and over the *rack* for a *conservative* monthly and down in a *fresh cool chair* to join the **counterattack**. Oh oh, say I, and hold fast to the chair *arm*: that one did it: **eviscerated! And then out and away** *into* the sunlight, my neck **prickling** with satisfaction.   (1960: 100)

The onomatopoeic 'plunk (oneself) down' is almost a conventional idiom for 'throw (oneself) down', or 'drop (something)'. 'Liberal' is a dead metaphor, now literal in the context of politics. 'Massive' is on its way to full conventionalization as 'big', though not yet in all semantic contexts (?'a massive laugh'; ?'a massive mouse'). 'Score a point', a sports metaphor for 'win an argument in debate' is not fully conventionalized for the debating context. 'Rack' for a contraption on which one hangs newspapers or magazines is fully conventionalized, thus literal, a dead metaphor; as is 'conservative' in the political context. The use of 'fresh cool (chair)' is perhaps semi-conventional for 'newly used'. But 'counterattack', another military metaphor for 're-sponse' in the context of politics, is a relatively fresh metaphoric usage. The use of 'arm' in the context of 'chair' is a dead metaphor. But 'eviscerated', here in the context of political debate, is still relatively fresh. 'Into (the sunlight)' is a dead metaphor, originally mapping a 3-D walled enclosure onto a more abstract, perhaps 2-D space. But '(neck) prickling (with satisfaction)' is a relatively fresh usage, not yet fully restricted to this particular semantic context.

Consider now a passage from the comic fiction writer (and practicing journalist) Carl Hiaasen (2002):

> Only two types of journalists choose to stay at a *paper* that's being **gutted** by Wall Street **whorehoppers**. One faction is comprised of editors and reporters whose skills are so *marginal* that they are lucky to be employed, and they know it. **Unencumbered** by any sense of duty to the readers, they are pleased to *forgo* the **pursuit** of actual news in order to *cut expenses* and **score points** with the **suits**. These fakers are eager to *pick out* in a *bustling* city room — they are at their best when arranging and attending *pointless* meetings, and at their **skittish**, in*decisive* worst **under the heat** of a **looming** *deadline*. Stylistically they *strive* for *brevity* and **froth**, *shirking* from stories that **demand** *depth* and *deliberation*, stories that might **rattle a few cages** and **raise a little hell**.   (2002: 202).

'Paper' is a dead metaphor used literally; but the use of 'gutted', a mapping from the butcher shop to business, is relatively fresh and not restricted to a single semantic context, as is 'whorehoppers'. 'Marginal' is a dead spatial metaphor. 'Unencumbered' is a resuscitated Latin metaphor now on the way towards re-conventionalization. 'Forgo' is a dead metaphor for 'choose not to', while 'pursuit' is perhaps still semi-live as a metaphor for 'search for'. Both 'cut' and 'expenses' are dead metaphors, the first relatively recent, the second harkening back to Latin. The sports metaphor 'score points' is still somewhat alive in its context here, as is 'suits' (for 'higher management'). Both 'pick out' (for 'identify') and 'bustling' (for 'busy') are on their way to full literality, as is 'pointless' (for 'purposeless'). 'Skittish' is still marginally fresh; '(in)decisive' is a dead Latin metaphor; and 'under the heat' is still a reasonably live usage, as is 'looming'. 'Deadline' is a conventionalized near-dead metaphor, as is 'strive', another martial metaphor and 'brevity', a mapping from space to time. 'Froth', on the other hand, is relatively alive. 'Shirking' (for 'avoiding') is near-dead and almost literal, but 'demand' is perhaps still somewhat alive in this context. Both 'depth' (in this context) and 'deliberation' (in all contexts) are dead metaphors, the latter from Latin. Finally, both 'rattle a few cages' and 'raise a little hell', while already idiomatic, are still fairly live usages, leastwise in their present context.

The degree of *contextual freedom* of metaphoric usage turns out to be a central issue, both methodological and theoretical. From a theoretical perspective, live metaphoric usage is not restricted to a single semantic context. Though it is, para-doxically, highly sensitive to its serendipitous *pragmatic* context. Multiple semantic targets can be construed as similar to — and thus metaphorically mapping onto — the very same semantic source domain; just as many semantic source-domains can map metaphorically onto the very same semantic target. It is the serendipitous con-strual of the discourse context that makes metaphoric language effective, that gives it its double edge — semantically accessible yet pragmatically fresh. In contrast, it is the relative predictability and conventionality of the semantic context that makes literal usage, well, so literal and so indifferent to its pragmatic context. Semantics is conventionalized context, or petrified pragmatics.

From a methodological perspective, the Aristotelian approach to metaphor is more heavily invested in studying the on-line *process* of metaphoric usage, rather than its ultimate *end-product*, the well-established metaphor. It focuses on the *con-tinuum*, thus on small incremental steps of on-line metaphoric behavior that lead from *a* through *b* and *c* eventually to *z*. And it attempts to understand, from an adaptive perspective, both the on-line process of fresh metaphoric usage and the protracted gradual process of conventionalization, idiom formation and metaphor extinction.

3.4.2. Lakoff *et al.'s* "conceptual metaphors"

An alternative view of metaphor has been advanced more recently by Lakoff and Johnson (1980), Lakoff (1987) and Lakoff and Turner (1989). To begin with, this ap-proach rejects the traditional Aristotelian view of metaphoric/figurative language as a species of analogy or similarity, interpreting Aristotle's perspective, I think er-roneously, as 'objectivist'.[2] Lakoff *et al.* suggest that stable, universal *conceptual met-aphors* underlie all specific instances of metaphoric usage. Such conceptual meta-phors group actual instances of metaphoric usage into 'families' whose members are said to share the same underlying cognitive structure. And a hierarchy of con-ceptual metaphor is suggested, whereby some are more generic and underlie fami-lies of more specific conceptual metaphors.

The cognitive structure of conceptual metaphors is said to be a *mapping* relation between *distinct cognitive domains*. Similarity — construed or otherwise — is pre-sumably not involved.[3] So that cross-domain relations are equations ("X is Y") ra-ther than similes ("X is like Y").

Conceptual metaphors are said to be stable, conventionalized, culturally en-trenched and largely human-universal (Lakoff and Turner 1989). They are, further, *automatically activated* during on-line metaphoric use (*ibid.*: 51). And such on-line activation presumably accounts for our understanding of non-literal meanings.

As an example of families of metaphoric expressions grouped under the same 'conceptual metaphors', consider (Lakoff *et al.* 1989):

(13)   **Conceptual metaphors:**
   a.   'learning is eating'
        'he spoon-fed them information'
        'she chewed on the idea for a while'
        'he swallowed (her version) whole'
        'that is a half-baked idea'
        'it'll take time to digest the information'
        'algebra whetted her appetite for math'
        'she had them eating out of her hand'
        'he just wants us to regurgitate his own ideas'
        'they soaked in everything she said'
   b.   'belief/knowledge is possession'
        'I have certain beliefs'
        'the acquisition of knowledge'
        'we all hold it true that ...'
        'he possessed an uncanny ability to ...'
        'I receive a double-message from her'
        'let go of your prejudices'
        'give away your belief'
        'I get your drift'
   c.   'understanding is perceiving'
        'I see your point'
        'I hear you'
        'to shed more light on the issue'
        'I was in a dark all through the discussion'
        'she saw through his lies'
   d.   'action is motion'
        'I barely got through college'
        'my studies hit a roadblock'
        'do it this way'
        'I'm stuck on this problem, can't go on'
        'he is holding her back'
        'he pushed me into doing it'
        'she walked him through the program'
        'he's walking a fine line'
        'she lacks direction'
        'the end of this project is in sight'
        'how's it going?'
        'the project is at a standstill'

As one peruses the large collections of examples cited as empirical support for 'conceptual metaphors', it slowly becomes clear that this approach is heavily invested in collecting and classifying — by intuitive judgements that make a considerable amount of sense — the *end-products* of metaphoric behavior. The overwhelming role of metaphoric behavior in the diachronic process of semantic and grammatical change is acknowledged (Sweetser 1990). But the large collection of examples are invariably cited *without* the specific communicative context in which they were actually produced. This leaves the actual process of metaphoric reasoning *in situ* largely obscured. The out-of-context examples purport to demonstrate the ubiquity of their underlying *long-distance* conceptual metaphors, rather than the much more specific *short-distance* semantic mappings that obtain during context-grounded metaphoric behavior.

As far as can be ascertained, the suggested cross-domain 'conceptual-metaphoric' mappings alluded to in this approach are not constructed for the occasion, for the specific context. They are already there, pre-wired into the mind/brain as part of the structure. In metaphoric behavior, these mappings are presumably *re-discovered* or exploited in specific contexts. Whatever element of serendipity that may exist in metaphoric usage, it is not a matter of fresh discovery, innovation or fresh construal, but rather of *recognizing* what is already there, of *acknowledging* what one already knows. In using a metaphoric expression, be it brand new, one merely matches — or sorts — serendipitous contexts with their appropriate cognitive templates.

Several vexing questions are prompted by the inexorable onward march of the 'conceptual metaphor' framework. How does one know how to perform the requisite matching between a context (target) and its underlying cognitive domain (source)? How does one sort contexts in order to assign them to their proper — relevant — conceptual metaphor? Is each context inherently matchable to a particular conceptual metaphors? Pre-sorted and bearing the right 'cognitive tag'? If so, by what principles or mechanisms? And — the bane of all algorithmic approaches to pragmatics — can the inventory of all possible contexts be predicted and assembled in advance of live communicative behavior *in situ*? And, last but not least, how does one decide in which context to launch into metaphoric usage, and in which to deploy a semantically-equivalent literal expression?

Another question that comes to mind is this: how does one account for the fact that one target domain can be metaphorically mapped onto multiple source domains via multiple conceptual metaphors, as in (culled from Lakoff *et al.* 1989):[4]

(14)   Multiple 'conceptual metaphors' underlying causation

	Metaphoric expression	Underl. conceptual metaphor
a.	'success comes from hard work'	'causes are spatial sources'
b.	'hard work brought about my success'	'causes are physical forces'
c.	'the death had an impact on me'	'being affected is being hit'
d.	'is there a link between coffee and cancer?'	'causes are links in a chain'
e.	'since he it me, I hit him'	'causes are temporal precedence'
f.	'his actions led me to filing a suit'	'causes are things that move you'

And likewise, how does that account for the fact that one source domain can map onto multiple target domains, as in (culled from Lakoff *at al*. 1989):

(15)   Metaphors mapping onto 'X is motion in space'

	Actual example	Source domain
a.	'He went from being a nice guy to being a monster'	(X = change of state)
b.	'He barely got through college'	(X = action)
c.	'Success comes from hard work'	(X = causation)
d.	'Apply force to the edge of the lid'	(X = force)
e.	'Tuesday is coming up fast'	(X = time moving to us)
f.	'The past is fast receding'	(X = time moving from us)
g.	'He moved towards adulthood'	(X = us moving to time)
h.	'She left her childhood behind'	(X = us moving from time)
i.	'Then the idea came to me'	(X = belief moving to us)
j.	'I came to believe in capitalism'	(X = us moving to belief)
k.	'From this we infer ...'	(X = inference)
l.	'She was moved by it'	(X = emotion)
m.	'No harm will come to you'	(X = damage)
n.	'She followed the instruction'	(X = compliance)
o.	'The baby arrived prematurely'	(X = birth)

What are the principles and/or mechanisms that constrain the proliferation of one-to-many and many-to-one cognitive mappings? Is there a role — and if so, what — to the communicative context in constraining such proliferation?

In a lexical-semantic network, all connections between nodes are in principle possible. Some are more likely, more common, more conventionalized and entrenched or more adaptive in some contexts, either in a particular culture or universally. But given a newly-construed communicative context, new connections can always be made. Does the 'conceptual metaphor' framework claim anything above and beyond the general *network* design of permanent semantic memory, the automatic activation of multiple senses within such a network, and the facilitatory or inhibitory effect of context?

At this point one is impelled, somewhat reluctantly, to make a methodological observation. The purported classification that assigns actual metaphors to their more 'generic conceptual' metaphors always makes sense, it seems reasonable. But the analytic method employed remains, essentially, that of the logician-philosopher. The vast collection of out-of-context metaphors, together with their classifiers, are obtained through the study of *competence* rather than of *performance*. And as such, it makes intuitive sense in much the same way that *syntactic deep structure* or *transformations* made sense, in another ubiquitous framework that relied primarily on the native's proverbial intuition (Chomsky 1965).

3.4.3. The cognitive evidence

One may divide possible empirical claims about the mental activation during on-line production and interpretation of metaphoric language into the following questions (following Gibbs 1994a, Gibbs *et al.* 1997):

(16) **Questions about mental activation during on-line metaphoric behavior**:
    a. Are literal senses of a metaphoric expression always activated?
    b. Is the intended (target) metaphoric sense always activated?
    c. What role does the context — both discourse-pragmatic and clause-semantic — play in these activations?
    d. Are the relevant conceptual metaphors always automatically activated?

Surprisingly, there is a reasonable consensus about questions (16a,b,c). Automatic activation of literal senses (16a) is a direct consequence of the early-onset (within 0.250 msecs from stimulus presentation) automatic activation of multiple sense of words (Meyer and Schwaneveldt 1976; Swinney 1979; Neeley 1990).

The activation of intended metaphoric senses (16b), at least in their valid contexts, is of course taken for granted when a metaphoric sense is either intended or understood, but is also well documented experimentally (see surveys in Gibbs 1994b; Cacciari and Glucksberg 1994).

A vast experimental literature also demonstrates both facilitatory and inhibitory contextual effects (16c), both in multi-sense activations (Meyer and Schwaneveldt 1971; Conrad 1974; Schwaneveldt *et al.* 1976; Swinney 1979; Tannenhaus *et al.* 1979; Norris 1986; Glucksberg *et al.* 1986; van Petten and Kutas 1987; Kintsch 1988; Tabbossi 1988; Gernsbacher and Faust 1991; McCandliss 1992; *inter alia*) and in the processing of metaphors and idioms (Gibbs *et al.* 1997; see general reviews in Gibbs 1994b and Cacciari and Glucksberg 1994).

None of these three empirical responses to questions (16a,b,c) bear in any specific way on question (16d) about the automatic mental activation of conceptual metaphor. On this, the experimental literature is ambiguous, inconclusive and sharply divided. The issue is reviewed by both Gibbs (1994b) and Cacciari and Glucksberg (1994), the former sympathetically, the latter skeptically. But sympathies aside, both sides suggest that conceptual metaphors *may* be activated in some contexts but not in others.

Perhaps the most revealing concession on the subject is made in the more sympathetic Gibbs *et al.* (1997), summarizing their study of mental activation during on-line processing of live idiomatic expressions:

> Furthermore, the quick speed with which people process idioms compared to literal uses of the same expression or [of] nonidiomatic equivalents *make it somewhat unlikely* that people are actually computing metaphorical mappings each time they read or hear idioms in discourse. What contextual conditions facilitate or inhibit the access of conceptual metaphors in language processing, at what point during the moment-by-moment processing of idioms are conceptual metaphors accessed, and how long the activation of conceptual metaphors persists when idioms are understood are important questions for future research. One possibility is that conceptual metaphors may be accessed at the point when one encounters *a key word* or uniqueness point, in an idiom ... *Our data do not tell us* whether people must compute or access and idiom's underlying conceptual metaphor in order to comprehend what the idiom figuratively means during on-line processing. (1997: 150; italics and brackets added)

The phrase 'key word' is indeed revealing, compatible as it is with what Cacciari and Glucksberg (1994) also suggest: That it is the activation of key words *in the natural context* of a metaphoric expression during live communication that activates connected nodes in the semantic network. And that such activation is experimentally indistinguishable from the presumed activation of underlying 'conceptual metaphors'.

As an illustration, consider first the pair of constructed examples in (17) below, where the metaphoric usage (17b) is a transparent instance of the ubiquitous conceptual metaphor "motion in time is motion in space". In both (17a) and (17b), a likely natural context is suggested in brackets:

(17) a. **Literal spatial motion:**
          [They were **riding back from the back forty**, dead tired, when they saw the fire.]
          They **raced from** the gate **to** the barn in record time.
      b. **Figurative temporal motion:**
          [They were **much younger than us**, but still]
          they **raced from** youth **to** senility in record time.

In both (17a) and (17b) 'race from ... to' automatically activates 'motion in space' regardless of context. In the literal (17a), both the discourse context ('riding back from the back forty') and the clausal context ('from the gate to the barn') are fully compatible with that activation. In the figurative (17b), however, the discourse context ('much younger than us') automatically activates the node 'time', and the clausal context ("youth to senility') automatically activates 'age' and thus further strengthens that activation. 'Motion', 'space' and 'time' are thus all automatically activated in the metaphoric usage (32b) without any need to invoke the a conceptual metaphor.

But does it work the same way in non-contrived metaphoric usage? Let us re-examine the first fiction passage cited above (Percy 1960):

> Down I *plunk* myself with a *liberal* weekly at one of the *massive* tables, read it from
> cover to cover, nodding to myself whenever the writer **scores a point**. *Damn right*, old
> son, I say, jerking my chair in approval. **Pour it on them**. Then up and over the *rack* for
> a *conservative* monthly and down in a **fresh cool chair** to join the **counterattack**. Oh
> oh, say I, and hold fast to the chair *arm*: that one did it: **eviscerated!** And then out and
> away *into* the sunlight, my neck **prickling** with satisfaction.   (1960: 100)

The live metaphor 'score a point' is preceded in its discourse context by 'with a liberal weekly', which automatically activates 'politics'. 'Score a point' itself automatically activates the literal sense of 'competitive sports'. All relevant semantic nodes of
the presumed conceptual metaphor 'politics is a competitive sport' are now activated without the need for any added provisions.

Next, the live metaphoric usage 'pour it on them', '(verbal) argument' has already
been activated in the preceding discourse, and the literal sense 'pour liquid' is now
activated. All relevant semantic nodes of the presumed conceptual metaphor 'arguing is pouring liquid on the interlocutor' are again activated without recourse to any
added provisions.

Next, in 'counterattack' automatically activates its literal martial sense. However,
the preceding discourse context had already activated 'politics'. All semantic nodes
of the presumed conceptual metaphor 'politics is warfare' are thus activated without
recourse to any special provisions.

Next, 'eviscerate' automatically activates its literal sense of 'butchery'. The preceding context had already activated 'politics' and 'argument'. All the relevant semantic
nodes of the presumed conceptual metaphor 'winning in politics is butchery' are
thus activated without recourse to any added provisions.

Finally, 'neck prickling' automatically activates its literal tactile sense. The preceding context had already activated 'political debates' and 'enjoy', and the clausal context keeps the latter active with 'satisfaction', a node closely-linked to 'enjoy'. All relevant semantic nodes of the presumed conceptual metaphor 'mental enjoyment is
like physical prickling of the neck' are now activated without recourse to any added
provisions.

The network design of the conceptual lexicon, together with the automatic activation of literal ('source') senses with their closely linked local node-clusters (frames,
scripts), together with the ever-present live discourse context that automatically activates figurative ('target') senses and their locally-clustered nodes (frames, scripts),
seems to account for the co-activation of literal and metaphoric senses during natural on-line processing — without any need for specific activation of 'conceptual
metaphors'.

3.4.4. The diachronic evidence: Metaphors and grammaticalization

As suggested earlier, one of the best-known instances of metaphoric extension
is that of grammaticalization, where erstwhile lexical words ('source') are re-
analyzed as grammatical morphemes ('target'). The role of metaphoric inference
in grammaticalization is widely conceded (Heine 1993, 1997, 2002; Heine and

Reh 1984; Givón 1973a, 1989; Sweetser 1990; Heine *et al.* 1991; Bybee *et al.* 1994; *inter alia*).

In this section I will describe in some detail two cases of grammaticalization. Each case involves a succession of small, local metaphoric-inferential steps whose motivating pragmatic context shifts along the continuum from one step to the next. In both cases, the original lexical source undergoes a gradual shift towards increased abstraction, a process sometimes subsumed under *semantic bleaching* (Givón 1979a), prior to its final shift to the target grammatical use. In each case, the original source and the ultimate target may indeed seem semantically distant, enough to be considered different — dissimilar — cognitive domains. But each of the actual step-wise metaphoric shifts along the continuum bridges over small semantic gaps between closely-linked domains that can indeed be considered similar.

Consider first the widely reported grammaticalization of the motion verb 'go' to the 'future/irrealis' tense/modality, a *bona fide* instance of the conceptual metaphor 'temporal motion is spatial motion' (Heine 1993, 1997; Givón 1973; Bybee *et al* 1994; *inter alia*):

(18) | Historical stage | Contextual–pragmatic inference |

a.   **Perfective spatio-temporal motion:**
She went to the barn (for some purpose)   volitional action ⊃ purpose

b.   **Perfective spatio-temporal motion with a purpose:**
She went to the barn to feed the horse   motion for purpose ⊃ purpose is focal

c.   **Perfective spatio-temporal motion for a purpose:**
She went (somewhere) to feed the horse   purpose ⊃ not yet accomplished

d.   **Imperfective (spatio-?) temporal motion for a purpose:**
She's going (there?) to feed the horse   imperfective ⊃ unrealized

e.   **Temporal motion toward purported action:**
She's going to feed the horse (tomorrow)   unrealized now ⊃ realized in the future

f.   **Temporal motion toward future action:**
She gonna feed the horse tomorrow

The verb 'go' does not shift directly from its oldest source domain 'motion toward spatial goal' (18a) to the eventual target domain 'motion towards temporal goal' (18f). Rather, the pragmatic inference [volitional action ⊃ purpose] first licenses the incidental use of purpose V-complement constructions (18b), the real source of the eventual 'future' sense.

The next inference is purely about the communicative process itself [motion for purpose ⊃ purpose is focal]. By gradual change of usage frequencies (Heine 2002), the figure/ground relation between the spatial motion and its purpose shift towards the latter, licensing (18c). The spatial goal is now incidental, the purpose event is now central.

The next inference [purpose ⊃ not yet accomplished] seems trivial. Nonetheless, it licenses the crucial shift of focus to the imperfective aspect (18d), the syntactic template for the 'future' construction.

The next inference, the seemingly trivial [imperfective ⊃ unrealized], completes the gradual semantic de-focusing of spatial motion, leaving behind purely temporal motion towards a yet-to-be-realized action (18e). The optional temporal adverb takes the entire construction under its scope, thus barring usages such as '*she is going now to feed the horses tomorrow'.

The last inference, [unrealized now ⊃ realized in future], consolidates the grammaticalized 'future' construction (18f), as is evident by the phonological contraction to *gonna*.

As Heine (2002) notes, the relevant communicative context, and thus contextual-pragmatic inferences, that drive diachronic change shifts from one step to the next along the continuum of grammaticalization. The description of the final product in (33) as a mapping between the spatial and the temporal domains is not an observation about the actual metaphoric process, but only about some imputed abstract competence.

One may as well note that motion in space is necessarily also motion in time (cf. Kant's *transcendental manifold*). That is, one cannot go from here to there without simultaneously also moving from now to then. The pervasive conceptual metaphor 'motion in time is motion in space' is thus *not* a mapping between two different conceptual domains. Rather, it is a multi-step bridge that begins with a source domain involving motion in *both* time and space. Gradual *semantic bleaching* of the more concrete feature 'space' leaves, at the end, only the more abstract features 'time'. Motion in space and motion in time are thus, among other things, somewhat similar. They have something in common — change over time.

The second example is more complex, involving a historical development that spanned ca. 600 years, whereby the verb 'get', in its 14th century sense of 'take' or 'obtain', became the grammatical marker of the GET-passive construction of late 20th century English. At least 11 distinct steps of semantic and/or syntactic re-analysis were involved in this protracted development. They are given, somewhat schematically, in (19) below (Yang and Givón 1994):

(19) a.   He got an axe   (simple transitive verb)
      b.   He got the axe **and went** to the barn   (incidental motion)
      c.   He got the axe to the barn   (causation of motion)
      d.   He got **the horse** to the barn   (expansion to animate objects)
      e.   He got **Joe** to the barn   (expansion to human causees)
      f.   He got Joe **to go** to the barn   (added verbal complement)
      g.   He got Joe **to fire** Mary   (expanded range of verbs)
      h.   He got Mary **to be fired**   (expansion to passive complements)

i.	He got **himself** to be fired	(expansion to reflexive structures)
j.	He got himself fired	(simplification of syntactic relics)
k.	He got fired	(simplification of syntactic relics)
l.	He got elected	(expansion to non-adversive uses)

Each of the shifts above represents a subtle adjustment to a new communicative context, accompanied by either change of syntactic structure (19a–b, b–c, e–f, g–h, h–i, i–j, j–k), change in the semantic range and/or usage frequency of the object (19c–d, d–e), or change in the semantic range and/or usage frequency of the complement verb (19f–g, k–l). Along this continuum, the communicative focus of the construction changes gradually, as does its syntax, as does the meaning of 'get' itself: from 'obtain' in (19a, b), to 'transport' in (19c), to 'lead' in (19d), to 'cause' in (19f, g, h, i, j), to the adversive-passive grammatical marker in (19k), to the generalized passive marker in (19l). The small metaphoric shifts that make up the seeming domain-to-domain leap in (19) pile up gradually, bridging in small local hops between adjacent — similar — domains.

3.5. Figurative language and semantic networks

We are now in a position to see how the contextual-pragmatic — Aristotelian — view of metaphoric behavior fits into the network model of permanent semantic memory sketched out earlier above. This turns out to be surprisingly straightforward. We already noted (cf. (12) above) that in different usage contexts, the same lexical word may shift its activation pattern slightly, so that some *marginal* nodes are activated only in limited contexts. In contrast, the activation pattern of the *coreprototype* node-cluster remains relatively stable across multiple contexts.

The prototype core of a word, the node-cluster that is automatically activated in all contexts, represents the word's most common, conventionalized *literal sense*. The marginal nodes, in contrast, are only activated in special, less frequent contexts. This is the activation pattern of normal *polysemy*, as in (20) below.

In live metaphoric use, both the core node-cluster (literal meaning) and the relevant marginal nodes are *co-activate*, the first by the expression itself, the second by the discourse context, as in (21) below.

As a metaphor becomes conventionalized, the frequency of co-activation increases, till the erstwhile metaphoric, context-dependent co-activation pattern becomes the automatic co-activation pattern of a *conventionalized idiom*. What used to be the context-triggered margin has now become a second context-free core. In conventionalized idiom use, two semantic cores are automatically co-activated by the idiomatic expression itself, as in (22) below, needing no extra context.

Finally, the old literal sense may gradually lose usage frequency, so that it is only activated infrequently, in special contexts. And such a process may progress to the point where the erstwhile idiom has become a *dead metaphor*. A new mental activation pattern has been stabilized. And the new literal sense is now activated automatically by the phonological form of the dead metaphor, as in (23) below.

On-line metaphoric behavior is, fundamentally, not all that different from the normal contextual adjustment that occurs every time one uses the same word, or the same syntactic construction, again and again in live communication.

The diachronic continuum between early polysemy and dead metaphor may be illustrated by the four diagrams (20)–(23). The black nodes are those that are automatically activated by the perceptual for from of the word or expression. The blank nodes are those that are activated only by the discourse context.

(20) **Early polysemy**:

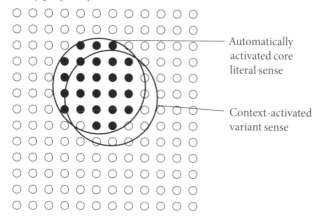

Automatically
activated core
literal sense

Context-activated
variant sense

(21) **Live metaphor**:

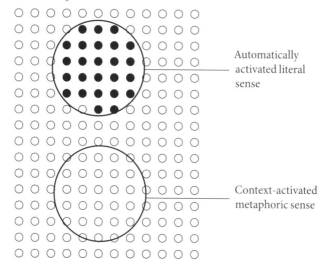

Automatically
activated literal
sense

Context-activated
metaphoric sense

(22) **Idiom:**

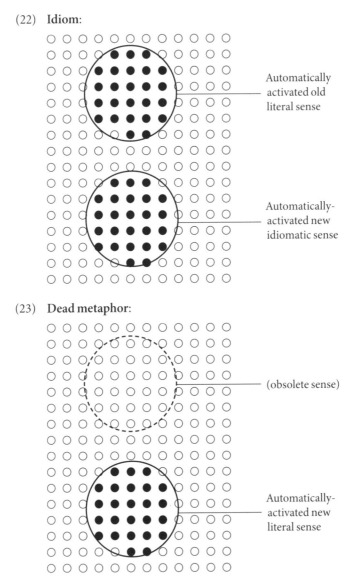

Automatically
activated old
literal sense

Automatically-
activated new
idiomatic sense

(23) **Dead metaphor:**

(obsolete sense)

Automatically-
activated new
literal sense

3.6. Adaptive motivation and frequency distribution of figurative language

Since the selection of metaphoric over semantically-equivalent literal expressions seems to be a matter of choice, one needs to inquire into the adaptive communicative motivation for metaphoric behavior. At least two adaptive explanations have been suggested, with possible interactions between them.

(a) **Experiential activation**

Metaphoric expressions, when compared to their literal equivalents, are "... more image-evoking and vivid." (Ortonyi 1980: 78). They recast "... abstract concepts in terms of the apprehendable." (Glucksberg and Keysar 1990: 15). What this claim amounts to, I think, is that many literal senses of metaphors, in particular those that are abstract, do not activate vivid *experiential* mental nodes, those that connect the dry semantic network to either *perceptual* or *affective* centers. In a fundamental way, it seems, network activation patterns do not by themselves guarantee meaningful meaning, they only guarantee different neuro-cognitive representation of different meanings. What makes a meaning more salient and vivid, what spices it up and brings it to life, what adds *arousal*, is the simultaneous activation of some non-semantic — perceptual or affective — experience.

(b) **Construal of novelty**

The second explanation may or may not be intended by Ortonyi's observation that "... Metaphors are means of expressing things that are literally inexpressible in the language in question." (Ortonyi 1980: 15). As noted earlier, metaphoric behavior appears to be the main vehicle of coining new senses from related — similar but not identical — pre-existing senses. This is what Cacciari and Glucksberg (1994: 469) refer to as *sense extension* and *sense creation*. This, of course, makes perfect sense in light of the claim that metaphoric behavior is a species of abductive-analogical reasoning, the kind of mental process that is at the very heart of all learning, discovery and the novel construal of experience.

If metaphoric behavior has a strong adaptive-communicative motivation, one would expect different text types, with different communicative goals, to have a different frequency distribution of live figurative usage. Consider first two genres of written communication that are loaded to the brim with new information — highbrow news reporting and scientific papers. Given motivation (b) above, one would expect them to be loaded with metaphoric language. In fact, they are not.

As an illustration of the low frequency of metaphoric usage in serious news reporting, consider an international news report in the New York Times International edition (Myre 2004: A3). Out of the 1300 lexical words in the 3-column half-page article, only three (3) live metaphoric expressions can be identified. This translates into *metaphoric density* of 3/1300 = 0.0023. And two of the metaphoric uses were direct quotes from interviewees:

(24) a. ... the case has been **simmering** for months ... [judicial proceedings ⊃ cookery]

b. ... Said Avraham Shochat, a member of the opposition labor party. "What happened is just an extra. He is **polluting the atmosphere** ..." [political malfeasance ⊃ pollution]

c. "It could be a question of how long Shinuy can **hold its nose** before it begins to lose credibility" he said. [political malfeasance ⊃ stink]

Consider next a page out of a technical report in a scientific volume (Posner 2004: 511). Out of the 370 lexical words used on one page, not a single live metaphor could be found. This translates into metaphoric density of 0/370 = 0.000.

Clearly, transacting new *episodic* information is not, by itself, an adaptive motivation for metaphoric usage. Metaphoric usage, it seems, is about *semantic* novelty, about *new senses*, about reorganizing the generic-cultural conceptual map. In a genre designed to transact high density new episodic information, frequent revision of the established senses of words may in fact be a distraction or even a cognitive impediment. From a compatible perspective, the other adaptive motivation for metaphoric language, perceptual-affective vividness, may also prove an impediment for a genre designed to appear objective and dispassionate.[5]

By way of comparison, consider the density of live metaphoric usage in one half page of W. Percy's *The Moviegoer* (1960: 147). Out of a total of 77 lexical words used, 13 live figurative uses — metaphor, simile, metonymy or comparison — can be found. That is, a metaphoric density of 13/77 = 16.%. Fiction is one place where one expects to find a high density of metaphoric language. This is so presumably because fiction is itself a deliberate contrast between the real and the imagined-but-could-be-real. It rises and falls on sucking — or suckering — readers into *imaginary yet plausible* scenes, so that they may care about the doings of characters who have never lived. And as means to an end, the activation of vivid perceptual and affective mental nodes is what makes the unreal as good as real.

3.7. Final reflections

The hybrid nature of mental categories is not the pragmatist's doctrinal whim, but a bio-adaptive strategy. From one adaptive perspective, prototype-like categories are designed to sort out and respond to the bulk of experiential tokens, and to do so rapidly and automatically with little regard to the fine nuances of context. But from another, the system must also allow for the slower and more deliberate processing of adaptively-relevant minorities of exceptional tokens. And the slow processing of such minorities is also an adaptive necessity. First, because outliers tend to be perceptually less salient or more ambiguous, and thus demand more careful scanning. And second, because both sorting and responding to outlier minorities depends heavily on the context. And therefore third, because scanning the context — the frame — is of itself much more costly. There is much more of it to scan, and the vast expanse of it is yet unstructured, and must be construed anew for the occasion.

Within biological populations, minorities, however statistically negligible, are sometime the very crux of adaptation. In this respect, slow and sluggish context-dependent processing, a strategy designed to take care of small minorities, is at the very heart of learning, discovery, change and innovation. From this perspective, the rather pedestrian, local, step-wise metaphoric behavior is vital for semantic change, conceptual innovation and the rise of abstract categories. This is not a linguistic fact about words and their meanings, but a cognitive fact about concepts and their adaptive change. To paraphrase Ernst Mayr, what makes a system truly live, what makes it biological rather than physical-chemical, is not its uniform bulk, but rather its potential for — however rare, however unpredictable — exception and variation.

Notes

* I am indebted to Sam Glucksberg, Bernd Heine, Mike Posner and Mick Rothbart for helpful comments on an earlier version of this chapter. They are, needless to say, absoved from responsibility for the final product.

1. Many philosophers and linguists, and in their wake a multitude of lay persons, assume, erroneously, that grammar is used primarily to code the structure of atomic propositions, (viz. Carnap's 1959 'logical syntax' or Chomsky's 1965 'deep syntactic structure'; *inter alia*). The reason why this assumption is so widespread has to do with the methodology of studying propositions, clauses and sentences in isolation from their communicative context.

2. In lumping Aristotle together with the rest of the 'objectivists' bogeymen, Lakoff and Johnson (1980) chose to ignore the fact that his approach to similarity was pragmatic, i.e. context-bound and non-objective (cf. *Metaphysics*; see discussion in ch. 1).

3. Again contra Aristotle (*Rhetoric*), who consider metaphor and metonymy to be sub-species of *simile*.

4. In the same vein, examples (28a,b,c) above, taken together, are an instance of one target domain, *cognition*, mapping onto three source domains via three conceptual metaphors (feeding, possession, perception). Are those three also mapped onto each other via some more-generic conceptual metaphor? If so, which is the source and which the target?

5. The pages of scientific texts are, of course, littered with the carcasses of dead Greek, Latin and Germanic metaphors.

CHAPTER 4

Grammar and other minds:
An evolutionary perspective

4.1. Sociality, communication and other minds*

In the preceding two chapters we noted several general facts about the effect of context on mental representation, thus about the pragmatic nature of mental categories. First, we noted that context is not an objective entity but rather a mental construct, the construed relevant *ground* vis-à-vis which tokens of experience achieve relatively stable mental representation as salient *figures*. Whatever stability mental representation possesses is due, in large measure, to the classification of tokens of experience into generic categories or types. In constructing such types, the organism practices an unavoidable measure of idealization. It glosses over, or averages out, much of the observed cross-token variability, or at least the portion of the variability that is deemed irrelevant. In doing this, the organism reveals itself to be a confirmed Platonist.

Next and more pertinent to other minds, we noted that neither social cooperation nor interpersonal communication can proceed meaningfully and efficiently unless one takes it for granted that one's generic mental categories are shared, to quite an extent, with those of one's interlocutor. That is, that roughly the same conceptual map of the universe, or at least the relevant portions thereof, is held in common by members of the same speech community. In the linguistic literature, this culturally-shared conceptual map is known as the *lexicon* (dictionary, encyclopedia). In the cognitive literature, it is known as *long-term semantic memory*.

While we acknowledge that the presumption of shared cognition is a pre-condition for cooperation and communication, the mental models we have dealt with thus far were not about the mind of any specific others, nor about the representation of specific episodic information. They are, rather, models of the culturally-shared *generic* universe of reference, the one we assume any of our interlocutors must share with us. This assumption requires no verbal confirmation during actual communication. It is taken for granted as an abductive inference:

(1) **Other minds as an inference from observed similarities**:
     If it looks like me, walks like me, talks like me, and otherwise displays all physical and behavioral signs of belonging to my intimate social group, then it must surely also share my cultural perspective on the universe. That is, it must have the same generic conceptual map of the world.

Inference (1) is a mundane application of *reasoning by feature association* and an inexpensive adaptive strategy at that. For, much like biological evolution in general, inference (1) merely extends into a novel functional domain an old, entrenched, presumably automated and perhaps genetically wired-in cognitive mechanism. Bio-organisms have been using this adaptive strategy for eons to infer categorial membership — from superficial visibles to adaptively-relevant invisibles. The mind of the other and its similarity to one's own is the most natural inference a social organism can make.

In this chapter we extend our investigation from the generic to the specific. That is, to mental models of the mind of *particular* interlocutors at *particular* times during on-going communication. The mental models we will consider here represent the interlocutor's transitory states of *belief* and *intention* in specific communicative contexts. Not just any communicative contexts, but those that are so common and so recurrent, and thus presumably so adaptively relevant, that they have become conventionalized, automated or *grammaticalized*. We will thus be dealing with the communicative function of grammar, hoping to flesh out in more concrete terms three old observations:

● Grammar is petrified cognition (Paul 1890);
● Grammar is an automated discourse processing strategy (Givón 1979a);
● Syntax is grammaticalized pragmatics (Langacker 1987).

That is, recasting these observations in terms of the automated construal of the interlocutor's shifting mental states during on-line communication.

4.2. Mental models

Cognitive psychologists have long recognized three major, distinct but closely interacting, systems of metal representation in the human mind/brain (Atkinson and Shiffrin 1968):

Cognitive label:	Communicative equivalent:
Permanent semantic memory	The generic lexicon
Episodic memory	The current text
Working memory and/or attention	The current speech situation

Not only are these three types of mental representation recognized for their specific cognitive-behavioral properties, but also for their specific brain locations. In the sections below I will briefly recapitulate our earlier discussion (ch. 3) of these three mental representational systems.

4.2.1. Permanent semantic ('procedural') memory

Much of the preceding two chapters was dedicated to the functional properties and structural organization of the generic lexicon. Its interaction with episodic memory are noted further below. The brain location of the lexical-semantic network has been, albeit tentatively, identified as left-inferior pre-frontal cortex (Posner and Pavese 1997; Abdulaev and Posner 1997), but older sub-cortical limbic areas are also strongly implicated (Tucker 1991, 2002). Experimental evidence also suggests that a single neuro-cognitive semantic network is responsible for representing both visual (pre-linguistic) and verbal (linguistic) concepts (Humphreys and Riddoch 1987, 1988, ed. 1987; Riddoch and Humphreys 1987a, b; Riddoch *et al.* 1988). This of course makes perfect sense from an evolutionary perspective (Givón 2002: chs 4, 5). It also parallels the cross-modal input into episodic memory (see directly below).

4.2.2. Episodic ('declarative') memory

Propositional-declarative information about unique events, states, situations or individuals, or about their concatenations in longer chunks of coherent discourse, is represented in episodic memory (Kintsch and van Dijk 1978; Gernsbacher 1990; Kintsch 1982, 1994; Ericsson and Kintsch 1997). Both visual and linguistic input are represented in this system, first in the sub-cortical limbic system (*hippocampus* and *amygdala*; Squire 1987; Squire and Zola-Morgan 1991; Petri and Mishkin 1994; Goodale 2000; Mesulam 2000). The hippocampus-based early episodic representation is the one most relevant to on-line human communication (Ericsson and Kintsch 1997).

The hippocampus-based early episodic memory, while a large capacity, is still a limited temporary-storage system. It is also an active processor where information is restructured and consolidated. For longer-term, more stable storage, episodic information is transferred to a more permanent memory in the front-cortical area (Squire 1987; Squire and Zola-Morgan 1991).

4.2.3. Working memory and/or attention

Working ('short term') memory represents what is available for *current activation* by the attentional system. It thus partially overlaps with the attentional system (Schneider and Chein 2003; Posner and Fan 2004; Mesulam 2000). Working memory is a limited storage-and-processing buffer of small capacity and short duration, where material is kept temporarily activated pending further processing decisions. It has a cross-modal conscious component that interacts with the *executive attention* (Schneider and Chein 2003; Posner and Fan 2004), as well as several modality-specific non-conscious components (visual, auditory, tactile etc.; Baddeley 1986, 1992; Shallice 1988; Gathercole and Baddeley 1993; Carpenter and Just 1988; Just and Carpenter 1990; Ericsson and Kintsch 1997; Treisman 1995; Treisman and De-Schepper 1996; DeSchepper and Treisman 1996; Treisman and Kanwisher 1998).

Material stored in the working-memory buffer must receive some type of attentional activation in order to reach longer-term episodic representation. Retrieval of information from episodic memory requires attentional re-activation, thus presumably bringing material back into some working-memory buffer. The retrieval cue may vary, depending on the type of information and the type of attentional activation that funneled the in-bound information to begin with (Treisman 1995; Treisman and Kanwisher 1998; Fernández-Duque 1999a,b; Thornton and Fernández-Duque 1999).

4.2.4. Interaction between memory systems

(a) **Semantic memory and episodic memory**

An asymmetrical two-way interaction holds between permanent semantic memory and episodic memory. First *developmentally*, memory traces of unique but similar tokens of experience are presumably responsible, in collaboration with innate capacities, for the eventual construction of generic concepts. Second, in *on-line processing* of unique experiences, entities, states or events are recognized as tokens of established, conventionalized generic types. That is, semantic memory must be co-activated with episodic memory if episodic traces of unique entities, states or events are to be meaningful.

(b) **Working memory and episodic memory:**

The interaction between working memory and episodic memory may be given schematically as flow chart (2) below:

(2) **Interaction between working memory/attention and episodic memory**
(adapted from Gathercole and Baddely 1993; Shallice 1988)

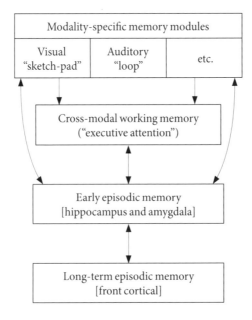

Other aspects of the interaction between working memory and episodic memory are discussed in Ericsson and Kintsch (1997).

4.3. Grammar

4.3.1. Developmental-evolutionary perspective

Grammar is probably the latest evolutionary addition to the mechanisms that drive human communication (Givón 1979a; 2002, ch.4; Lieberman 1984; Bickerton 1980, 1990; Li 2002). While the evolutionary argument remains necessarily conjectural, it is supported by a coherent body of suggestive evidence.

Ontogenetically, children acquire the lexicon first, using pre-grammatical (pidgin) communication before acquiring grammar (Bloom 1973; Bowerman 1973; Scollon 1976; Givón 1979a, 1990). Likewise, natural second language acquisition follows the same course but most often stops short of grammaticalization (Bickerton 1981, 1990; Bickerton and Odo 1976; Selinker 1972; Schumann 1976, 1978, 1985; Andersen 1979; Givón 1979a, 1990).

A well-coded lexicon can be acquired by many non-human species (Premack 1971; Gardner and Gardner 1971; Fouts 1973; Terrace 1985; Savage-Rumbaugh *et al.* 1993, 1998; Savage-Rumbaugh and Lewin 1994; Pepperberg 1991, 1999; Tomasello and Call 1997; *inter alia*). This supports the suggestion that the neuro-cognitive structures that underlie semantic memory are old pre-human, pre-linguistic structures (Givón 2002, ch. 4). In contrast, the communicative natural use of grammar in non-human species has never been attested. Nor has any success in teaching grammar to non-human species been reported (Premack 1971; Terrace 1985; Pepperberg 1991, 1999; Tomasello and Call 1997; Hauser 2000). Grammar as we know it thus seems a unique human capacity.

4.3.2. Grammar as structure

As a symbolic code, grammar is much more complex and abstract than the sensory-motor codes of the lexicon. At its most concrete, the primary grammatical signal involves four major coding devices:

(3)   **Primary grammar-coding devices**:
  - Morphology
  - Intonation:
    - clause-level melodic contours
    - word-level stress or tone
  - Rhythmics:
    - pace or length
    - pauses
  - Sequential order of words or morphemes

Some of the primary coding devices (morphology, intonation) are more concrete, involving the same sensory-motor channels that code the lexicon. But these concrete devices are integrated into a complex whole with the more abstract elements of the code (rhythmics, sequential order) that are, in all likelihood, second- or third-order constructs.

The most concrete element of the grammatical code, grammatical morphology, is a diachronic derivative of lexical words (Givón 1979a; Traugott and Heine eds 1991; Heine *et al.* 1991; Hopper and Traugott 1993; Bybee *et al.* 1994; *inter alia*).

The primary grammar-coding devices in (3) are in turn used to signal yet more abstract levels of grammatical organization:

  (4)   **More abstract levels of the grammatical code**:
    ● Hierarchic constituency
    ● Grammatical relations (subject, object)
    ● Syntactic categories (noun, verb, adjective; noun phrase, verb phrase)
    ● Scope and relevance relations (operator–operand, noun–modifier, subject–predicate)
    ● Government and control relations (agreement, co-reference, finiteness)

4.3.3. Grammar as adaptive function

The great complexity and abstractness of grammar is due in part to the complexity of its functional interaction with many other language-processing modules. It interacts intimately with semantic memory (lexicon), with propositional semantics (argument structure), with episodic memory (discourse coherence), with working memory and attention (Gernsbacher 1985; Givón 1991a), and with Broca's area (automated rhythmic-hierarchic routines; Greenfield 1991).

The functional correlates of grammar have been ill understood until recently, due to an entrenched structuralist methodology. In this tradition (Chomsky 1965), grammatical structures (clause-types) were culled from the intuition of the speaker-investigator and analyzed *qua* structures, in isolation from their communicative context. At best, one found them to be isomorphic with propositional semantics ('deep structures', Chomsky 1965).

Once grammar is studies in its natural adaptive context, the communicative function of both constructions and morphology can be pinpointed in highly specific ways (Givón 2001a). But the systematic deployment of grammar to signal mental representation of other minds is often obscured by the structuralist terminology employed by even the most functionally-inclined grammarians. It is also masked by the incipient empiricist mind-cast that often prevails in applying and interpreting text-distributional methods (Givón 1995, ch. 7). As a result of the latter, the communicative function of grammatical construction is often equated with the observable *discourse context* in which grammatical constructions appear, rather than with the *communicative goals* of the language-using mind.

In this and the three subsequent chapters, I would like to show how the discourse-coherence functions coded by grammar can be re-interpreted, rather transparently, as *perspective-shifting operations* (MacWhinney 1999, 2002). And that those, in turn, can be further re-interpreted as systematic manipulation (in production) or anticipation (in comprehension) of the *interlocutor's current states of belief and intention* (Givón 2001b).

The most common discourse-pragmatic domains coded by grammar are listed in (5) below (Givón 2001a).

(5)   **Discourse-pragmatic function of major grammatical systems**

    Structures: **Functions:**

    NP grammar   **Referential coherence**

a.	grammatical relations	referential coherence
b.	definiteness, reference	referential coherence
c.	anaphora, pronouns	referential coherence
d.	deictics	referential coherence
e.	pragmatic voice	referential coherence
f.	topicalization	referential coherence
g.	relativization	referential coherence, event grounding
h.	focus and contrast	referential coherence

    VP grammar   **Event coherence**

i.	tense	temporal grounding of event
j.	aspect	aspectual grounding of event
k.	modality	epistemic–deontic grounding of event
l.	speech acts	epistemic–deontic grounding of event

    Cross-clausal grammar   **Event/chain coherence**

m.	inter-clausal connectives	event grounding, chain grounding
n.	chain-initial adverbials	chain grounding
o.	presentative constructions	referential grounding, chain grounding

As can be seen in (5), some grammatical systems can function in more than one discourse-pragmatic domain. Thus, for example, relativization (5g) is part of the grammar of both referential coherence and event coherence. Tense (5i), aspect (5j) and modality (5k) are used to signal both temporal–aspectual–modal grounding and cross-clausal event coherence. And the grammar of inter-clausal connectives (5m) integrates devices that signal both referential coherence and event-coherence, albeit often at higher hierarchic levels.

4.3.4. Communication without grammar

The adaptive function of grammar comes into sharper relief when one notes that humans can, in some developmental, social or neurological contexts, communi-

cate without grammar. In such contexts, they use the well-coded lexicon together
with some rudimentary combinatorial rules. That is, they use *pre-grammatical
pidgin* communication (Bloom 1973; Bowerman 1973; Scollon 1976; Bickerton
1981, 1990; Bickerton and Odo 1976; Selinker 1972; Schumann 1976, 1978, 1985;
Andersen 1979; Givón 1979a, 1990). In reference to one such context, early child
communication (ca. 18 months of age), Bowerman (1973) observes:

> ... early child speech is 'telegraphic' — that is consists of strings of content words
> like nouns, verbs, and adjectives, and lacks inflections, articles, conjunctions, cop-
> ulas, prepositions and post-positions, and, in general, all functors or 'little words'
> with grammatical but referential significance ... (Bowerman 1973: 3–4)

As an example of coherent but largely pre-grammatical *child pidgin*, consider the
following two passages of interaction between a 29-month-old Spanish-speaking
boy and his father (Wise 1984; Givón 1990). In (6), high-frequency verb inflections
for first and second person already conform to the adult model:

(6) a. No sé.
         NEG know-**1s**
         'I don't know.'

     b. Ves?
         see-**2s**
         'You see?'

     c. Mira,   así   dos!
         look-IMPER/2s like.this two
         'Look, like this, two!'

     d. Sí, tuyo dos.
         yes, yours two
         'Yes, [there are] two [with] yours.'

     e. Aquí hay   campo.
         here have/NEUT room
         'Here there's room.'

     f. Así,   Papi!'
         like.this, Daddy
         'Like this, Daddy!'

In (7), the same invariant high-frequency verb form (3rd person sg.) is used regardless of number (7b) and person (7c), an oblique form of 'you' is substituted for the
nominative, and the plural noun suffix is dispensed with (7b):

(7) a. Mi pantalón está ...
         my pant   be-**3s**
         'My pants are ...'

     b. Aquí está   dos carro aquí.
         here be-**3s** two car here
         'Here there're two cars here.'

c. Aquí está tí, Papi.
   here be-**3s** you/OBL Daddy
   'Here you are, Daddy.'

d. Aquí está Guiguis arriba!
   here be-**3s** G. up
   'Here is Guiguis up there!'

As an example of coherent adult *second-language pidgin*, consider (8) below, spoken by an 80-year-old Japanese-English pidgin speaker in Hawaii (Bickerton and Odo 1976; Bickerton and Givón 1976; Givón 1990):

(8) ...oh me? ...oh me over there ... nineteen-twenty over there say come ... store me stop begin open ... me sixty year ... little more sixty year ... now me ninety ... nah ehm ... little more ... this man ninety-two ... yeah, this month over ... me Hawaii come-*desu* ... nineteen seven come ... me number first here ... me-*wa* tell ... you sabe gurumeru? ... you no sabe gurumeru? ... yeah this place come ... this place been two-four-five year ... stop, ey ... then me go home ... Japan ... by-n-by ... little boy ... come ... by-n-by he been come here ... ey ... by-n-by come ... by-n-by me before Hui-Hui stop ... Hui-Hui this ... eh ... he ... this a ... Manuel ... you sabe-*ka* ...

As an example of coherent narrative produced by an *agrammatic (Broca's) aphasia* patient, consider (9) below (Menn 1990: 165):

(9) ... I had stroke ... blood pressure ... low pressure ... period ... Ah ... pass out ... Uh ... Rosa and I, and ... friends ... of mine ... uh ... uh ... shore ... uh drink, talk, pass out ...

... Hahnemann Hospital ... uh, uh I ... uh uh wife, Rosa ... uh ... take ... uh ... love ... ladies ... uh Ocean uh Hospital and transfer Hahnemann Hospital ambulance ... uh ... half'n hour ... uh ... uh it's ... uh ... motion, motion ... uh ... bad ... patient ... I uh ... flat on the back ... um ... it's ... uh ... shaved, shaved ... nurse, shaved me ... uh ... shaved me, nurse ... [sigh] ... wheel chair ... uh ... Hahnemann Hospital ... a week, a week ... uh ... then uh ... strength ... uh ... mood ... uh ... up ... uh ... legs and arms, left side uh ... weak ... and ... Moss Hospital ... two week ... no, two months ..."

In the absence of morpho-syntactic structure, the bulk of coded clues for establishing text coherence in pre-grammatical discourse, above and beyond situational inferences (Kintsch 1992), are furnished by the lexicon. But a small set of cognitively-transparent ('iconic'; Haiman 1985a,b; Givón 1991c) 'rules' of *proto-grammar* are already evident in Pidgin communication (Givón 1990; 2002: ch. 4). Neither the lexical clues nor the 'rules' of proto-grammar disappear in fluent grammatical communication of native adults. Rather, vocabulary-cued processing remains a parallel channel alongside grammar (Kintsch 1992; Givón 1990, 1991c). And the cognitively-transparent ('iconic') conventions of proto-grammar are integrated with the more conventional rules of grammar.

The differences between pre-grammatical (pidgin) and grammatical communication are summed up in (10) below.

(10)   **Pre-grammatical vs. grammatical communication** (Givón 1979a; 1989)

Properties	Grammatical	Pre-grammatical
Structural:		
a. morphology:	abundant	absent
b. constructions:	complex, embedded	simple, conjoined
c. word order:	grammatical (subj/obj)	pragmatic (topic/comment)
d. pauses:	fewer, shorter	copious, longer
Functional:		
e. processing speed:	fast	slow
f. mental effort:	effortless	laborious
g. error rate:	lower	higher
h. context dependence:	lower	higher
i. processing mode:	automated	attended
j. development:	later	earlier
k. consciousness:	sub-conscious	more conscious

The heavy dependency of Pidgin communication on lexical vocabulary tallies with the fact that lexicon is acquired before grammar in both first and second language acquisition, as well as with the fact that more abstract vocabulary is the diachronic precursor of grammatical morphology in grammaticalization. Pre-grammatical children, adult Pidgin speakers and agrammatic aphasics comprehend and produce coherent multi-propositional discourse, albeit at slower speeds and higher error rates than those characteristic of grammatical communication. The identification of grammar with a more automated, language processing system has been suggested in Givón (1979a, 1989), Blumstein and Milberg (1983), and Lieberman (1984).

4.4. Grammar and other minds

4.4.1. The mental representation of context

In evolving its lexical and grammatical codes, human language had liberated itself, albeit only partially, from the tyranny of paying constantly attention to context. This partial liberation involved two separate waves of *partial automation* of language processing, whereby the two codes — lexical phonology and grammar — automatically activate mental structures that represent, systematically and reliably, the most relevant, and frequently-accessed aspects of the context. As a result, language production and comprehension has become faster, less error-prone, and less dependent on limited attentional resources.

Three distinct types of context are accessed systematically during human communication, and are thus good candidates for automation. The three correspond, rather transparently, to the three neuro-cognitive representation systems noted earlier above:

(11) Context types as cognitive representation systems:

Context	Representation system
The shared generic network	Permanent semantic memory
The shared speech situation	Working memory/attention focus
The shared current text	Early episodic memory

In this section, I will begin to flesh out the claim that grammar is used systematically, during on-line communication, to activate mental representations of the interlocutor's current states of belief and intention. The more traditional pragmatic terminology for tapping into the mind of the interlocutor is that of *shared context*. That is, the assumption that the mental representation that is currently activated in my mind is also currently activated in yours. In such a framework, the three types of contexts (11) represent three types of *grounds* for justifying the assumption of shared context during live communication.

We will examine here only a restricted set of examples that illustrate the role of grammar in accessing the three types of context (11); that is, the three types of mental representations of the mind of the interlocutor during ongoing communication. The discussion of many other grammar-cued systems will be deferred to the next three chapters (5, 6, 7). Our first set of examples pertains to the grammar of definite description.

4.4.2. Access to definite referents

In using definite grammatical cues, the speaker assumes that the referent, while not necessarily currently activated, is mentally *accessible* to the hearer. Such accessibility may depend on either one of the three cognitive systems that can represent the *shared context*. A definite referent is thus *grounded* to one (or more) of those representation systems.

4.4.2.1. *Grounding referents to the shared lexicon*
As noted earlier, the culturally-shared lexicon is coextensive with permanent semantic memory. During on-line communication, different nodes in this representational system in the mind of the hearer are activated by the speaker's use of different lexical words. Some of these words, however, are not generic, but rather have

unique referents that are *globally accessible* to all members of the relevant social unit. Part of knowing the meaning of the word is knowing that it has a unique referent. In using such words, the speaker needs to only mark them with a *definite* grammatical marker ('the'), which then signals to the hearer that there is no need to search further for unique reference. The automatically-activated lexical node itself will suffice.

(12)   **Globally-accessible definite referents**:

	Referent	Relevant social unit
a.	**The sun** came out.	All humans
b.	**The president** has resigned.	A nation-state
c.	They went to **the cemetery**.	A community
d.	**The river** is frozen over.	A community
e.	Call **the sheriff**!	A county
f.	**The Gods** must be angry.	A religion
g.	**Daddy** is home!	A family

The cuing of unique reference through grounding in the shared lexicon may also involve a mixed access system. In such a system, one referent is activated first via another type of shared context. Another referent is then activated automatically as a connected node of the first. This hybrid type of referential access is sometime called *framed-based* ('script-based'; Anderson, Garrod and Sanford 1983; Yekovich and Walker 1986; Walker and Yekovich 1987). Thus consider:

(13)   **Double-grounded 'frame-based' definite referents**:
    a.   My boy missed **school** today,
         he was late for *the bus.*
    b.   She showed us **this gorgeous house**,
         but *the living room* was too small.
    c.   She went into a **restaurant**
         and asked *the waiter* for *the menu.*

The word 'school' in (13a) automatically activates its cluster of connected nodes ('frame'), including in this culture 'bus'. The word 'house' (13b) automatically activates its cluster of connected nodes, among them 'living room'. The word 'restaurant' automatically activates, among others, 'waiter' and 'menu'. The speaker uses the definite article with the expectation that these concepts are not only accessible, but in this case also activated in the hearer's mind.

4.4.2.2. *Grounding referents in the shared speech situation*
When interlocutors share the same speech situation with others, referents within that space-time grid are, at least in principle, equally accessible to them. This entitles a speaker to assume that information that is accessible to him/her in the immediate speech situation, via visual or auditory channels, is also accessible to others who

share the same space-time grid. This is nothing but a mundane application of reasoning by feature association:

- Since both I and my interlocutor share the same speech situation, then if I have a mental model of entities that are accessible in this speech situation, then my interlocutor must have the same mental model.

In the grammar of definite reference, a number of well-known examples exist where the assumption of unique reference depends on equal access in the current speech situation. They all fall under the general label of *deixis* (pointing). The most common ones are:

(14) a. **Interlocutors**:
          I am telling **you** that …
      b. **Other referents**:
          No, she doesn't want **this** book, she wants **that** one.
      c. **Location**:
          There was no room for them **there**, so they came **here** instead.
      d. **Time**:
          He wanted to come **then**, but I told him to wait till **now**.

4.4.2.3. *Grounding referents in the shared current discourse*
By far the most common grounds, in human communication, for assuming that a referent is currently accessible to the interlocutor involves our presumption that the just-transacted current discourse is as mentally accessibility to the hearer as it is to us. That is, we assume that a mental trace of the just-transacted current text exists in, and is accessible to, our interlocutor's *episodic memory*.

When a referent is introduced into the discourse for the first time, the speaker assumes the existence of no such mental trace, and therefore marks the referent grammatically as *indefinite*. Subsequently, if the referent is deemed to be still accessible, various *definite* grammatical devices may be used, depending on further details of the discourse context. As a simple illustration, consider the narrative discourse in (15).[1]

(15) a. There was **this** man standing near the bar,
      b. but we ignored **him** and went on across the room,
      c. where **another man** was playing the pinball machine.
      d. We sat down and ordered a beer.
      e. **The bar tender** took his time,
      f. I guess **he** was busy.
      g. So we just sat there waiting,
      h. when all of a sudden **the man standing next to the bar** got up and …

In marking 'man', introduced for the first time in (15a), with the indefinite 'this', the speaker cued the hearer that he doesn't expect him/her to have an episodic mental trace of the referent. In coding the same referent with the anaphoric pronoun 'him' in (15b), the speaker assumes that the referent is not only accessible, but is still *currently activated* in the hearer's episodic memory.

Another referent is introduced for the first time in (15c), this time with the indefinite marker 'another'. 'The bar tender' is introduced for the first time in (15e) — but marked as *definite*. This is so because the prior discourse had activated 'bar', which then remained activated by the persistence of the narrated situation. And 'bar tender' is an automatically-activated connected node of the lexical frame 'bar' (see discussion of (13) above).

The continued reference with the anaphoric pronoun 'he' in (15f) again indicates the assumption that the referent is both accessible and currently activated.

Finally, the man introduced first in (15a,b), absent for five intervening clauses, is re-introduced in (15h). The use of a definite article suggests that the speaker assumes that this referent is still accessible to the hearer, but that the hearer's search in episodic memory is not going to be simple. Another man has been mentioned in the intervening (15c) as 'playing the pinball machine'. Both referents are assumed to still be accessible, and would thus compete for the simple definite description 'the man'. To differentiate between them, a *restrictive relative clause* is used, matching 'standing next to the bar' in (15h) with the proposition 'this man was standing near the bar' in (15a). In using this grammatical cue, the speaker reveals his/her assumption that the hearer still has an episodic trace of both the referent and the proposition in (15a).

4.4.3. Access to the interlocutor's deontic states

The narrative example (15) above reveals another important feature of our presumption of access to other minds. Our mental model of the mind of the interlocutor shifts constantly, from one clause to the next during live communication. As speakers release more information, they constantly update what they assume the hearer knows. They thus seem to possess a shifting mental model of the hearer's labile *epistemic* (knowledge) states. In this section we will show that speakers must also possess a shifting mental model of the hearer's labile *deontic* (intention) states.

The epistemic and deontic states we will consider here can be cued by several grammatical sub-systems, the bulk of which are to be discussed in ch. 6 below. The most conspicuous of these sub-systems, and the easiest to illustrate, is the grammar of *speech-acts*.

The study of speech-acts has traditionally centered on a set of *felicity conditions* or *use conventions* that are associated with the various speech-acts (declarative, imperative, interrogative, etc.). These conventions have had an illustrious history in post-Wittgensteinean philosophy, beginning with Austin (1962), Searle (1970), or Cole and Morgan (eds 1975), among many others. They are also known as *Gricean conditions* on — or *conventional implicature* of — speech-acts (Grice 1968/1975; Levinson 2000).

As an illustration, consider the following, somewhat schematic but still residually plausible, dialogue between speakers A and B:

(16) A-i: So she got up and left.
      B-i: You didn't stop her?
      A-ii: Would you?
      B-ii: I don't know. Where was she sitting?
      A-iii: Why?
      B-iii: Never mind, just tell me.

In the first conversational turn (16A-i), speaker A executes a *declarative* speech-act, which involves, roughly, the following presuppositions about hearer B's current mental states (in addition to the speaker's own mental states):

(17) a. **Speaker's belief about hearer's epistemic state**:
          • Speaker believes hearer doesn't know proposition (20A-i).
          • Speaker believes hearer believes that speaker speaks with authority about proposition (20A-i).
      b. **Speaker's belief about hearer's deontic state**:
          • Speaker believes hearer is well-disposed toward the speaker communicating to him/her proposition (20A-i).
      c. **Speaker's own epistemic state**:
          • Speaker believes he/she knows proposition (20A-i).
      d. **Speaker's own deontic state**:
          • Speaker intends to inform hearer of proposition (2A-i).

In the next turn (16B-i), B, now the speaker, executes an *interrogative* speech-act (yes/no question), which involves, roughly, the following presuppositions about hearer A's current mental states (as well as the speaker's own):

(18) a. **Speaker's belief about hearer's epistemic state**:
          • Speaker believes hearer knows the declarative proposition underlying question (16B-i).
          • Speaker believes hearer knows speaker does not know that proposition.
      b. **Speaker's belief about hearer's deontic state**:
          • Speaker believes hearer is willing to share their knowledge of that proposition.
      c. **Speaker's own epistemic state**:
          • Speaker is not certain of the epistemic status of the proposition underlying (16B-i).
      d. **Speaker's own deontic state**:
          • Speaker would like hearer to share their knowledge with him/her.

In turn (16B-iii), lastly, speaker B executes a *manipulative* speech-act, which involves, roughly, the following presuppositions about hearer A's current mental states (as well as the speaker's own):

(19) a. **Speaker's belief about hearer's epistemic state:**
 - The hearer believes the hearer knows that the desired event ('You tell me') is yet unrealized.

 b. **Speaker's belief about hearer's deontic state:**
 - Speaker believes hearer is capable of acting so as to bring about the desired event.
 - Speaker believes he hearer is well-disposed toward acting to bring about the desired event.

 c. **Speaker's own epistemic state:**
 - Speaker believes the desired event ('You tell me') is yet unrealized.

 d. **Speaker's own deontic state:**
 - Speaker would like the event ('You tell me') to come about.

At every new turn in the conversation (16), not only do the speaker's own belief-and-intention states change, but also his/her mental representation of the hearer's belief-and-intention states. And one would assume that a similar fast-paced adjustment also occurs in the hearer's mental model of the speaker's belief-and-intention states.

4.5. The selectivity of mental models

Earlier above (sec. 4.3.4) we noted that focal attention and working memory are both a highly selective entry channel into longer-term episodic representation. What is more, this selectivity makes episodic memory itself a highly selective repository of past experience, be it visual or verbal. We have also noted, (sec. 4.3.4. and (10) above) that grammar bears all the marks of a highly automated processing system. And one of the hallmarks of automation is decreased reliance on the conscious *executive attention* system.

Fluent speakers of human language are notoriously bad at giving a conscious account of why they have just used a particular grammatical construction. They are equally unreliable, with minor exceptions, at episodic recall of the grammatical form of just-produced discourse — once that discourse has left the short-term working-memory buffer (Barker 2004). Grammar is just like any other *skilled performance* executed by an *expert*. And as Socrates has discovered to his chagrin and eventual sorrow (and reported in both *Meno* and the *Apology*), experts are too skilled to know how or why they do things. They just do them.

Only few grammatical sub-systems can be recalled verbally and reliably from a just-concluded discourse, most conspicuously (Barker and Givón 2003):

- speaker/hearer alternations in conversational turns
- speech act value (declarative, interrogative, manipulative, negation)
- epistemic and deontic modal values (certainty, intent, obligation, evidence)

Otherwise, the rapid, fluent deployment of grammatical form is relatively sub-conscious. One can recall it only as long as the utterance remains within the sort-term working-memory buffer (auditory loop, visual sketch-pad; Gernsbacher 1985; Gathercole and Baddely 1993). Beyond that range, grammar is not, by and large, consciously retrievable from episodic-memory (Barker and Givón, forthcoming).

The subliminal nature of grammar, ever present but seldom recalled,[2] contrasts sharply with lexical and propositional information, which speakers tend to attend to consciously, store reliably in, and retrieve consciously from, episodic memory (Kintsch and van Dijk 1978; Gernsbacher 1985; Dickinson and Givón 1997; Barker and Givón 2003; Barker 2004). By automating a processing system, one tends to bar conscious access to it. The material can still be stored in a long-term bin, but it cannot be retrieved with conscious cues (Treisman 1995; Bar and Biderman 1998).

We have just established, albeit sketchily, that grammatical constructions are systematically associated with speakers' explicit mental models of their interlocutors' epistemic and deontic states. This is the only way the systematic communicative use of grammar can be explained. What is more, these mental models are wholly subconscious. They are seldom mentioned in episodic recalls of conversations (Barker and Givón 2003). But why?

Two complementary explanations suggest themselves:

- **Automaticity**: The speaker's shifting mental models of their own and the hearer's shifting mental states are constructed automatically, implicitly and subconsciously. Like other information reaching episodic memory without conscious attention, these mental models are inaccessible to conscious verbal recall, even if they do have episodic traces (Treisman 1995; Treisman and Kanwisher 1998; Fernández-Duque 1999a, b; *inter alia*).
- **Irrelevance**: Much of the information about the speaker's *and* hearer's shifting epistemic and deontic mental states is wholly irrelevant at any point in the discourse *except* during the fleeting moment of processing a particular conversational turn or clause. Storing that information in longer-term episodic memory, and making it consciously accessible at any other time, would serve no useful purpose. Indeed, it might interfere with the mental representations that are relevant at *that* — later — time.

These explanations also hold for why grammatical form itself is not stored in and retrieved from episodic memory, leastwise not consciously:

- its activation/use is automatic and thus sub-conscious; and
- it is relevant only in the discourse context in which it was originally transacted.

The coherence structure of discourse is profoundly re-shuffled in early episodic memory (Loftus 1980; Gernsbacher 1990; Ericsson and Kintsch 1997; Dickinson and Givón 1997; Barker and Givón 2003; Barker 2004). Recalling propositions from episodic memory clad in the same grammatical garb with which they entered would be a burdensome adaptive distraction (Givón 1995, ch. 8).

Grammar, it seems, is but a means to an end in language processing, an input/ output *translation code*. What is stored in the hearer's episodic memory, in addition to propositional information, is not grammatical structure itself, but what it stands for — multi-propositional coherence structure (Gernsbacher 1990). To echo Wittgenstein's ladder metaphor, once grammar has been used to get us where we need to go — coherent episodic representation of discourse — it is discarded. Carrying it any further would have been an adaptive burden.

4.6. Other minds in an evolutionary perspective

4.6.1. Overview

The discussion of so-called *Theories of Mind* was launched with a prescient article by Premack and Woodruff (1978) titled "Does the chimpanzee have a theory of mind?" While largely programmatic, Premack and Woodruff's article was brimming with theoretical and methodological insights. In a concluding line that anticipates empiricist objections, Premack and Woodruff (1978) suggested, perhaps tongue in cheek:

> Moreover — and we add this with more than facetious intent — it would waste the behaviorist's time to recommend *parsimony* to the ape. The ape could only be a mentalist. Unless he is intelligent enough to be a behaviorist.   (1978: 526; italics added)

The evolutionary import of the 1978 article was clear from the start, be it from the cross-species or cross-developmental comparative orientation, be it from the unabashed invocation of "naturalness" or "primitiveness" as key element in the mentalist account of inferences of other minds:

> The important point here is that assigning mental states is not a sophisticated or advanced act but a primitive one.   (*ibid.*: 525)

> having decided that behaviorism is *unnatural* because it requires suppressing *primitive inferences*, whereas theories of mind are *natural*.   (*ibid.*: 526; italics added)

The intensive discussion that follows has engendered too vast a literature for me to be able to review exhaustively here. This literature may be divided, roughly and with a generous allowance for overlaps, into six more-or-less distinct categories:

(a) **Theory of mind in human adults**:
    Gopnik and Wellman (1994); Whiten (ed. 1991); Dunbar (1998); Malle *et al.* (eds 2000), Fussell and Kreutz (eds 1998); *inter alia.*
(b) **Children's theory of mind**:
    Wellman (1990); Gopnik & Wellman (1992); Bartsch and Wellman (1995); Povinelli and deBlois (1992); Meltzoff (1999, 2000a, b); *inter alia.*

(c) **Autistic (children's) theory of mind:**
Baron-Cohen (1995); Baron-Cohen *et al.* (1995); Leslie and Frith (1988); Penner *et al.* (1989); Morton *et al.* (1991); *inter alia.*

(d) **Non-human primates' theory of mind:**
Povinelli and Preuss (1995); Povinelli and Eddy (1996a, b, c); Povinelli et al. (1990, 1992) Tomasello (1996); Tomasello and Call (1997); *inter alia.*

(e) **Theory of mind and the brain:**
Dunbar (1998); Baron-Cohen (2000); Morton *et al.* (1991); Meltzoff (2002b); *inter alia.*

(f) **Evolution of theory of mind:**
Byrne and Whiten (eds 1988); Povinelli & Preuss (1995); Mithen (1996); Dunbar (1998); Byrne (1998); Baron-Cohen (2000); Meltzoff 2000b; Meltzoff and Prinz (eds 2002); *inter alia.*

In her critical review of the research that imputes theories of minds to non-human primates, Heyes (1998) chose to take Premack and Woodruff at their literal word, interpreting their closing lines as a *parsimony* argument in philosophy of science. She pointed out, I think correctly, that Occam's Razor is hardly a winning argument in science, given that all other things are seldom equal. Her loud protestations notwithstanding, Heyes' review is a spirited articulation of traditional behaviorist rejection of mental categories. Now reluctantly conceded to humans, mental models of other minds — indeed of one's own mind — are still denied to our nearest kin. Heyes lists the various types of behavior that have been proposed as evidence for theories of mind in non-human primates as follows:

- imitation
- self-recognition
- social relationships
- deception
- role-taking
- perspective-taking

She then argues that in each case, a simpler, traditional *associationist* explanation accounts for the observed behavior.[3]

As many of Heyes' peer commentators noted at the time, the criterial bar she holds up is so high that only organisms capable of *verbal articulation* of their theories of mind could possibly clear it (Gray and Russell 1998; Slaughter and Mealey 1998),[4] and perhaps not even those (Gordon 1998; Kamawar and Olson 1998).

Spirited empiricism aside, much of the Theory of Mind literature since Premack and Woodruff's clarion call has been plagued by four abiding, and to my mind questionable, assumptions about mental models in general and mental models of other minds in particular. These assumptions have not always been explicit, but they nonetheless insinuate themselves into much of the discussion by *bona fide* mentalists.

(a) **Gapped evolution**: The Theory of Mind literature, including Heyes' own review, reveals a clear if sometime implicit Cartesian bias. It attempts, whether in cross-species or cross-developmental comparisons, to draw too sharp a line between species or developmental stages that have Theories of Mind, and those that don't. In the same breath, too sharp a line is drawn between mental capacities that qualify as Theory of Mind and those that don't. Whether intended or not, the discussion thus presupposes a profoundly non-Darwinian, non-gradualistic model of gapped evolution (Eldredge and Gould 1972). This model has been largely rejected by evolutionary biologists (Lande 1980, 1986).

(b) **Mega-modularity**: A natural concomitant of gapped evolution is an assumption, often implicit, that has bedeviled so-called Evolutionary Psychology from the very start: That the emergence of complex new mental capacities must perforce involve the concomitant emergence of brand new brain structures or mega-modules. This assumption disregards the two most common developmental trends in evolution, including brain evolution:

- **Terminal modification**: The gradual modification of an extant module to perform, at least initially, *both* its old function and a similar-but-not-identical new function.
- **Distributiveness**: The assembly of complex new modules from pre-existing simple ones, whereby the novelty is not the structures themselves, but their coordinated, spatio-temporally distributed activation pattern.

(c) **(Self-)consciousness**: The third silent partner in the discussion, invoked from the very start by the very label 'Theory of Mind', is a strong bias toward conscious — indeed self-conscious — mental models of both one's own mind and the mind of the interlocutor. This bias again flies in the face of the vast neuro-cognitive literature that documents the existence of unattended, subconscious mental models, as well as the complex interaction between attention and automaticity.[5]

(d) **Categorization and mental models**: Lastly, the Theories of Mind literature has tended, on the whole, to not avail itself of what is known about human categorization, and about the three neuro-cognitive capacities that serve as the most common repositories of mental models: Semantic memory, episodic memory and working-memory/attention.

My own take on the subject tends in the opposite direction from gapped evolution, mega-modularity and self-consciousness, harkening back to Premack and Woodruff's (1978) original gut instincts, that:

- The 'primitive' mechanisms that license what appears to be 'inferences' about other minds are old and well entrenched *evolutionary precursors* to both conscious (2nd-order) and self-conscious (3rd-order) mental representation.
- That such evolutionary precursors ('pre-adaptations') contributed to an incremental development of mental models, first of one's internal somatic states, then to one's visceral-emotional states, then to one's mind, and lastly of other minds.

- That as a result of this gradual incrementation, the neural mechanisms that support our more complex, higher-order mental models may well be distributive and multi-modular.
- And that the role of consciousness and executive attention must be examined as one component within the complex, multi-step development of these mental models.

The latter point is particularly important because grammar, the most complex and sophisticated — and most likely the most recent — evolutionary addition to the tool-kit of human representation and communication, is by and large a subconscious, automated processor of our mental models of other minds.

4.6.2. 'Reasoning' by feature association: The wrong metaphor?

As noted earlier above (ch. 2), reasoning by feature association is an ancient, entrenched concomitant of biologically-based categorization, the very core of the adaptive rationale for the evolution of generic mental categories. But however convenient the metaphors of 'reasoning' or 'inference' may be as illustrative devices, they are in fact somewhat misleading. For they mis-represent the underlying neuro-cognitive mechanisms involved in this species of 'reasoning'. Our habituated generic mental categories do not depend on rational conscious inferences such as (20) below:

(20) **Reasoning by feature association as an abductive inference**:
Category A has strongly-associated features a, b, c, d, etc.
Individual x is a member of category A.
Individual x possesses feature a.

Therefore individual x must also possess features b, c, d, etc.

Inferences such as (20) are convenient, schematic, post-hoc rationalizations of the *end product*, but they don't describe the *process*.

In the processing of conceptual-semantic categories, the adaptive ends of schematic feature-association inference like (20) are accomplished much more efficiently by *automatic activation* of the prototype node-cluster, an activation that may be triggered by few or even one salient core feature. 'Reasoning' by feature association is an automated, frequency-driven neuro-cognitive mechanism. It had served for eons of vertebrate evolution in the processing of external, somatic-internal and visceral-emotional referents. There is no reason to assume that it was not pressed into service in a like manner to process mental-internal referents. That is:

(21) If it looks like me, behaves like me and is my conspecific, then it must surely also possess my mental properties.

The only prerequisite for 'inference' (21) is that one has a mental representation of one's *own* epistemic and intentional states, and perhaps also that one is *as conscious* of one's mental state as one is of one's internal-somatic, motor states and external perceptual input. But whether fully conscious processing is implicated here remains to be empirically established.

4.6.3. Neurological incrementation: From old-brain to limbus to neo-cortex

The oldest area of our brain, the so-called *old brain* (hind-brain; medula and pons), is used in the current mammalian design to represent, primarily, *internal somatic* input; that is, the largely sub-conscious 'autonomous' bodily states (circulatory, digestive, pulmonary, glandular). In reptiles, the *fore-brain* was used to represent *external sensory* input, including *motor-sensory* input from the limbs. The proto-cortical *diencephalon*, the *thalamic* and *limbic* systems, mediate between the old ('reptilian') brain and the *neo-cortex* in the current mammalian design. The neocortex (telencephalon), in turn, was projected from various regions of the thalamic and limbic proto-cortex. It contains further — 'more cognitive' — elaborations of various older limbic systems (Martin 1985; Kelly 1985; Mesulam 2000). But almost all major cortical systems in primates still have sub-cortical limbic and/or thalamic components. So that the thalamic-limbic systems form the *core* and the neocortical projections the outer *shell* of complex, vertically-integrated, multi-modular distributive systems (Mesulam 2000; 1991, Tucker 2001, 2002). That is:

> . . . a new theoretical model of the cortex, what might be called a "core-and-shell" model. At the limbic core of the cortex are motivational [deontic] mechanisms, centered on the hypothalamus. Forming the shell or interface with the environment are the sensory and motor neocortical networks. Memory is organized through a reentrant arbitration, creating a functional resonance between the paralimbic networks of the core and the neocortical networks of the shell.   (Tucker 2001: 1–2)

This pattern of inter-connectivity may be given diagrammatically (Mesulam 2000):

(22) **Inter-connectivity between the limbic-thalamic 'core' and the neocortical motor and sensory 'shell'** (following Mesulam 2000)

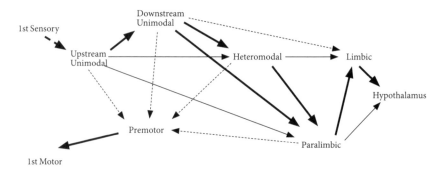

The representation of mental states of *volition/intention* (deontic) and *belief/knowledge* (epistemic) in the primate brain is still 'rooted' in the thalamic-limbic core (Tucker 1991, 2000, 2001; Mesulam 2000). In addition, the proto-cortical core also has 'downward' connections to somatic-visceral representation in the old brain.

It is of course possible to dismiss thalamic-limbic representation as 'not quite cognitive'. But given the profound core-shell connectivity and distributiveness of the major memory and attention networks, such strict dichotomy is untenable. Further, the transition from 'purely perceptual' to 'cognitive' representation in the primate visual cortex is gradual and multi-staged (Kaas 1989). And further, the major cognitive representation sub-systems of human language — semantic and episodic memory — are a transparent, recent evolutionary elaboration on the two 'streams' of visual processing system (Givón 2002: ch. 4). And both are rooted in limbic 'core' structures (Tucker 1991, 2000, 2001).

Finally, there is a body of evidence about the communicative behavior of Alex, an African Grey Parrot, who has not only acquired a considerable auditory/oral-coded English lexicon, including a number of abstract concepts, but also seems to be able to distinguish between declarative, interrogative and manipulative speech acts (Pepperberg 1991, 1999). Alex was also recorded rehearsing his English phonetics at night after being chided for faulty performance earlier in the day.[6] Thus, not only does this avian have representations of intentional belief states, but he appears to be conscious of having them, and thus perhaps even self-conscious. All of which is accomplished, largely, with a thalamic-limbic proto-cortex.

4.6.4. Transformations of the referent

It may perhaps be useful to consider a natural step-wise evolutionary progression whereby older mechanisms of mental representation have incremented slowly and gradually, with each step relying on the application of the same neuro-cognitive equivalent of 'reasoning' by feature association (20/21).

(23)   **Evolutionary precursors of mental models of other minds**:
   a-i.   external-sensory representation
   a-ii.   motor-sensory (limbs & muscles) representation
   a-iii.   internal-somatic ('autonomous') representation
   b.   internal visceral representation
   c.   internal affective representation
   d.   internal deontic (cum-epistemic) representation
   e.   internal epistemic representation

Arguments in support of such gradual progression are given below.

4.6.4.1. *The primitive vs. less-primitive representations*
It is not clear which of the three older representation systems — *external-sensory* (23a-i), *motor-sensory* (23a-ii) and *internal-somatic* (23a-iii) — precedes in evolu-

tion. In reptiles already, internal-somatic representation (23a-iii) is localized in the old brain, but both the external-sensory (23a-i) and motor-sensory (23a-ii) representations are localized in the thalamic-limbic proto-cortex, a split that persists in avians and mammals. Either one of these three or even all three could have been the evolutionary precursors of the more sophisticated *internal epistemic* representation (23e). What is more, *internal deontic* representation (23d) could have arisen gradually via *internal-somatic* (23a-iii), *internal-visceral* (23b) or *internal-affective* (23c) representation.

An intriguing body of evidence suggests the existence of a natural, and perhaps phylogenetically old, association between internal motor control, internal somatic representation and external visual representation. This involves first the work of Rizzolatti and associates on the co-activation of visual *mirror neurons*, a visual representation system that is interspersed within the primary motor cortex in both humans and non-human primates (Rizzolatti and Gentilucci 1988; Rizzolatti *et al.* 1996a,b; Rizzolatti and Arbib 1998; Rizzolatti *et al.* 2000).

More recently, a similar association between the visual and motor-gestural systems has been identified in the *ventral visual information stream*, earlier identified (Ungerleider and Mishkin 1982) as dedicated to the processing of a spatial relations and spatial motion (Milner and Goodale 1995, 1998; Gallese *et al.* 1999).

At the very least, these findings suggest overlapping activation mechanisms between the somatic-motor and external-perceptual representation systems. But since there are also strong feedback connections between the *primary motor cortex* (posterior-frontal) and the adjacent *somatic sensory* representational region (anterior-parietal), the external-sensory (23a–i) and the motor-sensory (23b-ii) representation systems are now connected via co-activation. This three-way connectivity suggests possible neural mechanisms for self-other analogy, imitation(Byrne 1998; Meltzoff 2002a, b) and thus perhaps, ultimately, empathy.

4.6.4.2. *From internal-somatic to visceral-emotional to deontic representation*

It is possible now to consider *internal-somatic* representation (23a-iii), an ancient old-brain capacity, as the evolutionary precursor of *internal-visceral* representation (23b) of hunger, pain or adrenaline arousal. And that, in turn, may be considered the evolutionary precursor of *internal-emotional* representation (23c) of urges, positive affect, fear or revulsion. And that, lastly, may be considered the evolutionary precursor of *internal deontic* representation proper (23d), such as volition, rejection and, ultimately, intention.

4.6.4.3. *From deontic to epistemic*

One of Premack and Woodruff's (1978) more intriguing suggestions was that the representation of deontic states (volition, intention) is somehow 'more primitive' than the representation of epistemic states (knowledge, belief). However intuitively appealing, this suggestion is somewhat implausible as it stands, since knowledge is already implicit in volition. To illustrate this, let us consider the volitional expression (24a), which necessarily presupposes the *realis* proposition (24b) while asserting the *irrealis* proposition (24c):

(24) a. I want to leave the room.
      b. I am in the room now   (R, presupposed)
      c. I will be outside the room later (IRR, asserted)

Both the presupposition (24b) and assertion (24c) are epistemic mental states, as are the propositional referents ('verbal complements') of intentional predicates in general.

Whether the epistemic state is realized (R) or unrealized (IRR) is hardly an issue, given that both memorized and imagined information is represented in the same limbic-based episodic memory system (hippocampus and amygdala). Whether the epistemic state is visual or verbal is not an issue either, since the limbic-based episodic memory system, originally set up as part of the visual information-processing system, is the locus of *both* visual and verbal early episodic memory (Mishkin 1978, 1982; Mishkin *et al*. 1984; Ungerleider and Mishkin 1982; Squire 1987; Squire and Zola-Morgan 1991; Petri and Mishkin 1994). Finally, the limbic-based episodic memory system is an ancient proto-cortical system shared by all primates.

There remains still a considerable residual appeal to Premack and Woodruff's conjecture about the 'primitiveness' of the deontic vis-à-vis the epistemic. This may be due to the connection between intention and 'primitive urges' (sec. 3.6.4.2. above). But even in the minuscule proto-cortex of the avian brain, a conscious attentional system seems to mediate 'primitive urges', tempering them with relevant epistemic information and with, perhaps, the weighing of possible consequences and alternative actions. That is, if the communicative behavior of Alex the African Grey parrot's is to be believed. What is more, at least two of the main attentional networks in humans still contain limbic and/or thalamic sub-modules (sec. 3.6.6.3. below).

The conjecture that deontic representation preceded epistemic representation in the evolution of mind may still be salvaged, albeit in a modified form. Epistemic representation may have appeared first as an obligatory component of deontic representation (viz. (23) above). Only later on did it *liberate* itself from this subordinate status. Cases of such liberation are widely attested in the diachronic rise of irrealis/future epistemic modalities out of precursor deontic verbs such as 'want' or 'must' (Heine 1993; Hopper and Traugott 1993; Bybee *et al*. 1994).

Support for this revised conjecture also comes from the observation that in spontaneous non-human communication, whether by avians, canines or primates, only *manipulative* speech-acts are used. That is, speech-acts where epistemic representation is embedded in, and thus subordinate to, deontic representation (see again sec. 3.4.3. above). In child development as well, early speech-acts are overwhelmingly manipulative. Unembedded declaratives emerge only later (Carter 1974; Bates *et al*. 1975, 1979).

4.6.4.4. *From perception to cognition*

We noted above the possible 'liberation' of epistemic representation from prior subordination to deontic representation. There may have been a similar 'liberation' in the rise of 'strictly-cognitive' representation from phylogenetically older perceptual-cum-cognitive representation. Thus, *seeing* and therefore knowing what is under the current focus of attention may have well been the evolutionary precursor of *remembering* what one doesn't see any more, or of *imagining* what one has never seen.

If this line of reasoning holds, it may suggest that longer-term memory systems are a later evolutionary elaboration of the modality-specific working-memory (cum attentional activation) system. The fact that to this day the latter is the gateway to the former is consonant with this conjecture. This is so because in general, older brain systems tend to be the input gateways to new ones that evolve as their later projections. The progression, in visual information processing, from eye to thalamus to neo-cortex (Hubel 1988) is of course a case in point.

4.6.5. The puzzle of consciousness

4.6.5.1. *How old is consciousness?*

I see no cogent basis for pinpointing the exact stage where consciousness — as distinct from self-consciousness — interjected itself into the representational equation. There is no compelling evidence to suggest that either avians or mammals are *not* conscious of, at the very least, the external (23a-i), motor (23a-ii) and somatic (23a-iii) referents of their deontic or epistemic states. That is, of their *1st-order framing* at least of referents that are present here-and-now. What is more, the human working memory (cum attention) system, including the conscious executive attention, deals with information that is either strictly here-and-now (if entering through sensory channels) or strictly now (if retrieved from episodic memory). Some neurological structure supporting conscious attention must already exist in avians, let alone mammals and primates. The capacity for consciously attending to *what* one sees, knows or wants, may be an old evolutionary adaptation.

Mishkin *et al.* (1984) have suggested that automated information processing is phylogenetically older than attended processing. Their arguments involve the fact that in the current primate brain, the oldest structures (old-brain) are fully automated before birth. The next oldest (thalamic-limbic systems) are not fully automated at birth, but become automated early in post-natal maturation. While the cortex, in particular its youngest frontal and pre-frontal regions, is automated last and only partially, allowing for life-long learning and skill acquisition. And last but no least, the conscious executive attention is a pre-frontal capacity.

I think there are good reasons to suspect that this argument is upside down, and that to the contrary, consciousness always precedes automaticity. To begin with, in both ontogenetic maturation and life-long learning, attended processing always precedes automaticity. Indeed, high-frequency of *attended* processing is a pre-condition for automation (Schneider 1985; Schneider and Chein 2003). It is highly unlikely that evolution bucks these developmental trends. As elsewhere (Gould 1977), a recapitulationist scenario is more plausible. The evolutionary sequence of the automation of brain regions does not indicate that automaticity is ontogenetically older than consciousness, but only that older brain regions had shifted earlier from attended to automated processing.

To the extent, then, that a central governing, modulating and context-scanning mechanism exists in any vertebrate nervous system, there is no reason to assume that it was not the functional analogue of the current primate conscious executive attention.

The most compelling claim that an organism lacks the functional equivalent of a conscious executive attention would require showing that all the circuits that mediate between sensory input and action output in the organism are fully automated. One has to go far down the evolutionary ladder, far below vertebrates, to find an organism that could possibly be that primitive. Such an organism would be utterly oblivious to finer shades of contextual variation. Its information processing system would be fully algorithmic, and would depend on purely Platonic categories that are immune to variation, learning and adaptive change. It is not clear how such a Cartesian creature — or caricature — could have ever existed, let alone evolved.

4.6.5.2. *How old is self-consciousness?*
How old in phylogeny is self-consciousness? That is, consciousness of one's mental states or *2nd-order framing*. The limbic-projected primate neo-cortical structures that support self-representation, mediated intentionality and the executive attention system are indeed late evolutionary elaborations. But to this day they are part of *distributive networks* that include 'core' thalamic-limbic components (Mesulam 2000; Tucker 2001; Schneider and Chein 2003; Posner and Fan 2004). At the very least, one cannot assume that self-consciousness must have arisen first at in its current neo-cortical location. As with consciousness, the precursor or functional equivalent of self-consciousness may have resided in pre-mammalian thalamic-limbic structures. This is certainly consonant with the evolutionary rise of the neo-cortical systems of visual, auditory, somatic-sensory and motor representation, all of which are later projections from older thalamic-limbic loci.

The distributive network of executive attention is represented pictorially in (25) below, following Schneider and Chein (2003). Of the five major components of the network, only two — the Goal Processor in the *dorso-lateral prefrontal cortex* (DLPFC) and the Attention Controller in the posterior-parietal cortex (PPC) — are neocortical. The other three are either paralimbic (the Activities Monitor in the *anterior cingulate cortex*), limbic (Episodic Storage in the *hippocampus*), or thalamic (the Gating and Report Relay in the *thalamus*).

(25)   **Brain locations of the major components of the executive attention network** (Schneider and Chein 2003)

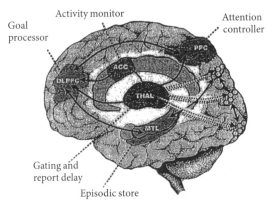

Of the two neocortical components, one — the posterior-parietal cortex (PPC) — is also the center of another attentional network, the one that controls the orientation of attention and keeps various options alive and available in cross-modal working memory (Mesulam 2002; Schneider and Chein 2003; Posner and Fan 2004). We will return to these two distributive networks of the executive attention in ch. 9 below.

There is, lastly, a theoretical argument that suggests that 1st-order framing — of sensory-external, somatic-sensory and internal-visceral input (23a) — is an evolutionary prerequisite for 2nd-order framing; that is, of framing the *output* of 1st-order framing. And likewise, that 2nd-order framing, of ones own affective, deontic and epistemic states (23c,d,e) is a prerequisite to 3rd-order framing, that of other minds. This argument does not, however, suggest absolute timing but only relative chronology.

4.6.5.3. *Consciousness and frames-within-frames: Russell's nightmare*
The difference between sub-conscious, conscious and self-conscious mental processes is not as easy to demonstrate as one would have thought. From a purely logical perspective, it seems a matter of hierarchy of frames akin to Russell's Theory of Types (ch. 1). The representation of sensory input (23a-i,ii,iii) is the *1st-order* frame. Representing one's 1st-order representation is a *2nd-order* frame. With each successive hierarchically-higher representation, another frame is added. Neat?

Alas, things get a bit messy when one adds consciousness to the equation. To begin with, consciousness does not add a frame whose scope is wider than that of sub-conscious cognition. It merely endows an erstwhile sub-conscious frame — be it 1st-order or 2nd-order — with a certain *quality*. No new referential domain is added.

Next, consciousness without self-consciousness — conscious 1st-order framing — would presumably involve awareness of a *sensory referent* (23a–i,ii,iii) but not of 'seeing', 'knowing' or 'wanting' that referent. That is, the mental frames 'see', 'know' and 'want' are imbued with consciousness, but they themselves remain outside the scope of that consciousness. This may make perfect mathematical sense in Russell's framework, but is it cognitively feasible? What exactly would it entail to be conscious of *what* one wants or knows but not of the *wanting* or *knowing*? How can one refrain from spreading consciousness upwards automatically to one's 2nd-order and 3rd-order frames? What plausible biological mechanism could enforce a Russellian injunction here?

Consider next the likely referents of older primal visceral feelings such as pain, hunger, adrenalin arousal, comfort or fear. Are they external vis-à-vis the representational system, or are they, reflexively, *both referent and representation*? If the latter, then by being conscious of the referent, one is automatically also conscious of the relevant *mental state* that represents the referent. That is, one is *self-conscious*.

Further, primal-visceral mental states are cognitively very intrusive and thus highly salient. Even if their referent could be somehow externalized, how can one be aware of such an intrusive referent without being aware of the equally intrusive primal visceral mental state prompted by the intrusive referent?

It may well be, lastly, that at least in principle one cannot constrain a pragmatic framing system from automatic recursive self-extension. Once an organism has framed an 'external' world, it has gained the capacity to frame its own framing mechanism. Cognition, like Pandora's box (or Chomsky's recursive embedding), can never be shut up once it has been opened. As a logician, Russell could legislate against any but first-order framing. Biological organisms are more likely to have some *selectional adaptive mechanisms* that constrain the proliferation of meta-frames and the attendant complexity above a certain upper bounds, but perhaps not below that bound.

4.6.5.4. *Descartes' receding line of defense: Verbally-reported consciousness*
Consciousness, or executive attention, may be an old pre-mammalian capacity. Can self-consciousness and its presumed supporting neurological mechanisms in the pre-frontal cortex of *homo sapiens* be a brand new capacity, developed only during the last 40,000 years in humans (cf. Baron-Cohen 2000)?

In the Theory of Mind literature, it has been taken for granted almost universally that self-consciousness — being aware of one's own mental processes — is the prerequisite for a 'real' Theory of Mind (e.g. Povinelli and Preuss 1995). And further, that this is the line that separates human from pre-human cognition (or autistic from normal cognition; or early-childhood from late-childhood cognition), with a certain hedge about our nearest kin. The insistence on drawing such sharp demarcation seems but the last, ever retreating, line of defense of the old Cartesian brick wall between 'us' and 'them'. But again and again, it seems, the only reason why 'they' could not have a Theory of Mind is because 'they' are incapable of reporting on it verbally.

4.6.6. The adaptive context of representing other minds

4.6.6.1. *Social cooperation*

The most important adaptive capacity a social cooperating species may need is the ability to forecast the behavior of one's conspecifics. Not only what they might be disposed to do in general, but what they will do right now, in the present context. The cheapest and most natural adaptive mechanism a social organism may have for predicting the social intentions of conspecifics is by extending the contextual scope of the entrenched adaptive strategy of 'reasoning' by feature-association. With such an extension, the most natural *null hypothesis* one could entertain is that one's conspecifics have a mind roughly like one's own, with similar deontic and epistemic capacities, and further, with the same causal goal-tree mappings between such mental capacities and future action.

4.6.6.2. *Communicative behavior*

Purposive communication is the use of some behaviors that may have been originally 'secular' as *speech acts*; that is, as a dedicated signaling system whose purpose is to induce others to comprehend what is in one's mind. Not only to comprehend, but hopefully also to spring into relevant action. Such behavior is inconceivable without a running on-line mental model, however subconscious, of the interlocutor's rapidly-shifting intentional and epistemic states. A purely associationist account of this capacity (e.g. Bloomfield 1933) would crash on the very same grounds as Quine (1951) and Premack and Woodruff (1978) have suggested. But, such purposive communicative behavior is an old pre-mammal capacity that is not fully automated even in avians (Ristau ed. 1991; Pepperberg 1999).

4.6.6.3. *The advent of human communication*

As noted earlier above, much of past discussion of Theory of Mind has tilted, whether explicitly or implicitly, towards equating 'real' Theory of Mind with the ability to report about it verbally, consciously. While expressing serious reservations about the validity of this Cartesian bias, one must nonetheless acknowledge the possibility that the rise of well-coded human communication may have had a profound impact on our species' ability to extend framing operations beyond their earlier bounds. Whether this extension turns out to be a matter of kind or degree is for the moment unclear and perhaps even irrelevant.[7]

(a) **Phonological words and semantic memory**
A great number distinct processing steps occur in rapid succession during lexical comprehension, and the early ones are all subconscious and automated. The auditory (for spoken words) or visual (for written words or visual objects) stages of language processing are highly automated, and do not reach conscious semantic representation till ca. 200–250 millisec after stimulus presentation (Swinney 1979; Treisman and Kanwisher 1998; Barker and Givón 2002).

The mere fact that human language has dedicated code units — the phonological words — that automatically activate conceptual nodes in semantic memory makes those units, as well as their mental referents, akin to *external* objects of perception. That is, phonological words are themselves available to conscious attention. Both auditory and written word-forms can be kept activated in respective working-memory buffers for ca. 2–5 seconds, an activation that can be extended by conscious rehearsal (Gathercole and Baddely 1993). Lexical concepts, including those with purely mental referents ('see', 'want', 'know'), can thus persist under the scope of conscious attention as if they were external objects of sensory perception. And this, in turn, may contribute to extending our consciousness to mental predicates, both to those referring to one's own mind and, eventually, to those referring to other minds.

(b) **Grammar and episodic memory**
As noted above (see also chs 5, 6, 7 below), the systematic on-line construction of mental models of the current epistemic and deontic states of one's interlocutor is the central adaptive motivation for the evolution of grammar. Specific grammatical constructions are used to code (in the speaker's mind) and cue (in the hearer's mind) specific mental models of the interlocutor's current (and rapidly shifting) mental states. This system is highly automated and sub-conscious, and by all available accounts also a relatively recent evolutionary addition (Bickerton 1981, 1990; Li 2002; Givón 1979a, 2002).

The phylogenetic recency and high automaticity of human grammar does not mean, however, that the construction of mental models of the interlocutor's current (and constantly shifting) mental states is necessarily a recent, human-specific capacity. It only means that the streamlining and *automation* of this capacity is recent and human-specific.

Likewise, the high level of automaticity of human grammar does not of itself indicate whether the same capacity in pre-human organisms was (or is) either subconscious, conscious or self-conscious. If anything, the absence of grammar may simply suggest that the underlying capacity of constructing mental models of other minds is more conscious in pre-human social organisms. As noted above, attended processing always precedes, and is the prerequisite to, automation in the developmental sequence (Schneider 1985; Schneider and Chein 2003). The coherent, efficient storage and retrieval of information — including coded communication — in episodic memory must have been given a tremendous boost by the evolution of grammar.

(c) **Declarative speech-acts**
Even with a well-coded lexicon, early childhood as well as non-human communication are heavily weighted toward manipulative speech-acts (Tomasello and Call 1997; Savage-Rumbaugh *et al.* 1993; Pepperberg 1991; Carter 1974; Bates *et al.* 1975, 1979). In contrast, the bulk of the grammatical machinery of human language is invested in coding declarative speech-acts (Givón 2001a). And at the use-frequency level, natural human discourse is tilted heavily toward declarative speech-acts (Givón 1995, ch. 2).

The emergence of declarative speech-acts, whose communicative goal is largely epistemic, may have enhanced the liberation of epistemic mental predicates from their erstwhile subordination to deontic predicates. And the separate and more explicit lexical representation of epistemic predicates may have, in turn, contributed towards heightened consciousness of these quintessential *mental framing* operators; first of those referring to one's own mental states; and then, by extension — reasoning by feature association — of those referring to the mental states of others.

(d) **Displaced spatio-temporal reference**
Both early childhood and primate communication are weighted heavily towards here-and-now, you-and-I, and this-or-that referents that are perceptually accessible within the immediate speech situation. Mature human communication is, in contrast, heavily tilted towards spatio-temporally displaced referents, states and events. In terms of use-frequency, again, human communication is heavily weighted toward *displaced reference*. This use-frequency bias is, in turn, reflected in the fact that much of our grammatical machinery is dedicated to communicating about displaced referents, states and events (Givón 2001a).

The immediate speech situation is mentally represented in the working memory-cum-attention system. Such representation shifts from one moment to the next, and is temporally unstable. In contrast, displaced referents, whether remembered or imagined, are more likely to be represented in episodic memory. Compared to working memory, episodic memory is a much more stable, long-lasting mental representation. And this *temporal stability* may have contributed toward the objectivization of verbally-coded referents, including mental predicates.

(e) **Multi-propositional discourse**
Lastly, early childhood and primate communication are overwhelmingly mono-propositional (Tomasello and Call 1997; Savage-Rumbaugh *et al.* 1983; Bloom 1973; Carter 1974; Scollon 1976; Bates *et al.* 1975, 1979). In contrast, mature human communication is, at the use-frequency level, overwhelmingly multi-propositional. This is reflected, in turn, in the fact that the bulk of the machinery of grammar is invested in coding multi-propositional (cross-clausal) coherence (Givón 2001a). What is more, grammar-coded discourse coherence pertains, primarily, to mental models of the interlocutors current epistemic and deontic states. The high automaticity of grammar may mean, among other things, that the evolution of grammatical communication was motivated, at least in part, by the strong adaptive pressure of having to deal with a rising frequency of *perspective shifting*.

The current processing rate of oral human discourse is ca. 1–2 per event clause (Barker and Givón 2002). Such a rate is, most likely, a whopping order-of-magnitude above what pre-human (or pre-grammatical) communicating species had to deal with. The automation, through grammar, of one's construction of mental models of the interlocutor's shifting epistemic and deontic states may be both the natural consequence of our species' accelerated reliance on communication and its facilitator.

Notes

* I am indebted to Brian MacWhinney, Mike Posner, David Premack and Don Tucker for helpful comments on an earlier version of the ms. Needless to say, they are all absolved from any responsibility for the final product.

1. This topic is discussed in much more detail in Chapter 5.

2. When Xenophon went to Delphi to consult the oracle prior to departing for his ill-fated *Anabasis*, the Pythia is reputed to have said: "Invoked or uninvoked, the God [Apollo] will be there". Grammar seems to enjoy the same measure of behind-the-scenes ubiquity.

3. Though, somehow, it seems to never occur to Heyes that her argument is a classical parsimony gambit, of the type she faults Premack and Woodruff (1978) for.

4. This is, in essence, how older children managed to clear the bar, by being able to furnish verbal accounts of their theories of minds.

5. There are some refreshing exceptions, however. Thus, Gordon (1998) in his commentary observes: ". . . Heyes seems to be asking: "Do they have a theory of mental states, with law-like generalizations, inferences from behavior to mental states, and so forth, or do they have only non-mentalistic resources? The thesis [is] that if it is a mentalistic resource then it is a theory in a full-blooded sense." (1998: 121)

6. Irene Pepperberg (in personal communication). See also Pepperberg (1999).

7. As noted earlier (chs 1, 2), the difference is logically arbitrary and depends on the construal of a relevant context.

Chapter 5

Referential coherence

5.1. Coherence as mental operations

Discourse coherence has traditionally been considered a property of the external product of communication, the oral or written *text* (Grimes 1975; Halliday and Hassan 1976; Longacre 1976). It has also been considered a property of the internal product of communication, the *mental text* stored in episodic memory (Mandler 1978; Johnson and Mandler 1977; Kintsch 1982; van Dijk and Kintsch 1983; Trabasso and van den Broeck 1985; Givón ed. 1983). While the approach pursued here is fully compatible with the latter, it involves a certain upping of the cognitive antes. That is, it proceeds from the properties of the text to the *mental operations* responsible for producing or interpreting the text (Kintsch and van Dijk 1978; Gernsbacher 1990; Kintsch 1994; Givón 1995, ch. 8). This perspective is in line with other dynamic accounts, be they developmental, of evolutionary or diachronic, that seek to understand the product by understanding the process (Givón 2002).

In the preceding chapter, we noted that the grammar of referential coherence may involve the speaker's implicit assumptions about the hearer's mental models of the *generic lexicon* (semantic memory), or of the *current speech situation* (working-memory or attention), or of the *current text* (episodic memory). In this chapter we will continue to probe into the latter two aspects of referential coherence. Since the current text is, by definition, in the midst of being produced and interpreted, the two mental representation systems that are most closely implicated here are (Ericsson and Kintsch 1997):

- working memory/attention
- early episodic memory

We will of course take it for granted that semantic memory remains involved in discourse coherence operations. To begin with, one type of referential coherence (globally-accessible definite referents) depends on the activation of generic-lexical networks. Further, grammar is only one processing channel available for discourse processing. The lexical-semantic channel does not get suspended in grammatical-ized language, but rather remains available (Kintsch 1992), given that it is automatically activated to begin with. This dependence on semantic — lexical and propositional — information for inferring discourse coherence is, of course, much more conspicuous in pre-grammatical Pidgin communication, as well as in pre-human communication (see ch. 4).

5.2. Coherence as grounding

5.2.1. Grounding in episodic representation

Coherence may be taken to mean continuity, connectivity or *grounding*. Following van Dijk and Kintsch (1978) and Kintsch (1982, 1994), I will take it for granted that the mental text represented in episodic memory has a sequential-hierarchic *network* structure. With this in mind, coherent episodic representation can be considered the chief guarantor of rapid on-line access to — and retrieval of — specific episodic-memory nodes during discourse production and comprehension. Such access depends, crucially, on the nodes' connectivity or *grounding* to other nodes in the network. During on-line discourse production and comprehension, both the speaker and hearer are busy connecting — or grounding — incoming lexical and propositional nodes to the pre-existing episodic structure of the current text.

From the hearer's perspective, such grounding guarantees three crucial adaptive imperatives of discourse processing:

- coherent on-line comprehension
- coherently structured episodic storage
- rapid subsequent access to the stored text.

From the speaker's perspective, using grammar to cue the hearer to establish well-grounded episodic structure guarantees the hearer's comprehension, thus successful communication. That is, the hearer's episodic representation may thus approximate the speaker's. Text comprehension thus depends crucially on the on-line creation of well-structured episodic representation (Gernsbacher 1990).

The use of grammar to cue the grounding of incoming information into the episodic representation of the current text involves two main directions:

- anaphoric (retrospective) grounding
- cataphoric (anticipatory) grounding

The first grounds incoming information into the already-existing mental text. The second establishes the structural foundations of the newly-arriving text.

5.2.2. Cataphoric grounding

5.2.2.1. *Truth and reference in the Real World*

An illustrious tradition, culminating in Logical Positivism, considered reference to be a mapping between referring linguistic expressions and entities in the Real World (henceforth RW; Russell 1905; Strawson 1950, 1964; Carnap 1956, 1959). From this objectivist perspective, the truth value of propositions containing referring expressions depends in part on whether the referring expressions in them do or don't map onto entities in the RW. As an illustration, consider:

(1)   a.   **The present king of France** is not bald
      b.   **The present queen of England** is not bald

(2)   a.   There is a king of France
      b.   There is no one that is both king of France and bald
      c.   There is a queen of England
      d.   There is someone that is both queen of England and not bald

According to Russell's approach to denotation, in asserting (1a) one asserts two contradictory propositions — the false (2a), and the true (2b). And further, the falsity
of (2a) is due to *failed denotation* of 'the present King of France' in (1a). In asserting (1b), on the other hand, one is not being contradictory. Rather, one asserts two
propositions, the truth of one (2c) being due to *successful denotation* of 'the present
Queen of England' in (1b), the truth of other (2d) being a matter of mere fact.

It is of course remarkable that human languages elect to code the referents in
(1a,b) with exactly the same grammatical device (syntactic subject, the definite article 'the'), paying no heed to denotation in the RW or the truth value of the propositions. In the same vein, human languages ignore RW-grounded denotation and
truth value in marking indefinite referents, as in:

(3)   a.   I rode **a unicorn** yesterday
      b.   I rode **a horse** yesterday

In matters of reference, it seems, the grammar of human language, or rather the
grammar-using mind behind it, marches to a different drum. Rather than ground
linguistic referents in the RW, we ground them in some verbally-constructed *Universe of Discourse*. Or, in the framework pursued here, we ground linguistic referents in the current discourse as represented in either (fleetingly) working memory/
attention or in (more lastingly) episodic memory.

5.2.2.2. *Referential intent*

It is of course true that the Universe of Discourse and the proverbial RW enjoy a
considerable overlap in normal human communication, which tends on the whole
to deal with extant human individuals and their everyday affairs. But when the two
worlds part company, the grammar of reference cheerfully disregards denotation
in the RW, opting to align itself with denotation in the Universe of Discourse. In
(3a), for example, the grammar first created a hypothetical referent in an imaginary
universe of discourse, then referred to it as if they were real.[1] In the same vein, consider:

(4)   a.   She's looking for *a horse*; **it** escaped last Friday
      b.   She's looking for *a horse*; **it** had better be white

In both (4a) and (4b), the pronoun 'it' is equally grounded to a referent ('a horse') in the pre-established Universe of Discourse. And while the grammar of English in this case does not distinguish between the real horse that escaped last Friday (4a) and the imagined white horse yet to be identified (4b), the speaker surely does. The speaker *intends* 'a horse' in (4a) to be interpreted as aspecific *referring* entity in the universe of discourse, but 'a horse' in (4b) to remain an imaginary, potential, *non-referring* one. In other languages (or in other varieties of English), the speaker's *referential intent* is explicitly marked by grammar (see further below).

The treatment of the referential contrast in (4a,b) by logicians harkens back to Aristotle who, in *De Sophisticis Elenchis*, observed that nominal expressions can be used in two main senses, one specific and referring (*sensus divisus*), the other generic and non-referring (*sensus compositus*). Carnap (1956, 1959) and Russell (1905) re-cast this contrast as one between the *existential* (referring) vs. the *universal* (generic, non-referring) quantifiers, respectively, as in:

(5)   a.   **Universal (non-referring):**
           All Greeks are bald = **For all** (x), if (x) is Greek, then (x) is bald
      b.   **Existential (referring):**
           Socrates is bald = **There exists** an (x), that (x) is Socrates,
           and (x) is bald

The choice of generic subjects to illustrate non-reference (5b) is somewhat unfortunate, since generic subjects in natural language tend to be highly referring, indeed topical. However, their proper domain of reference (universe of discourse) is not the universe of tokens but rather that of *types*. That is, the generic referent 'all Greeks' in (5a) tends to be used when the type 'Greeks' has already been established as *topical referent* in the preceding discourse.

5.2.2.3. *Reference and propositional modalities*

The effect of propositional modalities on the referential properties of nominals under their scope was initially noted by Quine (1953). A more detailed treatment of propositional modalities and their interaction with the grammar of tense-aspect will be deferred to ch. 6, below. The logical tradition (cf. Carnap 1956) recognized four propositional modalities — necessarily true, factually true, possibly true, not true. This division again goes back to Aristotle. The four logical modalities can be easily re-interpreted in communicative terms as their equivalent communicative modalities in (6) below. For the purpose of predicting the behavior of referents under modal scope, the four propositional modalities can be grouped into two mega-modalities, *fact* (true) and *non-fact* (non-true):

(6) **Propositional modalities**:

Communicative	Logical
Fact	*True*
a. Presupposition	Necessarily true (analytic)
b. Realis-assertion	Factually true (synthetic)
Non-fact	*Non-true*
c. Irrealis-assertion	Possibly true (no truth value)
d. NEG-assertion (negation)	Not-true (false)

The referential behavior of nominals under the scope of the four modalities is illustrated in (7) below:

(7) a. **Fact, Realis**:   She **saw** a dog
                                   ($\supset$ a particular dog; REF)
                                   (*$\supset$ any dog; *NON-REF)

     b. **Fact, Presupposition**: Because she **saw** a dog,...
                                   ($\supset$ a particular dog)
                                   (*$\supset$ any dog; NON-REF)

     c. **Non-fact, Irrealis**:   She **will** see a dog
                                   $\left\{\begin{array}{l}(\supset \text{a particular dog; REF}) \\ (\supset \text{any dog; NON-REF})\end{array}\right\}$

     d. **Non-fact, Negation**:   She **didn't** see a dog
                                   ($\supset$ any dog; NON-REF)
                                   She **didn't** see the dog.
                                   ($\supset$ a particular dog; REF)

The effect of propositional modalities on the referential behavior of nominals under their scope is then:

(8) **Reference and propositional modality**:
     a. Under the scope of **non-fact** modalities, nominals can be interpreted as *either* referring or non-referring.
     b. Under the scope of **fact** modalities nominals can *only* be interpreted as referring.

In more economical terms of markedness (default), (8) may be re-cast as:

(9) **Reference and propositional modality**:
     a. Nominals *may* be interpreted as non-referring only if they fall under the scope of a non-fact modality (marked).
     b. Otherwise they *must* be interpreted as referring (unmarked; default case)

The re-formulation of (8) into (9) takes account of the fact that human discourse tends to be, at the usage-frequency level, overwhelmingly about real rather than unreal events and referents (Givón 1995, ch. 2).

One common syntactic environment, nominal predicates (Donellan 1966), also behaves like a non-fact modality, allowing the contrast between referring and non-referring nominals. This is probably due to the fact that the habitual-timeless aspect used in nominal predicates denotes *no particular time*, and propositions in that mode refer to no particular events/states. For the purpose of reference, at least, the habitual-timeless aspect behaves like a non-fact modality:

(10) **Nominal predicates (habitual-timeless modality)**:
    a. **Referring:**   He's **a teacher** I met in college
                       (Context: You asked me who he was)
    b. **Non-referring:** John is **a teacher** by profession
                       (Context: You asked me what he did for a living)

The vast majority of lexical verbs carry an inherent *realis* modality, so that — unless under the scope of some explicit non-fact operator — their indefinite object must be interpreted as referring. It is therefore more economical to list the relatively few lexical verbs that carry an inherent *irrealis*, *negation*, or *presupposition* modality. Some of the more typical ones are:[2]

(11) a. **Inherent irrealis verbs:**
        want, like, look for, dream of, think of, believe in
    b. **Inherent negative verbs:**
        lack, refuse, decline, miss, fail
    c. **Inherent presuppositional verbs:**
        know, forget, regret, be happy, be good, learn, understand

5.2.2.4. *Reference vs. topicality*

So far, if one tests isolated clauses without their discourse context, it would seems that the referring vs. non-referring contrast is about the speaker's *referential intent*. And one could easily find languages (Turkish, Modern Hebrew, Mandarin Chinese, Krio, Sherpa, etc.) where special markers are accorded to indefinite nouns that are meant to refer, as contrasting with the unmarked non-referring nominal. In Bemba (Bantu; Givón 1973b), the referring vs. non-referring contrast cuts across the definitive/indefinite contrast. Thus consider:

(12) **Fact-realis:**
    a. **Referring:**   a-a-somine   **ichi**-tabo
                        s/he-PAST-read **REF**-book
                        'S/he read a/the book'
    b. ***Non-referring:** a-a-somine **chi**-tabo
                        s/he-read **N/REF**-book

(13) **Non-fact, irrealis:**
    c. **Referring:**   a-ka-soma   **ichi**-tabo
                       s/he-FUT-read **REF**-book
                       'S/he will read a/the particular book'
    d. **Non-referring:**   a-ka-soma   **chi**-tabo
                       s/he-FUT-read **N/REF**-book
                       'S/he will read a (some, unspecified) book'

(14) **Non-fact, negation:**
    e. **Referring:**   ta-a-a-soma   **ichi**-tabo
                       NEG-s/he-PAST-read **REF**-book
                       'She didn't read *the* book'
                       *'S/he didn't read a/*any* book'
    f. **Non-referring:**   ta-a-a-soma   **chi**-tabo
                       NEG-s/he-PAST-read **N/REF**-book
                       'S/he didn't read *any* book'

When the same morphological contrast is studied in its natural communicative context, a different picture emerges. The grammatical operator supposedly marking REF-indefinites as 'intended to refer' turns out to mark thematically important — *topical* — referents. That is, indefinite referents intended to *persist* in the subsequent discourse regardless of their logical referential status. In contrast, the grammatical operator supposedly marking non-referring nominals as 'not-intended to refer' turns out to mark thematically unimportant — *non-topical* — referents; that is, indefinite referents that are *not* intended to persist in the subsequent discourse. What we have here is a system of cuing *thematic importance* or *relevance* rather than logical status.

As a typical example of this contrast, consider the use of the referring-indefinite marker 'this' in spoken American English, as seen in a Dear Abby letter (Wright and Givón 1987):

(15) **The indefinite articles *a(n)* vs. this in English discourse:**

> Dear Abby: There's *this guy* I've been going **with** for near three years. Well, the problem is that **he** hits me. **He** started last year. **He** has done it only four or five times, but each time **it** was worse than before. Every time **he** hits me it was because **he** thought I was flirting (I wasn't). Last time **he** accused me of coming on to *a friend* of **his**. First **he** called me a lot of dirty names, then **he** punched my face so bad **it** left me with a black eye and black-and-blue bruises over half of my face. It was very noticeable, so I told my folks that the car I was riding in stopped suddenly and my face hit the windshield. Abby, **he**'s 19 and I'm 17, and already I feel like *an old married lady* who lets her husband push her around. I haven't spoken to **him** since this happened. **He** keeps bugging me to give **him** one more chance. I think I've given **him** enough chances. Should I keep avoiding **him** or what?
>
>   Black and Blue.

Of the three indefinite referents introduced for the first time into the discourse in (15), the one introduced by 'this' ('this guy') recurs again and again as the central character in the subsequent narrative (aside from the speaker herself). The indefinite referents introduced by 'a' — one logically referring ('a friend of his'), the other non-referring ('an old married lady') — do not recur in the subsequent text.

The *cataphoric persistence* of 'a'-marked vs. 'this'-marked indefinite referents has been studied in oral narratives produced by 8–12-year old native speakers of American English. The results are summarized in (16) below (Wright and Givón 1987).

(16)   **Mean cataphoric persistence (TP) of indefinite 'a'-marked and 'this'-marked subjects and objects in spoken English** (expressed as number of times the same referent recurred in the sub-sequent 10 clauses; Wright and Givón 1987)

Grammatical coding	Mean TP value	N	%
'this'-subject	6.95	**28**	65
'this'-object	2.40	15	35
TOTAL 'this'		43	100
'a'-subject	1.54	13	
'a'-object	0.56	**94**	88
TOTAL 'a'		107	100

A clear interaction can be seen in (16) between grammatical subjecthood and the indefinite article 'this': 65% of 'this'-marked referents appeared as subjects, while 88% of 'a(n)'-marked referents occurred as non-subjects. Indeed, the contrast of grammatical roles — subject vs. direct object vs. others — is one of the most reliable cataphoric grammatical signals for both indefinite *and* definite referents.

Referring-indefinite — highly topical — subjects most commonly appear in a special *existential-presentative* construction. Thus, 100% of the 'this'-marked subjects in (16) appeared in such a construction, as in, e.g.:

(17)   *There's this guy* who comes over to our house every night.

The cataphoric persistence of subject-marked vs. object-marked referents in a sample of five languages is given in (18) below. The data are expressed as a contrast between low-persistence referents, those that persist only 0–1–2 times (0–2) in the subsequent 10 clauses, and high-persistence referents, those that persist more than twice (>2) in the subsequent 10 clauses.

(18)   Cataphoric persistence of subjects and objects of transitive clauses in
Sahaptin, Panare, Bella Coola, Korean and Spanish (Givón 1995, ch. 6)

Persistence in the following 10 clauses

Language		0–2		>2		TOTAL	
		N	%	N	%	N	%
Sahaptin	Subject	9	19.6	37	**80.4**	46	100.0
	Object	21	**61.8**	13	38.4	34	100.0
Panare	Subject	9	31.0	20	**69.0**	29	100.0
	Object	19	**65.5**	10	34.5	29	100.0
Bella Coola	Subject	27	21.4	99	**78.6**	126	100.0
	Object	82	**65.1**	44	34.9	126	100.0
Korean	Subject	53	35.3	97	**64.7**	150	100.0
	Object	106	**72.0**	44	28.0	150	100.0
Spanish	Subject	19	19.0	81	**81.0**	100	100.0
	Object	70	**70.0**	30	30.0	100	100.0

5.2.2.5. *The cognitive interpretation of topicality*

Cataphoric persistence in subsequent text is of course only a heuristic measure. But a measure of what? In other words, what is the cognitive status of 'topicality'? The experimental literature, however meager (Gernsbacher 1990; Tomlin 1995, 1997) suggests that what is assessed here is *attentional activation*. Indefinite referents, those that are introduced into the discourse for the first time, are marked as topical when the speaker wants to cue the hearer to strong attentional activation of the referent, and thus salient coding in the currently-assembling episodic memory, and thus more efficient retrieval (Gernsbacher 1990; Givón 1991a).

Definite referents, those assumed to already have mental representation in the hearer's episodic memory, can also be marked by various grammatical devices as 'topical'. This is done when the speaker wants to facilitate the search and retrieval for such referents in the hearer's extant episodic memory when they had been previously topical; to re-code them as still topical in currently-assembling episodic memory.

Whether during initial coding (indefinite) or subsequent retrieval and re-coding (definite), the grammar of reference and topicality in human language is keyed delicately to anticipate the epistemic mental states of the interlocutor. As we shall see further below, the system as a whole is both extensive and very finely articulated.

5.2.3 Anaphoric grounding

5.2.3.1. *Activation, search and mental connectivity*
As already noted (ch. 4, sec. 4.4.2.), anaphoric referents are those for which the speaker assumes that the hearer already has a pre-existing *accessible mental representation*. The grammar of anaphoric reference cues the hearer about how to ground the current referent onto its co-referent node in the pre-existing mental representation.

We have further noted that the relevant mental representation may sometime be the current speech situation or the generic lexicon. Still, the bulk of the grammatical machinery used to cue hearers about the grounding of anaphoric referents involves the mental representation of the current discourse.

The grounding of anaphoric referents is a complex process that involves, at least potentially, three distinct mental operations:

(i) *Attentional activation* of the current referent in the working-memory buffer.
(ii) *Searching* for and *accessing* the referent's antecedent co-referent in the appropriate sub-network of episodic memory.
(iii) *Grounding*, i.e. establishing a *mental connection* between the antecedent co-referent in episodic memory and its current activated locus in working memory/attention.

Attentional activation (i) depends, at least in part, on whether the referent is topical, as well as on whether it is already available in working memory. Searching and accessing (ii) is only required if the referent is not currently active in working memory/attention. By default, a referent is still active in working memory if it appeared in the preceding clause. Grounding (iii) may involve real neural connections, or some form of cognitive indexing of co-reference. Whatever the neuro-cognitive mechanism is that marks the successive appearances of the same referent as "co-referent", it is one of the chief guarantors of discourse coherence.

Like referential coherence itself, (i), (ii) and (iii) above are integrated into the complex set of mental operations of discourse production and comprehension. The mental capacities relevant to referential coherence of the current discourse are (Gernsbacher 1990; Ericsson and Kintsch 1997):

- attention
- working memory
- early episodic memory

5.2.3.2. *Grammatical cues for anaphoric coherence*
A surprisingly large portion of the grammatical machinery of human languages turns out to partake in the cuing of referential coherence. Among those, the most conspicuous ones, cross-linguistically, are:

(19)   Main sub-systems in the grammar of referential coherence:

Without lexical nouns

   a.   zero, pronouns, pronominal agreement
   b.   same-reference (SS) vs. switch reference (DS) markers in clause-chaining

Combined with lexical nouns

   c.   determiners, articles, numerals
   d.   restrictive modifiers (adjectives, relative clauses)
   e.   grammatical case-roles (subject, direct object)
   f.   role-changing constructions (passive, inverse, antipassive, dative-shift)
   g.   existential-presentative constructions
   h.   word-order topicalizing devices (L/R-dislocation)
   i.   contrastive-topic devices (Y-movement, cleft clauses)

Several grammatical devices in (19) cue primarily *cataphoric* coherence (indefinite articles (19c); grammatical case-roles (19e); role-changing constructions (19f); existential-presentative clauses (19g)). Those have already been discussed above. A few devices cue primarily *anaphoric* coherence (19a). But many cue *both* anaphoric and cataphoric coherence (19b, c, d, h, i). This is, of course, natural, since such double-grounding constructions involve the *re-activation* of a currently inactive (but still mentally accessible) referent. That referent may have been topical in its *previous* discourse locus. Upon its re-emergence into the discourse, its *current* topicality must now be established.

5.2.3.3. *Referential continuity and anaphoric grounding*

One of the most telling diagnostics for the role of anaphoric grammatical devices in discourse processing is the heuristic text-based measure of *anaphoric distance* (AD). This measure assesses how far back in the preceding discourse, in terms number of clauses, the most recent antecedent co-referent of the current referent can be found. In table (20) below, the typical average AD values of some of the more common anaphoric-reference grammatical devices are given, together with some indication of the degree to which the text-measured populations cluster around their means.

(20)   **Comparison of mean anaphoric distance (AD) values and degree of categorial clustering of common anaphoric devices** (Givón 1995, ch. 8)

	Construction	Mean AD (# of clauses)	Degree of clustering around the mean
a.	Zero anaphora	1.0	100% at mean
b.	Unstressed pronouns	1.0	95% at mean
c.	Stressed pronouns	2.5	90% bet. 2–3 cl.
d.	Y-movement	2.5	90% bet. 2–3 cl.
e.	Cleft clauses	3.0	90% bet. 2–4 cl.
f.	DEF-noun	7.0	25% at 1.0 cl. 35% bet. 5.0–19 cl. 40% at 20+
g.	DEF-noun with restrictive modifier	10.0	55% bet. 5.0–19.0
h.	L-dislocated DEF-noun	15.0	60% a >20+ 13% at 10–19 25% at 4–9

One must emphasize that anaphoric distance (AD), much like cataphoric persistence (CP) earlier above, is but a *heuristic* measure. By itself, AD does not correlate directly with any mental operation. Rather, it is possible to interpret AD measurements as correlating with some mental entities — both structures and operations. But the case for such correlations must be established slowly and gradually, argued on firm theoretical grounds, and eventually supported by independent cognitive evidence.

The main division in (20) is between grammatical devices with no lexical noun, those that signal *maximal referential continuity* (20a, b), and devices where a lexical noun (or a stress pronoun) is used, those that signal *referential discontinuity* (20c–h):

- maximal continuity → • zero anaphora,
  - • unstressed pronoun

- discontinuity → • stressed pronoun,
  - • NPs with lexical noun

As an illustration of how this major distinction is deployed in text, consider the following passage of Western fiction. Of the referents that play any significant role in the narrative,[3] the maximally-continuous ones are bold-faced, the discontinuous ones are italicized.

(21)   **He** circled it wearily as a wolf, **[0]** studying it from all angles, and when finally **he** stopped within a dozen feet of *the dead man*, **he** knew much of what had happened at this place. *The dead man* had ridden a freshly shod horse into the playa from the north, and when **[0]** shot **he** had tumbled

from the saddle and *the horse* had galloped away. *Several riders* on unshod ponies had then approached the body and *one* had dismounted to [0] collect the weapons. *The clothing* had not been stripped off, nor was *the body* mutilated.   (L'Amour 1962: 7)

Cognitively, the maximally-continuous anaphoric devices signal the default choice of *continued activation* of the current topical referent. From the perspective pursued here, the currently activated topical referent is the *filing-label* under which incoming new information is attached. This filing-label marks the current *clause chain*, which is the next-higher hierarchic level of discourse structure above the clause. Clauses are the lowest filing level, into which lexical words are filed in linear order. Continuing activation thus means that until further notice, incoming information — words and clauses — will be filed into the same clause-chain, under the same filing-label, the currently activated topical referent.

Discontinuous anaphoric devices signal, at the very least, the *terminated activation* of the current topical referent and, if the discourse is not itself terminated, the *activation of a new topical referent*. Such minimal discontinuity, in reference but not in larger thematic units (the chain), is seen in the use of short-distance devices (20c, d, e). An example of the use of such a device, in this case the stressed pronoun 'one', can be seen in (21). The stressed pronoun 'one' terminates the activation of the previous topical referent ('several riders'), but the two subsequent clauses are still part of the same — continuing — chain.

Short-distance discontinuous anaphoric devices are often used as chain-medial switch-reference devices, in discourses where two topical participants switch back and forth. This may be illustrated in:

(22) a. Peter arrived first. A minute later Mary came in and took a table in the back.
      b. So **HE** decided to pretend he didn't see her,
      c. but then **SHE** got up and came over,
      d. and **HE** was so embarrassed and didn't know what to say,
      e. Then **SHE** just said hi & sat down.

Finally, long-distance discontinuous anaphoric devices, such as (20f, g, h), terminate the activation of both the current topical referent *and* the current clause-chain, and then activate a new topical referent, for which there is an extant mental trace. Thus, the full indefinite NP 'several riders' in (21) terminated the activation of the preceding topical referent 'the dead man', as well as of the previous chain of which 'the dead man' was the filing label. A new clause-chain is thus opened, with 'several riders' as its topical referent. This new chain is then terminated when 'the dead man', the topic of an earlier chain, returns at the onset of a new chain. Its return is only implicit, however, accomplished by the frame-based reference to 'the clothing' and 'the body'. Both of these referents find their anaphoric antecedent in the earlier occurrence of 'the dead man'.

Several long-distance anaphoric devices subsumed under (20f,g,h) find their anaphoric antecedent co-referent outside the current clause-chain. Thus, in addition
to their own de-activation and re-activation, they also cue the hearer to searching
for the antecedent co-referent *across* at least one chain boundary, or even across a
higher thematic boundary, that of the paragraph. As an illustration of one such long-
distance anaphoric device, L-dislocation (20h), consider (23) below, taken from an
informal conversation, where three examples are found in the speech of the main
speaker:[4]

(23) H: …Well my dad was born in Sherman, that's close to where […] is. He
          was born in Sherman in 1881, and he died in '75. Yeah. And ah, so, ah of
          course, **my great grandfather, they came in there**, I think, y'know, part
          of them from Tennessee and part of them from Illinois. And I don't re-
          ally know much about that far back … Tom. **But my grand-dad, he
          was a hard-shelled Baptist preacher**, and he just, y'know, farmed and
          ranched.
      T: In Texas?
      H: Yeah, yeah.
      T: So he was already in Texas?
      H: They must've come there when he was small, y'know, 'cause he spent …
      T: Your great grandfather moved and your grandfather was really raised
          in Texas.
      H: Yeah, yeah. In other words, about three generations of us … were in
          Texas …
      T: In Texas …
      H: And of course we eh, **my dad, all he ever did was farm and ranch** …

Lastly, long-distance anaphoric antecedent search in episodic memory may also
be guided by the use of restrictive modifiers. Thus, for example, the definite referent
'the dead man' in (21) finds its antecedent several chains earlier, where the discovery
of *a dead man* is broached for the first time. The restrictive modifier, be it an adjective or a relative clause, presumably guides the episodic-memory by matching the
previous occurrence of the same predication.

A modifier-guided co-referent search may also be motivated by *referential competition*, as in the use of a restrictive relative clause in (24h) below (see ch. 4). The
predication 'standing next to the bar' in (24h) is matched back to 'standing next to
the bar' (24a).

(24) a. There was **this man** [standing near the bar],
      b. but we ignored him and went on across the room,
      c. where **another man** was playing the pinball machine.
      d. We sat down and ordered a beer.
      e. **The bar tender** took his time,

  f. I guess he was busy.

  g. So we just sat there waiting,

  h. when all of a sudden **the man [standing next to the bar]** got up and ...

5.3. Use frequency, markedness and cognitive status

In traditional linguistic terms, the maximal-continuity anaphoric devices — zero-anaphor and unstressed/clitic pronoun — are the *least marked* devices, carrying the smallest phonological weight and lacking independent lexical status.[5] Their small physical size is, in turn, matched by their high *use frequency* in natural communication(Zipf 1935).

 As an illustration of the distributional facts, consider first the frequency distribution of zero/pronouns vs. full definite nouns in spoken Ute, spoken English, and two spoken English-based pidgins (Givón ed. 1983; 1984) in (25). (When the sample of full NPs also includes indefinite nouns, the predominance of zero/pronouns is a little less pronounced.)

(25) **Text frequency of clauses with anaphoric subject pronouns (incl. zero) vs. full subject nouns in spoken Ute, spoken English and two spoken English-based Pidgins** (Givón ed.1983, 1984)

	Zero/pronoun		DEF noun		TOTAL	
Language	N	%	N	%	N	%
Ute	288	**93.5**	20	6.5	308	100.0
English	540	**74.4**	185	25.6	725	100.0
Spanglish (pidgin)	109	**68.9**	54	31.1	163	100.0
Filipinglish (pidgin)	132	**73.3**	48	26.7	180	100.0

 Not surprisingly, referents occupying the subject grammatical role in the clause are much more likely to be coded as zero/pronouns, due to their high referential continuity and topicality. As an illustration, consider first the frequency distribution in Zacapultec Mayan (DuBois 1987):

(26)   The distribution of grammatical subjects, objects and 'others' in the zero-pronoun and full-NP categories in Zacapultec (from DuBois 1987)

| | Referent NP type | | | | | |
| | Zero/pronoun | | Full-NP | | TOTAL | |
Grammatical role	N	%	N	%	N	%
Transitive subjects	169	**93.9**	11	6.1	180	100.0
Intransitive subjects	136	**51.9**	126	48.1	262	100.0
All subjects	305	**60.0**	137	40.0	442	100.0
Direct objects	96	**54.3**	81	45.7	177	100.0
Others	24	13.4	154	**86.6**	178	100.0

As noted earlier above (18), the subject grammatical role is used to code the most *topical* (cataphorically persistent) referents in discourse. What the Zacapultec distributional data show is that transitive-subjects, predominantly human agents, also have the highest *anaphoric accessibility* — **93.9%** zero/pronouns. The intransitive subject slot, in contrast, is more commonly used to introduce new — anaphorically discontinuous — referents that are less likely to be human agents. Only **51.9%** of intransitive subjects are high-continuity (zero/pronoun), essentially matching the level of direct objects (**54.3%**). Referents coded as indirect objects of various types ('others') are mostly non-continuous, with only **13%** zero/pronouns.

The predominance of the subject-coded — thus continuous — referents in coherent text is also illustrated by the following distribution in spoken English narrative:

(27)   **Number of participant-referents per clause in spoken English narrative** (Givón ed. 1983)

# of referents per clause	N	%
1 (subject)	39	38.6
2 (subject and object)	54	53.4
3 (subject, object, other)	8	8.0
>3	—	—
TOTAL	101	100.0

The distribution of total NPs in the various grammatical roles in the text in (27) can be re-computed as:

(28) **Frequency distribution of various grammatical**
       NP roles in spoken English narrative

Grammatical role	N	%
Subject	101	59.0
Object	62	36.0
Others	8	5.0
TOTAL	171	100.0

The grammatical subject, the clause's most topical referent, codes the event participant that is the most *continuous* — both anaphorically and cataphorically. Subject-coded referents constitute 60% of all referents in our spoken English text. Direct objects, the clause's secondary topics, constitute the bulk of the rest (36%). Non-topical 'others' referents make up a negligible residue (5%). Because the more topical arguments are so anaphorically recurrent, few high-frequency topical referents predominate natural discourse, recurring again and again in the text. In contrast, the much more numerous non-topical referents tend to appear only once and then seldom recur (Wright and Givón 1987).

In terms of grammatical coding topical referents, tend to be predominantly subjects and predominantly zero/pronoun. And clause-chains in natural discourse tend to be equi-topic chains. In the cognitive framework pursued here, topical referents serve as the salient *filing labels* for their respective chains. As long as the same topical referent persists, the clauses containing it are filed under the same clause-chain node in episodic memory. And the termination of the current topical referent is most commonly associated with the termination of the current clause-chain.

5.4. Cognitive model

5.4.1. Preamble

In this section I sketch out more explicitly the cognitive interpretation of the grammar of referential coherence, an interpretation that has been developed gradually during the preceding discussion. I will take it for granted that the *verbal clause* that codes either a state or an event is the minimal unit for adding new language-coded information into episodic memory (Chafe 1994; Barker and Givón 2002). A clause in connected discourse tends to have one topical referent, most commonly its grammatical subject. The clause is, in turn, part of a larger thematic unit, the *clause-chain*, which is in turn part of a *thematic paragraph*, which is in turn part of an *episode*, etc. up to whatever hierarchic depth appropriate for the particular discourse.[6]

In the accretion of new information into episodic memory, the following conventions are observed:

(29) **Filing and storage conventions for episodic memory**:
   a. **Sequential-hierarchic structure**: Discourse stored mentally in epi-
       sodic memory is sequentially-hierarchically structured, with words
       stored linearly under their proper event/state clause nodes, clauses
       stored linearly under their proper chain nodes, chains under their
       proper paragraph nodes, paragraphs under their proper episode
       nodes, etc.
   b. **Topical referent**: Each clause has a *topical referent* that, most com-
       monly, serves as the topic for the entire clause-chain containing the
       clause.
   c. **Activated filing label**: The topical referent that persists through multi-
       clause chain serves as the chain's *filing label*.
   d. **Matching clauses to their proper chain-files**:
       Within each clause, that *topical referent* serves as the filing guide, mak-
       ing it possible for the clause to be filed under its proper chain node.
   e. **Continued file activation**: As long as incoming clauses continue to
       have the same activated topical referent, they continue to be filed un-
       der the same chain node.
   f. **Terminated file activation**: To *discontinue* filing incoming informa-
       tion into the chain, its filing label, the topical referent, must be de-acti-
       vated.
   g. **New file activation**: To open a new chain for filing incoming new in-
       formation, its filing label — a *new topical referent* — must first be acti-
       vated inside the first clause in the chain.
   h. **One open file at a time**: Only one filing label at a time can be activated,
       so that only one chain at a time can receive incoming new information.
   i. **Incoming new information**: The incoming new information is all the
       words in the clause except for its topical referent.

Since conventions (29) constitute a set of strong cognitive claims about the central
role of topical nominal referents in episodic information processing, it is perhaps in
order to ask why it is *nominal referents* — objects or persons, rather than locations,
times, or predicates — that are used so consistently as the filing labels in the incrementation of new information into clause-chains? Several factors conspire to make
this the most natural cognitive, developmental and evolutionary choice:

- Nominal referents are perceptually and cognitively salient, being typically concrete, durable, individuated, spatially compact, and often fast moving.
- Nominal reference is acquired earlier in language ontogeny.
- Nominal reference evolved earlier in language phylogeny.
- Nominal referents code culturally central entities, in particular those that are
  prototypically human-agents, (active, conscious, willful) or salient patients (concrete, compact, manipulable, useful).

Human communication seems to single out these cognitively and culturally salient entities as the important *topical entities* about which information chunks — predications — are transacted. But this information processing system bears the unmistakable footprints of a pre-linguistic evolutionary development. So that it is most likely that visual episodic information processing was already organized along similar lines (Barker and Givón 2002; Givón 2002: ch. 4). Salient, compact, durable, movable entities, occupying the roles of either active agent or impacted patient, have been serving for a long time as the *thematic guide-posts* around which events and states were organized, and eventually also multi-propositional discourse.

5.4.2. Cognitive operations

The grammar of referential coherence, in so far as it involves episodic mental representation of the current text, cues two major types of cognitive operations:

- **Attentional activation operations (cataphoric)**, whereby nominal referents are either activated, de-activated or re-activated in working memory/attention.
- **Search and grounding operations (anaphoric)**, whereby the episodic mental model of the current text is searched for the antecedent co-referent of the currently active topical referent, and a grounding connection between the two loci of the referent — working memory and episodic memory — is established.

Under attentional activation we subsume three possible processing instructions:

(30) **Main attentional processing instructions**:
    a. **Continue activation** of the currently active topical referent.
    b. **Terminate activation** of the currently active topical referent.
    c. **Activate** a currently inactive topical referent, by either:
      (i) activating a **new referent** (indefinite)
      (ii) re-activate an **existing referent** (definite)

Search and grounding operations apply only when a currently inactive definite referent with an accessible episodic-memory trace is being re-activated (30c-ii).

The main grammar-cued mental operations relevant to referential coherence are summarized in (31) below as a series of ordered binary choices. They are given here from the perspective of the speaker. That is, as the speaker's instructions to the hearer about how to manipulate either the hearer's working-memory/attention or the hearer's episodic memory of the current text. For each binary choice, one option is assumed to be the *default* ('unmarked', U) case, the one more frequent is natural communication and thus cognitively less costly. The other option, the *marked* case (M), is the one less frequent in natural communication and thus cognitively more costly.

(31)   **Major grammar-cued mental operations in referential coherence**
([U = unmarked = default; M = marked]

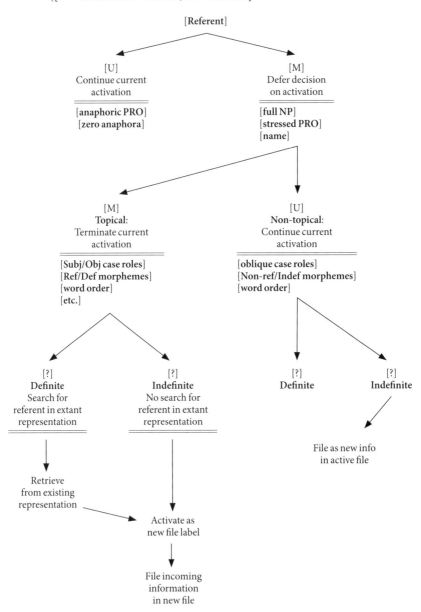

From the perspective of the hearer, the grammar-cued operations outlined in (31) can be rendered as the processing instructions in (32). These instructions are given in the form of conditional statements (if *p*, then *q*), with *p* standing for grammatical cue and *q* standing for mental operation.

(32)   **Major grammar-cued mental operations in referential coherence (hearer's perspective):**

a.   if ZERO/PRO → continue current activation (keep filing incoming
                    information under same node)
b.   if FULL NP → (i)   defer activation decision
                   (ii) determine referent's topicality
c.   if NON-TOPICAL → (i)   do not activate
                       (ii) continue current activation
d.   if TOPICAL → de-activate the current active node;
      then:
e.   if INDEFINITE → (i)   do not search for episodic antecedence;
                      (ii)   initiate a new text-node;
                      (iii)   activate the new referent/node;
                      (iv)   ground the new referent/node to the most
                              current text locus in episodic memory.
                      (v)   start filing incoming new information
                              under the new node.
f.   if DEFINITE → determine the source of definiteness:
                      (i)   **Speech situation** mental model;
                      (ii)   **Generic-lexical** mental model;
                      (iii)   **Episodic text** mental model
      then:
                      (iv)   search for antecedent co-referent in
                              appropriate mental model;
                      (v)   ground the antecedent to its co-referent
                              in the current text locus;
                      (vi)   initiate a new file-node labeled by the new
                              topical referent;
                      (vii)   activate the new referent node;
                      (viii) start filing incoming new information
                              under new node.

5.5. Discussion

The specific cognitive model presented above is a reasonably parsimonious interpretation of the distribution of grammar in text, as well as of the cross-linguistic distribution of syntactic constructions (Givón ed. 1983; 2001a). It is fully consonant with what is presently known about the neuro-cognition of working-memory, attention and early episodic memory. What is more, it makes highly specific, testable empirical predictions. It is nevertheless true that in the 14 years since this model has been first proposed (Givón 1991a), relatively few experimental studies have been carried out to either support or refute it. The scientific status of this model is, therefore, still that of a hypothesis awaiting dis-confirmation. The little experimental literature bearing on it at least in part (Gernsbacher 1990; Tomlin 1995, 1997) is fully consonant with the model's major tenets.

Whichever way one elects to formalize the deployment of grammar in the maintenance of referential coherence, it is fairly clear that the grammar-cued operations we have surveyed above involve the speaker's detailed forecasts about — thus mental model of — the hearer's rapidly-shifting *epistemic states*. And that those mental states pertain to two (and a half) major cognitive representation systems: working-memory, attention and early episodic memory. More recent experimental evidence (Barker and Givón 2003) suggests that the hearer's *deontic/intentional* states are also represented in episodic memory.

Because the hearer's epistemic and deontic states shift constantly during on-line communication, the speaker's mental models of the hearer's mind must shift just as rapidly, at the very least with each successive event/state clause. This fast rate of change suggests that these models are maintained in the speaker's *working-memory*, the mental capacity that most closely matches the flow-rate of ca. 1–2 seconds per clause (Barker and Givón 2002). This representation is most likely subliminal and highly automated, a suggestion consonant with the fact that it is almost entirely unavailable to conscious verbal recall (Barker and Givón 2003). The traditional 'Theories of Mind' assumptions that mental models of other minds need to be explicit, conscious or verbal, again seems to be questionable.

One of the most striking facts about discourse coherence in general and referential coherence in particular is the incredible amount of grammatical machinery that is expended on searching for the *antecedent co-referent* of the currently-activated topical referent (32f–i,ii,iii,iv) and then on *grounding* — mentally connecting — co-referent mental nodes (32e-iv), (32f-v). The connections created this way are often distant, transcending the admittedly-more-common connections between adjacent clause ('local coherence'). Such long-distance co-reference connections ('global coherence') may cut across chain, paragraph and episode boundaries, thus across the hierarchic node-structure of the mentally-stored text. There seems to be a strong adaptive pressure for such grounding, one that may be given as the following constraint:

(33)   **The anaphoric grounding constraint**:
       When an important topic is re-introduced into the discourse, mental
       access to the information filed under its antecedent text-location must
       be assured.

What is the adaptive (communicative) rationale for such a rigid constraint? The answer is, I think, reasonably transparent. If a recurrent referent is thematically important ('topical'), its topicality ('relevance') must be justified upon being re-activated in its current textual locus. As noted above, this type of justification is systematically furnished — and coded by grammar — for *indefinite* referents, that is, upon their first introduction into the discourse. The grammar marks them there as highly topical; they are then cataphorically grounded into the still-assembling new text.

But the information that justifies the topicality of a definite, anaphoric referent with prior text antecedence has *already* been furnished at least once before — at the locus of its *initial* occurrence in the text. Obligatory anaphoric grounding makes that information available again, and again, and again — at the referent's *subsequent* textual loci. The rigid provision for anaphoric grounding (33) thus dispenses with the need to re-assemble the information again and again from scratch every time a topical argument with an extant episodic trace returns into the discourse. The original relevance-justifying information is simply transmitted to each new text locus where the referent is re-activated.

Anaphoric grounding connections across the episodically-stored text are thus, in one sense, a time-saving device . They make it possible to tap into thematic information that has already been assembled and stored in the episodic mental model of the current discourse — when that information becomes relevant again. What constraint (33) suggests is an even more extensive reliance, during on-line communication, on mental models of the mind of the interlocutor.

Notes

1. As noted in ch. 1 (1.8.5), a logic-based approach to reference can divide the Universe of Discourse into various sub-universes, one of them real (RW), the others unreal. All linguistic referents can then be indexed to their respective worlds, and be then treated with the same truth-conditional grounding conventions. This approach was adopted by the proponents of *Possible Worlds Semantics* (later *Possible Worlds Pragmatics*, cf. Montague 1970) of the 1960s and 1970s. It is thus akin to the 'referential intent' framework discussed here.

2. For a more exhaustive listing of the distribution of propositional modalities in the various grammatical environments, see Givón (2001a: ch. 6).

3. Full-noun referents that are *thematically incidental* or unimportant were not bold-faced.

4. From the conversation of a retired New Mexico rancher, recorded ca. 1978 (Givón ed. 1983).

5. While the English writing system renders unstressed anaphoric pronouns as separate words, in the spoken language they meet all the criteria for verb prefixes (subject) or suffixes (object). For the relevant data and discussion see Givón (2002: ch. 3).

6. Multi-participant conversations with alternating turns vary enormously as to the degree, scope and complexity of their hierarchic structure, depending on the degree of collaboration (vs. competition) between interlocutors, length of individual turn and overall thematic coherence. But long thematically-coherent chunks of conversation have a similar sequential-hierarchic structure as narrative. For further discussion see Givón (ed. 1997).

CHAPTER 6

Propositional modalities

6.1. Propositions vs. speakers

The propositional modality associated with a verbal clause may be likened to a shell that encases it but does not tamper with the kernel inside. That kernel, the lexical and propositional information about the type of event/state and its participants, remains unaffected by the modal shell. Rather, to put this first in the most traditional terms of truth-conditional logic (Carnap 1956, 1959), the modality assigns various *truth values* to the proposition (necessary truth, factual truth, possible truth, or falsity; Carnap 1956, ch. V). Or, in the equally traditional terms of tense logic (Cocchiarella 1965; Scott 1970; Montague 1970), the modality indexes the proposition's temporal axis to either right now (present), to some real prior time (past), or to some unreal, imagined or potential time (e.g. future).

A more recent tradition in linguistics (Palmer 1979, 1986; Coates 1983; Bybee and Fleischman eds. 1995; *inter alia*) owns up to the fact that in natural language, modal shells are not really logical properties of propositions, but rather code the *speaker's attitude* toward the proposition.[1] But as I will suggest throughout this chapter, the speaker's attitude is, in turn, never just — not even primarily — about the proposition itself, but rather about the *hearer's attitude* towards the proposition *as well as* toward the speaker.

The more recent linguistic tradition owes much, whether directly or indirectly, to post-Wittgensteinian 'ordinary language' philosophers and their discussion of speech-acts (Austin 1962; Grice 1968/1975; Searle 1970; *inter alia*). Much like the grammar of speech-acts, with which modality intersects copiously, the grammar of propositional modalities is a prime domain where we can investigate how grammar involves the systematic on-line construction of mental models of other minds.

In traditional terms again, the speaker's *modal attitude* involves two types of judgements about the clause/proposition, and about the hearer's states of belief and intentionality:

- **Epistemic judgement**: matters of truth, probability, certainty, belief or evidence.
- **Deontic ('valuative') judgement**: matters of desirability, preference, intent, ability, obligation, manipulation or power.

Despite the traditional division, the two mega-modalities — epistemic and deontic — are never mutually exclusive in natural language, but rather interact in many specific ways, a fact that is already apparent in Grice's (1968/1975) *Maxims*. That is, the speaker's modal attitude during communication is seldom confined only to either the hearer's beliefs or the hearer's intention; most commonly it pertains to both. Put another way, epistemic matters are never transacted in a social-deontic vacuum.

A simple-minded example illustrates what is meant by the modal shell leaving the propositional kernel relatively unaffected; consider:

(1) a. Darla shot the tiger.   (epistemic = R-assertion)
     b. **It's too bad** that Darla shot the tiger.   (deontic = preference)
     c. **If** Darla shoots the tiger, ...   (epistemic = possibility)
     d. Darla **didn't** shoot the tiger   (epistemic = NEG-assertion)
     e. Darla **should** shoot the tiger   (deontic = obligation)
     f. Shoot the tiger, Darla!   (deontic = manipulation)
     g. **Did** Darla shoot the tiger?   (epistemic = uncertainty)

Through the various changes of its modal shell, the propositional kernel in (1), identifying 'Darla' as the subject-agent, 'the tiger' as the object-patient, and 'shoot' as the transitive event, persists relatively intact. Examples (1a–g) also illustrate the intermingling of epistemic and deontic modality. Thus, the deontic modality in (1b) is coupled with the epistemic modality of *presupposition*. The deontic modality in (1e, f) is coupled with the epistemic *irrealis*. The epistemic modality in (1g) is coupled with deontic attitude concerning the speaker's-hearer's mutual *obligations*, as are the supposedly purely-epistemic declaratives in (1a, c, d) (Grice 1968/1975).

6.2. Epistemic modalities

6.2.1. Recapitulation

As noted earlier (ch. 5), four major epistemic modalities bear the clearest functional — semantic, pragmatic — and grammatical consequences in natural language. In the logical tradition, these modalities go back to Aristotle's *De Interpretatione* (Barnes ed. 1984, vol. I), and more recently to Carnap (1956). The four are listed again in (2) below, together with their communicative equivalents (Givón 1982; 1995, ch.4).

(2) **Epistemic modalities:**

Logical	Communicative
Necessary truth	Presupposition
Factual truth	Realis assertion
Possible truth	Irrealis assertion
Non-truth	Negative assertion

The communicative interpretation of the four epistemic modalities may be given as (Givón 1982):

(3) The communicative re-definition of epistemic modalities:

    a. **Presupposition:**

       The speaker takes it for granted that the hearer accepts the proposition as *true without challenge*, either by definition, prior agreement or generic culturally-shared conventions, by being obvious to all present at the speech situation, or by having been asserted by the speaker and left unchallenged by the hearer.

    b. **Realis assertion:**

       The speaker *strongly asserted* the proposition to be true. *Challenge* from the hearer is deemed appropriate, although the speaker has *evidence* or other strong grounds for defending their *strong belief.*

    c. **Irrealis assertion:**

       The speaker *weakly asserts* the proposition to be either possible, likely or uncertain (epistemic), or required, desired or undesired (deontic). The speaker is *not* ready to back up their assertion with evidence or other strong grounds. *Challenge* from the hearer is readily entertained, expected or even solicited.

    d. **Negative assertion:**

       The speaker *strongly asserts* the proposition to be *false*, often in contradiction to the hearer's explicitly-expressed or assumed belief. At the very least, the speaker assumes that the hearer is familiar with the corresponding affirmative. A *challenge* from the hearer is anticipated, but the speaker has *evidence* or other strong grounds for defending their *strong belief.*

In addition to the assumptions noted in (3) about the hearer's epistemic states, other epistemic and deontic conditions may apply, depending on the speech-acts within which the epistemic modality is embedded.

Much like its epistemic sister, deontic modality may be divided into a great number of sub-modalities — volition, rejection, preference, fear, approval, disapproval, ability, power, obligation, manipulation, etc. Each of these sub-modalities in turn involve highly specific judgements made by the speaker about the hearer's epistemic and deontic mental states.

Lastly, the distribution of both epistemic and deontic modalities in various grammatical contexts is well documented and highly predictable cross-linguistically (Givón 1982, 1984, 2001a ch. 6). In the following sections we will deal only with some of those grammatical contexts.

6.2.2. Presupposition vs. assertion

A cursory inspection of even one of the sub-conditions in (3a) makes it clear that with the processing of each clause, the speaker's forecast of the hearer's mental model must change. This is because an R-assertion (3b), having been transacted without challenge from the hearer, immediately acquires the modal status of pre-supposition (3a).

Above and beyond the general communicative conventions in (3a), several grammatical constructions in most languages are dedicated towards cuing the hearer about presupposed information. At least in terms of use frequency, these constructions display a high concentration of presupposed clauses. They are, most conspicuously:

- restrictive relative (REL) clauses
- contrastive-focus constructions (cleft, stress-focus)
- verbal complements of factive verbs
- adverbial clauses
- main clauses with the pluperfect aspect

To illustrate the way some of these devices are used in natural communication, consider first a restrictive REL-clause modifying a referring-definite head noun. The presupposed information in the REL-clause matches closely its explicitly-asserted antecedent in prior text:

(4)   **Restrictive REL-clause with an explicit antecedent**:
      On Tet, the Vietnamese New Year, **nineteen Viet Cong guerilla commandos shot their way into the embassy** . . . [nine intervening clauses, crossing one paragraph boundary] . . . The commando force **that entered the embassy compound** was wiped out.   (McNeilley 2001: 11)

Neither the head noun nor its modifying restrictive REL-clause need to literally match their anaphoric antecedents in the prior text. Their anaphoric relation can also be accomplished by an — often protracted — chain of inference, as in:

(5)   **Restrictive REL-clause with an implicit antecedent**:
      Sun Tzu became a general for the King of Wu during the Spring and Autumn period in China (722–481 BC) and won great victories for him . . . [three intervening paragraph, including an episode boundary] . . . To hand down the wisdom **he gained from his years in battle** (*ibid.*: 3–5)

A restrictive REL-clause can also modify a referent introduced into the discourse for the first time, i.e. an indefinite (see ch. 5). Such a referent has no anaphoric antecedence in episodic memory, and thus its modifying REL-clause could not be, technically, presupposed. That is, it cannot have previously-asserted anaphoric antecedence in episodic memory. Such REL-clauses serve as *relevance anchors* for building up a salient episodic representation of the newly-introduced referent. The new referent itself may be marked as definite (6a). It may also be, technically, non-referring (6b):

(6) a. **Restrictive REL-clause modifying a new but definite-marked head**:
Whereas warfare deals only with the time **during which the country
is at war and is concerned essentially about the proper use of armed
forces**, statecraft deals with successfully navigating relationships between nations.   (*ibid*.: 5)

b. **Restrictive REL-clause modifying a non-referring indefinite head**:
Many city-states, countries, and empires have been built up by leaders **who leveraged their nation's unique history, geography and
assets** . . . These leaders were able to insure their state's ability to
survive.   (*ibid*.: 13)

The use of presupposed information in adverbial clauses may be seen in (7) below,
where the more-or-less-explicit propositional antecedent of the ADV-clause directly precedes it across a chain boundary:

(7) **Presupposed information in an ADV-clause**:
Napoleon's attempt to gain mastery of Europe embroiled the continent in
warfare from 1803 to 1815. This eventually led to all the great powers of
Europe combining against him. **After finally joining forces to defeat Napoleon**, the allies of the Sixth Coalition . . . met in Austria.   (*ibid*.:17–18)

As an illustration of the use of presupposed information in verbal complements of
factive verbs, lastly, consider:

(8) **Presupposed information in factive V-complements**:
Prior to the Napoleonic wars, armies were raised and supported by kings
and princes. Composed of multiple nationalities and a mix of loyal men and
mercenaries . . . [two intervening paragraphs] . . . For Prussia to combat this
new military model, Clausewitz and others recognized **that the eighteenth-
century methods of Frederick the Great were outmoded**   (*ibid*.: 37)

6.3. Tense

Tense appears, at first glance, to be an anchoring device of a relatively limited scope,
grounding states and events vis-à-vis the constantly shifting *time of speech*, an important component of the *current speech situation*. In this sense, tense has been recognized, if sometime implicitly, as part of the pragmatics of communication (Cocchiarella 1965; Scott 1970; Montague 1970). But as noted earlier, the constantly
shifting 'now' — the temporal axis of the current speech situation — is but a mental construct. In using tense markers in natural communication, speakers thus presuppose that their interlocutors keep a running mental model of the speech situation, and within it the time of speech, and can then place tense-marked events in
their proper temporal locus vis-à-vis the discourse's constantly-shifting time-axis
(Givón 2001a, ch. 6). That is, schematically:

(9) Tense and temporal deixis ('grounding')

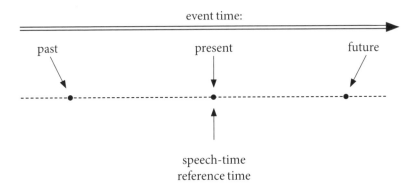

In natural communication in most languages, explicit grammar-cued temporal grounding of clauses tends to be done only at the beginning of clause-chains. This is consonant with the fact that chain-initial (or paragraph-initial) clauses are the prime location for *thematic re-orientation* in the discourse (see ch. 7), where new referential, spatial and temporal grounding is established. If such a locus is also dis-course-initial, the speaker acts to establish the hearer's temporal perspective from scratch. If it is discourse-medial, the speaker cues the hearer about changes in the thematic, referential, spatial or temporal perspective vis-à-vis the preceding chain.

As noted earlier (ch. 5), clause chains are characterized by high continuity of reference. The same is true of the chain's temporal continuity. Thus, once the chain has been temporally grounded (or re-grounded) by explicitly tense-marking its ini-tial clause, most languages use reduced marking, including zero, in the rest of the clauses in the chain — for as long as no further temporal re-orientation occurs.

In the same vein, many languages use an invariant marker that, in effect, cues the hearer that the same temporality (or aspectuality) persists as in the preceding clause. As an illustration of this, consider the use of the so-called *consecutive tense* in Swahili, following initial grounding to either *past* (10), *future* (11), *progressive* (12), or *perfect* (13) (Givón 2001a, ch. 18; original text from Mbotela 1934):

(10) a. . . . wa-Ingereza wa-**li**-wa-chukua wa-le   maiti,
             PL-British   3p-**PAST**-3p-take 2p-DEM corpses
          '. . . then the British took the corpses
      b. wa-**ka**-wa-tia   katika bao   moja,
          3p-**CONS**-3p-put on   board one
          put them on a flat board,
      c. wa-**ka**-ya-telemesha maji-ni   kwa utaratibu w-ote.
          3p-**CONS**-them-lower water-LOC of in-order 3p-all
          and lowered them steadily into the water . . .'

(11) a. . . . Wa-Ingereza wa-**ta**-wa-chukua wa-le   maiti,
          PL-British   3p-FUT-3p-take 2p-DEM corpses
          '. . . then the British will take the corpses
      b. wa-**ka**-wa-tia   katika bao   moja,
          3p-CONS-3p-put on   board one
          put them on a flat board,
      c. wa-**ka**-ya-telemesha maji-ni   kwa utaratibu w-ote.
          3p-CONS-them-lower water-LOC of   in-order 3p-all
          and lower them steadily into the water . . .'

(12) a. . . . Wa-Ingereza wa-**na**-wa-chukua wa-le   maiti,
          PL-British   3p-PROG-3p-take 2p-DEM corpses
          '. . . then the British are taking the corpses
      b. wa-**ka**-wa-tia   katika bao   moja,
          3p-CONS-3p-put on   board one
          putting them on a flat board,
      c. wa-**ka**-ya-telemesha maji-ni   kwa utaratibu w-ote.
          3p-CONS-them-lower water-LOC of   in-order 3p-all
          and lowering them steadily into the water . . .'

(13) a. Asubuhi siku ya pili
          morning day of two
          'In the morning of the second day
      b. tu-**me**-kwenda mto-ni   Ruvu,
          we-PERF-go   river-LOC Ruvu
          we went to the Ruvu river,
      c. tu-**ka**-mw-ita   mwenye mitumbwi
          we-CONS-him-call owner   canoes
          called the owner of the canoes
      d. tu-**ka**-mw-ambia: "Haya,   lete   mitumbwi",
          we-CONS-him-tell EXHORT bring-IMPER canoes
          and told him: "Hey, bring the canoes",
      e. tu-**ka**-vuka   wote pia   wapagazi na wanyampara na tajiri.
          we-CONS-cross all complete porters and guards   and trader
          and then crossed all together with porters, guards and trader . . .'

In re-grounding the temporal perspective at the beginning of a new chain, the speaker invariably reverts to fully-marked tense, as in (14a) and (14f) below. Once the temporal perspective has been re-established, the 'consecutive tense' is again used, as in (14b) and (14g) (*ibid.*):

(14) a. tu-**li**-po-fika,
      we-**PAST**-REL-arrive
      '...When we arrived,

    b. ni-**ka**-wa-ambia wapagazi: "Pang-eni   mizigo",
      I-**CONS**-them-tell porters   arrange-IMPER loads
      I told the porters: "Line up your loads",

    c. wa-**ka**-leta   mizigo,
      they-**CONS**-bring loads
      so they brought over their loads,

    d. wa-**ka**-i-panga   mahali pamoja,
      they-**CONS**-them-arrange place   together
      arranged them together,

    e. ni-**ka**-wa-ambia tena: "Haya ...".
      I-**CONS**-them-tell again EXHORT
      and I told them: "Now ...".

    f. Siku ya pili tu-**li:**-kwenda Viranzi,
      day of two we-**PAST**-go Viranzi
      The following day we moved on to Viranzi,

    g. ya tatu tu-**ka**-enda Kangeni ...
      of three we-**CONS**-go Kangeni
      and the next one on to Kangeni ...'

6.4. Aspect

In discussing tense above, we have indulged in a certain measure of simplification, obscuring the fact that tense in natural language, especially in coherent discourse, seldom if ever occurs by itself. Rather, grammatical tense-markers are always associated with another element of temporal perspective, *aspectuality*.

Three main grammar-coded aspectual contrasts are attested in many and perhaps most languages, all involving the shift of perspective from a more common one ('unmarked') to a less common one ('marked'):

- perfective vs. imperfective
- perfective/preterit vs. perfect
- remote vs. immediate/vivid

We will discuss them in order.

6.4.1. Perfectivity

The cognitive ('semantic') prototype of *event* is a fast, perceptually salient change, an action initiated by a volitional agent and whose consequences are registered upon a strongly-affected patient. The majority of verbs used in everyday human discourse are inherently *perfective*, depicting relatively fast-paced *actions* ('jump', 'tell', 'break', 'kick', etc.) A minority, however, is inherently *imperfective* ('think', 'want', 'be tall', 'know' etc.), depicting protracted physical or mental *states*.

Inherently-perfective verbs in discourse appear most commonly in the *unmarked* perfective aspect. Their grammar-marked imperfective forms are used on those less-frequent — *marked* — occasions when the speaker wishes to change the normal perspective of an event, construing it instead as a protracted on-going state; that is:

(15) a. **Perfective norm ('unmarked)**:
          She *broke* the window.
      b. **Imperfective counter-norm ('marked')**:
          She *was breaking* the window.

From a perfective perspective, an event is viewed *as if* from far away, as a compact, well-bounded small object. From an imperfective perspective, it is viewed *as if* from near by, as a protracted, unbounded span. These two perspectives may be illustrated diagrammatically as (Givón 2001a, ch. 6):

(16) a. **Perfective aspectual perspective**:

          point of view

      b. **Imperfective aspectual perspective**:

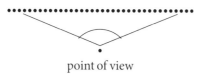

          point of view

In connected coherent discourse, the essentially-cognitive contrast between perfective and imperfective acquires another, discourse-pragmatic, dimension, that of *sequential* vs. *simultaneous*, respectively. Perfective-marked event clauses tend to depict events in a temporal sequence. Imperfective-marked state clauses tend to depict simultaneous — temporally overlapping — events. As an illustration, compare:

(17) a. **Perfective-sequential:**
          She came in, **ate lunch** and left.
      b. **Imperfective-simultaneous:**
          When he came in, **she was eating lunch**.

In the differential use of grammar-coded perfective vs. imperfective in discourse, the speaker manipulates the cognitive and communicative perspective from which s/he wishes the hearer to view the event/state. In cognitive terms, the speaker cues the hearer whether to view the proposition as either a compact event or a protracted state. In communicative terms, s/he cues the hearer about the relative temporal relations between adjacent clauses — sequentiality vs. simultaneity. In the latter case, most conspicuously, the speaker relies heavily on his/her mental model of where the hearer's temporal perspective is at any given moment of the current discourse.

6.4.2. Preterit, perfect and deferred relevance

The perfective/sequential or *preterit* aspect most commonly codes past events that are relevant at the time of their occurrence. This is by far the most common — *unmarked* — perspective in coherent natural discourse, where information is disclosed mostly whenever it is most relevant (Grice 1968/1975). The *perfect* or *deferred-relevance* aspect, on the other hand, tends to depict events that occurred earlier but are relevant later; indeed, events whose relevance is often deferred all the way to the *time of speech*. Thus contrast:

(18) a. **Preterit (normal) perspective:**
          Context: What did you do **then**?
          Response: I **ate** dinner.
      b. **Perfect (deferred-relevance) perspective:**
          Context: Would you like something to eat **now**?
          Response: Thanks, I **'ve already** eaten.

The difference in perspective between the perfective past (19a) and the present perfect (19b) may be depicted diagrammatically as, respectively:

(19) a. **Perfective-preterit perspective:**

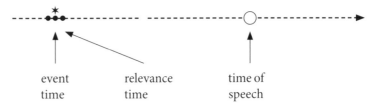

event   relevance   time of
time   time   speech

b. **Present-perfect perspective:**

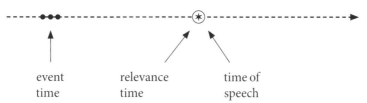

event	relevance	time of
time	time	speech

In connected discourse about past events, the much more frequently used (un-marked) perfective-preterit aspect codes sequential events narrated *in the same order* in which they occurred. The perfect-past (marked), in contrast, is used to code *out-of-sequence* events:

(20) a. **Preterit-perfective (in sequence):**
          She came in, **ate lunch**, waited a while and left.
      b. **Perfect-past (off-sequence):**
          She came in. **She had already eaten lunch**. So she waited and then left.

In using this grammar-coded contrast, the speaker once again manipulates the perspective from which s/he wishes the hearer to view the event, using the perfect grammatical form to cue the hearer's that the more common (unmarked) perspective on the event — relevance at time of occurrence and narration in natural sequence of occurrence — has been violated.

6.4.3. Immediacy and affect: Remote vs. vivid

In many and perhaps most languages, a subtle aspectual contrast is found, one that further specifies perfective-coded past events (or their concatenation), tagging them *as if* viewed either *remotely* or *vividly*. This distinction is to some extent remi-niscent of the contrast drawn above between the narrow-angled perfective (16a) and the wide-angled imperfective (16b). However, since it is the perfective past that is most commonly further tagged as either remote or vivid, one obviously deals here with a more subtle further elaboration of the perspective.

The *remote* vs. *vivid* distinction in English can be seen in the contrast between the preterit past and the simple (habitual) verb forms, when used in past-time nar-rative (so-called 'historical present'). In both spoken and written English, the 'simple' verb form renders events more immediate and vivid, as if one is somehow present on the scene and thus emotionally more affected. As an illustration, compare the same piece of narrative rendered in both aspects:

(21) a. **Remote:**
            So I **gave** him his instructions, and I **told** him to go ahead and do it.
            And he **said** he **would**. Y'know, I really **trusted** the guy, I **had** known
            him for a long time. Plus, he **was** taking notes all along. So I **figured** . . .
      b. **Vivid:**
            So I **give** him his instructions, and I **tell** him I **say** go ahead and do it.
            And he **says** he **will**. Hey, I really **trust** the guy, I**'ve** known him for such
            a long time. Plus he**'s** taking notes and all. So I **figure** . . .

There is a partial overlap between the aspectual contrast *vivid* vs. *remote* and the
genre contrast *oral* vs. *written* discourse, respectively. The vivid aspect is perhaps
used more commonly in oral narrative, and is perhaps more likely to be grammar-
coded in pre-literate cultures. But literary genres can easily appropriate this useful
perspective-shifting device, to the point where whole stories, essays and novels may
be written in the immediate aspect. As an example of a highly literate practitioner,
consider the following passage from a short story (Barthelme 1981):

(22) . . . His gifts *this* morning **include** two white jade tigers, at full scale, carved
      by the artist Lieh Yi, and the Emperor himself **takes** brush in hand to paint
      their eyes with dark lacquer; responsible officials **have** suggested that six
      thousand terra-cotta soldiers and two thousand terra-cotta horses, all full
      scale, be buried, for the defense of his tomb; the Emperor in his rage **orders**
      that three thousand convicts cut down all the trees on Mt. Hsiang, leaving
      it bare, bald, so that responsible officials **may** understand what **is** possible;
      the Emperor **commands** the court poets to write poems about immortals,
      pure beings, and noble spirits who by their own labor **change** night to day,
      and these sung to him; everyone **knows** that executions should not be car-
      ried out in the spring, even a child **knows** it, but in certain cases . . .

The first line in (22) also exhibits a common associated feature of the vivid aspect:
deictic grounding of referents (vis-à-vis either the speaker's location or time-of-
speech) as *proximate* — 'this' rather than 'that', 'here' rather than 'there', 'now' rather
than 'than'.

    As an illustration of the use of the *vivid* aspect in the more colloquial register
genre, consider the following example of direct-quoted uneducated speech, with
the *remote* (italicized) and *vivid* (bold-faced) aspects alternating in the very same
passage (Leonard 1990):

(23) . . . See, what *happened* . . . This's at the time I'**m** getting 'Freaks' ready for
      production. I'**ve** got a script, but it **needs** work, get rid of some of the more
      expensive special effects. So I **go see** my writer and we **discuss** revisions.
      Murray's good, he's been with me, he *wrote* all my 'Grotesque' pictures,
      some of the others. He's done I don't know how many TV scripts, hundreds.
      He'**s** done sitcoms, westerns, sci-fi, *did* a few 'Twilight Zone's . . . Only **now**

he **can't** get any TV work 'cause he's around my age and the networks **don't** like to hire any writers over forty. Murray **has** kind of a drinking problem, too, that **doesn't** help. **Likes** the sauce, **smokes** four packs a day . . . We**'re** talking — get back to what I want to tell you — he **happens** to mention a script he *wrote* years ago when he *was* starting out and never *sold.* I **ask** him what it's about. He **tells** me. It **sounds** pretty good, so **take** the script home and **read** it." Harry *paused.* "I **read** it again, just to be sure. My experience, my instinct, my gut, **tells** me I **have** a property here, that with the right actor in the starring role, I **can** take to any studio in town and practically write my own deal. This one, I **know**, **is** gonna take on heat fast. The next day I **call** Murray, **tell** him I**'m** willing to option the script.... (1990:86–7)

One consequence of our metaphor of narrow vs. wide *camera-angle*, used to characterize both the perfective/imperfective and remote/vivid aspectual contrasts, is of particular interest here. In the visual construction of space, a wide visual angle stands for either a *large* or a *near-by* object. From the *imperfective* (wide-angle) perspective, an on-going event is scrutinized from near by, with all gory detail open to inspection, as if the observer is located right *at the scene* and is thus emotionally more *engaged*. From the *perfective* (narrow-angle) perspective, the event is viewed from a *remote* vantage point, whereby the observer is emotionally more *detached*.

6.4.4. Correlation between modality, tense and aspect

While one could discuss modality, tense and aspect in isolation, in natural communication they are, at least at the level of use frequency, closely correlated. Their most common patterns of association are:

(24) **Association of modality, tense and aspect in natural communication**

Modality	Tense	Aspect	Markedness
Realis	past	perfective	unmarked
	present	imperfective	marked
		perfect	marked
Irrealis	future	(perfective)	marked
	(habitual)	imperfective	marked
	(repetitive)	imperfective	marked

By far the most common combined form in natural communication is the that of *realis–past–perfective*, the benchmark unmarked form. While much less common in text, *realis–present–imperfective*, *realis–present–perfect*, and *irrealis–future–perfective* are just as stable and well attested cross-linguistically. The status of the equally-stable *habitual/repetitive-imperfective* combination is somewhat murky. In terms of logical reference properties and lack of temporally-specified event, this combination resembles irrealis-assertion. In terms of high subjective certainty in communication, however, it often resembles realis-assertion. It is thus, like several other combinations, a modal hybrid.

6.5. Deontic sub-modes of irrealis

6.5.1. Preamble

The grammatical contexts most commonly associated with irrealis modality are (Givón 2001a: ch. 6):

- irrealis modal operators in declarative clauses
  - future
  - modal adverbs
  - modal auxiliaries
- irrealis non-declarative speech-act:
  - yes–no questions
  - manipulative speech-acts
- irrealis verbal complement
- irrealis relative clauses
- irrealis adverbial clauses

Most of these grammatical contexts will not be treated in great detail. In terms of mental models of other minds, of more interest are the irrealis environments where some *deontic* dimension is intermixed with the ever-present epistemic sub-mode. We will focus here on three grammar-coded communicative contexts associated with non-declarative speech-acts:

- the subjunctive mood
- yes–no interrogative speech-acts
- manipulative speech-acts

6.5.2. The subjunctive mood

6.5.2.1. *Preamble*

> Honey, I have an uh … unusual request … uh … Y'see, I've been on this uh … island … for a long time without uh … the companionship of a uh … female … So I been wonderin' … uh … if I *gave* you two coconuts …
>
> (Ed Sanders as "Robinson Crusoe" The Fugs, *It Crawled into my Hand, Honest*, Reprise Records RS-6305 (ca. 1967))

The subjunctive sub-mode of irrealis may conflate under the same grammatical form, at least in some languages, both sub-modes of irrealis (Givón 1994):

- **epistemic**: lower certainty (vis-à-vis future)
- **deontic**: weaker manipulation (vis-à-vis the imperative)

We will treat them in order.

6.5.2.2. *The subjunctive of lower certainty*

Consider, for example, the epistemic gradation in Spanish between the future and the subjunctive, with and without a lower-certainty modal adverb. In (25) below, the subjunctive form can only be used with the lower-certainty modal adverb:

(25)   a.   **Future without modal ADV = highest certainty**:
             ven**drá**.
             come/3s/FUT
             's/he will come'

       b.   **Future with modal ADV = lower certainty**:
             Quizá ven**drá**.
             maybe come/3s/FUT
             'Perhaps s/he'll come'.

       c.   **Subjunctive with epistemic ADV = lowest certainty**:
             Quizá **venga**.
             maybe come/3s/SUBJUN
             'Perhaps he **might** come'.

       d.   ***Subjunctive without epistemic ADV (ungrammatical)**:
             *mañana **venga**.
             tomorrow come/3s/SUBJUN

A similar gradation is obtained with the past-subjunctive form:

(26)   a.   **Past with no modal ADV = highest certainty**:
             se-murió
             REFL-die-PRET/3s
             'S/he died'

       b.   **Past without modal ADV = lower certainty**:
             tal vez se-murió
             perhaps REFL-die/PRET/3s
             'Maybe s/he died'.

       c.   **Past subjunctive with modal ADV = lowest certainty**:
             tal vez se-muri-**era**.
             perhaps REFL-die-PRET/SUBJUN/3s
             'Perhaps she may have died'

       d.   ***Subjunctive without modal ADV: (ungrammatical)**
             *ayer se-muri-**era**
             yesterday REFL-die-PRET/SUBJUN/3s

In yes–no-questions, the very same subjunctive form may be interpreted in two distinct modal senses, at least in some contexts — as a lower-certainty *epistemic* operator, or as a lower preference *deontic* operator:

(27) a. Future ('indicative') = **higher certainty:**
          (Piensas que) se-va   mañana?
          (think/2s that) REF-go/3s/FUT tomorrow
          '(do you think) she'll leave tomorrow?'
      b. Subjunctive = **lower certainty or weak preference:**
          Piensas que se-**vaya**   mañana?
          think/2s that REF-go/3s/**SUBJUN** tomorrow
          (i) 'Do you think s/he'**ll really** leave tomorrow?'
               (epistemic = lower certainty)
          (ii) 'Do you think s/he **should** leave tomorrow?'
               (deontic = weak preference)
      c. Subjunctive = **weak obligation:**
          Que se-**vaya**   mañana?
          that REF-/3s/**SUBJUN** tomorrow
          '**Should** s/he leave tomorrow?'

The deontic interpretations of both (27b-ii) and (27c) are, in some sense, intermediate between the epistemic and the deontic, embedded as they are under the scope of the largely epistemic yes–no question. What this suggests, I think, is that even in grammar-coded communication, which tends to be more categorial and discrete, it is not always easy to separate matters of certainty (epistemic) from matters of sociality and power (deontic). We will return to this issue further below. But even as an epistemic marker, the use of the subjunctive form reveals, once again, how finely speakers can calibrate their judgement of the level of assertive certainty that hearers may tolerate. Such fine calibration is presumably rooted in the speaker's judgement as to how certain the *hearer* is.

One may as well note, lastly, that the subjunctive of lower certainty is well established in English, as in the following finely-scaled examples of irrealis adverbial clauses:

(28) **Certainty scale for irrealis ADV-clauses in English:**

      Highest certainty

      a. **Irrealis 'when':**
          When she *comes*, we *will* consider it.
      b. **Irrealis 'if':**
          If she *comes*, we *will/may* consider it.
      c. **Subjunctive 'if':**
          If she ever *came*, we *would/might* consider it.
      d. **Counter-fact 'if'** (subjunctive):
          If she had *come*, we *would have/might have* considered it.

      Lowest certainty

6.5.2.3. *The subjunctive of weak manipulation*

The very same forms, in both Spanish and English, that is used to code the epistemic subjunctive of lower certainty are also used to code the subjunctive of weaker manipulation. Consider first direct manipulative speech-acts:

(29) a. **Imperative (familiar, stronger):**
          Ven!
          come/2s/IMPER
          'Come!'
      b. **Subjunctive (formal, polite/weaker):**
          Venga!
          come/2s/SUBJUN
          'Do come!'

Likewise, in a *hortative* (preference) use with 3rd person subjects:

(30) a. **Hortative:**
          Que venga!
          SUB come/3s/SUBJUN
          '**Let** him/her come!'
          'S/he *may/should* come'
      b. **Subjunctive of hope:**
          Ojalá   que venga!
          PREFER that come/3s/SUBJUN
          '*Let's hope* s/he *may/should/would* come!'
      c. **Subjunctive of preference:**
          Mejor que venga   pronto.
          better SUB come/3s/SUBJUN soon
          'S/he *had better/should/might as well* come soon'

The same deontic use is found in verbal complements of manipulation verbs, where the subjunctive contrast with the infinitive form of the verb (Givón 2001a, vol. II, ch. 12):

(31) a. **Infinitive complement (successful causation):**
          le-hicieron   callar-se
          3s/OBJ-made/3p shut-up/INF-REF
          'they made him/her *shut up*'
      b. **Infinitive complement (stronger manipulation):**
          le   mandaron callar-se
          3s/OBJ ordered/3p shut-up/INF-REF
          'They ordered him *to shut up*'
      c. **Subjunctive complement (weaker manipulation):**
          le   mandaron que se   callara
          3s/OBJ ordered/3p that REFL be.quiet/PAST/SUBJUN/3s
          'They told him that he *should keep quiet*'

What the use of the subjunctive of manipulation reveals once again, especially when contrasted with other grammatical forms that code varying manipulative strength, is not only the fine calibration of the speaker's deontic mental states, but also his/her assessment of the *hearer's* finely-shaded deontic states. Many languages invest a large amount of grammatical machinery in the finely-shaded coding of this modal continuum. In face-to-face communication, it seems, the grammar of deontic modality is rooted in finely-calibrated judgements of social relations of status, power, obligation, or politeness. We will return to these issues further below.

6.5.2.4. *The subjunctive of heightened affect*
In Spanish and other languages, the subjunctive form may invade an adjacent modal domain, that of *heightened affect*. The grammatical context for this is, at first inspection, somewhat contradictory, falling as it is under the scope of *factive* predicates. That is, predicates whose verbal complements are *presupposed*. Thus (Butt and Benjamin 1988):

(32) a. Les sorprendió que lo sup**iera**.
          them surprised/3s SUB it know/3s/PAST/**SUBJUN**
          'They were surprised that s/he *should* know/knew it'.

      b. No me soprende que vin**ieran**.
          NEG me surprises that come/**PAST/SUBJUN/3p**
          'It doesn't surprise me that the *should come*/came

      c. Me molesta que te   quej**es**   tanto.
          me bother/3s SUB REFL complain/2s/**SUBJUN** so
          'It bothers me that you (*should*) complain so much'.

      d. Me alegra   que te gust**e**.
          REFL cheer/3s SUB OBJ please/3s/**SUBJUN**
          'I'm happy that you (*should*) like it'.

      e. Fué   una lástima que no me lo dij**eras**.
          was/3s one pity   SUB NEG me it say/2s/PAST/**SUBJUN**
          'It was a pity that you didn't tell me!'

      f. Lo siento que est**é**   enfermo.
          it regret/I SUB be/3s/**SUBJUN** sick
          'I'm sorry that s/he is sick'.

While many of the factive predicates in (32) involve some deontic sub-mode of *preference* (32c, d, e, f), surprise or lack thereof (32a, b) is presumably an *epistemically rooted* emotional state.

6.6. The pragmatics of NEG-assertions

When one studies the communicative use of epistemic modalities, as summarized in (3) above, it becomes clear that NEG-assertion, reproduced in (3d) below, is not a simple Aristotelian or Carnapian truth-conditional operator:

(3) d. **Negative assertion**:

The speaker *strongly asserts* the proposition to be *false*, often in contradiction to the hearer's explicitly-expressed or assumed belief. At the very least, the speaker assumes that the hearer is familiar with the corresponding affirmative. A *challenge* from the hearer is anticipated, but the speaker has *evidence* or other strong grounds for defending their *strong belief*.

In addition to reversing the truth value of propositions, negation in natural language comes loaded with rich and subtle pragmatics, not only in matters epistemic but also, as we shall see below, in matters of social deontics.

Most conspicuous is, to begin with, the radically different communicative contexts in which NEG-assertions and their corresponding affirmatives are used. The difference is so striking that one may suggest, I think rightly, that affirmative and negative declaratives are two distinct *speech-acts* (Givón 1979a). Thus compare:

(33) A: -What's new?
      B: –Rod Page has just said my wife is a terrorist.
      A: –He did? That's terrible!

(34) A: –What's new?
      B: –Rod Page has just said my wife is **not** a terrorist.
      A: –Gee, was she **supposed to** be one?

The embedded NEG-assertion in (34) is odd in its present context, and rightly elicits a baffled response from the hearer, indicating that something was amiss in the speaker's presupposition about what the hearer was supposed to already know. What was missing, of course, was the hearer's familiarity with the corresponding affirmative *My wife is a terrorist*.

NEG-assertions are typically made on the tacit assumption that the hearer either has heard about, believes in, is likely to take for granted, or is at least familiar with the corresponding affirmative. In other words, when uttering a NEG-assertion, the speaker relies on the accessible mental trace in the hearer's mind of the corresponding affirmative.

NEG-assertions are indeed a curious epistemic hybrid:

- **Pragmatics**: The speaker *presupposes* the hearer's familiarity with, or even strong epistemic commitment to, a proposition.
- **Semantics**: But then the speaker goes ahead and *strongly denies* the truth of that proposition.

The corresponding affirmative that is pragmatically presupposed in the felicitous use of a NEG-assertion may be established explicitly in the preceding discourse, with the speaker him/herself first setting up an expectation and then contradicting it, as in:

(35) **Background**:   Joe told me he won $10,00 in the lottery,
   NEG-assertion: but later I found out he **didn't** .

The corresponding affirmative may also be contributed explicitly by the hearer in a preceding turn, as in:

(36) **Background**: A: I understand you're leaving tomorrow.
   NEG-assertion: B: I'm **not**. Who told you that?

The speaker may also rely, in his/her pragmatic presupposition, on specific knowledge about the hearer's general state of affairs or current state of mind. To illustrate this, consider the felicity of the three alternative responses by speaker B to the NEG-assertion made by speaker A:

(37) A: So you **didn't** leave after all.
   B   (i):   No, it turned out to be unnecessary.
      (ii):   Who said I **was** going to leave?
      (iii):   How did **you** know I was going to?

Finally, the speaker's pragmatic presupposition may also have a cultural-generic ontology, as in:

(38) a.   There was once a man who **didn't** have a head.
   b.   ?There was once a man who had a head.
   c.   ?There was once a man who **didn't** look like a frog.
   d.   There was once a man who looked like a frog.

The reason the negative in (38a) is pragmatically felicitous is because it reports a break from the generic norm. The reason why (38b) is pragmatically odd is because it merely restates the norm and thus harbors a *tautology*. Conversely, the negative in (38c) is a tautology that merely restates the norm. While the affirmative (38d) breaks the norm, and is thus pragmatically felicitous. Though if one happened to live in a universe where men had no heads, or where they most commonly resembled frogs, both felicity relations in (38) would be reversed.

   NEG-assertions, it seems, are a distinct speech-act, used with different communicative goals in mind than affirmative assertions, thus also with different assumptions about the hearer's current epistemic state. Affirmative assertions are used to communicate new information in contexts of the hearer's presumed *ignorance*. NEG-assertions are used in contexts of the hearer's presumed *error* or *misguided belief*.

6.7. Evidentiality

The phenomenon of *evidentiality* overlaps, at least in part, with epistemic modality, though in many languages the two are coded by two distinct grammatical subsystems. Rather than pertaining directly to epistemic certainty, grammaticalized

evidential markers code primarily the *evidential source* that can back up an assertion and, only indirectly, the *strength* or *reliability* of that evidence. It is the latter
that links evidentiality to subjective certainty through a chain of a mediating inferences:

> evidential source ⊃ evidential strength ⊃ epistemic certainty

Given the communicative re-definition of epistemic modalities (3), grammaticalized evidential marking is most likely to be found in strongly-asserted clauses,
those under the scope of either *realis-assertion* or, more marginally, NEG-*assertion*.
Clauses under the scope of *presupposition* are exempt from evidential marking because there is no need for supporting evidence. The hearer presumably agrees the
speaker and tenders no challenge, either because of shared definitions, general conventions, shared beliefs, or unchallenged prior assertion. Clauses under the scope
of *irrealis* are also exempt from evidential marking, in this case because they are
weakly-asserted and the speaker is not prepared to back them up with evidence.

The grammatical marking of evidentiality may be thus viewed as further, finer
specification of the epistemic range of high-certainty realis assertion . In this, evidentiality serves a similar modulating function as that of the subjunctive in the
weaker-certainty modal range of irrealis.

The most common grammar-coded evidential distinctions divide the source of
information into two broad categories:

- **access**: direct experience vs. hearsay vs. inference
- **sensory modality**: visual vs. auditory vs. others (for direct experience)

The strength or reliability of the evidence is then ranked along well-known universal hierarchies (Givón 1982; Chafe and Nichols eds 1986):

(39) **Hierarchies of evidential strength**:
  a. **Access hierarchy**:
    direct sensory experience > inference > hearsay
  b. **Sensory sub-hierarchy**:
    vision > hearing > others
  c. **Personal access hierarchy**:
    speaker > hearer > 3rd person
  d. **Spatial proximity**:
    near > far
  e. **Temporal proximity (tense/aspect)**:
    present > perfect/recent past > remote past

The most common grammar-coded evidential contrast is between directly-experi-
enced and indirect evidence (either hearsay or inference). This can be seen in the
contrast between two past-tense suffixes in Turkish (Slobin and Aksu 1982):

(40) a. **Past, directly witnessed:**
          gel-**di**
          come-**PAST/DIR.EV**
          'he came (as I directly witnessed)'
      b. **Past, hearsay or inferential:**
          gel-**miş**
          come-**PAST/INDIR.EV**
          'he came (as I hear, as they say)'
          'he came (as I infer)'
          'he came (to my surprise)'

In most evidential systems, a clause with first person subject (or object) is exempt from evidential marking because the speaker, being a participant in the event, presumably has *direct access* to the evidence (39c). As an example, consider Sherpa (Tibeto-Burman), where evidential contrasts are found in both the perfective/past and the progressive/present, but not in the irrealis/future, and only for third person subjects (Givón 1982):

(41) a. **Third person (direct evidence):**
          ti-gi   chenyi chaaq-**sung**
          3s-ERG cup   break-**PERFV/DIR.EV**
          's/he broke the cup'
      b. **Third person (hearsay or inference):**
          ti-gi   chenyi chaaq-**no**
          3s-ERG cup   break-**PERFV/INDIR**
          's/he broke the cup'
      c. **First person (no distinction):**
          ngyee chenyi chaaq-**yin**
          I/ERG cup   break-**PAST/1s**
          'I broke the cup'
      d. **Third person (direct evidence):**
          ti   lagha ki-yin   **no**
          3s/ABS work do-IMPFV **be/DIR.EV**
          's/he is working'
      e. **Third person (hearsay or inference):**
          ti   lagha ki-yin   **way**
          3s/ABS work do-IMPFV **be/INDIR**
          's/he is working'
      f. **First person (no contrast):**
          nga   lagha ki-yin   **way**
          I/ABS work do-IMPFV **be/1s**
          'I am working'

g. **Third person, irrealis (no contrast):**
  ti   lagha ki-**wi**
  3s/ABS work do-FUT
  's/he will work'

In terms of the assumptions the speaker makes about the hearer's epistemic or deontic states, the grammar of evidentiality as deployed in natural communication suggests, once again, that speakers can shift rapidly, from one clause to the next, their mental representation of the hearer's willingness to accept information with or without challenge and with or without supporting evidence.

6.8. Knowledge and power: The interaction between epistemics and deontics

6.8.1. Epistemic vs. deontic speech-acts

Pre-Socratic philosophers were both familiar with and interested in non-declarative speech-acts, given their wider pragmatic focus. In this connection, Haberland (1985) observes:

> Protagoras distinguishes four parts of discourse . . . namely "wish, question, answer and command" . . . Protagoras seems to have been interested in *speech acts*, not sentences in modern parlance. But . . . *it is statements* Plato is interested in.   (1985: 381; italics added)

Plato's role in narrowing philosophical interest to epistemic modality and thus declarative speech-acts is well documented. Haberland (1985) identifies the reason for Plato's narrowed focus as follows:

> For Plato . . . true knowledge — which, as he argues in this connection, does not coincide with perception — cannot aim at context-dependent truths; the truth of a sentence should not depend on who says it, in which situation, and to whom, and it should not, more specifically, depend on what the sentence is an answer to . . . But this interest of Plato's in statements . . . is again only understandable from a series of premises that are no longer self-evident. The first of these is that *truth is the main concern of the philosopher*. The second is that *analysis of language is ancillary to philosophical pursuits*. As a corollary from these two premises, we get that linguistic analysis is mainly concerned with truth as well. The third premise is that *truth is timeless and independent of context*.   (*ibid.*: 381–2; italics added).

As noted earlier (ch. 4), all speech acts involve assumptions that the speaker makes about *both* the epistemic and deontic mental states of the hearer (as well as of the speaker's him/herself). Nonetheless, the 3–4 major speech-acts that are most systematically coded by grammar in natural languages can be classified according to which of the two main sub-modalities is more focal in them:

(42)   **Speech-act**   **Dominant modality**

     Declarative   epistemic >> deontic
     Interrogative
         Yes–no-question   epistemic > deontic
         Wh-question   epistemic > deontic
     Manipulative   deontic >> epistemic

The 3–4 speech-acts in (42) are but the most common grammaticalized *prototypes*, the conventionalized, salient high-frequency peaks in a scalar, multi-dimensional *socio-cognitive* space. This continuum underlies the entire functional domain of speaker-hearer interaction, the so-called *communicative contract* as idealized in Grice's (1968/1975) conversational maxims. Along this continuum, the various speech-act prototypes shade into one another, a shading whereby the intensional balance of the speech-act is shifted gradually between epistemic and deontic.

As an illustration, consider first the continuum between *imperative* and *yes–no interrogative*:

(43)   **Most prototypical imperative**

    a.   Pass the salt.
    b.   Please pass the salt.
    c.   Pass the salt, would you please?
    d.   Would you please pass the salt?
    e.   Could you please pass the salt?
    f.   Can you pass the salt?
    g.   Do you see the salt?
    h.   Is there any salt around?
    i.   Was there any salt there?

    Most prototypical interrogative

In the same vein, consider the continuum between *imperative* and *declarative*:

(44)   **Most prototypical imperative**

    a.   Wash the dishes!
    b.   You better wash the dishes.
    c.   You might as well wash the dishes.
    d.   I suggest you wash the dishes.
    e.   It would be nice if you could wash the dishes.
    f.   It would be nice if someone could wash the dishes.
    g.   The dishes need to be washed.
    h.   The dishes are dirty.
    i.   The dishes were dirty.

    Most prototypical declarative

Likewise, consider the continuum between *declarative* and *yes–no interrogative*:

(45)   **Most prototypical declarative**

    a.   Joe is at home.
    b.   Joe is at home, I think.
    c.   Joe is at home, right?
    d.   Joe is at home, isn't he?
    e.   Is Joe at home?

     Most prototypical interrogative

Lastly, consider the continuum between *declarative* and *WH-interrogative*:

(46)   **Most prototypical declarative**

    a.   Joe called, and ...
    b.   What's-his-name called, and ...
    c.   Whoever it was that called, tell them ...
    d.   I don't know who called.
    e.   Who knows who called?
    f.   Who called?

     Most prototypical interrogative

What this finely calibrated continuum — calibrated in both grammatical form and epistemic balance — illustrates, once again, is that the epistemic and deontic modal strands of natural language, thus of natural communication and social interaction, are strongly intertwined.

6.8.2. The social deontics of knowledge

6.8.2.1. *Preamble*
The strong associations that hold between epistemic and deontic modalities may be expressed as the following one-way pragmatic inferences:

- truth ⊃ knowledge
- knowledge ⊃ certainty
- certainty ⊃ status
- status ⊃ power

None of these inferences is logically necessary. They are rather, *cultural-pragmatic norms* observed under the communicative contract. In the space below we will survey, albeit briefly, some of the social dimensions most commonly associated with the deployment of modality in natural communication.

6.8.2.2. *Certainty, authority and epistemic deference*
In the grammar of Japanese, the speech-act and modal value of propositions are marked by a large inventory of verb-final particles. Among those, one is used only by

women, who use it in *realis assertions*. When one assesses, experimentally, the degree of subjective certainly associated with that female-specific particle, it ranks consistently below the corresponding male-specific particle in terms of subjective certainty, as well as determination to fight off a challenge from the hearer (Tsuchihashi 1983).

More generally, Syder and Pawley (1974) observe that in facing an interlocutor of higher power, status or authority, speakers tend to scale down their expression of certainty, by using hedges that place assertions in a lower — irrealis — epistemic range. This is not done necessarily because of perceiving a contrary attitude on the part of the high-status interlocutor, but rather as a *hedge* against the possibility that the person of higher authority might hold a contrary belief. Such *epistemic deference* to power realities is a pervasive feature in most cultures.

6.8.2.3. *Authority, negation and politeness*

As noted above, the NEG-assertion is a *contrary* speech-act, used in denying the hearer's epistemic position. One would thus expect its use to be extremely sensitive to the perceived social position of the interlocutor. This seems to be the case universally, in the use of NEG-assertions in contexts where the interlocutor is perceived to be of higher status or power. Under such conditions, speakers tend to tone down their disagreement, couching their contrary opinion in a variety of softening devices. Many of these devices are sub-varieties of irrealis, as in:

(47)   a.   Quite, quite.
      b.   Yes, I see.
      c.   I see what you mean.
      d.   I suppose you got a point there.
      e.   Perhaps not quite so …
      f.   Perhaps you may wish to consider an alternative.
      g.   Well, I'm not sure about that, maybe …
      h.   Now if it were up to me, I would suggest …

In more traditional societies, it is often not easy to find overtly-marked NEG-assertions in speech directed even at social equals, let alone at perceived superiors or outsiders (Givón 2002: ch. 9). And in sub-cultures where overt negation is tolerated or even encouraged, as in academic or courtroom discourse, inter-personal hostility is quite often the consequence, whether intended or not (Givón 2002, ch. 10).

In small, intimate societies, people habitually negotiate the modality of their assertions in order to avoid head-on disagreement and thus overtly-negative speech-acts. This is reminiscent of Lewis' (1979) apt if anecdotal discussion of 'score-keeping in a language game'.

As an illustration of how this problem is handled in small, intimate societies, consider the *epistemic negotiation* between two long-time neighbors, Mrs. Phillip J. King and Momma, taken from a work of Southern fiction. In the first passage, the shifting topics whose truth value is negotiated are boldfaced, the manipulated epistemic-modal operators are italicized (Pearson 1985):

Mrs. Phillip J. King said he had been **dashing**, but Momma would not go along with dashing and said *to her mind* he had been **not unattractive**, but Mrs. Phillip J. King couldn't see fit to drop all the way from dashing to not unattractive, so her and Momma negotiated a description and arrived at **reasonably good looking**, which was mutually agreeable though it seemed for a minute or two that Mrs. Phillip J. King might hold out to have the reasonably struck from the official version. But Momma went on to tell her how she *thought* **his nose had a fanciful bend to it** which distracted Mrs. Phillip J. King away from the reasonably because, as she told Momma back, she *had always thought* his nose had a fanciful bend to it herself. Mrs. Phillip J. King called it **a Roman nose** and she said there wasn't anything uppity or snotty about it but it was purely **a sign of nobility**. And Momma said he *certainly* carried himself **like a Roman**, which sparked Mrs. Phillip J. King to *wonder if maybe* he had*n't* **come from Romans**, *if maybe* that wasn't why he was **a Republican**. But Momma said she *recalled* he was **a notable Democrat**. And Mrs. Phillip J. King said, *"Maybe* he was". And Momma said she *believed* so. And Mrs. Phillip J. King said *"Maybe* he was" again . . . I was not present when Mrs. Phillip J. King decided she couldn't let **reasonably good looking** rest peacefully and resurrected the whole business with the argument that **a moustache under that fancifully bent nose** *would have most certainly* made for **dashing**. But Momma could not see clear to allow for a moustache since there had not been one actually; however, Mrs. Phillip J. King insisted that i<u>f</u> Momma *could just imagine* **a finely manicured and dignified Douglas Fairbanks-style moustache** under that Roman nose then all of the rest of the features *would surely* come together and *pretty much* scream **Dashing** at her. But even with a moustache thrown in Momma could not sit still for any degree of dashing though Mrs. Phillip J. King campaigned rather fiercely for **Considerably Dashing** and then **Somewhat Dashing** and then **A Touch Dashing**, so Momma for her part felt obliged to retreat some from **reasonably good looking** and her and Mrs. Phillip J. King settled on **passably handsome** with Mrs. Phillip J. King supplying the **handsome** and Momma of course supplying the **passably**.   (1985: 191–2)

In the second passage, a wide range of evidential devices are deployed together with other epistemic operators, all aiming at the progressive upgrading of 'truth' (Pearson 1985):

"Pepsi Cola" she said. "Yes, I **believe** is was Pepsi Cola because **I'm near certain** it was Mr. Womble who ran the Nephi outfit". And Momma sat straight up and said, "Helen?". . . But Mrs. Phillip J. King just went straight on and said, "It **had to be** Pepsi Cola. He owned the bottling plant **you know** in Burlington. **I mean** his daddy, **now I don't think** he ever owned it himself, but his daddy did and made a killing putting out Pepsi Cola until he sold the business and made another killing doing that. **Momma said** it was just a ton of money that changed hands. **She was brought up in Burlington you know**". "But Helen", said Momma . . . "And **they tell me** his wife was just a gorgeous woman but not from around here . . . **Momma said** he went out and got one all the way from Delaware or Ohio, **she couldn't ever remember** exactly which, but **I imagine** it was Delaware since **P. J. tells me** . . . that Delaware is one of your urban states . . . and **P. J. says** there's plenty of money in Delaware mostly on account of the Duponts, and she **might have even been** a Dupont herself, anyway **I don't know** that she **wasn't** and she was **probably** from Delaware **I imagine**, which is where they all come from . . ." "Wasn't it cookies instead of Pepsi-Cola?" Momma wanted to know. "Didn't Mr. Alton's Daddy make those savannahs with white cream filling and those little oval shortbread cakes that came in the blue sack?" And Mrs. Phillip J. King got a little hot on account of the cream-filled savannahs and the shortbread cakes and she said to Momma, "Now Inez, he **might have** dabbled in cookies later but **I can tell you for a fact** it was Pepsi-Cola at the first because **Momma said** it was Mr. Womble at the Nehi and Mr. Foster at the Coca-Cola and Mr. Tod W. Smith at the Sundrop and Mr. Nance at the Pepsi-Cola, and **Momma herself told me** it was Pepsi-Cola that made him his money but **I don't ever recall** a whisper of cookies **passing her lips.**   (*ibid*.: 193–5)

6.8.2.4. *Certainty, modesty and politeness*
Questions of politeness and deference, with their complex culture-specific (as well as universal) detail, often wind up encroaching on epistemic space. Thus, Syder and Pawley (1974) note that some cultures seem to put a prime on the so-called *modesty principle*, whereby speakers as a matter of course profess to know less than they actually do, especially when the information may reflect favorably on their personal stature. It may well be that this culture-specific tendency is but a reflection of a more universal principle, already noted above:

(48)   **Subjective certainty vis-à-vis higher authority**:
        In communicating to an interlocutor of higher status, one downgrades
        one's own subjective certainty.

Lewis (1979) makes a similar observation couched in terms of a putative slave-master relationship.

6.8.2.5. *Knowledge, certainty, responsibility and blame*
In many cultures, perhaps in most, claiming *direct personal responsibility* for conveyed information may be a serious social error, a gambit that is avoided in all but the most intimate — thus well shielded — social contexts. Strong claims to direct authorship of transmitted information, with the attendant marking of high subjective certainty and strong evidential backing, are to be avoided. In carrying out communication under these cultural constraints, a variety of highly conventionalized strategies are used, including indirection, disclaimers, oblique attribution, impersonal/passive grammar, coding R-assertions as yes–no questions, negation or irrealis. While the structural devices may be the same as in some of the cases cited above, the guiding principle is perhaps different; roughly:

(49)   **The hazardous information principle**:
        a.   Knowledge is power, but power is responsibility.
        b.   Information may be coveted, it may also be hazardous and socially
              destabilizing.
        c.   Transmitting new information may yield a clear social advantage,
              but it also incurs risks.

d. Therefore, being identified explicitly as the author of information may be unwise, and must be avoided.

Principle (49) is particularly conspicuous in small, rural, geographically scattered communities, where residents of isolated homesteads are adept at cajoling fresh gossip, often malicious, out of the occasional visitor. In spite of their geographic scatter, such communities operate along the norms of the *society of intimates* (see ch. 2). In such societies, one's business is everybody's business, and the most mundane news is disseminated at lightning speed. The transmission of fresh gossip may indeed be the real purpose of one's visit. Yet the would be transmitter must tread lightly, lest s/he be pointed at later — often accusingly and perhaps by the very same host who warmed the information out of him/her — as the explicit author (see Givón 2002, ch. 9).

6.9. Summary: Propositional modalities and other minds

The deployment of grammar-coded propositional modality in natural communication reveals fine-tuned sensitivity on the part of speakers to the informational and social reality around them, most conspicuously to the constantly shifting epistemic and deontic states of their interlocutors. As in other grammar-coded domains, the pace is fast, the perspective is constantly shifting, and the performance is largely subconscious and automated, being part of the evolved, habituated skills of a social species. The adaptive scope of such skills is pervasive, pertaining as they do to how we live, behave, interact and communicate with our ever-present conspecifics.

Notes

1. As noted in ch. 1, for a truth-conditional logic to not founder upon self-inclusion paradoxes (Russell 1908), it cannot include its contextual shell. One of the most conspicuous subspecies of the contextual shell is, of course, the speaker's perspective. Carnap's (1956) relegation of this to the netherworld of pragmatics is of course the right move, given the goals of truth-conditional logic.

CHAPTER 7

Discourse coherence and clause chaining

7.1. Reorientation

In this chapter, last in our survey of grammar as a conventionalized tool for representing the interlocutor's mind during communication, we discuss a number of grammatical sub-systems that signal more *global* aspects of discourse coherence. That is, grammatical sub-systems that cue search-and-retrieval operations in episodic memory at the levels of the clause-chain or the paragraph. The two major sub-systems we discussed in the preceding chapters dealt, respectively, with the referential coherence of nominals and the tense-aspect-modal coherence of verbal clauses. These more concrete strands of coherence turn out to be fully integrated into the next-higher level of discourse coherence, the grammar of *clause-chaining*.

The thematic coherence of discourse bears some of the telltale signs of an *epiphenomenon*. One may liken it to a tapestry or to traditional music, in both of which more local, more concrete strands run as recurrent themes or *leitmotifs*. In signaling the various strands in discourse, lexicon and grammar share the functional load at various hierarchic levels. The more common coherence strands in natural discourse, and their relative coding reliance on either lexicon or grammar, are:

(1) **Well-coded discourse coherence strands**:

Strand	Coding vehicle		
Referents	grammar	>	lexicon
Location	lexicon	>>	grammar
Temporality	grammar	>	lexicon
Aspectuality	grammar	>	lexicon
Modality	grammar	>	lexicon
Voice perspective	lexicon	>>	grammar[1]
Actions/events	lexicon	>>	grammar

The paradoxical dual aspect of discourse coherence — multiple-stranded yet still a whole — is what Aristotle may have had in mind in his treatment of coherence in the *Poetics*, insisting first on the diversity of strands:

> The unity of plots does not consist, as some suppose, of having one man as its subject. An infinity of things befall that one man, some of which it is impossible to reduce to unity; and in like manner there are many actions of one man which cannot be made to form one action … (*Poetics* 8: 2322).

Still, Aristotle conceded the ultimate unity of the whole, coupling the concession with a classical methodological aside:

the story [...] must represent one action, a complete whole, with its several inci-
dents so closely connected that the transposition or withdrawal of any one of them
will disjoin and dislocate the whole. For that which makes no perceptible difference
by its presence or absence is no real part of the whole.   (*ibid.*)[2]

7.2. Clause chaining

7.2.1. Clauses, chains, and paragraphs

As noted earlier (chs 5, 6), the representation of discourse in episodic memory is
both sequential and hierarchic. The grammatical devices used during natural on-
line discourse production and comprehension may be viewed as *coherence signals*.
That is, as signals designed to cue the hearer about specific attentional and/or working-memory activation, mental connections, and search and retrieval operations in
episodic memory.

   The bulk of the grammatical devices used to signal discourse coherence pertain
either to grounding nominal referents into their proper clause (ch. 5), or to grounding clauses into their proper chain or, in a much more limited way, to grounding
chains into their proper paragraph. The use of grammar to cue discourse coherence
thus seems to be restricted to the lower levels of the hierarchic structure of episodic
memory. Relatively little grammatical machinery is expended on higher hierarchic
levels such as the paragraph, episode, etc..[3]

7.2.2. Major clause-types in the chain

The most general features of clause-chaining in coherent discourse, those that are
most systematically grammaticalized in natural language, pertain to the four most
salient positions that a clause may occupy within the chain:

- pre-initial (or grounding)
- chain-initial
- chain-medial
- chain-final

We will discuss the four in order.

(a) **Chain-grounding pre-initial clause**: A clauses in this position performs the
function of *coherence-bridge*, grounding the chain to the preceding discourse. Three
grammatical devices are most typically used in such clauses:

- pre-posed adverbial clauses
- pre-posed adverbial phrases
- L-dislocated noun phrases

All three furnish *local cataphoric links* to the directly-following chain-initial clause. In addition, they also signal more *global anaphoric links* to the preceding discourse, be it the preceding chain, paragraph, episode or even higher up in the hierarchic structure of the current text. Being in this way double-grounded, the chain-initial clause guarantees both the local and global connectivity of clause-chains in discourse. It bridges between the episodic trace of the current text (anaphoric) and the currently-assembling new information (cataphoric). And when the anaphoric connectivity of a new chain vis-à-vis the preceding chain is very high, the pre-initial grounding clause is often dispensed with.

(b) **Chain-initial clauses**: At this position, a clause launches the new chain, initiating its major coherence strands — topical referent, temporality, aspectuality, modality, speech-act, and, less often, a new narrator's perspective.[4] The grounding of chain-initial clauses is mostly local in both directions — anaphorically to the preceding chain-initial (grounding) clause, cataphorically to the following clause. Grammatically, such clauses tend to be highly finite (unreduced), with all coherence strands fully *marked* (referents, tense, aspect, modality and speech-act value). As the locus where these strands are launched for the rest of the chain, the chain-initial clause is particularly well grounded cataphorically.

(c) **Chain-medial clauses**: Clauses at this position are the most frequent and *unmarked* in coherent discourse. They carry the bulk of sequentially-presented new information in the chain, and display the highest level of *local anaphoric continuity* or grounding. Given that the next clause is very likely to be of the same type, chain-medial clauses are also strongly grounded cataphorically, strictly locally though perhaps by default. The grammatical marking of such clauses is most typically minimal or *least finite* (reduced), since most coherence strands continue as in the preceding clause.

(d) **Chain final clauses**: Clauses in this position terminate the thematic chain, be it in the more concrete terms of reference, tense, aspect, modality, speech-act, or in more abstract 'thematic' terms. The grounding properties of chain-final clauses are, as one would expect from their position in the chain, mostly anaphoric and only marginally cataphoric. Nonetheless, these clauses can signal some cataphoric information, such as the impending thematic break and the initiation of a new chain. In some grammaticalized clause-chaining systems, chain-final clauses also signal the type of new topical referent that will be initiated in the following chain ('cataphoric switch-reference'). Lastly, at least in one major clause-chaining type (in OV languages), the chain-final clause is the *most finite* (marked) clause type in connected discourse.

The overall structure of the chain and its grounding connections may be thus given, schematically, as (Givón 1987).

(2)   **Grounding and thematic continuity in the clause-chain**:

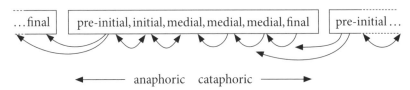

7.3. Pre-initial clauses ('coherence bridges')

Three major grammatical devices are most commonly used as pre-initial coherence bridges, all sharing the same general pattern of double grounding as noted above. We will survey them in order.

7.3.1. Pre-posed adverbial clauses

A pre-posed *adverbial subordinate* clause appears before its associated main clause; that is, pre-posed to it. The cataphoric links of such clauses to their following main clause are strictly local and semantically defined. These semantic local links may pertain, first, to *temporal relations*, either well marked in the ADV-clause itself (3), or implicit (4a). On occasion, the temporal relation depends on grammatical clues in the main clause (4b):

(3)   **Explicitly marked temporal links**:
    a.   **Precedence:**   **After** she entered, she saw him.
    b.   **Subsequence:** **Before** she entered, she saw him.
    c.   **Simultaneity:** **While** she **was** entering, she saw him.

(4)   **Less explicit temporal links**:
    a.   **Precedence:**   **When** she entered, she saw him.
    b.   **Subsequence:** **When** she entered, she **had already** seen him.
    c.   **Simultaneity:** **When** she **was** entering, she saw him.

Other local cataphoric semantic links that can also be explicitly marked:

(5):   **Conditional (irrealis):**   **If** you finish on time, you **can** have this.
      Conditional (subjunctive):   **If** you **did** that, they **would** lynch you.
      Conditional (counter-fact): **Had** he done that, he **would have** been fired.
      Concessive: **Though** she liked him, she decided he was not Mr. Right.
      Cause/reason: **Because** he liked her, he agreed.
      Imperfective participial: **Turning the corner**, she slowed down.
      Perfective participial: **Having eaten dinner**, he left.

Two quantified text studies, Thompson (1985) and Ramsay (1987), show the differential anaphoric and cataphoric links of pre-posed ADV-clauses, as compared with their *post-posed* equivalents; that is, those that follow their main clause. We will illustrate this first with examples from Thompson's (1985) study of purpose clauses in English. Consider first the contrast between a pre-posed and post-posed purpose clause in the same clause chain. The first is characteristically chain-initial, the second chain-medial (52):

(6) The Brendan was rushing madly farther and farther out to sea. **To slow her down**, we streamed a heavy rope in a loop from the stern and let it trail in the water behind us **to act as a brake**.   (Thompson 1985: 62)[5]

The pre-posed, chain-initial purpose ADV-clause in (6) is followed by a characteristic intonation break (,) and links anaphorically to both a referent in the preceding chain ('The Brendan' = 'her') as well as, more subtly, to previously described events ('rushing madly > 'slow her down'). Cataphorically, the zero subject of the purpose clause links to the adjacent main clause, where the co-referent 'we', the subject, persists as the main topic of the new chain.

As an illustration of how diffuse, implicit and farther-reaching the anaphoric links of a pre-posed ADV-clause can be, consider next (Thompson 1985):

(7) Tedium became our new enemy. Once or twice we glimpsed enough sun to make it worthwhile to hang the sleeping bags in the rigging and to try to dry our clothes. But usually the weather was too foggy or too damp for any success. And it was so cold that the next migrant to land on The Brendan, another water pipit, also failed to survive the night and perished. **To pass the time**, there was a shipboard craze for fancy rope work.   (*ibid.*: 63)

The pre-posed purpose clause in (7), 'To pass the time', refers to neither a specific event nor a specific subject/agent in the preceding four chains. Rather, it invokes the preceding thematic whole, a distillation of an entire passage. Nor is there a clear syntactic equi-subject constraint vis-à-vis the subsequent main clause, as there was in the pre-posed purpose clause in (6). Rather, the following main clause is itself an impersonal subjectless clause, with only an implicit allusion to 'the crew' or 'we'.

Essentially the same contrast between pre-posed and post-posed conditional ('if') and temporal ('when') ADV-clauses was reported by Ramsay (1987). Thus compare examples (8) and (9) below:

(8) **Pre-posed**:
     The early rehearsals tend to be in Italian. Mike Turner, the company's director, who was to conduct, was insistent on this. **If they knew Italian**, this would smooth things over the early rehearsal with Julia Contini.   (Ramsay 1987: 388)

(9)   **Post-posed**:
You can only split up **if you've been going together**.   (*ibid.*: 405)

In the same vein, compare the use of the two conditional ADV-clauses in the very same passage of a Western novel, one pre-posed and reaching diffusely back across several preceding chains, the other post-posed and narrowly focused on the directly-preceding main clause (L'Amour 1962):

(10)   The rifles spoke again from the sounding board of the rocks, racketing away down the canyons to fade at the desert's rim. Motionless upon a sun-baked slope, he waited while the sweat found thin furrows through the dust on his cheeks, but there was no further sound, no further shot, nor was there movement within the range of his vision … merely the lazy circle of a buzzard against the heat-blurred sky. **If they had not seen him already**, they would not see him **if he remained still**, and Shalako has learned his patience in a hard school.   (L'Amour 1962: 2)

7.3.2. Pre-posed adverbial phrases

To illustrate how shorter pre-posed adverbial phrases perform very much the same coherence-bridge function as larger adverbial clauses, contrast the chain-initial locative ADV-phrase 'In the West' in (11) below with the subsequent chain-medial post-posed ADV-clause 'after being translated'. (McNeilly 2001):

(11)   Japan was introduced to Sun Tzu's writing around 760 A.D. and her generals quickly absorbed the lessons. The three most well-known samurai — Oda Nobunaga, Toyotomi Hideyoshi, and Tokugawa Ieyasu — all mastered *The Art of War*. This mastery enabled them to transform Japan from a collection of feudal states into a single nation.
   In the West, The Art of War first made its appearance in 1772 **after being translated into French by a Jesuit**.   (McNeilly 2001: 5)

The pre-posed ADV-phrase 'In the West' cues the shift to a new location and contrasts it with the location of the preceding paragraph ('Japan'). Its cataphoric local connection links directly as the location of the subsequent chain-initial clause ('The Art of War made its appearance'). The next chain-medial ADV-phrase ('after being translated …'), in contrast, links narrowly and anaphorically to the preceding main clause ('made its first appearance'), furnishing its narrow temporal grounding.

   As an example of a pre-posed temporal ADV-phrase acting as a coherence bridge, consider:

(12)   This resulted in the loss of about a quarter of the civilian population of Germany, the elimination of much of the farmland, assets for production, housing, and food stores, and the loss of countless cultural treasures. **In the end**, much of Germany was left a wasteland.   (*ibid.*: 15)

The anaphoric links of 'In the end' reach back diffusely into the preceding several paragraphs describing the Thirty Years War. Its cataphoric link is strictly local, re-establishing the temporal axis for the chain-initial clause and thus for the new chain.

In principle, any short adverbial element could serve the chain-pre-initial coherence bridge function. Thus, consider the chain-initial appearance of two one-word adverbs, the first vaguely thematic ('furthermore'), the second evaluative ('unfortunately'):

(13)   **Furthermore**, they see tremendous value in the teaching of Sun Tzu and other ancient strategists and will deploy them to guide the Chinese ship of state. **Unfortunately**, for many professional soldiers and other interested in military strategy, it is not easy to master *The Art of War* and apply it directly to battles past, present and future.   (*ibid.*: 7)

7.3.3. Left-dislocation clauses

L-dislocation was discussed in ch. 5, above, in relation to the grammar of referential coherence. As noted there, L-dislocation cues the hearer to an anaphoric antecedent search that, most commonly, reaches back across several chains in the episodic memory of the current text. Its cataphoric link, in contrast, is strictly local, with a pronoun-marked co-referent in the very same clause. Thus recall, from an informal conversation:

(14)   H: ... Well **my dad** was born in Sherman, that's close to where [...] is. He was born in Sherman in 1881, and he died in '75. Yeah. And ah, so, ah of course, **my great grandfather, they came in there**, I think, y'know, part of them from Tennessee and part of them from Illinois. And I don't really know much about that far back, Tom. **But my grand-dad, he was a hard-shelled Baptist preacher**, and he just, y'know, farmed and ranched.

     T: In Texas?

     H: Yeah, yeah.

     T: So he was already in Texas?

     H: They must've come there when he was small, y'know, 'cause he spent ...

     T: Your great grandfather moved and your grandfather was really raised in Texas.

     H: Yeah, yeah. In other words, about three generations of us ... were in Texas ...

     T: In Texas ...

     H: And of course we eh, **my dad, all he ever did was farm and ranch** ...

The first anaphoric trigger in (14) is 'my dad'. Next, two L-dislocations pertain, technically, to referents with no explicit anaphoric antecedent, 'my great grandfather' and 'my grand-dad', respectively. However, the antecedent is there implicitly in both cases, by frame-guided cultural conventions (father > grandfather > great-grandfather). Only the third L-dislocation reaches back to an explicit anaphoric antecedent ('my dad'). In all three cases, the L-dislocation clause serves to establish a new topical referent for the chain that is thereby initiated.

7.4. Chain-initial vs. chain-medial clauses

We have seen many examples in (6)–(14) above of chain-initial clauses, with their strictly-local double-grounding links — both anaphoric and cataphoric. On the whole, their grammatical structure is not all that specialized, except for the fact that they tend to be highly marked (finite), with fully expressed arguments (referents, participants) and verbal modalities (tense, aspect, modality).

One type of chain-initial construction, however, is grammatically well-identified, the one that serves to introduce a brand new — referring indefinite — topical argument into the discourse. As an illustration of the paragraph-initial use of one type of construction, the *existential-presentative* clause, consider:

(15)   … **There's something I've been meaning to ask you** … Thing is, I'm not sure how to say **it**, **it**'s a bit embarrassing … Fact is, I'm not sure how you're going to take **this** … Well, heck, **it**'s been bothering me for such a long time, I reckon I better tell you about **it** …

In colloquial English, another functionally-equivalent presentative construction also exists, involving the use of an *extraposed* REL*-clause* as modifier of the newly-introduced REF-indefinite noun. Much like the existential-presentative clause, the REL-clause here supplies the *thematic justification* for the referent's salience, relevance or cataphoric topicality in the subsequent discourse. As an illustration consider:

(16)   … **This woman** came into my office yesterday **who had no shoes on**. It was freezing cold, but **she** didn't seem to mind, **she** just sat down and [0] started [0] talking and [0] kept going on, so finally I asked **her** if **she** didn't feel cold …

One of the most entrenched dogmas about English grammar, more pernicious for being largely tacit, is that conjoined chain-medial clauses in discourse are highly finite; that is, that they are grammatically fully marked. In fact, it is easy to show that English clause-chaining reflects the general principle noted earlier above — that chain-medial clauses tend to be the least-marked, least finite in discourse. This of course makes perfect sense, given that chain-medial clauses pack events/states where the main concrete strands of coherence (topical-referent, tense, aspect, modality, speech act) are the most continuous or anaphorically predictable.

We will illustrate this first with the more common type of clause-chaining in English, the one characteristic of VO languages. Consider first the aspectual change from imperfective to perfective in (17) below. The fully marked tense-bearing auxiliary 'was' is used once in the chain-initial clause, but is not repeated in the following chain-medial clauses; nor is the topical subject, coded as zero. A break in aspectual continuity in (17e), however, requires the initiation of a new chain, and the overt *full marking* of both aspect and subject pronoun, even if the latter remains the same.

(17) **Maximally-coherent imperfective-aspect chain**:
    a.   **She was** writ**ing** to her parents,
    b.   tell**ing** them about her new flat,
    c.   describ**ing** the furniture
    d.   and pok**ing** fun at the neighbors.

    Break in aspectual coherence:
    e.   **She** also **told** them …

    Unacceptable alternative following the break:
    e.   *, also **told** them …

The imperfective suffix -*ing* of course cannot be dispensed with even in the least finite chain-medial forms, being part of the word.

  In the same vein, the perfective/past suffix cannot be dispensed with either in the chain-medial clauses in (18) below, and for the same reason. Thus, consider the aspectual change from past/perfective to plu-perfect in (18e):

(18) **Maximally-coherent perfective-aspect chain**:
    a.   **He came** into the room,
    b.   **stopped**,
    c.   **saw** the woman on the couch,
    d.   **looked** at her briefly
    e.   and **wondered** why she was there.

    Break in action sequentiality:
    f.   **He had** been told about her …

    Unacceptable alternative following the break:
    f.   *, **had** been told about her …

Likewise in shifting modality (19e), marked by modal auxiliaries . Since the invariant bare-stem form of the verb follows English modal auxiliaries, a clearer instance of unmarked chain-medial verbs can be seen here:

(19) **Maximally coherent modal sequence**:
    a.   **She should** go there,
    b.   **stop** by,
    c.   **pick up** a pound of salami
    d.   and **take** it home.

Break in modal continuity:
e.   **She can** rest then …

Unacceptable alternative after the break:
e.   *, **can** rest then …

Lastly, consider the effect of a break in referential continuity when the modality remains the same (20e). The initiation of a new chain, and the full finite re-marking of the — continuing   verbal modality in the opening clause of the new chain — is still required:

(20)   **Maximally coherent initial sequence:**
a.   **He will come** into the room,
b.   **stop,**
c.   **see** the woman on the couch,
d.   **look** at her briefly
e.   and **wonder** who she was.

Break in referential continuity:
f.   Then **she will look** at him and …

Unacceptable alternative after the break:
f.   *, (she) **look** at him and …

As we shall see further below, English has another clause-chaining type with unmarked chain-medial clauses, one that is more common in OV languages.

7.5. Clause-level vs. chain-level conjunction

A combination of various intonational breaks (pauses) and marked conjunctions tend to be used in many if not most languages to signal the degree of thematic break between clauses. The intonational phenomena here are highly universal, and can be summarized as follows (Givón 1991b):

- A "comma" voicing break of approx. 100 msecs, coupled with a dip in intonation contour (pitch), tends to separate chain-medial clauses from each other.
- A "period" break of, most commonly of more than 100 msecs, coupled with a more pronounced intonation dip, tends to separate chains, i.e. follow chain-final clauses.
- Overt conjunction morphemes are less commonly used between chain-medial clauses. They are much more common between chains, where they may be either a suffix on the chain-final clause (OV type), a prefix on the first word of the next chain (VO type), or a prefix on the chain-final clause, as is often the case in English (VO type).

These generalizations may be summed as the following principle (Eisler-Goldman 1968):

(21)   **Correlation between cognitive and phonological continuity**:
The larger the cognitive-thematic break is in coherent discourse,
the more marked is that locus phonologically.

Principle (21) conforms to our earlier observation that the most highly-marked (finite) clauses in the chain are those at its two boundaries — either chain-initial (VO type) or chain-final (OV type). As a quick illustration of these tendencies, consider:

(22)   a.   **Comma+'and' conjunction**:
She came in, [0] stopped, [0] looked around **and** froze.
b.   **Period conjunction**:
She came in, [0] stopped **and** looked around. She froze.
c.   **Period+'then' conjunction**:
She came in **and** looked around. **Then** she froze.
d.   **Period+pre-posed-adverb conjunction**:
…She froze. **Later on** she woke up in a strange house…

As noted above, the boundary between larger thematic units, such as the chain, the paragraph or the episode, is where a larger number of coherence strands are most often discontinued. The correlation in written English narrative between clausal intonation breaks or marked conjunctions, on the one hand, and referential continuity on the other, was studied by Hayashi (1989). His findings are tabulated first in (23) below, expressed in terms of the percent of cataphoric discontinuity following the various conjunctions and/or punctuation marks.

(23)   **Cataphoric referential discontinuity associated with zero, comma,
period and paragraph indentation with 'and' and 'then' in English**
(Hayashi 1989)

Conjunction type	% subject switch (DS) across the conjunction
and	15
, and	70
. And	81
and then	16
, and then	36
. and then	100
, then	50
. Then	56
. PARAG/Then	100
comma (alone)	10
period (alone)	72

The punctuation devices in (23), written language's attempt to mimic intonation breaks, can be ranked in a rather predictable order, in terms of the degree of cataphoric referential continuity they signal, a ranking that reflects closely principle (21) above:

(24)   **Highest cataphoric continuity**

   zero
   comma
   period
   paragraph indentation

Lowest cataphoric continuity

Hayashi (1989) also studied the frequency association between the type of English conjunction — continuative vs. contrastive — and cataphoric referential discontinuity. The results are tabulated in (25) below.

(25)   **Cataphoric referential continuity and conjunctions type in written English** (Hayashi 1989)

Conjunction type	% subject switch (DS) across the conjunction
and (all punctuations)	29
, while	77
but (all punctuations)	85
, though	100
. Yet	100

While contrastive conjunctions show a powerful statistical association with referential discontinuity, discontinuity of other coherence strands, alone or in combination with referential discontinuity, may also trigger the use of contrastive conjunctions. As illustrations, consider:

(26)   a.   **Switch verb**:
            Mary sat down, **but** didn't eat
      b.   **Switch verb and subject (negation)**:
            Joe came, **but** Sally didn't
      c.   **Switch verb and object(negation)**:
            I found Sally, **but** not Joe
      d.   **Switch verb and subject**:
            Mary sat down, **but** Bruce stayed on his feet
      e.   **Switch verb and object**:
            Mary loved lettuce, **but** loathed spinach
      f.   **Switch verb, subject & object**:
            Mary played chess, **but** Bruce detested board-games

The notion 'contrast' or *counter-expectation* is always embedded in some context of pre-set expectations, whereby states, events or referents are expected to behave one way but in fact don't. The pre-set expectations may be normative-cultural, as in

(27a) below. They may also be set up for the occasion in the preceding discourse, as in (27b):

(27)   a.   **Generic-cultural expectations**:
            Mary had an IQ of 72 **but still** was a famous physicist
            Expectation: physicists have high IQ
       b.   **Anaphorically-set expectations**:
            Mary sat down **but** Bruce stayed on his feet
            Expectation: Mary and Bruce are similar or closely linked, thus
            expected to behave alike.

7.6. Chain-medial cataphoric switch-reference (DS) devices

As noted above, a high level of anaphoric continuity in all coherence strands is the hallmark of chain-medial clauses. On occasion, however, higher-level thematic continuity is maintained while referential continuity is broken. Many languages have special grammatical devices to indicate such chain-medial referential disruption. Some of those devices, such as contrastive pronouns and Y-movement clauses, were noted earlier (ch. 5, sec. 5.2.3.3.).

A relatively simple system of grammaticalized chain-medial cataphoric switch-reference may be seen in Miskitu (Chibchang). The least-marked participial ('infinitive') verb form is used to signal cataphoric *referential continuity* (SS) in many grammatical context, as in (Hale 1988, 1991):

(28)   a.   **Complement of modality verb**:
            Naha nani w-a-m-tla maki-**i**   ta krik-ri.
            we   PL house-your build-INF end break-PAST/1
            'We began to build your house.'
       b.   **Serial verb construction**:
            Baha uku-ka   pal-**i** wa-n.
            that vulture-CNSTR fly-INF go-PAST/3
            'The vulture flew away.' (lit.: 'The vulture left flying.')
       c.   **Aspectual auxiliary**:
            Kuh puht-**i**   saak-yang.
            fire blow-INF stand-1
            'I am blowing the fire.' (lit.: 'I stand blow the fire.')
       d.   **Serial verb plus auxiliary**:
            Yang nani utla   kum mak-**i**   banghw-**i** s-na.
            I   PL house one build-INF join-INF be-1
            'We are building a house.' (lit.: 'We are joining to build a house.')

In clause-chaining, the participial suffix is recruited, rather naturally, to signal chain-medial referential continuity (SS), a situation reminiscent of the use of the participial *-ing* suffix in the OV clause-chaining type in English (see below). In contrast, the most frequent finite *past/perfective* verb form, with the proper finite subject pronoun, was recruited to signal chain-medial *cataphoric switch-reference* (DS). This form was originally strictly a chain-final form. Thus (Hale 1988, 1991):[6]

(29) a. **Same-subject:**
          Baha ulu-ka   baut-i ik-amna.
          that wasp-CONSTR hit-INF kill-FUT/1
          'I will swat that wasp and kill it.'
      b. **Switch subject:**
          Man sula kum kaik-**ram**   plap-an.
          you deer one see-**PAST/2** run-PAST/3
          'You saw a deer and it ran.'
      c. **Switch subject:**
          Yang sula kum kaik-**ri**   plap-an.
          I   deer one see-**PAST/1** run-PAST/3
          'I saw a deer and it ran.'
      d. **Switch subject:**
          Aisi-k-i   Bilwi-ra ai blik-**an**   wa-ri.
          father-CNSTR-1 B.-to   me send-**PAST/3** go-PAST/1
          'My father sent me to Bilwi (Puerto Cabezas).'
          (lit.: 'My father sent me, and I went, to P.C.')

The use of the less-marked, non-finite participial form to signal cataphoric-SS in chain-medial clauses is essentially the same here as in the less-common clause-chaining type in English:

(30) Com**ing** into the room, look**ing** around and find**ing** no place to sit, she finally perch**ed** herself on the window sill.

Only the chain-final clause in (30) is finite and fully marked for referent ('she') and tense-aspect (perfective-past).

   Lastly, in some languages an *inverse* construction, such as the English Y-movement clause, can be recruited to signal chain-medial cataphoric switch-reference. The logic of such recruitment is reasonably transparent: Inverse clauses tend to code events in which the patient is more topical than the agent. That is, they code contexts where the more common topicality norm — agent > patient — is reversed. In texts with two equally-important participants, inverse clauses are thus used to signal the impending mid-chain topic switch: The *object/patient* of the preceding clause has now become the more topical referent, and is thus likely to persist, most commonly as *subject/agent*, in the next clause. Such 'recruitment' can be seen Sahaptin (Rude 1994):

(31)   a.   Continuity with 'proximate' subject:
   kúuu-xi vwána-pa shushansh i-q'ínunu-xan-a
   thus-same river-LOC stealhead 3/NOM/DIR-see-HAB-PAST
   '…the same way he [PROX] would see a stealhead [OBV] in the river

   ku i-pútya-xan-a   kwn-kínk
   and 3/NOM/DIR-spear-HAB-PAST that-INSTR
   and [PROX] would spear it [OBV] with it (the spear) …'

  b.   Switch from 'proximate' to 'obviate' subject:
   kuuk á-q'inun-a   xwúsaat inch'u-sha,
   then 3/ABS/DIR-see-PAST old.man sleep-IMPFV
   '…then he [PROX] saw an old man [OBV] sleeping,

   kuuk xwúsaat pá-q'inuun-a ku   pá-'n–a: …
   then old.man INV-see-PAST and INV-say-PAST
   the old man [OBV] saw him [PROX] and [OBV] said to him [PROX]: …'

  c.   Switch back from 'obviate' to 'proximate' subject:
   íkush pá-'un-a   xwúsaat-in
   thus INV-say-PAST old.man-OBV
   '…thusly the old man [OBV] said to him (Wild Cat) [PROX].

   ku   áw-n-a: …
   and 3/ABS/DIR-say-PAST
   And he (Wild Cat) [PROX] said to him (old man) [OBV]: …'

7.7. Recapitulation: clause chaining and other minds

The grammar of cross-clause and cross-chain coherence integrates most of the grammatical devices already surveyed in Chapters 5 and 6, above. With all coherence-cuing devices taken together, what emerges is an elaborate system of cues that speakers give hearers about highly-specific mental structures and operations, all directed at the three major cognitive systems in which the current text is represented during on-line communication: working-memory, attention and early episodic memory. While speakers and hearers are blissfully unaware of their grammar-cued communicative goals and operations, it is impossible to understand the great systematicity of their communicative behavior without conceding that during communication they must be working to construct their constantly-shifting, highly specific mental representations of their interlocutor's constantly-shifting epistemic and deontic states.

  The most likely locus of these grammar-cued mental models of other minds, given their fast-paced rate of change, is *working memory*, or at least a component thereof that is relevant for on-line discourse processing (Ericsson and Kintsch 1997). The fact that these mental models have been highly grammaticalized in human language indicates, at the very least, their high use-frequency, and adaptive utility.

Lastly, it may very well be that various aspects of mental models of the mind of the relevant other have already been automated in primate or other social species, albeit without the quintessentially-human phenomenon of grammar. This may be why it is so hard to demonstrate that 'they' are conscious of their 'theories of mind'. In terms of an evolutionary agenda, this may be another instance of an old story: Unless the light is moved to where the gold coin is more likely to be found, one may keep searching in vain under the same old street-lamp where the gold coin most assuredly never was.

Notes

1. For the lexical and grammatical cuing signals of narrator's voice ('perspective') in fiction, see Givón (2002: ch. 8).

2. Being the incorrigible methodologist that he was, Aristotle pointed out to the method of substitution and elimination that has proven reliable, to this day, in linguistics, discourse analysis and experimental psychology.

3. The most conspicuous exception is the use of proper names, either in reality or in fiction. This referential device is justified by high topicality at more global levels of coherence — say the chapter, the book, the work-place, or one's personal life.

4. The narrator's perspective ('voice') is more likely to remain the same over paragraphs, episodes or even higher chunks of discourse (Givón 2002: ch. 8). But an episode- or chapter-initial position is perforce also a chain-initial position.

5. From a novel by T. Severin (1978).

6. For more complex clause-chaining systems, see Givón (2001a: ch. 18).

Chapter 8

Community as other mind:
The pragmatics of organized science*

8.1. The scientist vs. the organism

In many obvious ways, organized science toils in the same vineyard and under similar handicaps as the cognizing biological organism. The history of philosophy attests to this, after a fashion, in repeatedly drawing close parallels between epistemology and philosophy of science (see Itkonen 1982, 2002). Indeed, the very same founders of epistemological empiricism (Aristotle) and rationalism (Plato) in the 4rd century BC have been repeatedly invoked by Inductivist and Deductivist philosophers of science, respectively, from the 2nd century AD onward. In this connection, Karl Popper (1959) acknowledges the historical affinity between the two trends of "growth of our knowledge", albeit in somewhat condescending terms:[1]

> For the most important way in which *common-sense knowledge* grows is, precisely, by turning into *scientific knowledge*. Moreover, it seems clear that the growth of scientific knowledge is the most important and interesting case of the growth of knowledge.
> It should be remembered, in this context, that almost all the problems of traditional epistemology are connected with the problem of the growth of knowledge. I am inclined to say even more: from Plato to Descartes, Leibniz, Kant, Duhem and Poincaré; and from Bacon to Hobbes and Locke, to Hume, Mill and Russell, the theory of knowledge was inspired by the hope that it would enable us not only to know more about knowledge, but also to contribute to the advance of knowledge — of scientific knowledge, that is.   (1959: 19; italics added)

In the same vein, the pragmatic middle ground in epistemology runs in parallel, and often merges, with the pragmatic middle ground in the philosophy of science, from Aristotle to Kant to Peirce to Hanson.

I would like to begin this chapter with a brief outline of pragmatics in the philosophy of science, an analog to the pragmatics of the individual learning mind. This re-statement follows, in the main, the earlier account in Givón (1989, ch. 8), though I have attempted here to make things a bit more concise and, hopefully, more coherent.[2] The main focus of this book, however, demands an eventual shift of emphasis, in anticipation of another parallelism, one evoked by the question:

- What is the equivalent in science of other minds?

Or, perhaps:

- Who is the scientist's relevant interlocutor?

The answer I intend to propose is sufficiently obvious, given two well-known works on the social dynamics of science — Kuhn (1962) and Lakatos (1978). The equivalent of the interlocutor in science is the *community of scholars*.[3] Which, even when not explicitly invoked, lurks about tacitly, whether in Popper's and Hanson's "current theory", in an objectivized version of Kuhn's "dominant paradigm", or in Lakatos'"research programme".

Like all analogies, the parallelism between organized science and the learning organism can be stretched only up to a point, beyond which one needs to concede some obvious differences:

- Science often runs on a much more protracted time-scale, with nothing remotely like the adaptive time-pressure imposed on behaving/cognizing organisms.
- The propositional knowledge of science is conscious, deliberately reasoned, and not automated.
- Philosophy of science emphasizes, perhaps overwhelmingly, the epistemic over the deontic.

Nonetheless, within bounds, the two domains, epistemology and philosophy of science, share the broad dynamics of (i) being always in the midst of the endless process of accretion of knowledge; and (ii) having always a *dialogic interaction* with some relevant interlocutor whose beliefs and intentions must be reckoned with.

8.2. Reductionist extremes in the philosophy of science

8.2.1. Preamble

Much like epistemology, philosophy of science has tended to oscillate, over its long history, between two reductionist extremes, deductivism (Rationalist) and inductivism (Empiricist). Like the proverbial blind men describing the elephant, each of the two reductionist schools undertook to focus almost exclusively on one aspect of the complex process of scientific inquiry, either *deductive inference* or *inductive inference*, de-emphasizing the other. What is more, both schools joined forces in trivializing — or mystifying — hypothesis formation and the central role taken by Aristotle's third mode of reasoning, *abductive inference*.

8.2.2. Deductivist accounts

The main difference between deductivists and inductivists hinges, as in epistemology, on the directionality of the relationship between facts (individual statements) and theories (general statements). But the distinction between individual and general statements (or 'concepts') is fundamental to both schools. From a cognitive perspective (empirical epistemology), the relation between the two is, transparently, isomorphic to the relation between *episodic/declarative* memory (statements about specific individual and/or events) and *semantic/procedural* memory (concepts; statements about general classes).[4]

With the distinction between facts and theories taken for granted, rationalists in the philosophy of science emphasized the aspect of knowledge accretion that depends on deductive inference. This is most conspicuous in the best practitioner of the genre, Karl Popper. Popper's vision of the overwhelming role of deduction in scientific inquiry is formulated in terms of the fundamental distinction between individual and universal statements (Popper 1959):

> Every application of science is based upon an inference from scientific hypotheses (which are *universal*) to *singular* cases, i.e. upon a *deduction* of singular prediction.   (1959: 64; italics added)

Indeed, Popper is more adamant about the inviolability of the individual-universal distinction than Carnap was in his late, more mature formulations, castigating Carnap:

> It is therefore not possible to abolish the distinction between individual concepts and universal concepts with arguments like the following of Carnap's: '... this distinction is not justified' he says, because '... every concept can be regarded as an individual or a universal concept according to the point of view adopted'.[5] Carnap tries to support this assertion '... that (almost) *all so-called individual concepts are* (names of) *classes*, just like universal concepts'. This last assertion is quite correct, as I have shown, but has nothing to do with the distinction in question.   (*ibid.*: 67)

The process of how universal concepts are arrived at, where the loyal opposition posits the central role of induction, is left deliberately vague in Popper's account. This is of course understandable, given that deduction itself cannot account for this, however central its role may be in Popper's rendition of the scientific cycle. Deduction is deployed, according to Popper, in the *testing*, not the assembling, of general theoretical statements:

> There can be no doubt that *we learn the use* of universal words, that is, of their *application* to individuals, by ostensive gestures and by similar means.   (*ibid.*: 65)

It is not that Popper does not know that phases other than deductive reasoning take their rightful place in scientific inquiry. It is, rather, that he considered them devoid of 'true' philosophical interest:

> I propose to look at science in a way which is slightly different from that favored by the various psychologistic schools: I wish to *distinguish sharply between objective science, on the one hand, and 'our knowledge' on the other*. I readily admit that only observation can give us 'knowledge concerning the facts', and that we can (as Hahn says) 'become aware of facts only by observation'.[1] But this awareness, this knowledge of ours, does not justify or establish the truth of any statement. I do not believe, therefore, that the question which epistemology must ask is '... on what does our *knowledge* rest? ... or more exactly, how can I, having had the *experience* S,

> justify my description of it, and defend it, against doubt . . . In my view, what episte-
> mology has to ask is, rather: How do we test scientific statements by their deductive
> consequences?   (1959: 97–8)

Popper's disdain for the 'psychological' closely parallels Carnap's and Wittgenstein's. This strong preference for 'logical' over 'psychological' — rational over naturalistic — epistemology is reminiscent of Chomsky's visceral disdain for the equally
naturalist 'performance', opting for the rational, abstract 'competence'.

Popper is at his sharpest as a critic of extreme inductivism. Much of the animus is
directed, perhaps aptly, at Wittgenstein's *Tractatus*:

> The positivist dislikes the idea that there should be meaningful problems outside
> the field of 'positive' empirical science — problems to be dealt with by genuine
> philosophical theory. He dislikes the idea that there should be a genuine theory of
> knowledge, an epistemology or a methodology[*1] . . . In the two years since the first
> publication of this book, it was the standing criticism raised by members of the Vi-
> enna Circle against my idea that a theory of method which was neither an *empir-
> ical science* nor *pure logic* was impossible: What was outside of these two fields was
> sheer nonsense.   (*ibid.*: 51; italics added)

It is hard to find a clearer statement of extreme reductionism in philosophy. And
likewise:

> only two kinds of statements exist for them: logical tautologies and empirical state-
> ments. If methodology is not logic, then, they will conclude, it must be a branch of
> some science — the science, say, of *the behavior of scientists at work*.   (*ibid.*: 52;
> italics added)

Popper points out the essential fallibility of induction as an instrument of generalization:

> According to this view, the logic of scientific discovery would be identical with in-
> ductive logic . . . It is usual to call an inference 'inductive' if it passes from *singu-
> lar statements* (sometime called 'particular statements'), such as accounts of the re-
> sults of observations or experiments, to *universal statements*, such as hypotheses or
> theories.   (*ibid.*: 27)

> positivists in their anxiety to annihilate metaphysics, annihilate natural science
> along with it. For scientific laws too, cannot be logically reduced to elementary
> statements of experience.   (*ibid.*: 36)

It is not clear, however, if Popper's complaint is akin to Quine's (1951). The point
may perhaps by clarified by a simple-minded example. Consider the putative inductive inference:

(1)   **Induction from particulars to the general**:
    a.   Socrates is Greek and bald.
    b.   Other encountered Greeks $x, y, z, \ldots n$ are also Greek and bald.

    c.   All Greeks are bald.

Two separate objections can be raised concerning the logical status of the inductive inference (1). First, one may indeed concede that knowledge of the general statement (1c) was derived through prior experience of the particular statements (1a) and (1b). But those statements already *presuppose* prior knowledge of the, equally general, generic classes 'Greek' and 'bald', and thus knowledge of their respective membership criteria — which are themselves *general statements*. Via inductive inference (1) we have created neither a new class 'bald' nor a new class 'Greek'. Rather, we have only *enriched* the pre-existing class 'Greek' by adding another necessary criterial feature to it, 'bald'. At its best, induction turns out to be a means of probing the association between criterial features of pre-existing general classes (e.g. adding a criterion, as in (1)). It further elaborates already known general statements. What it seems altogether incapable of doing is what empiricist have always wanted it to do — create general statements *di novo* out of individual experiences.

The second objection is handled more explicitly by Popper, who, like Wittgenstein and Perice, notes the inherent uncertainty — *leap-of-faith* — associated with induction; that is, generalizing from past to future experience, or from a small sample to the general population. Invoking none but Hume, Popper notes:

> that those instances ... of which we have had no experience [are likely to] resemble those of which we have had experience ... "... All probable arguments are built on the supposition that there is conformity betwixt the future and the past ..." (*ibid.*, appendix *vii: 369)

Wittgenstein (1918) made the same observation:

> the procedure of induction consists in accepting as true the *simplest* law that can be reconciled with our experience. This procedure, however, has no logical justification, but only a psychological one ... It is a hypothesis that the sun will rise tomorrow [based on the inductive observation of repeated instances of sunrise]: and this means that we do not *know* whether it will rise.   (1918: 143; brackets added)

Popper (1959) is somewhat of a mixed bag as deductivists go, at various points conceding interest in the pragmatics of science (see below). Deductivists in the social sciences, on the other hand, have taken much more reductive positions, often to the point of caricature. Thus Bach (1965), in extolling Chomky's position, sets up the stark opposition between extreme empiricism (the bad guys) and extreme rationalism (the good guys):

> Whereas the Baconian stresses caution and 'sticking to facts' with a distrust of theory and hypotheses ... The Keplerian emphasizes the creative nature of scientific discovery, the *leap to general hypotheses* — often mathematical in form, whose value is judged in terms of fruitfulness, simplicity and elegance ... The prevailing assumptions of American linguistics prior to 1957 were essentially Baconian in character ... [Chomsky's approach, on the other hand was a] deductively formulated method.   (1965: 113–14; brackets added)

Bach then likens the Chomkyan paradigm in linguistics to the 'good guys' in physics, quoting from Dirac's comments on Schroedinger:

> I think there is a moral to this story, namely, that it is more important to have beauty in one's equations than to have them fit the experiment.   (*ibid.*: 113–14)

In the same vein, Lees (1957) chimes in:

> Once it has developed beyond the prescientific stage of collection and classification of interesting facts, a scientific discipline is characterized *essentially* by the introduction of *abstract constructs* and theories and the validation of those theories by testing their predictive power.   (1957: 376; italics added)

Chomsky himself has, as a matter of habit, taken the process of discovery for granted, focusing almost entirely on how the general statement ('the grammar') accounts for ('predicts') all possible individual facts ('grammatical sentences'):

> By "grammar of the language L" I will mean a device of some sort (that is, a *set of rules*) that provides, at least, a complete specification of an infinite set of *grammatical sentences* of L and their structural description.   (1961: 6; italics added)

8.2.3. Inductivist accounts

Extreme inductivists in the philosophy of science can be just as smug and arrogant as their deductivist counterparts in dismissing empirical natural epistemology as 'primitive' and less worthy of the philosopher's attention, as compared with the more reflective, analytic accretion of scientific knowledge. Thus, in conceding the historical parallel between epistemology and the philosophy of science, Russell (1918) is unabashed about where his heart lies:

> It seems to me that when your object is not simply the study of the history or development of mind, but to ascertain the nature of the world, you do not want to go any further back than you are already yourself. You do not want to go back to the vagueness of the child or monkey, because you will find that quite sufficient difficulty is raised by your own vagueness ... There is one type of mind which considers that what is called *primitive experience* must be a better guide to wisdom than the experience of *reflective persons*, and there is the type of mind which takes exactly the opposite view ... It is quite clear that the educated person sees, hears, feels, does everything in a very different way from a young child or animal, and that this whole manner of experiencing the world and of thinking about the world is very much more analytic than that of a more primitive experience.   (1918: 181)

Russell is as clear as Popper about the fundamental distinction between individual and general statements, again underscoring parallels between the organism and the scientist:

> The first distinction that concerns us is the distinction between percepts and concepts, i.e. between objects of acts of perception and objects of acts of conception. *If there is* a distinction between particulars and universals, percepts will be among particulars, while concepts will be among universals.   (1911; in Russell 1956: 105; italics added)

After much hand waving, both logical and pseudo-empirical, Russell concedes a sense in which the distinction between the two types of knowledge does exist:

> We have thus a division of all entities into two classes: (1) particulars, which enter into complexes only as subjects of predicates or as the terms of relations, and, if they belong to the world of which we have experience, exist in time and cannot occupy more than one place at one time in the space to which they belong; (2) universals, which can occur as predicates or relations in complexes, do not exist in time, and have no relation to one place which they may not simultaneously have to another.   (1911; in Russell 1956: 124)

In his late-life reflection on the older formulation of the distinction, Carnap (1963) recapitulates the extreme formulation of his early empiricist years, founded on the availability of sense-derived atomic facts (individual statements):

> According to the original conception, the system of knowledge, although growing constantly more comprehensive, was regarded as a closed system in the following sense. We assumed that there was a certain rock bottom of the knowledge, the knowledge of the immediately given, which was indubitable. Every other kind of knowledge was supposed to be firmly supported by this basis and therefore likewise decidable with certainty. This is the picture that I had given in *Logischer Aufbau*. It was supported by the influence of Mach's doctrine of the sensations as the elements of all knowledge, by Russell's logical atomism, and finally by Wittgenstein's thesis that all propositions are truth-functions of the elementary propositions.   (1963: 57)

In explaining why the old strict-empiricist model had been later abandoned, Carnap goes on:

> Looking back at this view from our present position, I must admit that it was difficult to reconcile with certain other conceptions that we had at the time, especially in the methodology of science. Therefore the development and clarification of our methodological view led inevitably to an abandonment of the rigid frame of our theory of knowledge. The important feature of our methodological position was the emphasis on the hypothetical character of the laws of nature [general statements], in particular, of physical theories ... It was clear that the laws of physics could not possibly be completely verified. This led Schlick, under the influence of Wittgenstein, to the view that physical laws could no longer be regarded as general sentences but rather as rules for derivation of singular sentences ... The influence of Karl Popper's book *Logic der Forschung* worked in the same direction. Thus some of us, especially Neurath, Hahn and I, came to the conclusion that we had to look for a more liberal criterion of significance than verifiability.   (*ibid.*: 57)

The close resemblance of Carnap's later position to Popper's Hypothetico-Deductive (H-D) model is easy to discern. Particularly striking are (i) the hypothetical status of general statements (scientific theories); and (ii) the 'rules for derivation' mapping from general to particular statements. The latter are an obvious analogue to Popper's deductive reasoning in science, whereby possible individual facts are deduced as logical consequences of a hypothesis, i.e. as logically binding *predictions*;

then the 'more liberal' logical criterion of *falsifiability* is employed.

As one would expect, inductivists were as good as deductivists in ferreting out the exposed underbelly of their opponents' position. This goes back to Wittgenstein's celebrated trashing of deduction, in the *Tractatus* (1918):

> The propositions of logic are tautologies. Therefore the propositions of logic say nothing. (They are the analytic propositions).   (1918: 121)

Wittgenstein is, of course, concerned here with the ability of logical propositions to convey new information, a concern couched in terms of the prevailing Positivist *zeitgeist* — individual statements about objective reality:

> Tautologies and contradictions are not pictures of reality. They do not represent any possible situations. For the former admits *all* possible situations, and the latter *none*.   (*ibid.*: 69)

Wittgenstein next ties up the discussion of tautology and contradiction to the scale of three epistemic modalities (certain, possible, impossible), noting that an information-bearing proposition stands at neither extreme of the scale:[6]

> a tautology's truth is certain, a proposition's possible, a contradiction's impossible. Certain, possible, impossible: here we have the first indication of the *scale* that we need in the theory of probability.   (*ibid.*: 69–70; italics added)

Lastly, as noted above, Wittgenstein the flaming empiricist was as aware as his deductivist counterparts of the soft pragmatic underbelly of induction:

> the procedure of induction consists in accepting as true the simplest law that can be reconciled with our experience. This procedure, however, has no logical justification, but only a psychological one.   (*ibid.*: 143; italics added)

As in the case of deductivism, inductivism at its most reductive extreme crops up in the wild flower-beds of social science, where true believers have been just as adept at quoting *their* paragons of physics; as in, e.g., d'Andrade's (1965) quoting Newton:

> the best and safest method of philosophizing [doing science] ... seems to be, first to inquire diligently into the properties of things, and of establishing these properties by experiment, and then to proceed more slowly to hypotheses [theories] for the explanation of them.   (1954: 64)

In the same vein, L. Bloomfield, at the time a recent convert to Behaviorism, observed:

> the only useful generalizations about language are inductive generalizations.
>   (1933: 20)

And likewise in his review of Sapir's *Language* (Bloomfield 1922):

> we must study people's habits of language — the way they talk — without bothering about mental processes that we may conceive to underlie or accompany habits. We must dodge this issue by a fundamental assumption, leaving it to a separate investigation, in which our results will figure as data along the results of other social sciences.   (1922: 142)

And again in his critique of his mentor, Hermann Paul:

> The other great weakness of Paul's 'Principles' is in his insistence upon "psychological" interpretation . . . [and on] mental processes which the speakers are supposed to have undergone . . . The only evidence for these mental processes is the linguistic process; they add nothing to the discussion but only obscure it.   (1933: 17)

> In order to give a scientifically accurate definition of meaning for every form of the language, one should have to have a scientifically accurate knowledge of everything in the speakers' world . . . In practice, we define the meaning of a linguistic form, whenever we can, in terms of some other science.   (*ibid.*: 139–40)

> The mentalistic theory . . . supposes that the variability of human conduct is due to the interference of some non-physical factors, a *spirit* or *will* or *mind* . . . that is present in every human being . . . [and] is entirely different from material things and accordingly follows some other kind of causation or perhaps non at all.   (*ibid.*: 32–3)

8.3. The pragmatics of empirical science

8.3.1. Preamble

In one guise or another, pragmatics has been a silent partner in the philosophy of science ever since Aristotle. And as noted above, both avowed deductivists (Popper) and inductivists (Carnap) were forced to concede grounds to pragmatics. In the case of Carnap, this involved primarily the relaxation of the erstwhile-rigid boundary between factual and theoretical statements. In the case of Popper, the concessions were more extensive.

More to the point, pragmatics has been an integral part of the actual *practice* of science from the very start, most conspicuously again in Aristotle's practice of biology and bio-classification (see ch. 1). What the more mature recent accounts of organized science have done, beginning with Peirce, is bring pragmatics out into the open and inflict it upon philosophy of science, which until then had indulged in the very same reductionist excesses as had traditional epistemology.

I will begin by surveying the major junctures where pragmatics intrudes into the process of scientific inquiry. As we shall see further below, the intrusion is even more extensive.

8.3.2. Theory-laden facts

> Facts are not picturable, observable entities.
>
> (R. N. Hanson, *Patterns of Discovery*, 1958: 31)

As noted above, the stringent separation of factual ('particular') from theoretical ('general') statement had been the hallmark of both reductionist schools in philosophy of science. What pragmatist accounts have demonstrated, with arguments and case studies, is that the distinction, however useful, is in principle untenable. For, much like Kant's dialectic account of epistemology, data and theory define each other in science. So that at any given point, one may recruit one to re-define the other, and vice versa. That is, when fiddling with the theory, one takes the facts to be solid. Once the theory has been stabilized, one can — from a new vantage point — re-evaluate the solidity of the facts.

The most comprehensive account of this may be found in Hanson (1958), beginning with the rejection of the traditional Aristotlian view of objective, sensory-given facts. Hanson illustrates the frame-dependence of 'observed facts' with the following example from Biology:

> Imagine these two [scientists] observing a Protozoon — Amoeba. One sees a one-celled animal, the other a non-celled animal. The first sees Amoeba in all its *analogies* with different types of single cells: liver cells, nerve cells, epithelium cells. These have a wall, nucleus, cytoplasm, etc. Within this class Amoeba is distinguished only by its independence. The other, however, sees Amoeba's *homology* not with single cells, but with whole animals. Like all animals Amoeba ingests its food, digests and assimilates it. It excretes, reproduces and is mobile — more like a complete animal than an individual tissue cell.   (1958: 4; italics added)

Is either perspective wrong? Hardly. They are both right, each in a different theoretical context. In the same vein, one could cite the celebrated example from physics, whereby from one theoretical perspective and its attendant set of measurements (and instrumentation), the 'given' data of light are unmistakably waves; from another, they are particles. Again, both theoretical perspectives are valid, each revealing another aspect of the complex whole.

Another way in which data turn out, again and again, to be contaminated by theory is in the notoriously-pragmatic realm of *relevance*. As we will note further below, at many junctures in the cycle of scientific inquiry one has to weigh data against each other and decide which is more relevant for the 'purpose at hand'; with the 'purpose at hand' being, invariably, a theoretical construct. In this connection, returning to the amoeba, Hanson (1958) observes:

> This is not an experimental issue, yet it can affect experiment. What either man regards as significant questions or *relevant data* can be determined by whether he stresses the first or the last term of 'unicellular animal'.   (1958: 4–5; italics added).

In sifting through the data with theory-dependent criteria of *relevance* and *purpose*, the scientist merely recapitulates the bio-organism, which filter out large mounds of 'objective' data at any given moment, reducing them to small and thus manageable fractions — those that are most relevant — *at the moment, for the purpose at hand*. Both the scientist and the organism, in their respective domains, are highly selective in what they admit into evidence. And their selectivity has relatively little to do with the perceptual, objective status of the input data. The amount of available 'objective' data is, in both domains, staggering. Neither induction nor deduction could reduce those to a manageable, processable proportion. Only pragmatic — contextual, abductive — reasoning will accomplish that.

8.3.3. Abductive inference

At the center of any pragmatic account of knowledge incrementation stands abductive reasoning, being the instrument by which new hypotheses, new theoretical insights and illuminating explanations are put on science's table. As noted earlier (ch. 1), the Aristotelian provenance of abduction is to some extent murky. The lone explicit description in the *Prior Analytic II* seems relatively trivial, being an extension of Aristotle's standard version of deduction as explanation. In deductive inference, the middle term in the derivation — the general statement (*explanans*) — is as firm as a rock. In abductive reasoning ('reduction'), on the other hand, the middle term's connection to the third term (the conclusion; *explanandum*) is more tenuous:

> By reduction we mean an argument in which the first term clearly belongs to the middle, but the relation of the middle to the last term is uncertain though equally or more convincing than the conclusion; or again an argument in which the terms intermediate between the last term and the middle are few; for in any of these cases it turns out that we approach more nearly to knowledge. For example, let A stand for *what can be taught*, B for *knowledge*, C for *justice*. Now it is clear that *knowledge can be taught*; but it is uncertain whether *virtue is knowledge*. If now BC ['justice is knowledge'] is equally or more convincing than AC ['justice can be taught'] we have a reduction; for we are nearer to knowledge, since we have made an extra assumption, being before without knowledge that A belongs to C ['justice can be taught']. (*Prior Analytic* II, 25; J. Barnes ed. 1984: 110; italics added)

Put in clearer terms, perhaps:

(2) **Aristotle's 'reduction':**

a. knowledge can be taught   (certain prior statement)
b. ?justice is knowledge   (uncertain general statement/hypotheses)
———————————————————
c. ?justice can be taught   (uncertain conclusion; *explanandum*)

The oft-cited passage from the *Posterior Analytic II* is but a poetic metaphor. It does, however, evinces the flavor of how abduction is used in hypothesis formation or explanation:

> The particular facts are not merely brought together, but there is a new element added to the combination by the very act of thought by which they are combined ... The pearls are there, but they will not hang together until someone provides the string. (*Posterior Analytic* II. 19; cited from McKeon ed. 1941)

Hanson's interpretation of Aristotle's abduction harkens back to Peirce:

> Aristotle lists the types of inferences. These are deductive, inductive and one other called *apagoge*. This is translated as 'reduction'. Peirce translates it as 'abduction' or

'retroduction'. What distinguishes this kind of argument for Aristotle is that the relation of the middle to the last term is uncertain, though equally or more probable than the conclusion; or again an argument in which the terms intermediate between the last term and the middle are few. For in any of these cases it turns out that we approach more nearly to knowledge...since we have taken a new term. (1958: 85)

It is Peirce, rather than Aristotle, who sorts out the role of abduction in empirical science, as well as its relation to induction and deduction:

The first starting of a hypothesis and the entertaining of it, whether as a simple interrogation or with any degree of confidence, is an inferential step which I propose to call *abduction*...This will include a preference for any one hypothesis over others which would equally well explain the facts, so long as this preference is not based upon any *previous knowledge* [thus ruling out deduction] bearing upon the truth of the hypotheses, nor on any *testing* [hereby ruling out induction] of any of the hypotheses, after having admitted them on probation. I call all such inference by the peculiar name, *abduction*, because its legitimacy depends upon altogether different principles from those of other kinds of inference. (1940: 151; italics added)

Peirce takes great pains to differentiate abduction from induction, a worthy endeavor since many (including myself; cf. Givón 1979a, ch. 8) have at one time or another considered abduction a species of lower-certainty, weakened induction. Thus:

[*induction*] sets out with a theory and it measures the degree of concordance of that theory with fact. It never can originate any idea whatever. No more can *deduction*. All ideas of science come to it by way of *abduction*. Abduction consists in studying the facts and devising theories to explain them. Its only justification is that if we are ever to understand things at all, it must be in that way. Abductive and inductive reasoning are utterly irreducible, either to the other or to Deduction, or deduction to either of them. (C.S. Peirce, *Collected Writings*, 1934, vol. V: 146; italics added)

Peirce also notes the association between Aristotle's three modes of inference and his three epistemic modalities:

Deduction proves that something *must* be; Induction shows that something *actually is* operative; Abduction merely suggests that something *may be*. (*ibid*.: 171)

As for the precise role of abduction in hypothesis formation, Peirce's (1940) rendition is rather compressed:

The surprising fact C is observed; But if A were true, C would be a matter of course; Hence, there is a reason to suspect that A is true. (1940: 151)

The version given by Hanson (1958) is a bit more expanded, contrasting the pragmatic account with the putative inductivist and deductivist counterparts:

1. Some surprising phenomenon P is observed. 2. P would be explicable as a matter of course if H were true. 3. Hence there is reason to think that H is true. H cannot be retroductively [abductively] inferred until its contents is present in 2. Inductive accounts expect H to emerge from repetition of P. H-D [Popperian] accounts

make P emerge from some unaccounted-for creation of H as a 'high-level hypothesis'.   (1958: 86)

That is, if one may be forgiven deigning to improve on the great masters:

(3) **Abduction in hypothesis formation**:
  a. Puzzling facts *F* are incompatible with current Theory *T*.
  b. But facts *F* are fully compatible with Hypothesis *H*,
 (c. whose truth value is yet to be determined).
  d. That is, if Hypothesis *H* were the case,
  e. then facts *F* would be explained as a matter of course.

  f. Therefore Hypothesis *H* must be the case.

Peirce (1940) also locates deduction and induction within the empirical cycle:

> The operation of testing a hypothesis by experiment, which consists in remarking that, if it is true, observations made under certain conditions ought to have certain results, and then causing those conditions to be fulfilled, and noting the results, and, if they are favorable, extending a certain confidence to the hypothesis, I call *induction*.   (1940: 152)

In arguing against Popper's deductivism (H-D), Hanson (1958) foregrounds the role of abduction:

> Physicists do not start from hypotheses; they start from data. By the time a law has been fixed into an H-D system, really original physical thinking is over. The pedestrian process of deducing observation statements from hypotheses comes only after the physicist sees that the hypothesis will at least explain the initial data requiring explanation.[The] H-D account is helpful only when discussing the argument of a finished research report . . . the analysis leaves undiscussed the reasoning.   (1958: 71)

The order of application of the three modes of inference in the run-of-the-mill empirical cycle of investigation is then:

- **Abduction**: supposing a new hypothesis *H*, yet to be tested.
- **Deduction**: predicting testable logical consequences of *H*.
- **Induction**: testing the predicted consequences; then:
    if consequences are as predicted, one has failed to falsify *H*.
    if the consequences are not as predicted, *H* is thereby falsified.

The predicted — deduced — logical consequences of *H* are thus fully binding only in one direction, via *modus tollens*, leading to binding *falsification*:

$H \supset$ consequence
NEG-consequences $\supset$ NEG-*H*

Positive results, on the other hand, do not confirm *H*, but only fail to falsify it. So, for the moment and until further tests that may yet accomplish falsification, hypothesis *H* is safe.

Lastly, like Wittgenstein and Popper, Peirce concedes the inevitable residual uncertainty in the inductive 'leap of faith'. Though ascribing the consequent guesswork to abduction is perhaps not altogether enlightening:

> So long as the class sampled consists of units, and the ratio in question is a ratio between counts of occurrences, induction is comparatively a simple affair. But suppose we wish to test the hypothesis that a man is a Catholic priest, that is, has all the characters that are common to Catholic priests and peculiar to them. Now characters are not units, nor do they consist of units, nor can they be counted, in such a sense that one count is right and the other wrong. Characters have to be estimated according to their significance. The consequence is that there will be a certain element of guess-work in such an induction; so that I call it an *abductory induction*. (1940: 152)

8.3.4. Explanation

8.3.4.1. *Deductive 'explanations'*

The idea that a generalization or a statement of class-membership somehow counts as an explanation goes back to Aristotle's treatment of deduction in both the *Prior* and *Posterior Analytic*. Roughly:

(4) **Schema of deductive explanation:**
    a. antecedent particular facts
    b. general rule   (*explanans*)
    —————————————
    c. new puzzling facts   (*explanandum*)

The potential poverty of deductive explanation (4) becomes apparent in actual cases. Consider first the deductive explanation of the puzzling fact (5c) 'Socrates is bald':

(5) a. Socrates is Greek
    b. All Greeks is Bald (*explanans*)
    —————————————
    c. Socrates is bald   (*explanandum*)

On the one hand, if one did not know beforehand that the general statement (5b) ('middle term') was the case, one indeed gains *something* by relating the puzzling fact of Socrates' baldness (5c) to his membership in the class Greek (4a). The general statement (5b) thus allows the two hitherto disparate facts (5a) and (5c) to be linked, to *cohere*. On the other hand, one still doesn't *really* know why Socrates is bald, since one doesn't yet know why *all Greeks* are bald. Our deductive 'explanation', however useful in organizing hitherto disparate chunks of knowledge, turns out to be not much of an explanation, but at best a promissory note.

Deductive 'explanations' of this sort crop up repeatedly as pseudo explanations in popular and less-popular science. Consider, for example, the logical explanatory power of the pop-biology catch phrase 'survival of the fittest':

(6) a. Individual x is fittest
     b. All the fittest survive   (*explanans*)

     c. individual x survived   (*explanandum*)

The circularity of using (6b) as an explanation for (6c) is sufficiently obvious.

In the same vein, consider the explanatory power of 'reinforcement' in behaviorist psychology:

(7) a. Individual x repeatedly performed task y
     b. Repetition reinforces learning   (*explanans*)

     c. Individual x learned task y (*explanandum*)

Finally, consider the explanatory power of a standard statement in deductivist linguistics (Ross 1967):

(8) a. Structure x is a complex-NP.
     b. One can never copy out of complex-NPs   (*explanans*)

     c. One cannot copy out of structure x (*explanandum*)

In summing up the difficulty raised by the traditional Aristotelian notion of the general statement ('middle-term') of deduction being an 'explanation', Scriven (1962) observes:

> Hempel and Oppenheim's first mistake, then, lies in the supposition that by subsumption under a generalization one has automatically explained *something*, and that queries about this "explanation" represent a request for *further* and *different* explanation.   (1962: 97)

8.3.4.2. *Explanation as contextualization*

In a way, the pragmatic account of explanation is buried, as an embryonic vestige, inside Aristotle's account of deductive 'explanation'. This is so because the latter can achieve, at the very least, a *more general* account of the hitherto disparate facts. Indeed, all explanation is akin to placing erstwhile disparate facts in a *wider context*, so that what appeared at first blush accidental now becomes natural, understandable, taken as a matter of course. Thus (Scriven 1962):

> What is scientific explanation? It is a *topically unified* communication, the contents of which imparts *understanding* of some scientific phenomenon. And the better it is, the more efficiently and reliably it does this, i.e., with less redundancy and higher *over-all* probability. What is understanding? Understanding is, roughly, *organized knowledge*, i.e., knowledge of the *relations* between various facts and/or laws. These relations are many kinds — deductive, inductive, analogical, etc. (Understanding is deeper, more thorough, the greater the span of this relational knowledge).   (1962: 102; italics added)

Such complex *contextualization* is precisely what substantive new scientific hypotheses purport to accomplish. But they accomplish this by proposing something new and unprecedented, something uncertain and yet to be tested. Formal general statements such as Aristotle's middle term, however useful they may be in organizing disparate chunks of knowledge, only point out to *class-membership* relations among known facts. As Wittgenstein (1918) pointed out, however, they add no new knowledge into the system. They cannot; by definition.

8.3.4.3. *Causal explanation*

> The belief in causality is metaphysical. It is nothing but a typical metaphysical hypothesization of a well-justified methodological rule — the scientist's decision never to abandon his search for laws.
>
> (K. Popper, *The Logic of Scientific Discovery*, 1959: 248)

Traditional philosophers of science, whether inductivist or deductivist, have tended to rely almost exclusively on classical Newtonian physics for examples of scientific practice and, in particular, of causal explanation. Rather understandably, they tended to select cases of simple, chain-like, mechanical causation as paradigm examples of causal explanation. Here is how Russell (1948) describes it:

> Inference from experience to the physical world can ... be justified by the assumption that there are causal chains, each member of which is a complex structure ordered by the *spatio-temporal* [relation of] *com-presence* ... All members of such a [causation] chain are similar in structure.   (1948: 244; brackets and italics added)

The key term here is, of course, spatio-temporal *com-presence*, which one may as well re-christen as *co-occurrence*. But as simple as it may seem at first, causation turns out to be a theory-laden notion, a metaphysical construct that is inferred, often in complex and indirect ways, from various spatio-temporal co-occurrences, most often *subsequences*; and in particular from the *conditional asymmetries* of temporally-adjacent facts. Consider:

(9) **From temporality to conditionality to causality:**
   a. **Asymmetrical temporal association (subsequence):**
      (i) Event-type B never occurs unless it is preceded by A.
      (ii) Event-type A can sometimes occur without being followed by B.
   b. **Conditional logical association (necessity):**
      $B \supset A$ (but not necessarily vice versa)
   c. **Metaphysical explanatory leap (causality):**
      Therefore A must be the 'cause' of B.

A more realistic, pragmatic account of causal explanation, such as Hanson's, notes that members of a 'simple causation chain' are seldom if ever just the purported "... *discrete events bound to neighbouring events very much like themselves.*" (1958: 50) In an eloquent dissection of the ontology of causation, Hanson shows why this simple-chain model of causation is a caricature of science, either in modern physics or in the more complex yet biological and behavioral sciences:

> what we refer to as 'causes' are *theory-loaded* from beginning to end. They are not simple, tangible links in the chain of sense experience, but rather details in an *intricate pattern of concepts*.   (1958: 54; italics added)

And further:

> This is the whole story about necessary connection. 'Effect' and 'cause', so far from naming links in a queue of events, gesture towards *webs of criss-crossed theoretical notions*, information, and patterns of experiment ... The notions behind 'the cause x' and 'the effect y' are intelligible only against a *pattern of theory*, namely one which puts guarantees on inferences from x to y.   (1958: 64; italics added)

The idea that a simple, linear causal relation between facts can always be established is an oversimplification of how complex multi-variable science works. As Hanson (1958) notes, the only reason why a complex science can sometime give the misleading impression of simple causal chains is because of the simplifying methodology of *controlled experiments*. Such experiments are the standard fare of complex, multi-variable science, where causal connections and other dependencies cannot be determined from observing real-world conditions. Rather, one needs to abstract away from the real world. In a typical controlled experiment, all factors but two are either eliminated or held constant, effectively (if temporarily ...) being removed from consideration. One of the remaining two factors, the *independent variable* (A), is then manipulated. That is, its values are systematically varied. The effect of this manipulation on the values of the *dependent variable* (B) is then recorded. If the results are asymmetrical as in (9a), one is justified in calling the independent variable (A) the 'cause' and the dependent variable (B) the 'effect'.

In complex science, however, the controlled experimental procedure is repeated, with at least one of the variables being replaced by a hitherto untested one. And so on, often — it seems — ad infinitum. So that, gradually, a 'criss-cross pattern of connectivity' is established, whereby the simple notion of causal chain becomes submerged and modified beyond recognition. Eventually, as Hanson notes:

> To characterize such an enterprise as 'this happens, then that, then those things take place, which results in ...', is a bad caricature.   (1958: 67)

8.3.4.4. *Agency as a causal explanation*

The notions of *agency* and its associated inference of *intentionality*, so fundamental to the adaptive behavior of higher organisms, are conspicuous extensions of the 'metaphysical' causal reasoning in (9). Under the adaptive pressure of needing to predict the behavior of relevant entities, a bio-organism's first imperative is to understand. That is, to explain — by abductive reasoning — why entities behave the way they do. Agency is but an adaptive hypothesis:

(10)   **Agency as causal inference from motion under own power**:
- a.   **Inertia as norm**: Large classes of entities are mostly stationary.
- b.   **Motion under external cause**: Such entities seem to move only when other entities — external 'causes' — affect them.
- c.   **Motion without external cause**: But some entities seem to move without any visible external 'cause'.
- [d.   **Automorphic introspection**: What is more, I myself move when some internal 'urge' — called 'intention' — 'impels' me to do so.
- e.   **Inference of internal cause**: Those other entities must therefore move because of an *internal* 'cause', called 'intention'.
- [f.   **Reasoning by feature association**: Those other moving entities must have the same internal 'cause' called 'intention' as I do.

The abductive explanatory inference (10a–f) of intention, thus agency, is neither more nor less metaphysical than its antecedent external-cause explanation (9b). It is just a bit further along the complex, protracted endeavor of understanding, explanation and the accretion of knowledge. In the main, it merely extends Popper's *explanatory imperative* into an new adaptive domain. Most typically, such an extension is practiced by *purposefully moving organisms* who could benefit immensely from being able to predict the behavior of other moving organisms, who are adaptively crucial as either:

- sexually-or-socially cooperating conspecifics;
- hostile predators; or
- edible prey.

Most likely, the inference of 'intention' as internal causes is also propelled by *reasoning by feature association* (10d,f).

The 'metaphysical' category that arises out of (10), *intentionally-moving agent*, is as unimpeachable an explanatory abduction as can be found, in the sense that:

- It is highly predictive.
- It has strong feature associations between observable surface features and unobservable future behaviors. And
- It pertains to behaviors that are adaptively relevant, and can now be reliably predicted.

The abduction of the category 'intentionally-moving agent' thus abides by Popper's injunction for the scientist's decision never to abandon his search for laws. (1959: 248).

8.3.4.5. *Functional explanation*

> if a piece of wood is to be split with and axe, the axe must of necessity be hard; and, if hard, must of necessity be made of bronze or iron. Now exactly in the same way the body, which like the axe is an *instrument* — for both the body as a whole and its several parts individually have definite operations *for which they are made*; just in the same way, I say, the body if it is to do *its work*, must of necessity be of such and such character.
>
> (Aristotle, *De Partibus Animalium*,
> McKeon, ed., 1941: 650; italics added)

As noted earlier (ch. 1), functional explanations have been the *sine qua non* of scientific biology ever since Aristotle. In traditional philosophy of science, however, it has been frowned upon as an unseemly anthropomorphic manoeuver, an analogical heuristic at best: ascribing human intentionality to the behavior on non-human organisms! To wit (Hempel and Oppenheim 1948):

> One of the reasons for the perseverance of teleological considerations in biology probably lies in the fruitfulness of the teleological approach as a *heuristic device*: Biological research which was *psychologically motivated* by a teleological orientation, by an interest in purposes in nature, has frequently led to important results which can be stated in non-teleological terminology and which increase our scientific knowledge of causal connections between biological phenomena ... Another aspect that lends appeal to teleological considerations is their *anthropomorphic character*. A teleological explanation tends to make us feel that we really "understand" the phenomenon in question, because it is accounted for in terms of purpose, with which we are familiar from our own experience of purposive behavior. But it is important to distinguish between understanding in the *psychological* sense of a feeling of *empathic familiarity* from understanding in the theoretical, or cognitive, sense of exhibiting the phenomenon to be explained as a special case of some general regularity.   (Hempel and Oppenheim 1948: 17; italics added)

In a subsequent exercise of blatant know-nothingness, Hempel (1959) pays homage to the hallowed causal chains of physics, then notes this most quaint habit of behavioral scientists ('according to some, even in biology') to indulge in functional analysis:

> In the exact physical sciences, according to this view, all explanation is achieved ultimately by reference to causal or correlational antecedents; whereas in psychology and the social and historical disciplines — and, according to some, even in biology — the establishment of causal or correlational connections, while desirable and important, is not sufficient. Proper understanding of the phenomena studied in these fields is held to require other types of explanation. Perhaps the most important of the alternative methods that have been developed for this purpose is the method of *functional analysis*, which has found extensive use in biology, psychology, sociology and anthropology.   (1959: 121; italics added)

The condescension runs the gamut from 'anthropomorphic' to 'heuristic' to 'analogical' to 'impressionistic' to 'non-objective' to 'unproven' to 'mushy', depending on the time, place and discipline. Whole core disciplines founded upon 19th century Darwinian functionalism — Cultural Anthropology, Psychology, Linguistics — have become mired in silly non-sequitur argumentation, whereby anti-functionalist and anti-evolutionary predilections seem to go hand in hand; and where the argument is often an improbable amalgam of the positivist's *'prove it'* and the deductivist's *'derive it'*.

In my earlier foray into this topic (Givón 1989: ch. 8) I undertook to belabor the obvious, an enterprise that has become increasingly unrewarding. The grounds where this battle is being fought most actively at the moment is neither Anthropology, where the battle has essentially been lost, nor Linguistics, where a pal of smoke hangs over both warring camps, but rather Psychology, where a biology-minded, anthropologically-aware intellectual venture has been vigorously defining itself as 'Evolutionary Psychology' (Barkow *et al.* eds 1992; Whiten and Byrne eds 1997; *inter alia*). While the exact details may vary, and on occasion even rankle sympathetic evolutionists (see e.g. Gray *et al.* 2004), the foundational motivation of Evolutionary Psychology is unimpeachably Darwinian: What is good for the body is good for the soul. If the brain has evolved, so must have the mind, with all its attendant human-specific flowers — cognition, sociality, culture, language, art. And since the real heart of evolution, its *sine qua non*, remains adaptive selection, Aristotelian-Darwinian functionalism is the name of the game.

To close this topic, let me quote one of the more apt passages from the late S. J. Gould (1980), arguing against a recent minor spike of structuralism in evolutionary biology:

> the fascination generated by Dawkins'[7] theory arises from some bad habits of Western scientific thought — from attitudes (pardon the jargon) that we call *atomism*, *reductionism*, and *determinism*. The idea that wholes should be understood by decomposing into "basic" units; that properties of microscopic units can generate and explain the behavior of macroscopic results; that all events and objects have definite, predictable, determined causes. These ideas have been successful in our study of simple objects, made of few components, and uninfluenced by prior history.... But organisms are much more than amalgamations of genes. They have an [evolutionary] history that matters; their parts interact in complex ways. Organisms are built by genes acting in concert, influenced by environments, translated into parts that selection sees and parts invisible to selection. Molecules that determine the properties of water are poor analogues to genes and bodies. I may not be a master of my fate, but my intuition of wholeness probably reflects biological truth. (Gould 1980: 77–8; brackets added)

8.4. Multiple loci of pragmatic inference in the empirical cycle

> The game of science is, in principle, without end. He who decides one day that sci-
> entific statements do not call for any further tests, and that they can be regarded as
> finally verified, retires from the game.
>
> (K. Popper, *The Logic of Scientific
> Discovery*, 1959: 53)

While Peirce, and Hanson in his wake, single out the use of abductive inference during one particular phase of the empirical cycle, hypothesis formation, one might as
well note that pragmatic/abductive inference is resorted to at many other points
during on empirical investigation, where it is interspersed among various deductive and inductive phases of the inquiry. In (11) below, the Peirce-Hanson rendition
of the low-level cycle of empirical investigation is recapitulated schematically.

(11)   **The Peirce-Hanson scientific cycle recapitulated:**
   a.   **Fact-driven initial impetus ('the puzzle'):**
        "Strange facts F are incompatible with current theory T".
   b.   **Leaping to hypothesis ('the mystery'):**
        "Hypothesis H will account for ('explain') both the old fact compat-
        ible with T and the strange and incompatible facts F".
   c.   **Abductive inference ('gambler's leap to faith'):**
        "Therefore hypothesis H must be the case".
   d.   **Deductive consequences ('predictions'):**
        "Hypothesis H has the logical consequences C (C-i, C-ii, C-iii .... C-n)"
   e.   **Testability ('ways and means'):**
        "Given the present means, only a small sub-set of C are empirically
        testable".
   f.   **Relevance ('where to start'):**
        "Given that even the testable sub-set of C is still large, and given time
        and means limitations on inductive testing, the more central ('more
        relevant') logical consequences of H must be tested first".
   g.   **Inductive testing ('roll of the dice'):**
        "By experimental or other means, the conditions under which conse-
        quences C (beginning with C-i) should obtain are created, and the re-
        sults (presence or absence of C-i) are recorded.
   h.   **Inductive inference ('validity'):**
        "Since the results are often distributional rather than categorial, in-
        ferential statistics is employed to determine the degree of fit of the
        results to the predictions. A decision must be then made about the ac-
        ceptable level of error probability that they may be tolerated".
   i.   **Failure to falsify:** "If prediction C-i is the case, one has failed to falsify
        hypothesis H, and must now proceed to test consequences C-ii, C-iii
        etc. (back to (11g))".

    j.   **Falsification ('modus tollens'):**
       "If prediction C-i is not the case, hypothesis H is thereby falsified".
    k. **Reconsideration and modification ('back to square one'):**
       "The degree of damage to H by the falsification of C-i must now be
       determined: How central was C-i to H? Can H be modified to stand
       without C-i but still explain the initial puzzling facts F? (go back to
       (11b))".

In addition to the initial abductive leap to hypothesis (11a,b,c), pragmatic inferences of various sorts must intervene at a number of other points during the empirical cycle (11). To begin with, the determination of both the testability (11e) and
relevance (11f) is a matter of contextual-pragmatic judgement. Neither inductive
nor deductive reasoning could contribute much to such determinations.

Next, determining the tolerable error level in inferential statistics (11h) is a quintessential pragmatic judgement, whereby the level of risk-of-embarrassment one
is willing to tolerate is determined in a logically-arbitrary fashion. There is nothing
magical about 0.05 or 0.01 probability of a correlation being due to chance. It is a
matter of *psychological resilience*, of how much risk of betting on a losing horse one
is willing to tolerate.

Next, the decision about how many times one should try and fail to falsify a hypothesis, and how many of the hypothesis' testable logical consequences must be up-
held before one is satisfied and quits recycling (11i), is purely pragmatics. That is, as
Popper (1959) has rightly observed, the game is indeed — in principle — endless.[8]

Lastly, the reconsideration and modification phase (11k) is loaded with pragmatic judgements of multiple sorts: How central ('relevant') was the falsified prediction? How badly damaged is the hypothesis? Is retaining the hypothesis in a
modified form preferable to dumping it and starting from scratch?

8.5. The social pragmatics of science: Community as other minds

We come, lastly, to the question raised at the beginning of this chapter — what is the
analog in science to the mind of the interlocutor in social cooperation and communication? What exactly does "context as other minds" mean in science? The answer,
I believe, is fairly transparent. What is more, it is implicit in both Popper's and Hanson's formulations. All one needs to remember is that the extant Theory T does not
reside in some abstract epistemic space, but rather is subscribed to — ardently, as a
system of beliefs — by a substantial portion of an extant scientific *community*.

It is within such a context that one may talk about the 'sociology of science'. But
alas, the term is not always used with the purest motives. Consider, for example,
Kuhn's (1962) discussion of the community of scientists who subscribe to the same
theory — *paradigm* — during a period of 'normal science'. Kuhn is downright dis-
dainful of such a community, viewing it as conservative, small-minded and retro-

grade. He pooh-poohs the 'puzzles' that such a community elected to 'solve' as trivial and self-serving:

> one of the things a scientific community acquires with the paradigm is a criterion for choosing problems that, while the paradigm is taken for granted, can be assumed to have solutions. To a great extent these are the only problems this community will admit as scientific or encourage its members to undertake.   (1962: 37)

What ails Kuhn is, of course, an old complaint in social science, the ranting and raving against the alleged conservatism of the Popperian requirements — formulating explicit hypothesis, drawing their testable logical consequence, and abiding by some orderly methodological constraints and induction-dependent–however temporary — validation. In Kuhn's rendition, this boils down to:

> A paradigm can, for that matter, even insulate the community from those socially important problems that are not reducible to the puzzle form, because they cannot be stated in terms of the conceptual and instrumental tools that the paradigm supplies.   (*ibid.*)

What Kuhn pines for, in contrast, is the 'revolutionary science' of great discoveries, the grand cataclysms that overthrow the repressive paradigmatic shackles of 'normal science'. The impetus for such 'revolutionary science' are not lowly 'puzzles', but rather grand 'anomalies' — a logically arbitrary pragmatic judgement-call if there ever was one:

> Discovery commences with the awareness of anomaly, i.e. with the recognition that nature has somehow violated the paradigm-induced expectations that govern normal science.   (*ibid.*: 52–3).

Kuhn's histrionic version of science is as conspiratorial as it is over-dramatized, in equal measures egocentric and undignified.[9] But sociology need not lead to triviality, as is shown in the equally-social vision of Lakatos, whose rendition of the community of science — the *Research Programme* — is considerably broader than either Popper's or Kuhn's. In particular, Lakatos (1978) suggests that the requirements of logical consistency offered by Popper are often ignored in real scientific practice, where a community may make considerable progress holding on to its theoretical guns in the face of glaring internal contradictions. Rather than dump an old theory some of whose predictions have been falsified, the community continues to adhere to and embellish it:

> some of the most important research programmes in the history of science were grafted onto older programmes with which they were blatantly inconsistent. For instance, Copernican astronomy was 'grafted' on to Aristotelian physics, Bohr's programme on to Maxwell's. Such grafts are irrational for the justificationist and for the naive falsificationist, neither of whom can countenance growth on inconsistent foundations.   (1978: 56)

What Lakatos advocates, rather passionately, is deferring logical closure, ignoring falsification, and stretching the phase of competition between logically-incompatible theories. In this sense, Lakatos' vision of competing *communities* of science is profoundly Darwinian:

> The history of science has been and should be a history of competing research pro-
> grammes (or, if you wish, 'paradigms'), but it has not been and must not become
> a succession of periods of normal science: the sooner competition starts, the bet-
> ter for progress. 'Theoretical pluralism' is better than 'theoretical monism': on this
> point Popper and Feyerabend are right and Kuhn is wrong.   (*ibid*.: 69)

Given the schematic structure of the low-level empirical cycle (11), one could now point out that at every phase of the cycle, the scientist addresses, be it implicitly, the mind-cast of his/her *relevant community of scholars*. And that the scientist's expect-ations about that communal mind-cast — the mind of the relevant other — change from one phase of the cycle to the next. In this sense, the progression of scientific inquiry is reminiscent of the progression of natural discourse. And as there, the pre-vailing communal mind-cast, and the arguments raised against it, involve both epi-stemic and deontic mental states.

- **Hypothesis-formation (11a, b, c)**: At this phase of the investigation, the scientist addresses a community strongly disposed to believe in current Theory T, and to disbelieve the speculative, abduction-spawned Hypothesis H. The scientist, how-ever, banks on the dramatic impact on the communal mind of the puzzling Facts F (11a), and in particular on their manifest logical incompatibility with Theory T. The scientist also banks, presumably, on the vivid if tentative theoretical demon-stration that Hypothesis H can accommodate both the puzzling facts F and the range of facts traditionally accommodated by Theory T (11b).

As Lakatos (1978) notes, proponents of new hypotheses are not likely to sway many pre-set minds. Nonetheless, the arguments for Hypothesis H are clearly pitched in the context of the anticipated communal mind-cast. The proponent(s) of a new hy-pothesis may also tend to under-estimate the community's *deontic* commitment to the current Theory T. And this may account for the fact that in the early stages, ar-guments for a new hypothesis tend to be heated and emotionally loaded. What the proponents of Hypothesis H are up against is not only the pre-set epistemic habits of the community, but also its deontic commitment to the status quo.

Kuhn (1962) over-dramatizes to the point of caricature the difference between 'normal' and 'revolutionary' science, in suggesting that all non-revolutionary hy-potheses are trivial, and that the current 'paradigm' licenses them because they can do it no harm. More likely, there is no discrete categorial distinction between 'normal' and 'revolutionary ' hypotheses, but rather a continuum. New hypothe-ses may challenge lower, higher or higher-yet nodes in the hierarchic structure of the current theoretical edifice. And the *deontic resistance* the new hypothesis faces may be, rather naturally, directly proportionate to the hierarchic level at which it is pitched.

- **Deduced logical consequences (11d):** Here the proponents of *H* clearly presuppose — and then address — the community's commitment to deductive logic, and thus to theories free of internal contradiction. In this regard, while Russell's (1908) insistence on logical consistency may be an idealization, Lakatos (1978) dismissal of the need to worry about logical consistency is perhaps an exaggeration, hinting more at the community's *deontic recalcitrance* than *epistemic laxity*.

- **Testability and relevance (11e, f):** Here the proponents of new Hypothesis *H* are on notoriously tricky — contextual pragmatic — grounds. But their arguments are nonetheless pitched at some anticipated communal pragmatic norms. First, the norms concerning what can be tested given the currently available ways-and-means (11e). Second, the community's normative understanding of the hierarchic structure of current Theory *T*. And third, the community's normative, and most likely scalar, deontic commitment to the various tenets of current Theory *T* at its respective hierarchic levels.

- **Inductive testing (11g, h):** Here the proponents of new Hypothesis *H* operate in the context of the community's anticipated mind-cast, often deontic, about the importance of quantified correlational studies (11h), the expected level of sampling variability (and the community's tolerance thereof), and the community's tolerance of error probabilities in inferential statistics.

- **Failure to falsify (11i):** At this presumably-deductive phase of the investigation, the proponent of new Hypothesis *H* labor in the context of, first, the community's logical sophistication — how well does the community understand Popper's (1959) argument that one never verifies a theory, but only, tentatively, fails to falsify it? And second, tricky pragmatic grounds again — how many predictions of hypothesis *H* will the community insist on testing before enough is enough? And the answer to the latter most likely depends on the community's entrenched deontic commitment to current theory *T*.

- **Falsification (11k):** As noted earlier, falsification of a single prediction — especially at a relatively low level of the hierarchic theoretical edifice — is not necessarily the death knoll for a new hypothesis. But while Lakatos's (1978) position may be somewhat extreme, the burden certainly rests on the shoulders of the new hypothesis' proponents, who must argue, in the context of the community's presumed epistemic and deontic predilections, why the falsification is not yet fatal, and how hypothesis *H*, perhaps in a modified form, may yet be salvaged from early extinction.

One way or another, the practice of scientific inquiry is undertaken, at each phase of the empirical cycle, within the context of an anticipated communal mind-cast. The scientist, whether explicitly or implicitly, is always engaged in a dialog with one or more putative interlocutors in his/her relevant community of science. In this sense, Popper's 'endless game of science' is very much like the biological organism's unending quest for gradual incrementation of knowledge. Not any old organism, but rather, specifically, the social organism as it undertakes to learn from his/her conspecifics via social interaction and communication.

Notes

* I am indebted to my good friend Esa Itkonen for his critical reading of an earlier version of the manuscript. He is, naturally, absolved of any responsibility for the way I chose to interpret his remarks.

1. Popper's condescension to 'common-sense knowledge' is reminiscent of his fellow Viennese expatriate (and fellow reductionist) Carnap's condescension to pragmatics, that poor, messy step-sister of the worthier, clean, logical semantics (see ch. 1).

2. This is also an opportunity to fix up the rather sloppy treatment of philosophy of science in an earlier work (Givón 1979a: ch. 1).

3. In homage to the intellectual winds of the 1960s and Paul Goodman's charming if by-now-somewhat-faded utopianism.

4. As mature cognitive neuroscience makes it reasonably clear, neither one can proceed without the other at any given point of knowledge accretion. In other words, some species of Kantian-pragmatic dialectics must always be taken for granted. Individual organisms are never at a cognitive point zero (*tabula rasa*). Nor is, for that matter, the scientist, whose current theory and current facts are always there, at any given point.

5. Carnap thus argues as a pragmatist, conceding that what looks like an individual fact from a top-down perspective may look like a general theory from a bottom-up perspective. The history of science and the evolution of naturalistic knowledge are, of course, replete with erstwhile theories that, after repeated failure to falsify, became solid facts.

6. While Wittgenstein's major preoccupation here is *not* information theory but rather probability, the two are intimately connected, as is apparent from the immediate turn to semiotics: "Tautology and contradiction are the limiting cases — indeed the disintegration — of the combination of signs." (1918: 71) Wittgenstein never translates the logical context of tautology vs. contradiction to the information-theory context of *totally old* vs. *totally new* information, respectively. Nonetheless, his discussion implicitly pre-sages just that. Thus: "Contradiction is that common factor of propositions which *no* proposition has in common with another. Tautology is the common factor of all propositions that have nothing in common with one another ... Contradiction is the outer limit of propositions; tautology is the unsubstantial point at their center." (1918: 79)

7. Gould was reviewing Dawkins' (1976) *The Selfish Gene*, which short-changed the role of adaptive behavior in natural selection.

8. Biological organisms are, of course, faced with the very same pragmatic choice. However, for them the consequences of betting on the wrong horse are much more severe. The tried-and-true stable categories of mundane reality that survived the brutal test of natural selection have undergone millions of cycles of repeated failure-to-falsify tests. And the genetic lines of all the organisms who betted wrong are extinct.

9. An even more extreme version of the ranting-and-raving that passed, at a certain juncture, for 'sociology of science' may be seen in Feyerabend's *Against Method* (1975), a work that soon joined Kuhn, Foucault and Rohrty (and by an unfortunate co-option also the 'late' Wittgenstein) in licensing the 'post-modern' relativist revolt against the methodological constraints of anthropocentric, male-chauvinist, bourgeois science.

CHAPTER 9

The adaptive pragmatics of 'self'

9.1. Preamble*

> If now the form ['essence','definition'] of the living being is *the soul*, or part [aspect] of the soul, as would seem to be the case, seeing at any rate that when the soul departs, what is left is no longer an animal, and that none of the parts remain what they were before, excepting in mere configuration.
>
> > (Aristotle, *De Partibus Animalium*; in J. Barnes ed., 1984: 997; italics and brackets added)

This chapter, as well as the next, extends the pragmatic agenda somewhat beyond its traditional domain. What makes the topic worthy of inclusion is pragmatics' common thread — context. And, more specific to this book, context as the construed mind of the other.

Personality, or the self, can be viewed from a number of perspectives. To begin with, there are clear *genetic* parameters that make each of us unique, not only physically but also mentally. In conceding this — that some facets of one's personality must be genetically encoded and thus innate — one merely concedes what has been taken for granted throughout this book: that the mind, much like the body, is a product of adaptive evolution.

Another perspective on personality is that of *self-consciousness* or self-representation — the seat of consciousness, the once-and-future Holy Grail of cognitive neuroscience. A great number of serious scholars are busy trying to unpack, and perhaps some day even resolve, this mystery (see ch. 4). The fate of traditional dualism and its modern antithesis, physical or neural reductionism, hangs in the balance, as does the scientific account of life on earth.

Above the melee hovers Aristotle's enigmatic perspective, still beckoning, perhaps as the third — emergentist, dialectic — way. With the Philosopher, perhaps, one allows that yes, the *anima* is more than just the sum of the neural hardware where it is said to 'reside'. But still no, it cannot exist outside the body, nor does it, strictly speaking, inhabit the body as a 'resident'. Rather, it *emerges* from and in the body as the self-appointed agent of bio-teleology, claiming possession, taking over the management. But the *mechanism* that executes the self's teleology should be confused with neither the *teleology* itself nor its *agent*. To quote a wise woman:

> The cognitive view, to put it simply, maintains that between behavior and the brain there is a legitimate level of description: the *mind* . . . the cognitive approach attempts to explain behavior by a set of mental processes and mechanisms . . . that . . . can be mapped on to brain processes.   (Uta Frith 1991: 16–17)

An *x* that maps onto *y* cannot be identical to *y*, lest one be mired in tautology.

Lastly, there is the self as a *social construct*, beginning with the fact that a person is not a logical monolith impervious to contextual pressures, but rather a multi-faceted complex that is capable of revealing different faces in different adaptive contexts. At least in principle, one may argue — especially if some of those adaptive contexts are highly frequent and conventionalized — a single 'self' may not exist. Rather, each person harbors a multiplicity of 'selves' that reside under a single corporeal roof in some kind of domestic arrangement that is neither wholly harmonious nor hopelessly unwieldy, but is rather, for the bulk of the tasks at hand, a workable *adaptive compromise*.

Under this framework, if the multiple 'self' is conscious of itself, this is accomplished by internalizing — presumably through *social feedback* — the various context-induced public selves it presents to others; or at least the more frequent and conventionalized ones. Such a complex 'self' may well be conscious of only one of its multiples at any given time — the one relevant in the current context, given the notorious parsimony of conscious attention.

9.2. The essentialist self

In an article published some four years ago one of my favorite science writers, Malcolm Gladwell, reviewed a popular — indeed ubiquitous and seemingly indestructible — theory of personality, henceforth referred to as the *essentialist* theory of the self. In his review, Gladwell (2000) reported that in the face of considerable evidence to the contrary, people tend to make, in the first few seconds of encountering a stranger, snap holistic judgements about that person's 'essence' — what they are *really* like. Such judgements are made, most commonly, after exposure to a single, restricted context, one in which the stranger reveals only a limited range of his/her rich behavioral repertoire. Faced with such restricted information, people undertake to predict the stranger's behavior in multiple, hitherto-unobserved contexts.

The limited context on which Gladwell's article focuses is that of job interviews. And the empirical research he reports appears to suggest that, first, essentialist snap judgements are ubiquitous (Ambady *et al.* 2002). And second, that in the majority of cases such judgements turn out to be woefully unpredictive of a person's behavior in a wider range of other contexts.

In reporting on empirical research by N. Ambady, Gladwell observes:

> The observers, presented with a ten-second silent video clip, had no difficulty rating the teachers on a fifteen-item checklist of personality traits. In fact, when Ambady cut the clip back to five seconds, the ratings were the same. They were even the same when she showed her raters just two seconds of videotape.   (Gladwell 2002: 70)

> Ambady's next step led to an even more remarkable conclusion. She compared those snap judgements of teacher effectiveness with evaluations made after a full semester of classes, by students of the same teachers. The correlations between the two, she found, were astoundingly high.   (*ibid.*)

The culprit, according to Gladwell's learned sources, turns out to be, *mutatis mutandis*, irrationality. This time around, irrationality comes under a forbidding label supplied by social psychologists — the *Fundamental Attribution Error*, an apparent close kin to Tversky and Kahneman's (1974) equally irrational 'heuristics and biases'. To wit:

> Bernieri and Ambady believe that the power of first impressions suggests that human being have a particular kind of *prerational* ability for making searching judgements about others . . . Thinking only gets in the way. "The brain structures that are involved are very *primitive*" Ambady speculates. All of these *affective* reactions are probably governed by the lower brain structures.   (*ibid.*: 71; italics added)

The giveaway line in Gladwell's report, the one that locates the presumed 'irrationality' of our essentialist theory of the self within a wider — evolutionary — perspective, runs as follows:

> That most basic of human rituals — the *conversation with a stranger* — turns out to be a minefield.   (*ibid.*: 84)

But of course, our innate heuristics and biases, not only those that involve 'primitive' 'affective' domains but also those that pertain to the most sophisticated higher-end cognitive strategies, did not evolve in a society where conversation with strangers was the most basic human ritual. Rather, they evolved, over 6 million years of separate hominid-line evolution, in the exclusive confines of *the society of intimates*, where all communication and cooperation took place among members of the intimate, small, kin-related group, and where interaction with strangers was overwhelmingly hostile and took place only at the group's territorial boundary of (see 9.5.2. below, as well as ch. 2 above and Givón and Young 2002). In that society, the exclusive social venue of hominids till the advent of agriculture and sedentary habitation ca. 8,000 BC, one communicated *only* with people one knew intimately and exhaustively, people about whom one could use, reliably, the tried-and-true calculus of *reasoning by feature association*: If you know one trait of the person — their identity and kin-relation to you — the rest of their traits, in particular their behavior toward you in most relevant social contexts, were highly predictable.

Until the relatively recent — and gradual — dissolution of the society of intimates, an essentialist theory of self was highly predictive, and adaptive. There was nothing irrational or primitive about it.

9.3. The multiple self

9.3.1. Henrik Ibsen and Erving Goffman

Near the end of Henrik Ibsen's monumental poetic play, *Peer Gynt*, the eponymous hero, at the end of an audacious life, not to mention at the end of his frayed moral tether, is stumbling, lost and deflated, through a dark forest. At a clearing, holding up an onion in his hand, Peer Gynt proceeds to deliver a monologue that sums up, in the most graphic terms, the *contextual theory of the multiple self* (Ibsen 1867): [1]

> You are no emperor, but an onion!
> So now, my good Peer, I shall peel you away,
> neither tears nor entreaties will my verdict sway.
>   [He takes an onion and strips it skin by skin]
> There goes the battered, dry outer peel —
> the shipwrecked seaman on a lifeboat's keel.
> This one, the wanderer — scrawny and thin
> still bearing the scent of the old Peer Gynt.
> Next, underneath, comes the gold-mining clown —
> the juice, if there ever was any, is gone.
> Now this rough-skinned fellow has known better days —
> he's the fur-trapping hunter of Hudson Bay's.
> The next wears a crown — oh perish the thought!
> Out, Prince of Trolls! Nought come to nought!
> Next the archaeologist, short but still potent.
> Next, juicy and plump, the all-knowing prophet —
> ripe and mellifluous, reeking of lies,
> would bring bitter tears to an honest man's eyes.
> Now this, curled and soft, is the loose man of leisure,
> living his life of unbridled pleasure.
> The next looks unhealthy, streaked with black —
> Cleric or Slaver? Take your niggers back!
>   [He peels off several layers at once]
> What an incredible number of peels!
> Will one ever get to the heart of the deal?
>   [He pulls the whole anion apart]
> Damn it, we won't! For, right down to the core,
> there's nothing but layers and layers and more.   (1867: 191)

An apocryphal tradition attributes to the late Erving Goffman the following observation, one that sums up perhaps most succinctly the contextual theory of the multiple self:

> A personality is but the sum total of all the
> public faces a person presents over a lifetime.

As far as I have been able to ascertain, this *bon mot* is not to be found, leastwise verbatim, in Goffman's most likely source, *The Presentation of Self in Everyday Life* (1959). Nonetheless, the entire book is predicated on the proposition that a person's social communication with his/her conspecifics, most conspicuously with strangers, is nothing but an elaborate stage performance; and that people as a matter of course tailor their self-presentation to fit the — perceived, construed — current social context ('setting'). In other words, to fit what they perceive as their audience's expectations.

A telling quotation from Park (1950) frames Goffman's dark vision of life and social communication as a stage, and thus his implicit contextual theory of the multiple self:

> It is probably no mere historical accident that the word *person*, in its first meaning, is a mask. It is rather a recognition of the fact that everyone is always and everywhere, more or less consciously, playing a role ... It is in these roles that we know each other; it is in these roles that we know ourselves.   (1959: 19; italics added)[2]

Within this framework, Goffman views all public self-presentations as *essentialist simulations* in which the presenter conspires, whether consciously or subconsciously, with his/her gullible and equally-essentialist audience. It is indeed our ingrained, naive, essentialist folk-theory of the self that makes the performance so natural and convincing to both performer and audience. They *both* want to believe:

> First, individuals often foster the impression that the routine they are presently performing is their *only* routine or at least their *most essential* one. As previously suggested, the audience, in their turn, often assumes that the character projected before them is *all there is* to the individual.   (*ibid.*: 48; italics added)

Goffman's vision of social life as a succession of 'settings' in which context-determined 'selves' are 'presented'; and of the 'self' as an epiphenomenal composite of one's multiple, contextually-tailored performances, is highlighted by a citation from none but William James:

> we may practically say that he has many different social selves as there are distinct *groups* of persons about whose opinion he cares. He generally shows a different side of himself to each of these different groups.   (*ibid.*).[3]

Always the sly, reluctant theorist, Goffman comes closest to an explicit contextual theory of the self in his closing notes:

> In this report, the individual was divided by implication into two parts: he was viewed as a *performer*, a harried fabricator of impressions involved in the all-too-human task of staging a performance; he was viewed as a *character*, a figure, typically a fine one, whose spirit, strength and other sterling qualities the performance was designed to invoke. The attributes of the performer and the attributes of the character are of a different order, quite basically so, yet both sets have their meaning in terms of the show that must go on.
>
> First, character. In our society the character one performs and one's self are

> somewhat equated, and this self-as-character is usually seen as something housed within the body of its possessor, especially in the upper parts thereof, being a nodule, somehow, in the biopsychology of personality. I suggest that [essentialist] view is an implied part of what we are all trying to present, but provides, just because of this, a bad analysis of the presentation. The performed self was seen as some kind of an image, usually credible, which the individual; on stage and in character effectively attempts to induce others to hold in regard to him. While this image is entertained *concerning* the individual, so that a self is imputed to it, this self itself does not derive from its possessor, but from the whole scene of his action. The scene, in turn, has the attributes of local events that are then interpreted by witnesses. A correctly staged and performed scene leads the audience to impute a self to a performed character, but this imputation — this self — is a *product* of a scene that comes off, and is not the *cause* of it. The self, then, as a performed character, is not an organic thing that has a specific location, whose fundamental fate is to be born, mature, and to die; it is a dramatic effect arising diffusely from a scene [context] that is presented, and the characteristic issue, the crucial concern, is whether it will be credited or discredited.   (*ibid.*: 252–3; brackets added).

Having dispensed with the stage-constructed *presented self* as but a contextually simulated *front* for a cannily-scripted character, and having described the performer as a wily context-adjusting simulator, Goffman leaves us perplexed: Who *is* that cunning simulator him/herself, really? Since s/he is such a keen, conniving, successful dissembler, what hidden 'self' governs — as string-puller — such a superb super-agent? Who is the whip-cracking circus master? The homunculus? Does s/he have any inherent, stable *essential* attributes that enable him/her to be so successful, and in particular to be so aptly selective in zooming in on the right context? How does s/he, in a flash of inspired construal, tailor the right context-fitting essentialist-and-real-looking character so expertly that the — admittedly gullible and cooperative — audience is suckered into deeming the performance credible? Who is the *resident agent* in charge of such a commanding performance, this bravura, this *tour de force*?

On this issue, Goffman is surprisingly reticent; though at first he appears to concede the presence of a real-sounding — cognizing, goal-directed — agent behind the mask:

> Let us turn now from the individual as *character* performed to the individual as *performer*. He has a capacity to learn, this being exercised in the task of training for a part. He is given to having fantasies and dreams, some that pleasurably unfold a triumphant performance, others full of anxiety and dread that nervously deal with public discreditings in a public front region. He often manifests a gregarious desire for teammates and audiences, a tacit considerateness for their concerns; and he has a capacity for deeply felt shame, leading him to minimize the chances he takes of exposure.   (*ibid.*: 253)

But does that self have any stable inherent attributes *apart from* those directly required for putting on a good show? On this, alas, Goffman fizzles out in a lame empiricist hedge:

these attributes of the individual *qua* performer are not merely a depicted effect of particular performances; they are psychobiological in nature, and yet they seem to arise out of intimate interaction with the contingencies of stage performance.   (*ibid.*, 253–4)

'Psychobiological in nature' surely entails essential, indeed *innate*, personal attributes. But 'arise out of the intimate interaction', however attractively emergentist it may sound, leaves us in limbo. The only innate attributes of the 'self', so it seems, are those directly involved in his/her behavior *qua* performer — his/her ability to learn, plan, agonize over and put on a rousing good show.

9.3.2. Faust, Freud and the multiple self

The multiple-self theory of personality has been, under one guise or another, a well-known construct in and of social psychology. In his introductory essay to an edited volume on the subject, Jon Elster (1985) catalogues the variegated phenomenology that may be subsumed under the multiple self:

- **The loosely-integrated self**: A person may be viewed through the analogy of a firm whose sub-units may have achieved a considerable measure of independence, and where a centripetal overall direction is countered by equally vigorous centrifugal forces, such as striving for independence, creative initiative, and cravings for control, credit and reward.
- **Holding contradictory beliefs**: A person may hold contradictory beliefs, but they are activated in mutually-exclusive contexts. The seeming logical conflict between those contradictory belief (or contradictory goals) may thus never grate; and the logically-incompatible versions of reality (or goal structure) may not impinge on each other — as long as they are not activated simultaneously under the same beam of conscious attention.[4]
- **Self deception**: Two parts of a person are so well segregated from each other that one may endeavor to hide knowledge from, or even actively deceive, the other.[5]
- **Weakness of will**: A deontic split whereby one part of the person, labeled "the will", holds some goals, but another part holds contradictory goals. The latter is strong enough to override the "weak will" and thus prevail.
- **Faustian parallel selves**: Here Elster cites Faust's celebrated soliloquy 'Two souls, alas, dwell in my breast' as a model of a person torn between conflicting, logically incompatible, "personalities". Opting for one, it appears, would always have the sad consequences of relinquishing the other. In Faust's case, the split is the traditional Christian-Cartesian one between the elevated, God-given, soaring eternal soul and the base, indulgent, sinning, temptation-prone, perishable animal body (Goethe, *Faust*, W. Kaufmann, tr.):[6]

> Two souls, alas, dwell in my breast,
> One striving to forsake the other.
> The one hanging, in life's full lust

> Onto the world, claws clinging fast.
> The other rising with righteous zest
> Rarified heavenly spheres to quest.   (*ibid*.: 145)

- **Freudian-Hierarchic selves**: The 'person' is arrayed in conflicting levels, with a lowly *id* full of immediate, local urges and craves, and a higher, strategic *ego* in charge of future planning, goal management, conflict resolution and rational control.
- **Successive selves**: Changes in personality — both deontic and epistemic — may occur over time, so that "the same person" may indeed subsume a succession of mutually-incompatible 'selves'.
- **Public ('social') vs. private ('selfish') selves**: The private, selfish, hedonistic *homo economicus* vs. the social, moral, normative *homo sociologicus*.

However real the reported phenomena may be, the various versions recounted by Elster and his associates are transparent metaphoric exercises in folk epistemology or folk taxonomy of the mind in conflict. Only a few of the papers in the volume (most conspicuously Quattrone and Tversky 1985) report empirical results. And the psychologist's, economist's or philosopher's abiding bias is seldom far from the surface. So that in each case, the contrast between a more desirable vs. less desirable personage is fairly transparent. These biases may be summed as follows:

(1)   **Implicit valuation of components of the multiple self**

Category	Desirable	Undesirable
Hierarchic:	higher	lower
Agentive:	controller	controlled
Strategic:	ego	id
Quantitative:	single	multiple
Moral:	spiritual/God	carnal/nature
Social:	altruistic	selfish
Perspective:	complete	partial
Temporal:	current	prior
Cognitive:	rational	irrational

What comes out of these comparisons is somewhat unsettling: The most learned exponents of the multiple-self theory are in fact strongly biased towards the undivided, integrated *essentialist* self.

9.4. The impaired self

In the preceding section, somewhat to our shock, we discovered that the exponents of the contextual theory of the multiple self — be they Goffman in his theoretical reticence or the social psychologists with their implicit ameliorist agenda — are, whether consciously or not, *crypto essentialists*, with barely submerged predilections for one facet of the multiple self over the other. Two spirits, it seems, dwell within their breast, but the twain shall never part — the one an ur-Platonic invariant essentialist, the other an ur-Aristotelian context-adjusting empiricist.

In this section I will survey some of the facts culled from studies of two well-known personality disorders. In each case, I will suggest, one of the twin aspects of the self — the context-adjusting multiple or the invariant essence — has taken sway to the relative exclusion of the other.

9.4.1. Schizophrenia: The unconstrained multiple

As the discerning reader may have by now surmised, I have been gravitating, however slowly and tentatively, towards a complex middle-ground view of the self. In this framework, a central, controlling — essentialist — circus master selects, marshals and presents the various *dramatis personae* in the appropriate social contexts, given his/her construal of his/her audience expectations; that is, given his/her construal of the relevant epistemic and deontic mind-sets of the interlocutor.

About the same time Malcolm Gladwell's article appeared, Paul Lysaker, a clinical psychiatrist, in a forum sponsored by the Institute for Cognitive and Decision Sciences, University of Oregon, presented an analysis of the cognitive and communicative behavior of schizophrenics (Lysaker 2000; see also Lysaker *et al.* 1995a, b; Lysaker and Lysaker 2000; Bell and Lysaker 1995). The symptomatic cutoff line between schizophrenia and 'mere' severe depression, the most predictive diagnostics, turned out to be a disruption in 'dialogue quality'. On the truly-schizophrenic side of the scale, one finds only minimal monologue, cacophony, complex monologue or serial monologue. With the common denominator being, inevitably, *contextually inappropriate self-presentation*. Whether socially or communicatively, the schizophrenic appears to be endowed with a frail or altogether missing central controller. The ubiquitous circus master, the one even Goffman in his empiricist reticence couldn't quite deny, is not presenting the right cast members in their appropriate settings.

A more recent study (Klein 2003) probed the neuro-cognition of patients exhibiting the so-called 'borderline personality disorder' (BPD), a less-severe disorder akin to schizophrenia, in which the clinical symptoms include "unstable emotions, difficulty maintaining relationships and a high probability of self-inflicted damage" (Klein 2003: 190). In his study, Kline suggests that the source of disruption in BPD patients may be traced to part of the executive-attention control system, specifically to the sub-module responsible for cognitive *conflict resolution*. The very same conclusion was reached by Posner *et al.* (2002, 2003). The most specific impairment exhibited by BPD patients tends to be related to the part of the attentional network system that regulates conflict resolution:

> This shows an abnormality in the ability of the patients to exert control of their conflicting cognition and emotions (Bush, Luu & Posner 2000).   (Klein 2003: 1098).

The most specific neurological locus of the attentional-network impairment in BPD is the *anterior cingulate cortex*. Impairments comparable to those of BPD patients were also observed in stroke patients with lesions in the same brain area (Damassio 1994). And the very same sub-module of the attentional network, the *anterior cingulate cortex* responsible for executive control, has been more recently implicated in schizophrenia (Wang *et al.* 2004, ms).

The anterior cingulate cortex is part of the distributive, multi-module network of the *executive-attention* control system. Within this network (also including several sub-cortical regions), the *anterior cingulate cortex* is charged with evaluating competing alternatives — cognitive inputs or affective urges — and limiting attentional activation to a single competitor, presumably the one that is contextually more relevant (epistemic) or preferable (deontic).

In a recent review, Schneider and Chein (2003) identify five major sub-modules in the distributive network of executive attention, out of which the most germane to the disruption in BPD and schizophrenia are the three cortical sub-modules:

- **The Goal Processor**, located in the *dorso-lateral pre-frontal cortex* (DLPFC), the presumed locus of goal preferences, and closely linked to executive attention-control (Roberts, Robbins and Weiskrantz 1998).
- **The Attention Control** processor, located in the *posterior parietal cortex* (PPC), the presumed mechanism of selective shifting of attention. This mechanism activates most specifically under conditions of rapid shifts of attention due to competing inputs (Corbetta *et al.* 2002; LaBar *et al.* 1999).
- **The Activity Monitor**, located in the *anterior cingulate cortex* (ACC) and perhaps the most central mediating component of the executive attention circuit. The ACC evaluates competing alternatives stored in the PPC-based Attentional Control system, (presumably with some top-down input from the dorso-lateral pre-frontal cortex-based Goal Processor (DLPFC)). The ACC-based processor thus helps direct conscious attention to the contextually-appropriate input, and is also involved in overriding inappropriate automatic responses. It also responds to errors, as well as to high-level conflicts between task demands and habitual (automated) responses (Carter *et al.* 1998; MacDonald *et al.* 2000; van Veen *et al.* 2001; Kerns *et al.* 2004).

The rough brain location of these five sub-modules may be seen in (2).

(2) **Distributive network of executive attention system** (from Schneider and
Chein 2003)

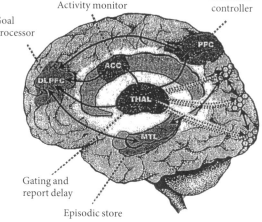

Tentatively, then, one may suggest that both the extreme case of schizophrenia and
the milder case of BPD are due to a disruption of the central, controlling, *essentialist*
component of the self. Competing alternatives — alternative presentations — may
indeed be represented elsewhere in the system (longer term in the *hippocampus*;
shorter term in the *posterior parietal cortex*). But the central mechanism that evaluates and adjudicates amongst them is disrupted, so that the multiples now interject
themselves at inappropriate times and into inappropriate — centrally unvetted and
uncontrolled — contexts.

9.4.2. Autism: The unyielding essence

It has become somewhat fashionable in recent years to interpret autism, and within
is the high-end Asperger Syndrom (Frith ed. 1991; Volkmar *et al.* 1996), as a disruption of a so-called 'Theories of Mind' module (Baron-Cohen 1989, 1990; Baron-Cohen *et al.* 1985; Frith 1989a, b, 1991; Leslie 1987; Leslie and Frith 1988; *inter alia*).
That is, of the ability to represent or frame mental states, first of oneself but especially of others. While this is certainly a striking feature of autism and Asperger,
there are several prominent, and equally consistent, feature of autism-Asperger that
have relatively little to do with social interaction, communication or mind-framing.
Taken together, the latter all point toward a more general disruption, one that may
subsume the mind-framing symptoms as one of its direct consequences.

  In order to put this point across, one may divide the most commonly-listed behavioral symptoms associated with autism-Asperger into two main groups: those
that clearly implicate mind-framing ((3) below); and those that clearly don't ((4)
below).[7] The two lists below are culled from Frith's (1991) admirable state-of-the-

art review. The items in list (3) are related, in one way or another, to mind-framing, either of one's own mind (2nd order) or of the minds of others (3rd order). They thus require no further discussion:

(3)   **Mind-framing impairments (2nd or 3rd order)**
      Gazing and shared attention
      Social interaction
      Social norms
      Empathy
      Sensitivity to others
      Language/communication
      Odd speech patterns/intonation/gestures(?)
      Use of personal pronouns
      Pretend play
      'Theories of mind' (perception, knowledge, belief)

More germane to the discussion here are commonly-observed behavioral features of autism-Asperger that seem to have nothing to do with social interaction or communication (3rd order framing), nor with framing of one's own mind (2nd order framing). Rather, they all involve, in one way or another, interaction with 'external', 'objective' input (1st order framing):

(4)   **Seemingly not mind-related impairments (1st order)**
      Inability to disengage attention
      Perceptual hyper- or hypo-sensitivity
      Compulsive fixation on physical objects
      Compulsive repetitive motion/gesture
      Fanatical pursuit of 'strange' interests
      Rigidity, rule-boundedness, pedantry
      Intolerance to change of routine
      No concept of non-literal meaning
      Problems with ambiguous/multiple meanings
      Inability to integrate details into overview framework

These features have one striking common denominator — the general inability to reframe; a pragmatic rigidity; inability to shift perspective; a predilection for staying within a single, fixed context; therefore the inability to adjust behavioral responses to vagaries of ever-shifting context. In sum, a fixed, invariant, unyielding 'self'.

In her review, Firth (1991) comes tantalizingly close to recognizing this *meta-pragmatic* ontology of autism, citing first symptomatic similarities to the so-called "semantic-pragmatic disorder"; but even closer by implicating Sperber and Wilson's (1986) 'relevance'. However, "relevance" by itself is not an explanation. For our ability to construe relevance is, in turn, dependent on our more general ability to construe the *relevant context*, to *shift perspective*, to *re-frame*. Such a capacity is prerequisite to all cognitive framing operations, be they 1st, 2nd or 3rd order. Which brings us back, rather naturally, to the human attentional system.

Earlier attempts to localize the impaired neurological module in autism implicated general frontal-lobe regions in a way that partially overlapped with schizophrenia (Frith 1991). More recent studies present a rather different picture. In their overview survey of three attentional networks, Posner and Fan (2004 ms) distinguish between three separate but partially-overlapping *attentional networks*, distinct both functionally-behaviorally and anatomically (see also Duncan and Owen 2000):

(5) **Major attentional networks** (after Posner and Fan 2004)

    Function/behavior   **Chief neurological locus**

    (a) Orienting/fixate   Posterior/dorsal parietal cortex (PPC)
                      (and other area)

    (b) Executive control   Anterior cingulate cortex (ACC)
                      Dorso-lateral pre-frontal cortex (DLPFC)
                      (and other areas)

    (c) Alert   Locus coruleus, right frontal cortex, parietal
                      cortex

Earlier above, we noted that the disruption in BDP and schizophrenia traces back, primarily, to network (5b), implicating most particularly the *anterior cingulate cortex* module of the executive attention system, in its capacity of selector between conflicting inputs. Schizophrenics, it seems, do not select according to contextual propriety ('relevance'). But it is network (5a), centered on the *posterior/dorsal parietal cortex*, the one involved in the orientation-fixation-disengagement of attention, that seems to be implicated in autism-Asperger. In this connection, Landry and Bryson (2004 ms) compared visual-attentional fixation and disengagement in normal, down-syndrom and autistic children, noting that (see also Bryson *et al.* 1996):

> children with autism had marked difficulty disengaging from one or two competing stimuli. Evidence is also provided for a more subtle problem in executing rapid shifts of attention to a stimulus in either side of space.   (Landry and Bryson 2004: 14 of ms)

And further:

> in autism difficulties disengaging a shifting attention are consistent with claims that attention is overly focused and charcterized by narrow "beam" or "spotlight" (Bryson *et al.* 1990; Rincover and Ducharme 1987).   (*ibid.*: 17 of ms)

Landry and Bryson (2004 ms) conclude that the neurological capacity implicated in autism-Asperger is, more likely, a *general attentional mechanism* rather than a domain specific social-communicative function such as 'theories of mind':

> Our finding implicates a general rather than a domain-specific (i.e., uniquely social) processes.   (*ibid.*)

On the face of it, the cognitive capacity at the root of autism-Asperger impairments seems to be the exact converse of the one implicated in schizophrenia: The central, essentialist, controlling 'self' seems to be overly strong, invariant, rigid and unselective; it pays scant attention to adaptively-relevant contextual variation, but rather maintains a rigid perspective; so much so that one is tempted to implicate the Selector module itself, Schneider and Chein's (2003) Activity Monitor component of executive attention, the *anterior cingulate cortex* (network (5b)). That is, in schizophrenia the executive appears to be too weak; in autism, too strong.

In fact, however, the culprit in autism-Asperger is more likely to be the executive selector's close collaborator within the executive attention network — the fixator-diengager-orientor — the *pragmatic zoom lens* located in the *posterior/dorsal parietal cortex* (network (5a)). Autistic-Asperger people appear to operate from a fixed, rigid perspective, and have a great difficulty adjusting their perspective to fit the vagaries of the rapidly-shifting context. Put another way, they have difficulty in contextual construal, or re-framing.

It is now clear why the social-communicative difficulties in autism-Asperger are so striking: In order to frame one's mind (2nd order), one needs to first *disengage* the perspective settings (attention) from their more stable framing of the external world (1st order). And going on to frame other minds (3rd order) is another order-of-magnitude jump in framing complexity. As noted elsewhere above (chs. 4, 5, 6, 7), human communication at its present evolutionary stage is founded upon rapid perspective shifting vis-à-vis the construed mental states of the interlocutor. A general impairment in shifting attention — i.e. perspective — would have profound ramifications for such a system.

As several studies have noted (Posner and Fan 2004; Duncan and Owen 2000), the two attentional networks in question partially overlap. Most conspicuously, in the *posterior parietal system*, central to the orienting–fixating–disengaging network (5a), also partakes, as an input buffer, in the executive-attention control network (5b) (Schneider and Chein 2003).

9.5. The complex self as an adaptive strategy

9.5.1. Evolutionary incrementation in framing complexity

As noted earlier (ch. 2), the cognitive adaptations that culminated in our central nervous system presupposed, from the very start, some capacity for contextual adjustments and cognitive re-framing. Neither the gradual evolution of biologically-based mental categories, nor contextually-flexible on-line responses to variable and oft-novel external input (1st order framing), nor individual life-time learning, could proceed without such a *pragmatic framing* capacity; that is, the ability to tell figure from ground, the relevant from the less-relevant, the urgent from the less-urgent, or the preferable from the undesirable. At whatever level of their evolutionary tree, bio-organisms could never be 100% automata. By definition.

A gradual increase in self-direction and behavioral control sooner or later requires, or at the very least greatly benefits from, the rise of 2nd order framing — the ability to take account of, and eventually modulate and control, one's own *internal* — eventually mental — states of knowledge and intention. As suggested earlier above (ch. 4), the 'sense of the self' may be phylogenetically old, and may have evolved gradually. All indications are that it must predate sociality and communication, given that it carries a clear adaptive payload and requires no social feedback.

The advent of social cooperation and communication must have upped the adaptive antes considerably. The ability to re-frame one's mind (2nd order) could now be recruited, perhaps with the help of the ubiquitous mechanism of reasoning by feature association (Meltzoff 2002), to create 3rd-order mental representations, those of the mind of the other. This new species of mental representation may, in turn, engender profound *feedback effects* on one's older — 2nd-order — self-representation. This is so because the mind of the other also harbors, among its epistemic and deontic states, adaptively-relevant representations of one's own mind — the interlocutor's 3rd-order representations. And so, to the extent that one is cognizant of other minds (3rd-order framing), one sooner or later also becomes enmeshed — for perfectly valid adaptive reasons — in a much more complex *4th-order* self-representation.

Last but not least, adjusting one's behavior to the ebb and flow of the social context almost invariably militates for tailoring one's public self-presentation in ways that, up to a point, are reminiscent of Goffman's stark vision of behavior in public.

9.5.2. Between intimates and strangers

It is striking as well as highly relevant that both Goffman and the social scientists, in their investigation of the multiple self, concern themselves primarily with *public* social behavior *among strangers*. But as noted earlier (ch. 2), during their protracted evolutionary history — 6 million years of a separate hominid line — human societies have been, invariably, *societies of intimates*. Such societies are characterized by small group size, kin-based structure, daily face-to-face contact, low socioeconomic differentiation, consensual non-hierarchic polity, great territorial stability and geographic isolation, slow cultural change, high informational stability and homogeneity — and thus a *high rate of shared knowledge*, both cultural-generic and episodic-specific. One of the strongest features of these hunter-and-gatherer societies is that one almost *never communicates with strangers*, but only with intimates. And those intimates are well known to each other over a lifetime of mutual observation and social traffic in multiple contexts. What is more, the inventory of social contexts in such a society is restricted, highly conventionalized, and well-known to all members.

However valid Goffman's vision may be — of life as a perpetual stage — for the current *society of strangers*, it is clearly an inappropriate model of public interaction in the society of intimates, where all members know each others' repertoire of 'public presentations' inside out; and where they have all had ample opportunity to run the calculus of strong feature association exhaustively, and to winnow out the chaff of two-faced false pretense from the essentialist wheat. In a small village society, including small-town USA, you can't hide who you *really* are. Everybody knows.[8]

Our innate predilection for self-concept have been set, primarily, overwhelmingly, during the long evolutionary tenure of the society of intimates. An *essentialist* theory of the self, with its calculus of *strong feature association* and thus *high behavioral predictability* in multiple conventionalized contexts, is the adaptive hallmark of such a society. Especially that it is reinforced by the highly adaptive and evolutionarily prior, entrenched *prototype-like mental categories*.

9.5.3. Other minds and the ontology of 'self'

The evolution of our self-concept seems to recapitulate, to some extent, the evolution of mental categories. The complex mental construct that appears to have emerged — an untidy melange of 1st-, 2nd- and 4th-order representations — is reminiscent of the Kantian compromise in epistemology, and of prototype-like categories in cognition. It displays features of both extreme theories of self — the invariant Platonic essentialist and the contextually-adjustable, publicly-performed multiple. Not only that, but the attendant neurology support *both* extremes, accommodating the multiplicity of conflicting urges and representations (in the *posterior parietal cortex*) and the controlling circus master (in the *anterior cingulate cortex*). Once again, evolution appears to have conspired to frustrate the predilections of simple-minded reductionists, having created a classical complex, hybrid — muddled and impure but still eminently serviceable — adaptive compromise. That our representation of the mind of the other (3rd order) rebounds and eventually transforms our own self-representation (2nd order) into a 4th-order construct is but an adaptive consequence of being a social, cooperative, communicating species.

As suggestive as Goffman's vision may be, it is in a way upside down. The interesting thing about context-tailored public presentation of the self's multiple facets is not how we deceive strangers with our cleverly-fabricated false *personae* (true as this may be on occasion), but rather how our 4th-order self-framing owes much to the feedback we receive from repeated, long-term interactions with *intimates*. That we see ourselves in part the way *they* see us is one consequence of our having developed the capacity to represent *their* mind; and conversely, to take advantage in our self-representation of their capacity to represent *our* mind.

9.5.4. Internalized other minds as a social-restraint mechanism

It may appear, following the discussion directly above, that our capacity for socially-sensitive self-representation (4th-order framing), that is, for incorporating into our self-representation at least some facets of how we presume others see us, is just another quirky spandrel, an unintended fringe benefit of our clearly-adaptive capacity to represent other minds (3rd-order framing). Before such a conclusion is adopted by acclamation, however, it may be worth noting that our capacity for 4th-order self-framing may itself have considerable adaptive benefits: It may have provided us with an entrenched bio-cognitive mechanism for *social restraint*.

Denizens of the old society of intimates have always been highly sensitive to perceived social feedback from conspecifics during face-to-face interaction. So much so that they have apparently made such feedback a lasting feature of their neuro-cognitive design, internalizing and incorporating it into their own self-representation. Goffman's multi-faceted publicly-performed 'self' may thus be not the smoke-and-mirrors production of a devious anti-social schemer, but rather an integral part of an evolved mechanism for enhancing sociality and cooperation.

Notes

* I am indebted to Mick Rothbart, Sara Hodges, John Orbell, Mike Posner and members of the Institute's Evolution Group for many helpful comments on an earlier version of the manuscript.

1. Peter Watts' translation from the original Norsk is admirable in its erudition, as well as in its adherence to original meaning and, indeed, to literal word selection. Alas, this is sometime accomplished at the expense of both rhyme and meter, two conspicuous features of Ibsen's lush, classicist poetic style. I have taken the liberty to tamper with Watts version in order to restore some flavor of the original's poetic form, as well as make some of the oblique references to Peer Gynt's variegated past *personae* a bit more transparent. My guidance in taking this regrettable license was A. Schlonsky's bravura Hebrew translation, the first version of the play/poem — in an aptly lush stage production — I encountered in my youth. For a glimmer of how the onion soliloquy would have sounded in the original stage Norsk, I am indebted to my old friend Thorstein Fretheim's inimitable rendition in the Oslo summer of 1995, based on the University edition (Ibsen 1963).

2. Park (1950): 247. This preposterous approach to etymology and metaphor is ubiquitous, namely that meanings never really change; that metaphors remain forever attached, by their resilient umbilical cord, to the literal meaning that first gave them life (cf. Lakoff and Johnson 1980; see ch. 3); that by digging out the words' etymology one has unearthed its primordial *ur*-sense. The all-time worst offender of this genre of reasoning was probably Nietzsche, in whose *The Genealogy of Morals* (1887) one finds the following, mind-boggling passage: "The clue to the correct explanation was furnished me by the question "What does the etymology of the terms for good in various languages tell us?" I discovered that all these terms lead us back to the same conceptual transformation. The basic concept is always *noble* in the hierarchical, class sense, and from this developed, by historical necessity, the concept of *good* embracing nobility of mind, spiritual distinction." (1887: 162)

3. James (n.d.) *The Philosophy of William James*: 128–9.

4. A well-known theory of personality, the *Theory of Cognitive Dissonance* (Festinger 1957), held considerable sway in the early 1960s. By the end of the decade, it became somewhat

scaled down, presumably with the realization that conflicting cognitive schemata are seldom accessed simultaneously (Abelson *et al.* 1968).

5. Ed Sadalla (in personal communication) notes that the best strategy for deceiving others is sincere self-deception; by which he means, I take it, that the two conflicting 'selves' are totally unaware of each other's incompatible epistemic and deontic states. Whether a mentally healthy person is capable of this fête of hide-and-seek remains, in my mind, an open question.

6. I plead guilty of tampering just a bit with Kaufmann's translation.

7. A third, minuscule group (iii) of symptoms seem to straddle the fence — no sense of humor, no common sense — and could belong to either list.

8. Kilpatrick *et al.* (2002) observe that during the first year of marriage, spouses are highly empathic and adjustable, displaying great willingness to accommodate the multiple facets of their partners and keep revising their model of the other. As repetition and familiarity set in and cumulate, however, spouses tend to revert to an increasingly stereotypical-fixed — essentialist — mental model of their partners.

CHAPTER 10

The pragmatics of martial arts

In memoriam, M. Ho'o

10.1. Preamble

At first glance, the martial arts seem an odd choice, perhaps as odd as the theory of personality, for inclusion in a book on pragmatics. A closer inspection reveals, however, that — given the focus of this book on context as other minds — the martial arts and, for that matter, strategic thinking in general, are a natural fit. In both communication and warfare, one's moves depend, at any decision-making juncture, on the ever-present — explicit or implicit — mind of *the other*, a mind crammed-full of currently-relevant but ever-shifting epistemic and deontic states.

 With an interesting difference, though: In the competitive context of combat, the other mind in question is not that of a cooperating interlocutor anxious to comply with Grice's maxims, but rather of a *hostile adversary* with incompatible goals and less-than-transparent beliefs. Indeed, the goal-trees of the two combatants, taken together, are much closer to the zero-sum, winner-take-all end of the scale. Consequently, the mind-reading deployed in both strategic thinking and martial engagement is more in line with so-called *Machiavellian Intelligence* (Byrne and Whiten eds 1988; Whiten and Byrne eds 1997). Still, these differences should not obscure the fact that strategic thinking and tactical action are just as dependent as cooperation and communication as they are on a realistic assessment of the mind of the other. In this respect, Whiten's (1997) choice of title — *the Machiavellian mind-reader* — is indeed apt.

10.2. Adaptive realism: There shall be weeping and wailing and gnashing of teeth

On an overcast Saturday morning sometime in the winter of 1979, Marshall Ho'o, my first Tai Chi Chuan *si-fu*, came to Bronson Park in Hollywood and unleashed upon his unsuspecting cohorts one of his most memorable Saturday Morning Specials, opening up with the Scriptural quote:[1]

> There shall be weeping and wailing and gnashing of teeth.

What followed was a rambling, impassioned harangue delivered in a harsh and choppy fashion, with the old man visibly agitated. Even for those of us who had sat through years of Marshall's Sermons on the Mound, this one, fondly known thereafter as the Weeping-Wailing-and-Gnashing-of-Teeth (WWGT) harangue, was a doozie.

In reflecting twenty-five years later on what we heard that morning, I still puzzle over what exactly the old man was after. The WWGT harangue seemed so incongruous with the bland Southern California winter, so out of tune with the relaxed mood of the audience.

The puzzle of WWGT eventually dissolved, leastwise for me, in a rather natural fashion. The old man was sounding the wake-up call, the traditional *a l'arm*: 'Stop playing self-indulgent games', he was telling us, 'get real, get ready to assume the responsibility for your own life'. What this son of the rough turn-of-the-century Sacramento Chinatown slum was telling us was that life, however gentle and groovy we may have willed it to be (given the *zeitgeist*), was harsh, for real, dead serious. He was reminding us about what both the Eastern and American-Indian traditions know as *The Way of the Warrior*.

Tai Chi has always been many things to many people. Aside from its well-documented martial origins, it has been viewed as a slo-mo meditation, a panacea for all that ails you, a regimen of physical fitness, a mind-body yoga (*Chi Kung*), even a dance form.

By the late 1970s, the prevailing ethos around the National Tai Chi Chuan Association and its various off-shoots has swung away full tilt from the martial roots of the discipline. The aging flower children of Bronson Park and their younger spiritual descendants were giving up on the Fat Man's [2] exacting insistence that the form, however soft and ethereal-looking, was still rooted in the concrete imperatives of hand-to-hand combat. To the draft resisters and lotus eaters of the 1960s, whose experience of war and famine and life-and-death seldom extended beyond the front end of the cathode tube, the preoccupation with warfare seemed silly, anachronistic, irrelevant. Tai Chi Chuan had successfully incorporated itself into the spirituality-cum-fitness consciousness of the Me Generation.

Marshall Ho'o was of course not alone in attempting to remind us that life was for real. In his third book, *Journey to Ixtlan*, Carlos Castañeda (1972) had earlier on attempted to do the same. To quote his — most likely fictitious — teacher Don Juan:

> Death is our eternal companion, it is always to our left, at an arms length.   (1972: 33)

And:

> The thing to do when you're impatient is to turn to your left and ask advice from your death … Your companion is there, watching you.   (*ibid.*: 34)

And likewise:

> Death is the only wise adviser we have … Whenever you feel … that everything is going wrong and you're about to be annihilated, turn to your death and ask.   (*ibid.*)

Castañeda had traced the same theme in his second book, *A Separate Reality* (1971), making the connection between death-the-companion and living like a warrior abundantly explicit:

> When a warrior has acquired patience, he is on his way to will. He knows how to wait. His death sits with him on his mat, they are friends. His death advises him, in mysterious ways, how to choose, how to live strategically.   (1971: 151)

But why should Bronson Park's young and beautiful in the prime of their life concern themselves with the invisible grim reaper sitting next to them on the mat? To their left? Why indeed?

10.3. The paradox of Karma

How can one square off the fact that life can be so staggeringly random and, at the same breath, the product deliberate choice? The Western mind abhors this contradiction as it abhors all others, striving to reduce life's complexities to simple causal chains. And so, when the Hindu concept of *Karma* transmutates into our Western context, it is often rendered as pre-ordination, destiny, or luck-of-the-draw: I am who I am, and tough luck for me if I have turned out to be a fool. Tough luck for you if I have turned out to be a jerk. Don't blame me, I am not in control. It's my Karma.

Living like a warrior is an anathema to this self-serving rendition of Karma. Karma for the warrior does not only mean facing up to the inevitable with stoicism and grace. It also means shouldering the burden of choice-making and the responsibility for all of one's choices, the lucky as well as the disastrous.

Living like a warrior — thus Marshall's WWGT — turns out to be about accepting not only one's quotient of blind luck, but also the consequences of having made one's choices. Or, as Castañeda puts it in *A Separate Reality* (1971)

> To be a warrior a man has to be, first of all and rightfully so, keenly aware of his own death. But to be concerned with death would force any one of us to focus on the self, and that would be debilitating. So the next thing one needs to be a warrior is detachment. The idea of imminent death, instead of becoming an obsession, becomes an indifference.   (1971: 150)

In his *Journey to Ixtlan* (1972), Castañeda observes that taking responsibility for one's choices is the crux of The Way of the Warrior:

> When a man decides to do something he must go all the way … but he must take responsibility for what he does.   (1972: 39)

And likewise:

> In the world where death is the hunter, my friend, there is no time for regrets or doubts. There is only time for decisions.   (1972: 40)

It is indeed easy to make choices at leisure. But the warrior must make them under duress, in real-action time.

10.4. Tao and Wu-Wei

In practicing Tai Chi Chuan as a martial art, one must understand the discipline's ancient roots in the Taoist pragmatic doctrine of human conduct. This doctrine hinges on the paradoxical concept of *Wu-Wei* ('no do'), which in turn emanates from the metaphysics of the *Tao*. The intimate link between the two — one cornerstone of Taoist metaphysics, the other the foundation of Taoist ethics — is evident in the Taoist penchant for talking about them simultaneously, in the same sutra, often in the same breath.

In the *Tao Teh Ching*,[3] Tao — the inherent directionality of the universe (natural drift, gradient, gravity, entropy, The Way) — is conceived of as the non-controlling ultimate natural cause:

> Tao never acts,
> Yet through it all is done.   (TTC, 37)

In human affairs, the Taoist is enjoined to emulate Tao — perceive the inherent directionality of each situation and align himself with it:

> To strive is to oppose Tao,
> He who opposes Tao dies young.   (TTC, 55)

The ruling metaphor of Taoist ethics is that of water, gravity's pliable servant:

> Be like water,
> It quenches all thirst
> Yet lays no claim,
> It flows to the lowest place
> And thus rejoins Tao.   (TTC, 8)

Particular scorn is reserved in Taoist ethics for arbitrary, unmotivated action:

> Those who aim to win the world
> And bend it in their image
> Will fail.
> The world is God's vessel,
> It cannot be re-made.
> To tamper is to spoil,
> To grab is to lose touch.   (TTC, 29)

Conversely, much faith is invested in yielding to the inherent directionality of the force-field:

> Yield and you shall remain whole,
> Bend and you shall become straight,
> Be empty and you shall be filled,
> Wear out and you shall be renewed,
> Have nothing and you shall have all.   (TTC, 22)

10.5. *Wu-Wei* as paradox

Wu-Wei is commonly misunderstood as an injunction to 'do nothing', an exhortation to passivity or monastic quietism. If this were the right interpretation, one would be hard-pressed to accept Tai Chi Chuan, flower of Taoist practice, as a martial art. The *Tao Teh Ching* does indeed point to *Wu-Wei* as the ultimate strategy:

Attain the utmost by Wu-Wei.   (TTC, 16)

This is, however, not a call to inaction, but only a warning against *arbitrary action*, action that goes against the grain. In this respect, Taoist ethics is profoundly utilitarian and conservationist:

To strive is to oppose Tao,
He who opposes Tao dies young..   (TTC, 55)

Wu-Wei is indeed a doctrine of human action, but action of a peculiar sort. If one acts against Tao, one winds up threshing about needlessly, wastefully. Acting in accord with the Tao is natural, effortless, economical. The would-be sage is urged to emulate the supreme Master Carver:

The Master Carver never carves..   (TTC, 28)

And likewise:

A good traveler leaves no tracks,
A good speaker is never heckled,
A good trader needs no scales,
A well-shut door requires no bolt.   (TTC, 27)

The paradox of *Wu-Wei* — how can one make deliberate choices, then act, and still live by *Wu-Wei*? — is only an apparent one. *Wu-Wei* is an invitation to *motivated action*, action that conforms with the inherent directionality of both the universe at large and the situation at hand. Before acting, one must first recognize which way the Tao blows, and only then act — with the flow. Put another way, one's action must take account of the *context*.

10.6. *Wu-Wei* as strategy

Many sutras of the *Tao Teh Ching* deal with military strategy. In accord with *Wu-Wei*, they all caution the warrior against precipitous, arbitrary action:

A wise general attains his goals and stops,
He doesn't fight past victory,
He wins but never rubs it in,
Gains but never boasts,

Scores but regrets it,
Conquers but deplores brute force.   (TTC, 30)

Victory is a funeral.   (TTC, 31)

The indebtedness of Taoist military strategy to the ethics of *Wu-Wei* is particularly obvious in the repeated exhortation to yield rather than attack. These passages constitute the foundation of Tai Chi Chuan as a martial art, as well as the earliest tactical manual of guerrilla warfare:

Do not invade but rather be invaded,
Retreat a foot rather than advance an inch,
March without formation,
Be ready without preparing,
Advance without charging,
Be armed without weapons..   (TTC, 69)

When two armies are evenly matched,
Whoever yields, wins.   (TTC, 69)

How does the sea control the rivers?
By keeping low.   (TTC, 66)

The Tao Teh Ching is not focused on military strategy. But the writings of one of Lao Tse's most celebrated contemporaries, Sun Tzu's *The Art of War* (henceforth AOW), most assuredly was. And the first principle of Sun Tzu is directly derived from the Taoist's *Wu Wei*:

For to win one hundred victories in one hundred battles is not the acme of skill.
To subdue the enemy without fighting is the acme of skill.   (AOW, III.3: 226)

And in the same vein:

To capture the enemy's army is better than to destroy it. (*ibid.*)

In practicing Tai Chi as a martial art, the strategy of *neutralization* likewise flows directly from the Taoist's *Wu Wei*; as does the strategy of absorbing the opponent's energy and recycling back, the avoidance of hard blocks, the preference for oblique angles and cyclic deflection.

The kind of contextually-motivated action implicit in *Wu-Wei* puts the main onus on one's perception, recognition, anticipation — of the opponent's action, therefore intent. This is only natural in the martial context, where action is often instantaneous, and where the adaptive consequences of the wrong move may be often catastrophic. Warfare is notoriously fluid and subject to constant, unpredictable shifts. Anticipating change and adjusting to it, expecting the unexpected and acting accordingly, are the essence of mature martial arts like Tai Chi Chuan. The entire practice is thus predicated on anticipating the opponent's mind, and then acting unexpectedly. Not surprisingly, Sun Tzu counsels the very same:

Speed is the essence of war;
take advantage of the enemy's unpreparedness;
travel by unexpected routes
and strike him when he takes no precaution.   (AOW, XI.29: 280)

Like neutralization, the Tai Chi Chuan strategy of *yielding* is equally rooted in *Wu-Wei*; again, not in *Wu Wei* as a prescription for passivity but as a call to motivated action. In the martial domain, the motivating context for one's action is always the opponent's action — or better yet, its anticipation. That is, anticipating the opponent's *intent*. The *Tai Chi Classics* (henceforth TCC)[4] make it clear, however, that yielding is not an absolute principle but rather a motivated one, subject to the vagaries of the construed context:

When the opponent is hard, I am soft.
That is called *yielding* (tsou).
When the opponent retreats, I follow.
That is *adherence* (nien).
When the opponent moves quickly, I respond quickly.
If he moves slowly, I respond slowly.   (TCC: 32)

When the opponent rises, I am already taller.
When he sinks, I am already lower.
When he advances, I am far ahead.
When he retreats, I am right upon him.   (TCC: 34)

When the opponent has moved, I have already moved.
When the opponent has not moved, I have already not moved.   (TCC: 57)

Only acute perception of the opponent's actions and extreme anticipation of his/her intent can sustain such paradoxical demands of timing, whereby one must act first but still appear to be reacting.

10.7.   The paradox of the invisible leader

Wu-Wei as a military strategy is closely linked to the Lao Tse's view of political leadership, best given as the paradox of the invisible leader. The *Tao Teh Ching* picks up this theme periodically, weaving a delicate line between ethics, political theory and military strategy:

The best leader people barely notice,
The next best they love and praise,
The next best they fear,
The next they hate …
 …When a wise leader is done,
People say "We did it ourselves".   (TTC, 17)

Tao never acts
Yet through it all is done.
If rulers did likewise,
The world will turn of its own accord.   (TTC, 37)

How does the sea control the rivers?
By keeping low.
A chief among men
Must speak as their inferior.
He who leads must walk behind.   (TTC, 66)

When the ruler is dull and lazy,
The people are snug and content.
When the ruler is smart and busy,
The people are bitter and restless.   (TTC, 58)

The invisible leader leads from behind, following, disclaiming. Whether this is a realistic vision remains a matter of conjecture. I have often wondered whether Marshall's repeated — forever ambivalent — experiments with democracy in the Association may have sprung from an awareness of the spiritual and ethical perils of explicit leadership.

Sun Tzu's description in *The Art of War* of the 'disinterested' military leader is reminiscent of Lao Tse:

> the general who in advancing does not seek personal fame, and in withdrawing is not concerned with avoiding punishment ... is the precious jewel of the state ... [Li Chuan: Such a general has no personal interest.   (AOW, X.19: 274)

10.8. The yoga of form

At the heart of all yogas lies the manipulation of visible, accessible means to reach invisible, intangible ends. The eternal paradox of all yogic practices has always been this: How could one cultivate so assiduously tangible external forms without neglecting their intangible internal essence? In *Journey to Ixtlan* (1972), Castañeda's Don Juan frames this paradox as follows:

> Take that rock for instance. To look at it is *doing*. To see it is *not-doing*.   (1972: 188)

Within Castañeda's framework, our universe comprises of two separate if parallel realities. The *Tao Teh Ching* is just as explicit on this, from the very start:

The Tao that can be told in words
Is not the real Tao,
Names that can be given
Are not the real names.   (TTC, 1)

Yogic practices necessarily involve action, so that while orienting toward the ultimate reality, the practitioner cannot afford to dismiss its external manifestations. In the yogic tradition, one reaches transcendent ends by manipulating available mundane means. The *Tao Teh Ching*, in spite of its overriding commitment to the ultimate, formless Tao, is not a rejectionist doctrine when it comes to the world of external forms. It is, if anything, unabashedly utilitarian:

> Thirteen spokes unite at the hub,
> But the wheel hinges on its empty hole.
> Clay is molded into a cup,
> But the space within is what is filled.
> Walls and a roof make a house,
> But the hollow inside is where you live.
> Thus, while the tangibles have their purpose,
> It is the intangible that is sought.   (TTC, 11)

10.9. The ritualization of form

The form of all human inventions is chosen for a purpose, be the invention an implement, an institution or a custom. The forms of human artifacts are thus profoundly *adaptive*, in very much the same sense as are the forms of biological organisms. They are constrained by the *purpose* for which they were constructed. This idea, as well as the profound analogy between bio-organisms and man-made artifacts, was recognized long ago by Aristotle, in his discussion of the structural design of bio-organisms (see chs 1, 8). The analogy Aristotle drew, between the animate body and man-made implements, rings true to this day; as does the governing principle of adaptive functionalism — the isomorphism between form and function:

> if a piece of wood is to be split with an axe, the axe must of necessity be hard; and, if hard, it must of necessity be made of bronze or iron. Now exactly in the same way the body, which like the axe is an *instrument* — for both the body as a whole and its several parts individually have definite operations for which they are made; just in the same way, I say, the body if it is to do its *work* [function], must of necessity be of such and such character.   (*De Partibus Animalium*, McKeon ed.: 650; brackets and italics added)

In both biology and culture, the occasional dissolution, over time, of a natural form-function mapping is a well known phenomenon, called *fossilization* or *ritualization*. Ritualization is an ingredient of all complex life-based systems. Once a complex structure has evolved to support a complex function, it can assume a life of its own — in part. So that not all structural details have a transparent functional motivation.

But complete ritualization of an erstwhile motivated system goes far beyond that. It involves the dissolution of all functional constraints on the liberated form. Once such constraints have been removed, two things happen, often in tandem:

• The practice or form becomes formalistic, meaningless.
• Arbitrary changes in the form may now be introduced with impunity.

The liberation of form from function often leaves the practitioner with a euphoric sense of absolute freedom. The history of modern art, dance, literature and music bears sad testimony to the self-indulgent narcissism that can spring from such freedom.

The practice of Tai Chi Chuan in total detachment from its martial roots may be pretty, artistic, therapeutic, spiritual, liberating, or just plain fun. But it still is profoundly barren and bereft of meaning. Once the original adaptive constraints have been discarded, once the form cannot be tested in its relevant adaptive space — in real-time actual combat, in sparring with a conscious opponent whose unpredictable moves cannot be choreographed in advance — any inspired guru may come along and change the form into, in principle, anything.

The *Tao Teh Ching* offers some cogent reflections on ritualization. It does so in the context of rejecting the Confucian system of well-ordered social institutions that had, in Lao Tse's view, become empty and ritualistic. Lao Tse singles out for particular scorn the Confucian notion of *Li*, variously translated as 'morals', 'standards', 'etiquette', 'propriety', 'ritual' or 'ceremony'. The *Li*-based Confucian code of human conduct is seen as arbitrary and ritualistic, something that is only resorted to when natural — adaptive — motivation is lost:

> When Tao is lost, 'compassion' arises,
> When 'compassion' is lost, *Li* arises,
> *Li* is the death of loyalty and honesty
> And the beginning of chaos.   (TTC, 38)

As Lao Tse saw it, the Tao, the universal, inherent natural motivation, supersedes the conventionalized notions of Justice and Compassion. In this vein, the kin-based, reward-laden Confucian code is disparaged:

> When the Six Relations are lost,
> 'Kind fathers' and 'devoted sons' appear.   (TTC, 18)

The Six Relations stand for natural kinship, the deep loyalty that springs from the Tao and requires neither justification nor exhortation nor reward. The behavioral imperatives of the Confucian Code, Lao Tse suggests, are only necessary when natural kinship is disregarded.

10.10. Complexity: Seven paradoxes

As we have seen throughout (but esp. ch. 8), the sweet siren song of reductionism is, alas, ever-present, casting its seductive spell. What I would like to do in this section is treat our Western aversion to paradoxes, our inherent recoil from logical contradiction (cf. Russell's *Theory of Types*, ch. 1), as an analogical stand-in for our well-documented penchant for *reductionism*. In this case, the analogy is reminiscent of the paradox of the self (ch. 9): On the surface, two contradictory aspects of a complex system beckon toward two alternative reductive accounts of the apparent complexity. If we resist the temptation to chose either one or the other, however, if we eschew simple linear causation, we find out that an integrated, interactive, dialectic system in fact explains the complex whole much better (chs 8, 9). This is what I have referred to, repeatedly throughout this book, as *adaptive compromises* in both biological and cultural evolution, whereby the complex design of the whole responds to and integrates together conflicting adaptive demands. In this respect, Taoist or martial-art paradoxes make a fascinating collection of cases-in-point.

10.10.1. The paradox of *Yin* and Yang

At the heart of the Taoist approach to just about anything lies the mother of all paradoxes, the principle of the *reconcilable contraries* or *unity in diversity*. Here is how the *Tao Teh Ching* puts it:

> Yin is the back of all,
> Yang is its face,
> From the union of the two
> The world attains its balance.   (TTC, 42)

The paradox of Yin and Yang pervades the practice of Tai Chi Chuan: How can one be both hard and soft? Both yielding and adhering? Both light and heavy? Both fast and slow? Both attentive and diffuse? Both deeply-rooted and instantly mobile? That is, both Yin and Yang?

The *Tai Chi Classics* offer the following observations, not all of them easy to interpret:

> Tai Chi comes from Wu Chi
> And is the mother of Yin and Yang.
> In motion they separate,
> In stillness they fuse   (TCC: 31)

> Sinking to one side is being responsive;
> Being double-weighted is being stagnant.   (TCC: 38)

> Insubstantial and substantial
> Should be clearly differentiated.   (TCC: 24)

Are these prescriptions paradoxical? The answer lies, of course, in the practice of Tai Chi Chuan as a *dynamic*, dialectic, pragmatic system. Spatially first, one can differentiate within the body, at any given moment, between substantial and insubstantial poles, heavy and light, rooted and mobile. But one could also recognize various degrees and mixes as the spatial distribution of opposites shifts over time, especially when one adjusts to the actions, or presumed intentions, of the adversary.

Temporally, one must be ready to shift instantaneously from Yin to the Yang and vice versa. As a fighting form, Tai Chi Chuan is tenable only in the context of motion and constant adjustment to *the adversary as context*. 'Is this form correct?' is a meaningless question outside this dynamic context.

This approach to form springs from the contextual-pragmatic doctrine of *Wu-Wei*. A posture or an action can only be judged relative to its motivating context, the action or intention of one's adversary. This observation tends to get lost when form is ritualized and made fixed, absolute, 'correct'.

10.10.2. The paradox of discreteness and continuity

Much like the substantial and insubstantial, discreteness and continuity appear irreconcilable at first glance. How could one observe the precision of discrete forms and still execute the seamless transition from one discrete form to another? This dilemma of Tai Chi Chuan is the same one that stymied both Plato and Aristotle. The latter, constrained by logic, made a less-than-happy attempt to resolve this issue in his classification of bio-organisms.[5] But in dynamic reality, whether of natural mental categories (ch. 2) or of Tai Chi Chuan practice, both discreteness and continuity must be accommodated. As the *Tai Chi Classics* make abundantly clear:

Tai Chi Chuan is like a great river,
Rolling on unceasingly (TCC: 25)

Let the postures be without breaks or holes,
hollows or projections,
discontinuities or continuities of form (TCC: 20)

Like all paradoxes, stasis and change are only in conflict as long as one maintains a rigid reductionist perspective. But as a dynamic discipline — martial or otherwise — Tai Chi Chuan is meaningless from such a perspective. As we shall see directly below, the natural perspective of Tai Chi Chuan is very much like that of biological organisms — *dynamic equilibrium*. Within such a perspective, discrete postures are meaningful — useful, defensible, correct — not because of how they stand alone, but for their place in the sequence of fluid motion. That is, in context.

10.10.3. The paradox or rootedness and lightness

The *Tai Chi Classics* impose another stringent demand on motion and stasis in Tai Chi Chuan, one that appears, at first glance, straight forward:

When one part moves,
All parts move.
When one part is still,
All parts are still.   (TCC: 57)

But if all parts are either at motion or in stasis, how is that reconcilable with the need to distinguish between the substantial (static, maximally rooted) and the insubstantial (dynamic, maximally weightless)?

The notion of balance in Tai Chi Chuan is founded upon the paradox of dynamic equilibrium. How does a single body gain maximal fluidity and buoyancy while retaining maximal gravity and 'seeking the lowest'? How does the fully polarized body — Yin on one side, Yang on the other — retain its balance? The answer is, of course, that it does not do so in stasis, only in motion. Much like categorial means in cognition (ch. 2), fixed postures are only abstract reference points along the continuum of motion. The reason why the Yin side is not vulnerable is because it can change instantly into a rooted, substantial Yang. The reason why the Yang side is not stagnant and sluggish is because it can change in a flash into the light, insubstantial Yin.

The scourge of *double weightedness*, failure to establish dynamic polarity, is shunned not because of the uselessness of either an all-Yin or an all-Yang posture, but because of the decreased potential for change. The well polarized body is thus a necessary ingredient of dynamic equilibrium.

10.10.4. The paradox of speed and consciousness

In practicing Tai Chi Chuan, one must seek the elusive middle ground between stagnation and unconsciousness. Stagnation is what happens when the practice is slowed down so much that continuity and flow are lost. Unconsciousness is what happens when the practice is speeded up so much that *conscious attention* begins to skip over smaller — automated — segments of time and motion. The practice of Tai Chi Chuan as a yoga of time and consciousness is paradoxical:

- How can one practice slow Tai Chi and still avoid stagnation?
- How can one practice fast Tai Chi without losing consciousness?

The paradox is, of course, inherent to the concept of timing in Tai Chi Chuan as a martial art. Again, from the *Tai Chi Classics*:

When the opponent rises, I am already taller.
When he sinks, I am already lower.
When he advances, I am far ahead.
When he retreats, I am right upon him.   (TCC: 34)

Many practitioners interpret the difference between the 'Inner School' (Tai Chi, Pa Kua, Hsin Yi) and 'Outer School' (Kung Fu, Shaolin Boxing) erroneously as the difference between slow and fast motion. My *Choi Lai Fut* teacher, Howard Lee, said it best when he denied the relevance of such a difference:

> Tai Chi is nothing but slow Kung Fu,
> Kung Fu is nothing but fast Tai Chi.

Or, as the *Tai Chi Classics* reminds us, speed is never fixed, but rather is determined by the speed of the opponent's actions, thus mind:

> When the opponent has moved, I have already moved.
> When the opponent has not moved, I have already not-moved.   (TCC: 57)

The initial slow pace in practicing in Tai Chi Chuan is only a means to an end:

- It trains one's attention (consciousness) to remain focused on smaller and smaller — eventually infinitesimal — segments of continuous motion.
- It promotes yielding and softness.
- It facilitate the yoga of Chi Kung.

What is at issue here is not speed, but the circulation of the so-called *Chi* and the deployment of consciousness.

At the other pole, fast practice is only useful if *Chi* and consciousness continue to permeate the smallest segment of time and motion. The challenge of 'fast' Tai Chi — thus of all forms of the 'Outer School' — is in keeping conscious attention focused on smaller and smaller time-and-motion frames. Ultimately, there are both benefits and pitfalls to both slow and fast practice. Ultimately, Tai Chi Chuan is not a slo-mo practice, but rather a *flexible speed* practice, adjusted to context.

10.10.5. The paradox of attention and automaticity

As noted repeatedly above (chs 2, 4, 9), in human perception, cognition and motor activity repeated performance of the same task in perfecting one's skill eventually leads to *automation* of the most repeated, predictable elements of the performance.[6] The gradual change from the initial slow, laborious, error-prone, attention-demanding performance to the eventual fast, skilled, low-error routinized performance is a universal process that takes place in the development of all mental and physical skills. It is a necessary ingredient in the acquisition of skilled language, reading, typing, dance, art or musical performance. Most students and teachers of the martial arts are well aware of this.

Like all useful tools, however, automaticity incurs certain costs. This is best put in form of another paradox:

- How can one practice repeatedly, to fluent perfection without losing consciousness?

This predicament is built into the neurological fabric of skilled performance. Repetition and familiarity breed automaticity and sub-consciousness, the twin sisters of contempt. And in the course of automation, attention is systematically bumped upwards from the smaller, lower segments of time-and-motion.

The challenge of practiced, fluent, error-free Tai Chi is the same one that faces an accomplished professional musician. How does one counter universal physiological, neurological and cognitive tendencies? How does one continue to deploy *Chi* and consciousness over the entire performance — down to the smallest fraction of time-and-motion — in spite of having become a skilled performer? Or, in the context of a martial art, how can one extend one's sensitivity to the opponent's actions and intents to smaller and smaller segments of time?

10.10.6. The paradox of diffuse attention

The reason why attention gives way to automaticity in the acquisition of complex skills is not a caprice of neuro-physiology, but rather a natural consequence of what attention and consciousness are — an energy-demanding rare commodity. There is only a limited amount of conscious attention to go around, and the various sub-systems of the organism are in constant competition for it. By automating low-level, repeating, predictable segments of a performance, one is able to retain and re-deploy consciousness to more global tasks, ones that are less predictable, more ambiguous, more in need of contextual adjustment and discrimination.

The general properties of conscious attention yield another paradox in the practice of Tai Chi Chuan as a martial art:

• How can one attend fully to one direction without losing one's attention to all other directions?

The answer is that maintaining peripheral attention is indeed fiendishly difficult and perhaps even physiologically untenable; but that a martial art — any martial art — cannot be practiced without somehow solving this paradox. For your opponent, if s/he is a worthy adversary, is striving just as hard to gain surprise and unpredictability, and to decipher *your* mind. The goal of conquering the paradox of diffuse attention is to retain enough tactical flexibility — so that one could adapt one's mind-speed to the opponent's.

10.10.7. The paradox of fixed-form practice

The last paradox is, I suppose, mostly a challenge to the non-martial practice of Tai Chi Chuan, practice without a real opponent. It involves the inertia generated by repeated practice of a set form, and the difficulty of maintaining the kind of flexibility, openness, context-sensitivity and instant adjustment to change that the *Tai Chi Classics* recommend. While visualizing a 'ghost' opponent may help, the only way I know of fostering and maintaining the requisite *contextual openness* is through free-form sparring with a real-time, unpredictable, live opponent.

10.11. Closure

My late teacher Marshall Ho'o paid repeated homage to Tai Chi Chuan as a martial art. Yet something very funny occurred every time he would demonstrate martial applications: He would revert to 'Outer School' (Kung Fu, Judo) moves. This was rather striking when you sparred with him. Did Marshall have faith in Tai Chi Chuan as a martial art? This is a question I have never been able to resolve to my full satisfaction. But it seems to me that severing the connection between 'inner' Tai Chi, the yoga, and 'outer' Tai Chi, the martial art, is a lapse of faith whereby neither aspect benefits. The martial art is deprived of its vital inner core. The yoga is bereft of its most concrete tools, let alone its creative paradoxes. These paradoxes are not mind games, but rather *performance puzzles* that, just maybe, have concrete biological solutions.

Whatever solutions there may be to these age-old paradoxes, they can only be revealed through practice. And the practice must be informed of the 'outer' roots of Tai Chi Chuan as a martial art. That is, as a discipline founded upon the presence of a real, on-line adversary-interlocutor whose constantly-shifting epistemic and deontic states, and concomitant actions, must be anticipated. Fortunately though not fortuitously, the speed of human motor performance tends to dovetail, on the whole, with the speed of visual perception and event cognition.[7]

Notes

1. The exact passage in Matthew (King James rendition), turns out to be either "... there shall be wailing and gnashing of teeth." (13.42; 13.50) or "... there shall be weeping and gnashing of teeth."(22.13; 24.51; 25.30). I confess I prefer Marshall's version. Besides, I have never been able to quote verbatim either.

2. Yang Jen-Fu, the last major exponent of the Yang school of Tai Chi Chuan, taught his last master class in Shanghai in 1935 and died in 1936. Most major transmission lines of the Yang school to the United States — Dung Yin-Jit, Cheng Man-Ching, Chen Wei-Ming, Chu Fong-Chu — can be traced back to the Fat Man's last master class in Shanghai.

3. The *Tao Teh Ching* (Book of the Tao) is attributed to Lao Tse. All quotation here are from my own translation (copyright 1972, Shaolin-West Foundation, Ignacio, Colorado).

4. The version of the *Tai Chi Classics* I quote here is from Lo, Inn, Amacker and Foe (1979).

5. As a practicing biologist and a keen observer of nature, Aristotle was struck by the graduality of change and growth. His logic, however, demanded discrete categories — either A or non-A but no murky in-between.

6. For an overview of this subject see again Shiffrin and Schneider (1977), Schneider and Shiffrin (1977), Posner (1978), Kahneman (1973), Schneider (1985), Schneider and Chein (2003), Posner and Fan (2004), *inter alia*.

7. See Barker and Givón (2002). What makes this dovetailing neurologically feasible are two cortical loci where motor and visual representations interlace and are co-activated: the mirror neurons in the pre-frontal B5 region (Rizzolatti *et al.* 1996; Gallese *et al.* 1999), and the dorsal visual stream (Milner and Goodale 1995, 1998; Gallese *et al.* 1999).

References

Abelson, R.P., E. Aronson, W.J. McGuire, T.M. Newcomb, M.J. Rosenberg and P.H. Tannenbaum (eds, 1968) *Theories of Cognitive Consistency: A Source-Book*, Chicago: Rand McNally.

Abdulaev, Y.G. and M.I. Posner (1997) "Time-course of activating brain areas in generating verbal associations", *Psychological Science*, 8.1.

Ambady, N., F. Bernieri and I. Richeson (2000) "Toward a histology of social behavior: Judgemental accuracy from thin slices of behavior", in M.P. Zenna, ed., *Advances in Experimental Social Personality*, 32:201–72.

Andersen, R. (1979 "Expanding Schumann's pidginization hypothesis", *Language Learning*, 29.

Anderson, A.S.C. Garrod and A.J. Sanford (1983) "The accessibility of pronominal antecedents as a function of episode shift in narrative discourse", *Quarterly J. of Experimental Psychology*, 35a.

Ackrill, J.L. (tr. & ed., 1963) *Aristotle's Categories and De Interpretatione*, Oxford: Clarendon Press.

Aristotle, *Categories*, in J. Barnes (ed. 1984).

Aristotle, *De Anima*, in J. Barnes (ed. 1984).

Aristotle, *De Interpretatione*, in J. Barnes (ed. 1984).

Aristotle, *De Partibus Animalium*, in J. Barnes (ed., 1984).

Aristotle, *De Generationem Animalium*, in J. Barnes (ed. 1984).

Aristotle, *De Sophisticis Elenchis* ('Sophistical Refutations'), in J. Barnes (ed. 1984).

Aristotle, *Historia Animalium*, in Barnes (ed. 1984).

Aristotle, *Metaphysics*, in R. Hope (tr. & ed. 1960), Ann Arbor: University of Michig-an Press.

Aristotle, *Nicomachean Ethics*, in J. Barnes (ed., 1984).

Aristotle, *Poetics*, in J. Barnes (ed 1984).

Aristotle, *Posterior Analytic*, in J. Barnes (ed. 1984); see also McKeon (ed. 1941).

Aristotle, *Prior Analytic*; in J. Barnes (ed. 1984).

Aristotle, *Rhetoric*, in J. Barnes (ed. 1984).

Atkinson, R.C. and R.M. Shiffrin (1968) "Human memory: A proposed system and its control processes", in K.W. Spence and T. Spence (eds) *The Psychology of Learning and Motivation*, vol. 2, New York: Academic Press.

Attneave, F. (1959) *Application of Information Theory to Psychology*, New York: Holt.

Austin, J. (1962) *How to Do Things with Words*, Cambridge: Harvard University Press.

Bach, E. (1965) "Structural linguistics and the philosophy of science", *Diogenes*, 51.

Baddeley, A.D. (1986) *Working Memory*, New York: Oxford University Press.

Baddeley, A.D. (1992) "Working memory: The interface between memory and cognition", *J. of Cognitive Neuroscience*, 4.3: 281–8.

Bar, M. and I. Bederman (1998) "Subliminal visual priming", *Psychological Science*, 9.6.

Barker, M. (2004) *Effects of Divided Attention on Verbal Episodic Memory*, PhD dissertation, University of Oregon, Eugene (ms).

Barker, M. and T. Givón (2002) "On the pre-linguistic origins of language processing rates", in T. Givón and B.F. Malle (eds 2002).

Barker, M. and T. Givón (2003) "The representation of conversation in episodic memory: Information vs. interaction", *TR no. 03–1*, Institute of Cognitive and Decision Sciences, University of Oregon.

Barker, M. and T. Givón (forthcoming) "Memory for grammar".

Barkow, J.H, L. Cosmides and J. Tooby (1992) *The Adapted Mind: Evolutionary Psychology and the Generation of Culture*, Oxford: Oxford University Press.

Barnes, J. (ed. 1984) *The Complete Works of Aristotle*, Bolingen Series LXXI, Princeton, NJ: Princeton University Press.

Baron-Cohen, S. (1989) "The autistic child's theory of mind: a case of specific developmental delay", *J. of Child Psychology and Psychiatry*, 30:285–98.

Baron-Cohen, S. (1990) "Autism: A specific cognitive disorder of 'mind-blindness'", *International Rev. of Psychiatry*, 2:79–88.

Baron-Cohen, s. (1995) *Mindblindness: An essay on Autism and Theory of Mind*, Cambridge, Mass.: MIT Press.

Baron-Cohen, S. (2000) "The evolution of a theory of mind", in M. Corballis and S.E.G. Lea (eds) *The Descent of Mind*, Oxford: Oxford University Press.

Baron-Cohen, S. and U. Frith (1985) "Does the autistic child have a 'theory of mind'?", *Cognition*, 21:37–46.

Barthelme, D. (1981) "The Emperor", *The New Yorker*, January 26, 1981, p. 32.

Bartsch, K. and H.M. Wellman (1995) *Children Talk about the Mind*, Oxford: Oxford University Press.

Basso, K. (1972) "To give up words: Silence in Western Apache Culture", in P.P. Giglioni (ed.) *Language and Social Context: Selected Readings*, London: Penguin Books.

Bates, E. (1976) *Language in Context: The Acquisition of Pragmatics*, New York: Academic Press.

Bates, E., L. Camioni and V. Volterra (1975) "The acquisition of performatives prior to speech", *Merrill-Palmer Quarterly*, 21.

Bates, E., L. Benigni, I. Bretherton and V. Volterra (1979) *The Emergence of Symbols: Cognition and Communication in Infancy*, New York: Academic Press.

Bates, E. and B. MacWhinney (1979) "A functionalist approach to the acquisition of grammar", in E. Ochs and B. Schieffelin (eds 1979).

Bell, M.D. and P.H. Lysaker (1995) "The relation of psychiatric symptoms to work performance for persons with severe mental disorder", *Psychiatric Services*, 46:508–11.

Bickerton, D. (1975) "Creolization, linguistic universal, natural semantax and the brain", University of Hawaii, Honolulu (ms).

Bickerton, D. (1977) "Pidginization, Creolization, language acquisition and language universals", in A. Valdman (ed.) *Pidgin and Creole Linguistics*, Bloomington: Indiana University Press.

Bickerton, D. (1981) *Roots of Language*, Ann Arbor, Mich.: Karoma.

Bickerton, D. (1990) *Language and Species*, Chicago: University of Chicago Press.

Bickerton, D. and T. Givón (1976) "Pidginization and syntactic change", in *CLS 12*, University of Chicago: Chicago Linguistics Society.

Bickerton, D. and C. Odo (1976) *Change and Variation in Hawaiian English*, vol. I: *The Pidgin*, NSF Final Report (grant GS-39748), Honolulu: University of Hawaii (ms).

Bloom, L. (1973) *One Word at a Time: The Use of Single Word Utterances Before Syntax*, The Hague: Mouton.

Bloomfield, L. (1922) "Review of E. Sapir's *Language*", *The Classical Weekly*, 18.

Bloomfield, L. (1933) *Language*, New York: Holt, Rinehart and Winston.

Blumstein, S. E. and W. Milberg (1983) "Automatic and controlled processing in speech/language deficits in aphasia", *Symposium on Automatic Speech,* Minneapolis: Academy of Aphasia.

Bolinger, D. (1977) *The Forms of Language*, London: Longmans.

Bonner, J. T. (1988) *The Evolution of Complexity*, Princeton, NJ: Princeton University Press.

Bostock, D. (1994) "Plato on understanding language", in S. Everson (ed. 1994).

Bowerman, M. (1973) *Early Syntactic Development*, Cambridge: Cambridge University Press.

Brody, B. (ed. 1970) *Readings in the Philosophy of Science,* Englewood Cliffs, NJ: Prentice-Hall.

Brown, P. and S. Levinson (1978) "Universals of language usage: Politeness phenomena", in E. Goody (ed.) *Questions and Politeness: Strategies in Social Interaction*, Cambridge: Cambridge University Press.

Brown, P. and S. Levinson (1979) "Social structure, group and interaction", in K. Schere and H. Giles (eds) *Social Markers in Speech*, Cambridge: Cambridge University Press.

Bryson, S. E., R. Landry and J. A. Wainwright (1996) "A componential analysis of executive function in autism: Review of recent evidence", in J. A. Burack and J. T. Enns (eds) *Attention, Development and Psychopathology*, New York: Guilford Press.

Bryson, S. E., J. A. Wainwright and I. M. Smith (1990) "Autism: A developmental spatial neglect syndrome?", in J. Enns (ed.) *The Development of Attention: Research and Theory*, Amsterdam: Elsevier.

Buchler, T. (1939) *Charles Peirce's Empiricism*, London: Kegan Paul.

Bush, G., P. Luu and M. I. Posner (2000) "Cognitive and emotional influences in the anterior cingulate cortex", *Trends in Cognitive Science*, 4:215–22.

Butt, J. and C. Benjamin (1988) *A New Reference Grammar of Modern Spanish*, London: Edward Arnold.

Bybee, J. and S. Fleischman (eds 1995) *Modality in Grammar and Discourse*, TSL #32, Amsterdam: J. Benjamins.

Bybee, J., W. Pagliuca and R. Perkins (1994) *The evolution of Grammar: Tense, Aspect and Modality in Languages of the World*, Chicago: University of Chicago Press.

Byrne, R. W. (1998) "Learning by imitation: A hierarchic approach", *Behavior and Brain Sciences*, 21:667–721.

Byrne, R. W. and A. Whiten (eds 1988) *Machiavelian Intelligence: Social Expertise and the Evolution of Intellect in Monkeys, Apes and Humans*, Oxford: Oxford University Press.

Cacciari, C. (1993) "The place of idioms in a literal and metaphoric world", in C. Cacciari and P. Tabbossi (eds 1993).

Cacciari, C. and S. Glucksberg (1994) "Understanding figurative language", in M. A. Gernsbacher (ed. 1994).

Cacciari, C. and P. Tabbossi (eds 1993) *Idioms: Processing, Structure and Interpretation*, Hillsdale, NJ: Erlbaum.

Carnap, R. (1950) "Testability and meaning", New Haven, Conn.: Graduate Philosophy Club, Yale University, pp. 419–71.

Carnap, R. (1956) *Meanining and Necassity*, Chicago: University of Chicago Press.

Carnap, R. (1959) *The Logical Syntax of Language*, Patterson, NJ: Littlefield, Adams & Co.

Carnap, R. (1963) *The Philosophy of Rudolph Carnap*, La Sallre, IL: Open Court.

Carpenter, P. A. and M. A. Just (1988) "The role of working memory in language comprehension", in D. Klar and K. Kotovsky (eds) *Complex Information Processing: The Impact of Herbert Simon*, Hillsdale, NJ: Erlbaum.

Carter, A. (1974) *Communication in the Sensory-Motor Period,* PhD dissertation, University of California, Berkeley (ms).

Carter, C.S., T.S. Braver, D.M. Barch, M.M. Botvinick, D. Nolls and J.D. Cohen (1998) "Anterior cingulate cortex, error detection, and online monitoring of performance", *Science,* 280 (5364):747–9.

Castañeda, C. (1971) *A Separate Reality,* New York: Pocket Books.

Castañeda, C. (1972) *Journey to Ixtlan,* New York: Pocket Books.

Chafe, W. (1970) *Meaning and the Structure of Language,* Chicago: University of Chicago Press.

Chafe, W. (1994) *Discourse, Consciousness and Time: Displacement of Conscious Experience in Speaking and Writing,* Chicago: University of Chicago Press.

Chafe, W. and J. Nichols (eds 1996) *Evidentiality: The Linguistic Coding of Epistemology,* Norwood, NJ: Ablex.

Chase, W.G. and K.A. Ericsson (1981) "Skilled memory", in J. Anderson (ed.) *Cognitive Skills and their Acquisition,* Hillsdale, NJ: Erlbaum.

Chase, W.G. and K.A. Ericsson (1982) "Skill and working memory", in G. Bower (ed.) *The Psychology of Learning and Motivation,* vol. 16, New York: Academic Press.

Chase, W.G. and H.A. Simon (1973) "Perception in chess", *Cognitive Psychology,* 4.

Chomsky, N. (1961) "On the notion 'rule of grammar'", in *The Structure of Language and its Mathematical Aspects,* Providence, RI: American Mathematical Society.

Chomsky, N. (1965) *Aspects of the Theory of Syntax,* Cambridge, Mass.: MIT Press.

Chomsky, N. (1966) *Cartesian Linguistics,* New York: Harper and Row.

Chomsky, N. (1968) *Language and Mind,* New York: Harcourt, Brace and World (revised edition, 1972).

Coates, J. (1983) *The Semantics of Modal Auxiliaries,* London: Croom Helm.

Cocchiarella, N. (1965) *Tense and Modal Logic: A Study in the Typology of Temporal Reference,* University of California, Los Angeles, PhD dissertation (ms).

Cole, P. (ed. 1978) *Pragmatics, Syntax and Semantics,* vol 9, New York: Academic Press.

Cole, P. (ed., 1981) *Radical Pragmatics,* New York: Academic Press.

Cole, P. and J. Morgan (eds) (1975) *Speech* Acts, Syntax and Semantics 3, New York: Academic Press.

Collins, A.M. and E.F. Loftus (1975) "A spreading activation theory of semantic processing", *Psychological Review,* 82.

Collins, A.M. and M.R. Quillian (1972) "How to make a language user", in E. Tulving and W. Donaldson (eds) *Organization of Memory,* New York: Academic Press.

Conrad, C. (1974) "Context effects in sense comprehension: A study of the subjective lexicon", *Memory and Cognition,* 2.

Corbetta, M.N., J.M. Kincade and G.L. Shulman (2002) "Neural systems for visual orienting and their relationships to spatial working memory", *J. of Cognitive Neuroscience,* 14.3:508–23.

Cresswell, M.J. (1972) "The world is everything that is the case", *Australian Journal of Philosophy,* 50.1.

Damassio, A. (1994) *Descartes Error: Emotion, Reason and the Human Brain,* New York: Putnam.

d'Andrade, E.N. (1954) *Sir Isaac Newton: His life and Work,* Garden City, New York: Doubleday.

Dascal, M. (1987) "Defending literal meaning", *Cognitive Science,* 11.

Dascal, M. (2004) "*Ex pluribus unum?* Patterns in 522+ Texts of Leibnitz's *Zamtliche Schriften und Briefe*, VI.4", University of Tel Aviv (ms).

Davidson, D. and G. Harman (eds 1972) *Semantics of Natural Language*, Dordrecht: Reidel.

Dawkins, R. (1976) *The Selfis Gene*, New York: Oxford University Press.

Denier van der Gon, J. J. and J. P. Thuring (1965) "The guiding of human writing movement", *Kybernetic*, 2.

deWaal, F. (1982) *Chimpanzee Politics: Power and Sex among the Apes*, London: Unwin Paperbacks/Counterpoint.

Diamond, J. (1999) *Guns, Germs and Steel*, New York: Norton.

Dickinson, C. and T. Givón (1997) "Memory and conversation", in T. Givón (ed.) 1997.

Diels, K. H. (1969) *Die Frangmenten der Vorsokratiker, herausgegeben von Walter Kranz*, 3 vols, Dublin and Zurich: Weidman.

Dik, S. (1978) *Functional Grammar*, Amsterdam: North Holland.

Donellan, K. (1966) "Reference and definite descriptions", *Philosophical Review*, LXXV.

Dreyfus, H. L. (1972) *What Computers Can't Do*, New York: Harper & Row.

DuBois, J. (1987) "The discourse basis of ergativity", *Language*, 63.4.

Dunbar, R. I. M. (1992) "Co-evolution of neocortex size, group size and language in humans", *Brain and Behavioral Sciences*, 16.4.

Dunbar, R. M. (1998) "The social brain hypothesis", *Evolutionary Anthropology*, 6.5.

Duncan, J. and A. M. Owen (2000) "Common regions of the frontal lobe recruited by diverse cognitive demands", *Trends in Neuroscience*, 23:475–83.

Eisler-Goldman, F. (1968) *Psycholinguistics: Experiments in Spontaneous Speech*, New York: Academic Press.

Eldredge, N. and S. J. Gould (1972) "Punctuated equilibria: An alternative to physical gradualism", in T. J. M. Schoopf (ed.) *Models in Paleobiology*, San Frsancisco: Freeman, Cooper & Co.

Elster, J. (1985) "Introduction", in J. Elster (ed. 1985).

Elster, J. (ed. 1985) *The Multiple Self*, Cambridge: Cambridge University Press.

Epstein, W. and I. Rock (1960) "Perceptual set as an artifact of recency", *American J. of Psychology*, 73.

Ericsson, K. A. and W. Kintsch (1997) "Long-term working memory", *Psychological Review*, 102:2.

Ervin-Tripp, S. (1970) "Discourse agreement: How children answer questions", in J. Hayes (ed.) *Cognition and the Development of Language*, New York: Wiley & Son.

Everson, S. (1994) "Introduction", in S. Everson (ed., 1994).

Everson, S. (ed. 1994) *Companion to Ancient Thought, 3: Language*, Cambridge: Cambridge University Press.

Fernández-Duque, D. (1999a) "Processing of object identity, location and change in the absence of focused attention", *TR no. 99–03*, Institute of Cognitive and Decision Sciences, University of Oregon, Eugene.

Fernández-Duque, D. (1999b) *Automatic Processing of Object Identity, Location, and Valence Information*, PhD dissertation, University of Oregon, Eugene (ms).

Festinger, L. (1957) *A Theory of Cognitive Dissonance*, Evanston, Ill: Row, Peterson.

Feyerabend, P. (1975) *Against Method: An Outline of an Anarchic Theory of Knowledge*, New York: The Humanities Press.

Fillmore, C. (1971) "How to know whether you're coming or going", in K. Hylgaard-Jensen (ed.) *Linguistik 1971*, Athenäum-Verlag.

Fouts, R.S. (1973) "Acquisition and testing of gestural signs in four young chimpanzees, *Science*, 180.

Frith, U. (1989a) *Autism: Explaining the Enigma*, Oxford: Blackwell.

Frith, U. (1989b) "Autism and theory of mind" in C. Gilberg (ed. 1989).

Frith, U. (1991) "Asperger and his syndrom", in U. Frith (ed. 1991).

Frith, U. (ed. 1991) *Autism and Asperger Syndrom*, Cambridge: Cambridge University Press.

Fussell, S.R. and R.J. Kreuz (eds 1998) *Social and Cognitive Approaches to Interpersonal Communication*, Mahwah, NJ: Erlbaum.

Futuyma, D.J. (1986) *Evolutionary Biology* (2nd edition), Sunderland, MA: Sinauer.

Gallese, V., L. Craighero, L. Fadiga and L. Fogassi (1999) "Perception through action", *Psyche*, 5.21 (July 1999).

Gardner, B.T. and R.A. Gardner (1971) "Two-way communication with an infant chimpanzee", in A. Schrier and F. Stollnitz (eds) *Behavior of Non-human Primates*, New York: Academic Press.

Garfinkel, H. (1972) "Remarks on ethnomethodology", in J. Gumperz and D. Hymes (eds 1972).

Garrod, S.C. and A.J. Sanford (1994) "Resolving sentences in discourse context: How discourse representation affects discourse understanding", in M.A. Gernsbacher (ed. 1994).

Gathercole, S.E. and A.D. Baddeley (1993) *Working Memory and Language*, Hillsdale, NJ: Erlbaum.

Gazdar, G. (1979) *Pragmatics: Implicature, Presupposition and Logical Form,* New York: Academic Press.

Geach, P.T. (1962) *Reference and Generality*, Ithaca, New York: Cornell University Press.

Geertz, C. (1972) "Linguistic etiquette", in J.B. Pride and J. Holmes (eds) *Sociolinguistics*, London: Penguin Books.

Geertz, C. (1973) *The Interpretation of Cultures*, New York: Basic Books.

Gernsbacher, M.A. (1985) "Surface information loss in comprehension", *Cognitive Psychology*, 17.

Gernsbacher, M.A. (1990) *Language Comprehension as Structure Building*, Hillsdale, NJ: Erlbaum.

Gernsbacher, M.A. (ed. 1994) *Handbook of Psycholinguistics*, New York: Academic Press.

Gernsbacher, M.A. and M.E. Faust (1991) "The mechanism of suppression: A component of general comprehension skills", *J. of Experimental Psychology: Learning, Memory and Cognition*, 17.2.

Gernsbacher, M.A. and T. Givón (eds 1994) *Coherence in Spontaneous Discourse*, TSL 31, Amsterdam: J. Benjamins.

Gibbs, R. (1984) "Literal meaning and psychological theory", *Cognitive Psychology*, 8.

Gibbs, R. (1987) "What does it mean to say that a metaphor has been understood?", in R.S. Haskell (ed.) *Cognition and Symbolic Structure: The Psychology of Metaphoric Transformations*, Norwood, NJ: Ablex.

Gibbs, R. (1994a) *The Poetics of Mind: Figurative Thought, Language and Understanding*, New York: Cambridge University Press.

Gibbs, R.W. (1994b) "Figurative thought and figurative language", in M.A. Gernsbacher (ed. 1994).

Gibbs, R., J.M. Bogdanovich, J.R. Sykes and D.J. Barr (1997) ""Metaphor in idiom comprehension", *J. of Memory and Language*, 37.

Gilberg, C. (ed. 1989) *Diagnosis and Treatment of Autism*, New York: Plenum.

Givón, T. (1973a) "The time-axis phenomenon", *Language*, 49.4.

Givón, T. (1973b) "Opacity and reference in language: An inquiry into the role of modalities", in J. Kimball (ed.) *Syntax and Semantics* II, New York: Academic Press.

Givón, T. (1979a) *On Understanding Grammar*, New York: Academic Press.

Givón, T. (1979b) (ed.) *Discourse and Syntax, Syntax and Semantics,* vol. 12, New York: Academic Press.

Givón, T. (1982) "Evidentiality and epistemic space", *Studies in Language*, 6.1.

Givón, T. (1983) (ed.) *Topic Continuity in Discourse: Quantified Cross-Language Studies*, TSL 3, Amsterdam: J. Benjamins.

Givón, T. (1984) ""Universals of discourse structure and second language acquisition", in W. Rutherford (ed.) *Language Universals and Second Language Acquisition*, TSL 5, Amsterdam: J. Benjamins.

Givón, T. (1985) (ed.) *Quantified Studies in Discourse, Text*, 5.1/2.

Givón, T. (1987) "Beyond foreground and background", in R. Tomlin (ed. 1987).

Givón, T. (1989) *Mind, Code and Context: Essays in Pragmatics*, Hillsdale, NJ: Erlbaum.

Givón, T. (1990) "Natural language learning and organized language teaching", in H. Burmeister and P. Rounds (eds) *Variability in Second Language Acquisition: Proceedings of the 10th Second Language Research Forum (SLRF)*, Eugene: University of Oregon.

Givón, T. (1991a) "The grammar of referential coherence as mental processing instructions", *Linguistics*, 30.1.

Givón, T. (1991b) "Serial verbs and the mental reality of 'event': Grammatical vs. cognitive packaging", in E. Traugott and B. Heine (eds) *Approaches to Grammaticalization*, TSL 19.1, Amsterdam: J. Benjamins.

Givón, T. (1991c) "Isomorphism in the grammatical code: Cognitive and biological considerations", *Studies in Language*, 15.1.

Givón, T. (1994) "Irrealis and the subjunctive", *Studies in Language*, 18.2.

Givón, T. (1994) (ed.) *Voice and Inversion*, TSL #30, Amsterdam: J. Benjamins.

Givón, T. (1995) *Functionalism and Grammar*, Amsterdam: J. Benjamins.

Givón, T. (1997) (ed.) *Conversation: Cognitive, Communicative and Social Perspectives*, TSL 34, Amsterdam: J. Benjamins.

Givón, T. (2001a) *Syntax*, vol. I, II, Amsterdam: J. Benjamins.

Givón, T. (2001b) "Toward a neuro-cognitive interpretation of 'context'", *Pragmatics and Cognition*, 9.2.

Givón, T. (2002) *Bio-linguistics: The Santa Barbara Lectures*, Amsterdam: J. Benjamins.

Givón, T. and B. F. Malle (eds 2002) *The Evolution of Language out of Pre-Language*, TSL 53, Amsterdam: J. Benjamins.

Givón, T. and P. Young (2002) "Cooperation and interpersonal manipulation in the society of intimates", in M. Shibatani (ed. 2002).

Gladwell, M. (2000) "The New-Boy Network", *The New Yorker*, 5–22–2002, pp. 68–86.

Glenberg, A. M., P. Kruley and W. A. Langston (1994) "Analogical processing in comprehension: Simulation of a mental model", in M. A. Gernsbacher (ed. 1994).

Glucksberg, S. (1991) "Beyond literal meaning: The psychology of allusion", *Psychological Science*, 2.

Glucksberg, S. (1993) "Idiomatic meaning and allusional content", in C. Cacciari and P. Tabbossi (eds 1993).

Glucksberg, S. and B. Keysar (1990) ""Understanding metaphoric comparison: Beyond similarity", *Psychological Review*, 97.

Glucksberg, S., B. Keysar and M.S. NcGlone (1992) "Metaphor understanding and accessing conceptual schemata: Reply to Gibbs", *Psychological Review*, 99.

Glucksberg. S., F.J. Kreutz and S.H. Rho (1986) "Context can constrain lexical access: Implications for models of language comprehension", *J. of Experimental Psychology: Learning, Memory and Cognition*, 12.

Goethe, J.W. *Faust*, tr. (1961) by W. Kaufmann; New York: Anchor Books (ppbk).

Goffman, I. (1959) *The Presentation of the Self in Everyday Life*, New York; Doubleday/Anchor Books (ppbk).

Goffman, E. (1963) *Behavior in Public Places*, Glencoe, IL: The Free Press of Glencoe.

Goffman, E. (1967) *Interaction Rituals*, Garden City, New York: Doubleday.

Goffman, E. (1971) *Relations in Public*, New York: Basic Books.

Goffman, H. (1974) *Frame Analysis*, Cambridge, Mass.: Harvard University Press.

Goffman, H. (1976) "Replies and responses", *Language and Society*, 5.

Goodale, M.A. (2000) "Perception and action in the human visual system", in M.S. Gazzaniga (ed.) *The New Cognitive Neuroscience*, 2nd edition, Cambridge, Mass.: MIT Press.

Gopnik, A. and H.M. Wellman (1992) "Why the child's theory of mind is really a theory", *Mind and Language*, 7.

Gopnik, A. and H.M. Wellman (1994) "The theory theory", in L.A. Hirschfeld and S.A. Gelman (eds) *Mapping the Mind: Domain Specificity in Cognition and Culture*, New York: Cambridge University Press.

Gordon, R.M. (1998) "The prior question: Do human primates have a theory of mind?", peer commentary on Heyes (1998), *Behavior and Brain Sciences*, 21, p. 120.

Gould, S.J. (1977) *Ontogeny and Phylogeny*, Cambridge, Mass: Harvard University Press.

Gould, S.J. (1980) *The Panda's Thumb*, London: Pelican.

Gray, C. and P. Russell (1998) "Theory of mind in non-human primates: Question of language?", peer commentary on Heyes (1998), *Behavior and Brain Sciences* 21, p. 121.

Gray, R.D., M. Heaney and S. Fairhall (2004) "Evolutionary Paychology and the challenge of adaptive explanation", in K. Sterelny and J. Fitness (eds) *From Mating to Mentality: Evaluating Evolutionary Psychology*, London/New York: Psychology Press.

Greenfield, P.M. (1991) "Language, tools and brain: The ontogeny and phylogeny of hierarchically organized sequential behavior", *Behavior and Brain Science*, 14.4.

Grice, H.P. (1968/1975) "Logic and conversation", in Cole and Morgan (eds 1975).

Grillner, S. (1975) "Locomotion in vertebrates–central mechanisms and reflex interaction", *Physiological Review*, 55.

Grimes, J. (1975) *The Thread of Discourse*, The Hague: Mouton.

Gumperz, J. (1977) "Sociocultural knowledge in conversational inference", in M. Saville-Troike (ed.) *Linguistics and Anthropology*, Washington, D.C.: Georgetown University Press.

Gumperz, J. and D. Hymes (eds 1972) *Directions in Sociolinguistics*, New York: Holt, Rinehart and Winston.

Gumperz, J. (1982) *Discourse Strategies*, Cambridge: Cambridge University Press.

Haberland, H. (1985) "Review of Klaus Heinrich, *Tertium Datur, J. of Pragmatics*, 9.2/3.

Haiman, J. (1985a) *Natural Syntax*, Cambridge: Cambridge University Press.

Haiman, J. (1985b) (ed.) *Iconicity in Syntax*, TSL #6, Amsterdam: J. Benjamins.

Hale, K. (1988) "Misumalpan verb sequencing constructions", paper read at the Chibchan Session, AAA Annual Meeting, Phoenix (ms).

Hale, K. (1991) "Misumalpan verb-sequencing constructions", in C. Lefebvre (ed.) *Serial Verbs: Grammatical, Comparative and Cognitive Approaches*, SSLS 8, Amsterdam: J. Benjamins Session.

Halliday, M.A.K. (1967) "Notes on transitivity and theme in English", *J. of Linguistics*, 3.

Halliday, M.A.K. and R. Hassan (1976) *Cohesion in English*, English Language Series, 9, London: Longman's.

Hamilton, E. and H. Cairns (eds 1961) *Plato: Collected Dialogs*, Princeton, NJ: Princeton University Press, Bollingen Series LXXI.

Hanson, R.N. (1958) *Patterns of Discovery*, Cambridge: Cambridge University Press.

Hauser, M. (2000) *Wild Minds*, New York: Henry Holt.

Haxton, B. (2001) *Fragments: The Collected Wisdon of Heraclitus*, New York: Viking.

Hayashi, L. (1989) "Conjunctions and referential continuity", University of Oregon, Eugene (ms).

Heine, B. (1993) *Auxiliaries: Cognitive Forces and Grammaticalization*, New York: Oxford University Press.

Heine, B. (1997) *Cognitive Foundations of Grammar*, New York: Oxford University Press.

Heine, B. (2002) "On the role of context in grammaticalization", in I. Wischer (ed.) *New Reflections on Grammaticalization*, TSL 49, Amsterdam: J. Benjamins.

Heine, B. and M. Reh (1984) *Grammaticalization and Reanalysis in African Languages*, Hamburg: Helmut Buske Verlag.

Heine, B., U. Claudi and F. Huennemeyer (1991) *Grammaticalization: A Conceptual Framework*, Chicago: University of Chicago Press.

Heller, J. (1962) *Catch-22*, London: Transworld Corgi (ppbk, 1970).

Hempel, C. (1959) "The logic of functional analysis", in L. Gross (ed.) *Symposium on Sociological Theory*, New York: Harper & Row (in B. Brody ed. 1970).

Hempel, C. and P. Oppenheim (1948) "Studies in the logic of explanation", *Philosophy of Science*, XV (in B. Brody ed. 1970).

Heraclitus, *Fragments*, in B. Haxton (tr. and ed. 2001).

Herman, R., S. Grillner, P. Stein and D.G. Stuart (eds 1976) *Neural Control of Locomotion*, vol. 18, New York: Plenum Press.

Heyes, C.M. (1998) "Theory of mind in non-human primates", *Behavioral and Brain Sciences*, 21.

Hiaasen, C. 2002) *Basket Case*, New York: Knopf.

Hinttika, J. (1967) "Individuals, possible words and epistemic logic", *Nous*, 1.

Hopper, p. (1987) "Emergent grammar", *BLS* **13**, Berkeley: Berkeley Linguistics Society.

Hopper, P. (1991) "On some principles of grammaticalization", in E.C. Traugott and B. Heine (eds 1991), vol. I.

Hopper, P. and E. Traugott (1993) *Grammaticalization*, Cambridge: Cambridge University Press.

Horn, L. (1972) *On the Semantic Properties of Logical Operators in English*, University of California, Los Angeles, PhD dissertation (ms).

Hubel, D. (1988) *Eye, Brain and Vision*, New York: Scientific American Library.

Humboldt, W. von (1836) *Linguistic Variability and Intellectual Development*, tr. G.C. Buck (1971), Coral Gables, FL: University of Florida Press.

Humphreys, G.W. and J.M. Riddoch (1987a) "Introduction: Cognitive psychology and visual object processing", in G.W. Humphreys and J.M. Riddoch (eds, 1987).

Humphreys, G.W. and J.M. Riddoch (eds 1987b) *Visual Object Processing: A Cognitive Neuropsychological Approach*, London: Erlbaum.

Humphreys, G.W. and M.J. Riddoch (1988) "On the case of multiple semantic systems: A reply to Shallice", *Cognitive Neuropsychology*, 5.1.

Ibsen, H. (1867) *Peer Gynt*, tr. by P. Watts, London: Penguin Classics (ppbk; 1966; reprinted 1970).

Ibsen, H. (1963) *Peer Gynt: Et Dramatisk Dikt*, Oslo: Universitetsforlaget.

Itkonen, E. (1982) "Change of language as a prototype of change of science", in A. Alqvist (ed.) *Papers from the Fifth International Conference on Historical Linguistics*, Amsterdam: J. Benjamins.

Itkonen, E. (2002) "Grammaticalization as an analogue of hypothetico-deductive thinking", in E. Wisher and G. Diewald (eds) *New Reflections on Grammaticalization*, Amsterdam: J. Benjamins.

James, W. (n.d.) *The Philosophy of William James*, New York: Random House.

Jespersen, O. (1924/1965) *Philosophy of Grammar*, New York: Norton.

Johnson, N. S. and J. M. Mandler (1977) "Remembrance of things parsed: Story structure and recall", *Cognitive Psychology*, 9.

Just, M. A. and P. A. Carpenter (1992) "A capacity theory of comprehension: Individual differences in working memory", *Psychological Review*, 99.1.

Kaas, J. H. (1989) "Why does the brain have so many visual areas?", *J. of Cognitive Neuroscience*, 1.2.

Kahneman, D. (1973) *Attention and Effort*, Englewood Cliffs, NJ: Prentice-Hall.

Kahneman, D. and A. Treisman (1984) ""Changing views of attention and automaticity", in D. Parasuraman (ed.) *Varieties of Attention*, London: Academic Press.

Kant, I. *Critique of Pure Reason*, in N. K. Smith (tr. 1929/1973).

Kamawar, D. and D. R. Olson (1998) "Theory of mind in young human primates: Does Heyes' task measure it?", peer commentary on Heyes (1998), *Behavioral and Brain Sciences*, 21, p. 122.

Karttunen, L. (1974) "Presupposition and linguistic context", *Theoretical Linguistics*, 1.2.

Katz, J. J. (1977) *Propositional Structure and Illocutionary Force*, New York: Crowell.

Katz, J. J. and J. A. Fodor (1963) "The structure of a semantic theory", *Language*, 39.

Keenan, E. L. (1969) *A Logical Base for for a Transformational Grammar of English*, University of Pennsylvania, PhD dissertation (ms).

Keenan, E. L. (1972) "Two types of presupposition in human language", in C. Fillmore and T. Langendoen (eds) *Studies in Linguistic Semantics*, New York: Holt, Rinehart and Winston.

Kelly, J. P. (1985) "Anatomical basis of sensory perception and motor coordination", in E. R. Kandell and J. H. Schwartz (eds) *Principles of Neural Science*, 2nd edition, New York: Elsevier.

Kemp, J. (1968) *The Philosophy of Kant*, Oxford: Oxford University Press.

Kerns, J. G., J. D. Cohen, A. W. MacDonald III, R. W. Cho, V. A. Stenger and C. S. Carter (2004) "Anterior cingulate conflict monitoring and adjustment control", *Science*, 303 (2–13–04):1023–1026.

Kilpatrick, S. D., V. L. Bissonette and C. E. Rusbult (2002) "Empathic accuracy and accommodative behavior among newly married couples", *Personal Relationships*, 9.4:369–93.

Kintsch, W. (1977) "On comprehending stories", in M. S. Just and P. Carpenter (eds) *Cognitive Processes in Comprehension*, Hillsdale, NJ: Erlbaum.

Kintsch, W. (1982) "Memory for text", in A. Flammer and W. Kintsch (eds) *Text Processing*, Amsterdam: North Holland.

Kintsch, W. (1988) "The role of knowledge in discourse comprehension: A construction-integration model", *Psychological Review*, 95.

Kintsch, W. (1992) "How readers construct situation models for stories: The role of syntactic cues and causal inference", in A. F. Healy, S. Kosslyn and R. M. Shiffrin (eds) *Essays in Honor of William K. Estes*, Hillsdale, NJ: Erlbaum.

Kintsch, W. (1994) "The psychology of discourse processing", in M. A. Gernsbacher (ed. 1994).

Kintsch, W. and T. van Dijk (1978) "Toward a model of text comprehension and production", *Psychological Review*, 85.

Kiparski, C. and P. Kiparski (1968) "Fact" in M. Bierwisch and B. Heidolph (eds) *Progress in Linguistics*, The Hague: Mouton.

Klein, R. N. (2003) "Chronometric explorations of disordered minds", *Trends in Cognitive Science*, 7.5 (May 2003).

Koffka, K. (1935) *Principles of Gestalt Psychology*, New York: Harcourt, Brace.

Kripke, S. (1963) "Semantic considerations in modal logic", *Acta Philosophica Fennica*, 16.

Kripke, S. (1972) "Naming and necessity", in D. Davidson and G. Harman (eds 1972).

Kuhn, T. (1962) *The Structure of Scientific Revolutions*, Chicago: University of Chicago Press.

LaBar, K. S., D. R. Gleitman, T. B. Parrish and M.-M. Mesulam (1999) "Neuroanatomic overlap of working memory and spatial attention networks: A functional MRI comparison with subjects", *Neuroimage*, 10.6:695–704.

Labov, W. (1972a) *Sociolinguistic Patterns*, Philadelphia: University of Pennsylvania Press.

Labov, W. (1972b) "Rules for ritual insults", in D. Sudnow (ed.) *Studies in Social Interaction*, New York: The Free Press.

Lakatos, I. (1978) *The Methodology of Scientific Research Programmes*, Philosophical Papers, vol. I, Cambridge: Cambridge University Press.

Lakoff, G. (1987) *Women, Fire and Dangerous Things*, Chicago: University of Chicago Press.

Lakoff, G., J. Espenson and A. Goldberg (1989) *Master Metaphor List* (unpublished draft), Cognitive Linguistics Group, UC Berkeley.

Lakoff, G. and M. Johnson (1980) *Metaphors We Live By*, Chicago: University of Chicago Press.

Lakoff, G. and M. Turner (1989) *More than Cool Reason: A Field Guide to Poetic Metaphor*, Chicago: University of Chicago Press.

L'Amour, L. (1962) *Shalako*, New York: Bantam (ppbk).

Lande, R. (1980) "Microevolution in relation to macroevolution", *Paleobiology*, 6.2.

Lande, R. (1986) "The dynamics of peak shifts and the pattern of morphological evolution", *Paleobiology*, 12.4.

Landry, R. and S. E. Bryson (2004) "Impaired disengagement of attention in young children with autism", *J. of Child Psychology and Psychiatry* (in press).

Langacker, R. (1987) *Foundations of Cognitive Grammar*, Stanford: Stanford University Press.

Lao Tse, *Tao Teh Ching* (Book of the Tao), translated with an introduction by T. Givón, Ignacio, CO: Shaolin-West Foundation.

Lee, C. J. (1990) "Some hypotheses concerning the evolution of polysemous words", *J. of Psycholinguistic Research*, 19.

Lees, R. B. (1957) "Review of Chomsky's *Syntactic Structures*", *Language*, 33.

Lehrer, A. (1990) ""Polysemy, conventionality and the structure of the lexicon", *Cognitive Linguistics*, 1.

Leonard, E. (1990) *Get Shorty*, New York: Dell.

Leslie, A. M. (1987) "Pretense and representation: the origins of 'a theory of mind'", *Psychological Review*, 94:412–26.

Leslie, A. M. and U. Frith (1988) "Autistic children's understanding of seeing, knowing and believing", *British J. of Developmental Psychology*, 6.

Levinson, S. (1983) *Pragmatics*, Cambeidge: Cambridge University Press.

Levinson, S. (2000) *Presumptive Meaning*, Cambridge, Mass.: MIT Press.

Levy, D. (1979) "Communicative goals and strategies: Between discourse and syntax", in T. Givón (ed. 1979b).

Lewis, D. (1972) "General semantics", in D., Davidson and G. Harman (eds 1972).

Lewis, D. (1979) "Score keeping in a language game", *Journal of Philosophical Logic*, 8.

Li, C. N. (2002) "Missing links, issues and hypotheses in the evolutionary origin of language", in T. Givón and B. F. Malle (eds 2002).

Lieberman, P. (1984) *The Biology and Evolution of Language*, Cambridge, Mass: Harvard University Press.

Limber, J. (1973) "The genesis of complex sentences", in T. Moore (ed.) *Cognitive Development and the Acquisition of Language*, New York: Academic Press.

Linde, C. (1974) *The Linguistic Encoding of Spatial Information*, PhD dissertation, Columbia University (ms).

Lloyd, G. E. R. (1996) *Aristotelian Explorations*, Cambridge: Cambridge University Press.

Lo, P.-J., M. Inn, R. Amacker and S. Foe (1979) *The Essence of T'ai Chi Ch'uan*, Richmond, CA: North Atlantic Books.

Loftus, E. (1980) *Eyewitness Testimony*, Cambridge, Mass.: Harvard University Press.

Longacre, R. (1976) *Anatomy of Speech Notions*, Lisse: Peter de Ridder Press.

Lysaker, P. H. (2000) "Neurocognition, narrative and the structure of dialogue in schizophrenia: Theoretical and clinical implications", paper presented at the University of Oregon, Eugene (ms).

Lysaker, P. H. and J. Lysaker (2000) "Psychosis and the disintegration of dialogical self-structure: Problem posed by schizophrenia for the maintenance of dialogue", *British J. of Medical Psychology*,.

Lysaker, P. H., M. D. Bell, W. S. Zito and S. M. Bioti (1995a) "Social skill impairments at work: Deficit and predictors of improvement in schizophrenia", *J. of Nervous and Mental Disease*, 183: 688–92.

Lysaker, P. H., M. D. Bell and J.G. Goulet (1995b) "The Wisconsin card sorting test and work performance in schizophrenia", *Psychiatric Research*, 56:45–51.

MacDonald, A. W. III, J. D. Cohen, V. A. Stegner and C. S. Carter (2000) "Dissociating the role of the dorsolateral prefrontal and anterior cingulate cortex in cognitive control", *Science*, 288 (5472):1835–1838.

MacWhinney, B. (1999) "The emergence of language from embodiment", in B. MacWhinney (ed.) *The Emergence of Language*, Mahwah, NJ: Erlbaum.

MacWhinney, B. (2002) "The gradual emergence of language", in T. Givón and B. F. Malle (eds 2002).

Malle, B., L. J. Moses and D. A. Baldwin (eds 2000) *Intentionality: A Key to Human Understanding*, Cambridge: MIT Press.

Mandler, J. M. (1978) "A code in the node: The use of story schemata in retrieval", *Discourse Processes*, 1.

Martin, J. H. (1985) "Development as a guide to the regional anatomy of the brain", in E. R. Kandell and J. H. Schwartz (eds) *Principles of Neural Science*, 2nd edition, New York: Elsevier.

Mayr, E. (1969) *Populations, Species and Evolution*, Cambridge: Harvard University Press.

Mayr, E. (1976) *Evolution and the Diversity of Life*, Cambridge, Mass.: Harvard University Press.

Mbotela, J. (1934) *Uhuru wa Watumwa*, London: Nelson [1966 edition].

McCandliss, B.D. (1992) "Understanding text when words have several meanings: Do inappropriate meanings have an influence?" Unpublished Research Thesis, University of Oregon, Eugene (ms).

McCormack, E.R. (1985) *A Cognitive Theory of Metaphor*, Cambridge, Mass.: MIT Press.

McKeon, R. (ed., 1941) *The Basic Works of Aristotle*, New York: Random House (22nd printing, 1970).

McNeilly, M. (2001) *Sun Tzu and the Art of Modern Warfare*, Oxford: Oxford University Press.

Meltzoff, A.N. (1999) "Origins of theory of mind, cognition and communication", *J. of Communication Disorders*, 32:251–69.

Meltzoff, A.N. (2002a) "Imitation as a mechanism of social cognition: Origins of empathy, theory of mind and the representation of action", in U. Goswami (ed.) *Blackwell Handbook of Child Cognitive Development*, Oxford: Blackwell Publishers.

Meltzoff, A,N, (2002b) "Elements of a developmental theory of imitation", in A.N. Meltzoff and W. Prinz (eds 2002).

Meltzoff, A.N. and W. Prinz (eds 2002) *The Imitative Mind: Development, Evolution and Brain Bases*, Cambridge: Cambridge University Press.

Menn, L. (1990) "Agrammatism in English: Two case studies", in L. Menn and E. Obler (eds 1990).

Menn, L. and E. Obler (eds 1990) *Agrammatic Aphasia* (3 vols), Amsterdam: J. Benjamins.

Mesulam, M.-M. (2000) *Principles of Behavioral and Cognitive Neurology*, New York: Oxford University Press.

Meyer, D.E. and R.W. Schwaneveldt (1971) "Facilitation in recognizing pairs of words: Evidence of a dependence between retrieval operations", *J. of Experimental Psychology*, 90.

Meyer, D.E. and Schwaneveldt, R.W. (1976) "Meaning, memory structure and mental processes", *Science*, 192:27–33.

Milner, A.D. and M.A. Goodale (1995) *The Visual Brain in Action*, Oxford: Oxford University Press.

Millner, D.A. and M.A. Goodale (1998) "The visual brain in action", *Psyche*, 4.12 (October 1998).

Mishkin, M. (1978) "Memory in monkeys severely impaired by combined but not by separate removal of amygdala and hippocampus", *Nature*, 273.

Mishkin, M. (1982) "A memory system in the monkey", *Philosophical Soc. of London [Biol.]*, 298.

Mishkin, M., B. Malamut and J. Bachevalier (1984) "Memories and habits: Two neural systems", in G. Lynch and J.L. McGaugh (eds), *Neurobiology of Learning and Memory*, New York: Guilford Press.

Mithen, S. (1996) *The Prehistory of Mind*, London: Penguin.

Montague, R. (1970) "Pragmatics and intensional logic", *Synthese*, 22 (reprinted in D. Davidson and G. Harman eds, 1972).

Morris, C. (1938) *Foundations of of the Theory of Signs*, Chicago: University of Chicago Press.

Morris, C. (1963) "Pragmatism and logical empiricism", in Carnap (1983).

Morton, J., U. Frith and A.M. Leslie (1991) "The cognitive basis of a biological disorder: Autism", *Trends in Neuroscience*, 4.

Myre, G. (2004) "Corruption inquiry may pose political hazard for Sharon", *The New York Times International*, Thursday January 22, 2004, p. A3.

Neeley, J. H. (1990) "Semantic priming effects in visual word recognition: A selective review of current findings and theories", in D. Besner and G. Humphreys (eds) *Basic Processes in Reading: Visual Word Recognition,* Hillsdale: Erlbaum.

Nietzsche, F. (1887) *The Genealogy of Morals,* in F. Golffing (tr. & ed.) *Friedrich Nietzsche: The Birth of Tragedy and The Genealogy of Morals,* New York: Doubleday/ Anchor ppbk (1956).

Norris, D. (1986) "Word recognition: Context effects without priming", *Cognition,* 22.

Nunberg, G. (1979) "The non-uniqueness of semantic solutions: Polysemy", *Linguistics and Philosophy,* 3.

Ochs, E. K. (1979) "Social foundations of language", in R. Freedle (ed.) *New Directions in Discourse Processing,* vol. 3, Norwood, NJ: Ablex.

Ochs, E. and B. Schieffelin (eds 1979) *Developmental Pragmatics,* New York: Academic Press.

Oh, C.-K. and D. Dinneen (eds, 1979) *Presupposition, Syntax and Semantics,* 11, New York: Academic Press.

Ortonyi, A. (ed. 1979) *Metaphor and Thought,* Cambridge: Cambridge University Press.

Ortonyi, A. (1980) "Some psycholinguistic aspects of metaphor", in R. P. Honeck and R. R. Hoffman (eds) *Cognition and Figurative Language,* Hillsdale, NJ: Erlbaum.

Palmer, F. (1979) *Modality and the English Modals,* London: Longmans.

Palmer, F. (1986) *Mood and Modality,* Cambridge: Cambridge University Press.

Park, R. E. (1950) *Race and Culture,* Glencoe, ILL: The Free Press.

Paul, H. (1890) *Principles of the History of Language,* tr. H. A. Armstrong, London: Swan Sonnenschein & Co.

Pearson, T. R. (1985) *A Short History of a Small Place,* New York: Ballantine (ppbk).

Peirce, C. S. (1931) *Collected Writings,* vol. I, Cambridge, Mass.: Harvard University Press.

Peirce, C. S. (1934) *Collected Writings,* vol. V, Cambridge: Harvard University Press.

Peirce, C. S. (1940) *The Philosophy of Peirce,* ed. by J. Buchler, New York: Harcourt, Brace.

Penner, J., U. Frith, A. M. Leslie and S. Leekam (1989) "Exploration of the autistic child's theory of mind: Knowledge, belief and communication", *Child Development,* 60.

Pepperberg, I. M. (1991) "A communicative approach to animal cognition: A study of conceptual abilities of an African Grey Parrot", in C. A. Ristau (ed. 1991).

Pepperberg, I. M. (1999) *The Alex Studies: Cognitive and Communicative Abilities of Grey Parrots,* Cambridge, Mass: Harvard University Press.

Percy, W. (1960) *The Moviegoer,* New York: Vintage International (1998 ppbk edition).

Petri, H. L. and M. Mishkin (1994) "Behaviorism, cognitivism and the new psychology of memory", *American Scientist,* 82.

Pinker, S. (1989) "Language acquisition", in M. I. Posner (ed. 1989).

Plato, *Cratylus,* in E. Hamilton and H. Cairns (eds 1961).

Plato, *Hippias Major,* in Woodruff (ed. 1982).

Plato, *Meno,* in E. Hamilton and H. Cairns (eds 1961).

Plato, *Phaedo,* in E. Hamilton and H. Cairns (eds 1961).

Popper, K. (1934/1959) *The Logic of Scientific Discovery* (revised edition, 1868), New York: Harper & Row.

Posner, M. I. (1978) *Chronometric Explorations of Mind,* New York: Oxford University Press.

Posner, M. I. (1986) ""Empirical studies of prototypes", in C. Craig (ed.) *Categorization and Noun Classification,* TSL #7, Amsterdam: J. Benjamins.

Posner, M. I. (ed., 1989) *Foundations of Cognitive Science,* Cambridge, Mass.: MIT Press.

Posner, M. I. (2004) "The achievements of brain imaging: Past and future", in N. Kanwisher and J. Duncan (eds) *Attention and Performance XX,* New York: Oxford University Press.

Posner, M. I. and S. W. Boies (1971) "Components of attention", *Psychological Review*, 78.

Posner, M. I. and J. Fan (2004) "Attention as an organ system", Dept. of Psychology, University of Oregon (ms).

Posner, M. I. and S. Keele (1968) "On the genesis of abstract ideas", *J. of Experimental Psychology*, 77.

Posner, M. I. and R. Klein (1971) "On the function of consciousness", *Fourth Conference on Attention and Performance*, University of Colorado, Boulder (ms).

Posner, M. I. and O. Marin (eds 1985) *Attention and Performance, XI*, Hillsdale, NJ: Erlbaum.

Posner, M. I. and A. Pavese (1997) "Anatomy of word and sentence meanings", paper presented at the *Colloquium on Neuroimaging of Human Brain Functions*, M. Posner and M. Raichle, orgs, *Nat. Acad. of Scie. USA*, Irvine, CA, May 1997 (ms).

Posner, M. I., M. K. Rothbart, N. Vizueta, K. N. Levy, D. E. Evans, K. M. Thomas and J. F. Clarkin (2002) "Attentional mechanisms of borderline personality disorder", *Proc. National Academy of Science USA*, 99.25:16366016370.

Posner, M. I., M. K. Rothbart, N. Vizueta, K. M. Thomas, K. N. Levy, J. Fossella, D. Silbersweig, E. Stern, J. Clarkin and O. Kernberg (2003) "An approach to the psychobiology of personality disorders", *Development and Psychopathology*, 15:1093–1106.

Posner, M. I. and C. R. R. Snyder (1974) "Attention and cognitive control", in R. L. Solso (ed.) *Information Processing and Cognition: The Loyola Symposium*, Hillsdale, NJ: Erlbaum.

Posner, M. I. and R. E. Warren (1972) "Traces, concepts and conscious constructions", in A. W. Melton and E. Martin (eds) *Coding Processes in Human Memory*, Washington, DC: Winston & Sons.

Povinelli, D. J. and S. deBlois (1992) "Young children's understanding of knowledge formation in themselves and others", *J. of Comparative Psychology*, 106.

Povinelli, D. J. and T. M. Preuss (1995) "Theory of mind: Evolutionary history of a cognitive specialization", *Trends in Neuroscience*, 18.9.

Povinelli, D. J. and T. Eddy (1996a) "What young chimpanzees know about seeing", *Monographs of the Society of Research on Child Development*, 61.247.

Povinelli, D. J. and T. Eddy (1996b) "Factors affecting young chimpanzees' recognition of attention", *J. of Comparative Psychology*, 110.

Povinelli, D. J. and T. Eddy (1996c) "Chimpanzees: Joint visual attention", *Psychological Science*, 7.

Povinelli, D. J., K. E. Nelson and S. T. Boysen (1990) "Inference about guessing and knowing by chimpanzees (Pan troglodytes)", *J. of Comparative Psychology*, 104.

Povinelli, D. J., K. E. Nelson and S. T. Boysen (1992) Comprehension of role reversal in chimpanzees: Evidence of empathy?", *Animal Behavior*, 43.

Power, M. (1991) *The Egalitarians: Human and Chimpanzee*, Cambridge: Cambridge University Press.

Premack, D. (1971) "Language in chimpanzee", *Science*, 172.

Premack. D. and G. Woodruff (1978) "Does the chimpanzee have a theory of mind?", *Behavioral and Brain Sciences*, 1.4.

Purtill, R. L. (1968) "Identity through possible worlds", *Nous*, 2.

Quattrone, G. A. and A. Tversky (1985) "Self-deception and the voter's illusion", in J. Elster (ed. 1985).

Quillian, M. R. (1968) "Semantic memory", in M. Minsky (ed.) *Semantic Information Processing*, Cambridge, Mass.: MIT Press.

Quine, w. van O. (1951) "Two dogmas of empiricism", *Philosophical Review*, 60.

Quine, W. van O. (1953) "Reference and Modality", ch. 8 of *From a Logical Point of View*, Cambridge: Harvard University Press.

Ramsay, V. (1987) "The functional distribution of pre-posed and post-posed 'if' and 'when' clauses in written discourse", in R. Tomlin (ed. 1987).

Riddoch, M. J. and G. W. and Humphreys (1987a) "Visual optic processing in a case of optic aphasia", *Cognitive Neuropsychology*, 4.

Riddoch, M. J. and G. W. Humphreys (1987b) "Picture naming", in G. W. Humphreys and J. M. Riddoch (eds 1987).

Riddoch, M. J., G. W. Humphreys, M. Coltheart and E. Funnell (1988) "Semantic systems or system? Neuropsychological evidence reexamined", *Cognitive Neuropsychology*, 5.1.

Rincover, A. and J. M. Ducharme (1987) "Variables influencing stimulus over-selectivity and "tunnel vision" in developmentally delayed children", *American J. of Mental Deficiency*, 91:422–30.

Ristau, C. A. (1991) (ed.) *Cognitive Ethology*, Hillsdale, NJ: Erlbaum.

Rizzolatti, G. and M. A. Arbib (1998) "Language within our grasp", *Trends in Neuroscience,* 21.

Rizzolatti, G., L. Fadiga, L. Fogassi and V. Gallese (1996a) "Premotor cortex and the recognition of motor actions", *Cognitive Brain Research*, 3:131–41.

Rizzolatti, G., L. Fadiga, M. Matelli, V. Bettinardi, E. Paulescu, D. Perani and F. Fazio (1996b) "Localization of grasp representation in humans by PET: 1. Observation vs. execution", *Experimental Brain Research*, 111.

Rizzolatti, G., L. Fogassi and V. Gallese (2000) "Cortical mechanisms subserving object grasping and action recognition: A new view on the cortical motor functions", in M. S. Gazzaniga (ed.) *The New Cognitive Neuroscience*, 2nd edition, Cambridge: MIT Press.

Rizzolatti, G. and M. Gentilucci (1988) "Motor and visual-motor functions of the premotor cortex", in P. Rakic an W. Singer (eds) *Neurobiology of Neocortex*, Chichester: Wiley.

Roberts, A. C., T. W. Robbins and L. Weiskrantz (1998) *The Pre-Frontal Cortex: Executive and Cognitive Functions*, Oxford: Oxford University Press.

Rosch, E. (1973a) "On the internal structure of perceptual and semantic categories", in T. E. Moore (ed.) *Cognitive Development and the Acquisition of Language*, New York: Academic Press.

Rosch, E. (1973b) "Natural Categories", *Cognitive Psychology*, 4.

Rosch, E. (1975) "Cognitive representation of semantic categories", *J. of Experimental Psychology: General*, 104.

Ross, J. R. (1967) *Constraints on Variables in Syntax*, PhD dissertation, MIT (ms).

Rothbart, M. and M. Taylor (1992) "Category labels and social reality: Do we view social categories as natural kinds?", in R. Semin and K. Fiedler (eds) *Language, Interaction and Social Cognition*, London: Sage Publ.

Rude, N. (1994) "Direct, inverse and passive in Northwest Sahaptin", in T. Givón (ed. 1994).

Russell, B. (1905) "On denoting", in Russell (1956).

Russell, B. (1908) "Mathematical logic as based on a theory of types", in Russell (1956).

Russell, B. (1911) "The relations of universals and particulars", in Russell (1956).

Russell, B. (1918) "The philosophy of logical atomism", in Russell (1956).

Russell, B. (1948) *Human Knowledge*, London: Routledge.

Russell, B. (1956) *Logic and Knowledge*, London: Routledge.

Sachs, H., E. Schegloff and G. Jefferson (1974) "A simplest systematic for the organization of turn-taking in conversation", *Language*, 50.4.

Sanford, A. J. and S. C. Garrod (1994) "Selective processing in text understanding", in M. A. Gernsbacher (ed. 1994).

Sapir, E. (1921) *Language*, (1929 edition) New York: Harcourt, Brace & Co., Harvest Books.

Schank, R. and R. Abelson (1977) *Scripts, Goals, Plans and Understanding*, Hillsdale, NJ: Erlbaum.

Savage-Rumbaugh, S. and R. Lewin (1994) *Kanzi: The Ape at the Brink of the Human Mind*, New York: Wiley and Sons.

Savage-Rumbaugh, S., J. Murphy, R.A. Sevcik, K.E. Brakke, S.L. Wiliams and D.M. Rumbaugh (1993) *Language Comprehension in Ape and Child, Monographs of the Society for Research in Child Development*, serial #233, vol. 58, nos 3–4.

Savage-Rumbaugh, S., S.G. Shanker and T.J. Taylor (1998) *Apes, Language and the Human Mind*, Oxford and New York: Oxford University Press.

Schieffelin, E. (1976) *The Sorrow of the Lonely and the Burning of the Dancer*, New York: St. Martin's Press.

Schmidt, R.A. (1975) "A schema theory of discrete motor skills", *Psychological Review*, 82.

Schmidt, R.A. (1980) "Past and future issues in motor programming", *Research Quarterly for Exercise Sports*, 51.1.

Schneider, W. (1985) "Toward a model of attention and the development of automatic processing", in M.I. Posner and O. Marin (eds 1985).

Schneider, W. and J.M. Chein (2003) "Controlled and automatic processing: Behavior, theory, and biological mechanism", *Cognitive Science*, 27:525–59.

Schneider, W. and R.M. Shiffrin (1977) "Controlled and automated human information processing, I: Detection, search and attention", *Psychological Review*, 84.

Schumann, J. (1976) "Second language acquisition: The pidginization hypothesis", *Language Learning*, 26.

Schumann, J. (1978) *The Pidginization Process: A Model for Second Language Acquisition*, Rowley, Mass.: Newbury House.

Schumann, J. (1985) "Non-syntactic speech in Spanish-English basilang", in R. Andersen (ed.) *Second Language Acquisition: A Cross-Linguistic Perspective*, Rowley, Mass.: Newbury House.

Schwaneveldt, R.W., D.E. Meyer and C.A. Becker (1976) "Lexical ambiguity, semantic context, and visual word recognition", *J. of Experimental Psychology: Human Perception and Performance*, 2.

Scollon, R. (1976) *Conversations with a One-Year Old Child*, Honolulu, HA: University of Hawaii Press.

Scott, D. (1970) "Advice on Modal Logic", in K. Lambrecht (ed.) *Philosophical Problems in Logic*, Dordrecht: Reidel.

Scriven, M. (1962) "Explanations, predictions and laws", in H. Feigl and G. Maxwell (eds) *Minnesota Studies in the Philosophy of Science*, III; reprinted in B. Brody (ed. 1970).

Searle, J. (1970) *Speech Acts*, Cambridge: Cambridge University Press.

Selinker, L. (1972) "Interlanguage", *International Review of Applied Linguistics*, 10.

Severin T. (1978) *The Brendan Voyage*, New York: McGraw-Hill.

Shallice, T. (1988) *From Neuropsychology to Mental Structure*, Cambridge: Cambridge University Press.

Shannon, C. and W. Weaver (1949) *The Mathematical Theory of Communication*, Urbana, IL: University of Illinois Press.

Shapiro, D.C.A. and R.A. Schmidt (1980) "Schema theory: Recent evidence and developmental implications", in J.A.S. Kelso and J.E. Clark (eds) *The Development of Movement Control and Coordination*, New York: Wiley.

Shapiro, D. C. A., R. F. Zernicke, R. J. Gregor and J. D. Diestel (1980) "Evidence for generalized motor program using gait pattern analysis", *J. of Motor Behavior.*

Shapiro, M. (1983) *The Sense of Grammar*, Bloomington: Indiana University Press.

Shibatani, M. (ed. 2002) *The Grammar of Causation and Interpersonal Manipulation*, TSL 48, Amsterdam: J. Benjamins.

Shiffrin, R. and W. Schneider (1977), "Controlled and automatic information processing, II", *Psychological Review*, 84.

Short, T. L. (1981) "Semeiosis and intentionality", *Transactions of the Charles S. Peirce Society*, 17.

Silberbauer, G. (1981) "Hunters/gatherers of the central Kalahari", in R. Harding and G. Teleki (eds) *Omnivorous Primates: Gathering and Hunting in Human Evolution*, 455–98, New York: Columbia University Press.

Simon, H. A. and C. A. Kaplan (1989) "Foundations of cognitive science", in M. I. Posner (ed. 1989).

Slaughter, V. and L. Mealey (1998) "Seeing is not (necessarily) believing", peer commentary on Heyes (1998), *Behavioral and Brain Sciences*, 21, p. 130.

Slobin, D. and A. Aksu (1982) "Tense, aspect and modality in the use of the Turkish evidential", in P. Hopper (ed.) *Tense-Aspect: Between Semantics and Pragmatics*, TSL 1, Amsterdam: J. Benjamins.

Smith, E. E., L. J. Rips and E. J. Shoben (1974) "Semantic memory and psychological semantics", in G. Bowers (ed.) *The Psychology of Learning and Motivation*, vol. 8, Hillsdale, NJ: Erlbaum.

Smith, N. K. (tr. 1929/1973) *Emmanuel Kant's Critique of Pure Reason*, London/New York: Macmillan (reprinted 1973).

Sperber, D. and D. Wilson (1986) *Relevance: Communication and Cognition*, Cambridge, Mass.: Harvard University Press.

Spitzer, M. (1999) *The Mind Within the Net: Models of Learning, Thinking and Acting*, Cambridge, Mass: MIT Press.

Squire, L. R. (1987) *Memory and Brain*, Oxford: Oxford University Press.

Squire, L. R. and S. Zola-Morgan (1991) "The medial temporal lobe memory system", *Science*, 253.

Stiles, D. (1994) "On evolutionary ecology and cultural realities", *Current Anthropology*, 35.4.

Strawson, P. (1950) "On referring", *Mind*, 59.

Strawson, P. (1964) "Identifying reference and truth-values", *Theoria*, XXX.

Sun Tsu, *The Art of War*, tr. by S. B. Griffith, in McNeilley (2001).

Sweetser, E. (1991) *From etymology to Pragmatics: Metaphorical and Cultural Aspects of Semantic Structure*, Cambridge: Cambridge University Press.

Swinney, D. A. (1979) "Lexical access during sentence comprehension: (Re)consideration of context effects", *J. V. L. V. B.*, 18.

Syder, F. and A. Pawley (1974) "The reduction principle in conversation", Auckland University, Auckland, New Zealand (ms).

Tabbossi, P. (1988) "Accessing lexical ambiguity in different sentence contexts", *J. of Memory and Language*, 324–40.

Tannenhaus, M. K., J. M. Leiman and M. S. Seidenberg (1979) "Evidence for multiple stages in the processing of ambiguous words in syntactic contexts", *J. V. L. V. B.*, 18.

Terrace, H. S. (1985) "In the beginning there was the "name"", *American Psychologist*, 40.

Thompson, S. (1985) "Grammar and written discourse: Initial vs. final purpose clauses in English", in T. Givón (ed. 1985).

Thornton, I.M. and D. Fernández-Duque (1999) "An implicit measure of undetected change", TR no. 99–02, Institute of Cognitive and Decision Sciences, University of Oregon.

Tomasello, M. (1996) "Do apes ape?", in C.M. Heyes and B.G. Galef (eds) *Social Learning: The Roots of Culture*, New York: Academic Press.

Tomasello, M. and J. Call (1997) *Primate Cognition*, Oxford and New York: Oxford University Press.

Tomlin, R. (ed. 1987) (ed.) *Coherence and Grounding in Discourse*, TSL 11, Amsterdam: J. Benjamins.

Tomlin, R. (1995) "Focal attention, voice and word order", in P. Downing and M. Noonan (eds) *Word Order in Discourse*, TSL #30, Amsterdam: J. Benjamins.

Tomlin, R. (1997) "Mapping conceptual representation into linguistic representation: The role of attention in grammar", in J. Nuyts and E. Pederson (eds) *Language and Conceptualization*, Cambridge: Cambridge University Press.

Trabasso, T. and P. van den Broek (1985) "Causal thinking and the representation of narrative events", *J. of Memory and Language*, 24.

Traugott, E.C. and B. Heine (eds 1991) *Approaches to Grammaticalization* (2 vols), Amsterdam: J. Benjamins.

Treisman, A. (1995) "Object tokens, attention and visual memory", *Attneave Memorial Lecture*, University of Oregon, Eugene, April 1995.

Treisman, A.M. and B. DeSchepper (1996) "Object tokens, attention and visual memory", in T. Inui and J. McClelland (eds) *Attention and Performance XVI: Information Integration in Perception and Communication*, Cambridge: MIT Press.

Treisman, A.M. and N.G. Kanwisher (1998) "Perceiving visually presented objects: Recognition, awareness, and modularity", *Current Opinion in Neurobiology*, 8:218–26.

Tsuchihashi, M. (1983) "The speech-act continuum: An investigation of Japanese sentence-final particles", *J. of Pragmatics*, 7.4.

Tucker, D.M. (1991) "Developing emotions and cortical networks", in M. Gunnar and C. Nelson (eds), *Developmental Neuroscience, Minnesota Symposium on Child Psychology*, vol. 24, Hillsdale, NJ: Erlbaum.

Tucker, D.M. (2002) "Embodied meaning: An evolutionary-developmental analysis of adaptive semantics", in T. Givón and B.F. Malle (eds 2002).

Turing, A.M. (1950) "Computing machinery and intelligence", *Mind*, 59.

Turnbull, C.M. (1968) "Contemporary societies: The hunters," in D.L. Sills (ed.) *International Encyclopedia of the Social Sciences*, Vol. 7, pp. 21–6. New York: Macmillan.

Tversky, A. and D. Kahneman (1974) "Judgement under uncertainty: Heuristics and biases", *Science*, 185: 1124–1131.

Tweedale, M. (1986) "How to handle problems about forms and universals in Aristotle's work", Auckland University, NZ (ms).

Ungerleider, L.A. and M. Mishkin (1982) "Two cortical visual systems", in D.G. Ingle, M.A. Goodale and R.J.Q. Mansfield (eds) *Analysis of Visual Behavior*, Cambridge: MIT Press.

van Dijk, T.A. and W. Kintsch (1983) *Strategies of Discourse Comprehension*, New York: Academic Press.

van Petten, C. and M. Kutas (1987) "Ambiguous words in context: An event related potential analysis of the time course of meaning activation", *J. of Memory and Language*, 26.

van Veen, V., J.D. Cohen, M.M. Botvinick, V.A. Stenger and C.S. Carter (2001) "Anterior cingulate cortex, conflict monitoring, and levels of processing", *Neuroimage*, 14.6:1302–1308.

Volkmar, F. R., A. Klin, R. Schultz, R. Bronen, W. D. Marans, S. Sparrow and D. J. Cohen (1996) "Asperger syndrom", *J. of the American Academy of Child and Adolescent Psychiatry*, 35.1:118–23.

Walker, C. H. and F. R. Yekovich (1987) "Activation and use of script-based antecedents in anaphoric reference", *J. of Memory and Language*, 26.

Wallace, A. F. C. (1961) *Culture and Personality*, New York: Random House.

Walzer, R. and M. Frede (tr. and eds 1985) *Galen: Three Treatises on the Nature of Science*, Indianapolis: Hackett.

Wang, K., J. Fan, Y. Dong, C.–Q. Wang and M. I. Posner (2004) "Selective impairment of executive attention in schizophrenia", Dept. of Psychology, University of Oregon (ms).

Wellman, H. (1990) *Children's Theories of Mind*, Cambridge: MIT Press.

Whiten, A. (1991) (ed.) *Natural Theories of Mind*, Oxford: Blackwell.

Whiten, A. (1997) "The Machiavellian mindreader", in A. Whiten and R. Byrne (eds 1997).

Whiten, A. and R. W. Byrne (eds 1997) *Machiavellian Intelligence II*, Cambridge: Cambridge University Press.

Whiting, W. C., R. F. Zernicke, T. M. McLaughlin and R. J. Gregor (1980) "The recognition and correlation of human movement patterns", *J. of Biomechanics*, 13.

Whorf, B. L. (1950) "An American Indian model of the universe", *I. J. A. L.*, 16.

Whorf, B. L. (1956) *Language, Thought and Reality: Collected Writings*, ed. by J. B. Carroll, Cambridge, Mass.: MIT Press.

Williams, B. (1994) "Cratylus theory of names and its refutation", in S. Everson (ed. 1994).

Winograd, T. (1970) *A Computer Program for Understanding Natural Language*, PhD dissertation, Dept. of Mathematics, MIT.

Wisdom, J. (1956) *Other Minds*, Oxford: Blackwell (2nd edition).

Wise, F. (1984) "Word order and referential distance: A study of Spanish first-language acquisition", University of Oregon, Eugene (ms).

Wittgenstein, L. (1918) *Tractatus Logico Philosophicus*, tr. by D. F. Pears and B. F. McGuinness, New York: The Humanities Press.

Wittgenstein, L. (1953) *Philosophical Investigations*, New York: MacMillan.

Woodburn, J. (1982) "Egalitarian societies", *Man*, 17.3.

Woodruff, P. (1982) *Plato, Hippias Major*, Indianapolis: Hackett Publishing Co.

Wright, A. and T. Givón (1987) "The pragmatics of indefinite reference", *Studies in Language*, 11.

Yekovich, F. R. and C. H. Walker (1986) "The activation and use of scripted knowledge in reading about routine activities", in B. K. Britton (ed.) *Executive Control Processes in Reading*, Hillsdale, NJ: Erlbaum.

Zipf, G. (1935/1965) *The Psychobiology of Language*, Cambridge, Mass.: MIT Press.

Index

A

abduction 205, 206, 207, 208
abductive inference 11, 21, 26, 91, 196, 205, 215
abductive reasoning 52, 73
abductory induction 208
accessability 70
activation 134
adaptation 50
adaptive compromise 39, 222, 249
adaptive context 54, 120
adaptive function (of grammar) 96, 97
adaptive middle 46
adaptive motivation 86
adaptive realism 239
adaptive utility 193
adverbial clause(s) 152, 153, 164, 180, 182
adversary (context) 250, 254
affective representation 103
agency 211, 212
agent 221, 226
agrammatical aphasia 99
Aksu, A. 169
Amacker, R. 254
Ambady, N. 222, 223
amygdala 93, 94
Anabasis 123
analogical reasoning 11, 35, 73
analogy 8, 18, 72
anaphora 136
anaphoric (pronoun) 104, 139
anaphoric accessibility 140
anaphoric coherence 134
anaphoric devices 137
anaphoric distance 136
anaphoric grounding 126, 134, 135, 146, 147
anaphoric links 181
Andersen, R. 95, 97
Anderson, A. 102
antecedent co-referent 146
anterior-cingulate cortex 117, 230, 233, 234, 235, 236
Apology (Socrates) 106
apriori synthetic 24
Aristotelian tradition (metaphor) 72
Aristotle 4, 9, 10, 11, 12, 13, 17, 18, 19, 20, 21, 23, 29, 35, 39, 59, 72, 88, 128, 150, 179, 194, 195, 196, 205, 206, 208, 213, 221, 247, 250
aspect 156, 161
aspectual continuity 187
aspectual perspective 157
aspectuality 156, 181
Asperger (syndrom) 231, 234

associationist (explanation) 109
assertion 151
Atkinson, R. C. 66
atomic features 45
attended processing 49, 116
attention 92, 93, 94, 100, 125, 127, 134, 193, 222, 252, 253
attentional activation 133, 134, 143
Attneave, F. 12
Austin, J. 32, 104, 149
authority (deontics) 173
autism 231, 234
automated processing 49, 116
automatic activation 70, 79, 111
automaticity 107, 252
automation 253

B

Bach, E. 199
Baddeley, A. 93, 107
Barker, M. 106, 107, 120, 122, 141, 146
Baron-Cohen, D. 109, 119, 231
Barkow, J. H. 214
Barthelme, D. 160
Basso, K. 62
Bates, E. 115, 121
behaviorism 202
behaviorist(s) 23
Bickerton, D. 95, 97, 98, 99, 121
biological evolution 59
biologically-based representation 40
Bloom, L. 95, 97, 122
Bloomfield, L. 30, 120, 202
Blumstein, S. E. 100
Bolinger, D. 32
Borderline Personality Disorder 229
Bowerman, M. 95, 97
Broca's aphasia 99
Broca's area 96
Bryson, S. E. 233
Bybee, J. 82, 96, 115, 149
Byrne, R. 109, 114, 214, 238

C

Cacciari, C. 72, 79, 80, 87
Call, J. 95, 109, 121, 122
camera angle 161
Carnap, R. 4, 36, 37, 88, 126, 128, 149, 150, 177, 197, 198, 201, 203, 220
Carpenter, P. 93
Carter, A. 115, 121, 122

Castañeda, C. 240, 241, 246
cataphoric continuity 181, 190
cataphoric discontinuity 198
cataphoric grounding 126, 135
cataphoric links 181
cataphoric persistence 132
cataphoric switch-reference 181, 191, 192
categorial clustering 136
categories 9, 39
categorization 59, 110
causal explanation 210, 211
causal inference 212
causality 210
causation 211
cause-reason (clauses) 182
central (members) 40
certainty 173, 176
Chafe, W. 32, 141
chain-final clause 180
chain-grounding clause 180
chain-initial clause 180, 181, 186
chain-medial clause 180, 181, 186, 191, 192
change 50
Chase, W. 48
chi 240, 252, 253
Chi Kung 240
child pidgin 97
Choi Lai Fut 252
Chomsky, N. 4, 43, 45, 64, 79, 88, 96, 198, 199, 200
chunking 48
classification 9
clause(s) 67, 180
clause-chain(s) 182
clause-chaining 179, 180, 191, 193, 194
clause-types 180
clustering (around the mean) 46, 49
Coates, J. 149
Cocciarella, N. 149, 153
coding devices (grammar) 95
cognition 7, 116
cognitive continuity 189
Cognitive Dissonance Theory 237
cognitive interpretation (of grammar) 133
cognitive mapping 71
cognitive model 141
cognitive neuroscience 36, 220, 221
cognitive operations 143
cognitive psychology 35
cognitive representation (system) 65
cognitive science 36
coherence 67, 68, 125, 146, 179
coherence bridge(s) 182
coherence signals 180
coherence strands 179
Cole, P. 104
Collins, A, M. 69

communication 8, 63, 97, 219, 235
communicative behavior 120
communicative function (of grammar) 92
communicative goals 96
communicative isolation 57
community of scholars 196
community of science 216, 218
competence 14, 64, 79, 198
complex self 234
complexity 248
comprehension 126
concepts 65
conceptual lexicon 65, 81
conceptual innovation 88
conceptual metaphor(s) 75, 76, 77, 78, 79, 80, 81, 82
concessive (clauses) 182
consciousness 221
conditional (clause) 182
conditional asymmetries 210
conditional reasoning 53
conditionality 210
conflict resolution 229
Confucian code 248
conjunction(s) 188, 189, 190
conscious attention 222, 251
consciousness 110, 111, 118, 251
consecutive (tense/aspect) 154, 155
consensual leadership 58
constructivist(s) 25
context 1, 8, 14, 71, 72, 75, 100, 123, 209, 239, 250
context-dependent (categories) 26
context types 100
contextual framing 1
contextual freedom 75
contextual inference 82, 205
contextual judgement 1
contextual reasoning 205
contextual theory of multiple self 224
contextualization 209
continued activation 137, 143
continuity 250
contradiction 202
contradictory beliefs 227
contrary speech-act 174
contrast 190
contrastive focus 152
conventionalized idiom(s) 84
cooperation 63, 237
counter-expectation 190
counter-fact (clauses) 164, 182
criterial features 46
cross-clausal grammar 97
cross-propositional coherence 68
cultural evolution 59
cultural-pragmatic norms 173

cultural relativism 29
cultural uniformity 57
current discourse 147
current speech situation 153

D

Damassio, A. 230
d'Andrade, E. N. 202
Darwin, C. 35, 50
Dascal, M. 37
Dawkins, R. 214, 220
dead metaphor(s) 73, 74, 84, 88
de-alienation 61, 62
declarative (speech-acts) 105, 121, 172, 173
declarative clauses 162
declarative memory 66, 93, 197
deduction 197, 204, 207
deductive consequences 215
deductive explanation 208
deductive inference 196
deductive logic 5, 28
deductivism 207
deductivist(s) 195, 196, 214
deep structure 96
deferred relevance (aspect) 158
definite 102, 103, 104, 144, 145, 153
definite referents 102, 133
definiteness 70
deictic grounding 160
deixis 103
Democritus 19
denotation 127
deontic (modality) 162, 172
deontic judgement 149
deontic representation 113, 114
deontic speech-acts 171
deontic state(s) 104, 105, 106, 114, 146, 177, 193, 218, 239, 254
Descartes, R. 119
developmental pragmatics 34
dialecticians 15
dialectics 220
dialogic interaction 196
Diamond, J. 56, 60
Dickinson, C. 107
diffuse attention 252
Dik, S. 32
direct access (evidentiality) 170
directly witnessed (evidentiality) 170
discourse coherence 66, 67, 125, 179
discourse context 96
discourse-pragmatic function 97
discourse processing 92
discreteness 250
displaced reference 122
diversity 64
dominance hierarchies 57

dorso-lateral prefrontal cortex 117, 230, 233
DuBois, J. 139, 140
Dunbar, R. I. M. 108, 109
Duncan, S. 234
dynamic equilibrium 250, 251

E

Eddy, T. 109
eidon 22
Eisler-Goldman, F. 188
Eldredge, N. 110
Elster, J. 227
emergence 44
emergent grammar 44
Empedocles 19
empirical cycle 215
empirical science 203, 206
empiricism 23, 199
empiricist(s) 23, 37, 196, 201, 202
episodic memory 66, 92, 93, 94, 100, 103, 115, 121, 125, 127, 134, 137, 141, 143, 193, 197
episodic mental model 147
episodic recall 106
episodic storage 126
epistemic modality 104, 150, 162, 168, 172, 206
epistemic certainty 169
epistemic deference 173
epistemic judgement 149
epistemic negotiation 174
epistemic operators (grammar) 163, 174
epistemic representation 113, 114, 126
epistemic speech-acts 146
epistemic state(s) 104, 105, 106, 111, 114, 146, 177, 193, 218, 239, 254
epistemic strength 169
epistemology 195, 196, 198, 203
Ericsson, A. 66, 93, 95, 125
essence 22
essentialism 51, 52, 55
essentialist(s) 229
essentialist self (theory) 222
ethnography of speech 23
event cognition 254
event coherence 97
evidential devices (grammar) 175
evidential source 169
evidential strength 169
evidentiality 168, 171
evolution 50
evolutionary biology 35, 36, 214
evolutionary perspective 91, 108
evolutionary precursors 110, 113
evolutionary psychology 214
excluded middle (law of) 44
executive attention 111, 118
existential-presentative (construction) 132

existential quantifier 128
explanation 11, 205, 206
explicit mental models 107
experiential activation 87
explanatory imperative 212

F
fact(s) 196, 203
fact (modality) 128, 129
factive verbs 152, 153
factual truth (modality) 150
falsifiability 202
falsification 207, 216, 217, 219
family resemblance 42, 43
Faust 227
feature association 46, 52, 59, 91, 236
felicity conditions 104
Fernández-Duque, D. 94, 107
Festinger, L. 237
Feyerabend, P. 220
figurative language 84, 86
figure-ground 11, 35, 40, 91
Fleischman, S. 149
Fodor, J. A. 64
Foe, S. 254
foraging economy 57
form 246, 247
formal pragmatics 37
fossilization 247
Foucault, M. 220
Fouts, R. 95
frame-based (definite) referents 102
framing 1, 234
framing complexity 234
frequency 11, 139
frequency distribution 27, 42, 43, 47, 86
Fretheim, T. 237
Frith, U. 109, 221, 231, 232, 233
Freud, S. 227
Freudian self 228
function 11, 247
functional explanation 213
functionalism 19, 31, 214
Fundamental Attribution Error 223
future (tense) 161, 162
Futuyma, D. 50

G
Gallese, V. 114, 254
gapped evolution 110
Gardner, B. T. 95
Gardner, R. A. 95
Garrod, S. 102
Gathercole, P. 93, 94, 107
Gazdar, G. 13
Geertz, C. 30, 37
general classes 199

generative grammar 44
generativity 43
generic (cultural) knowledge 57, 58
generic mental categories 111
generic-lexical networks 125
generic lexicon 69
Gentilucci, M. 114
Gernsbacher, M. A. 66, 93, 96, 107, 108, 125, 126,
    132, 146
Gibbs, R. 72, 79, 80
Gladwell, M. 222, 223, 229
global coherence 146, 194
globally accessible referents 102
Glucksberg, S. 72, 79, 80, 87
Goedel's Theorem 3
Goethe, J. W. 227
Goffman, E. 62, 224, 225, 226, 228, 229, 235, 237
Goodale, M. A. 93, 254
Goodman, P. 220
Gopnik, A. 108
Gordon, R. M. 109, 123
Gould, S. J. 110, 117, 214, 220
gradual change 18
graded membership 46
grammar 69, 91, 92, 95, 96, 100, 108, 121, 135,
    144, 145, 171, 179, 194, 200
grammatical code 96
grammatical communication 100
grammatical cues 134, 144, 145
grammatical devices 180
grammatical morphology 95
grammatical object 140
grammatical relations 96
grammatical subject 140, 141
grammatical systems 97
grammaticalization 73, 81
grammaticalized language 125
Gray, R. D. 214
Greenfield, P. 96
Grice, H. P. 32, 104, 149, 172
Grimes, J. 125
group size 56
grounding 102, 103, 126, 134, 146, 181, 182
grounding operations 143

H
Haberland, H. 171
habitual (tense/aspect) 161
Haiman, J. 99
Hale, K. 191, 192
Halliday, M. A. K. 32, 125
Hanson, R. N. 195, 196, 203, 204, 205, 206, 207,
    210, 211, 215
Hassan, R. 125
Hauser, M. 95
Hayashi, L. 189, 190
hazardous information principle 176

hearer's attitude 149
hearer's belief 150
hearer's intention 150
heightened affect (subjunctive) 166
Heine, B. 81,82,96,115
Hempel, C. 213
Heraclitus 15
Heyes, C. M. 109,123
hierarchic structure 60
hippocampus 93,94,117,231
historical present (tense/aspect) 159
Ho'o, M. 239,240,254
Hopper, P. 44,45,96,115
Hsin Yi 251
Hubel, D. 116
human communication 120,143
Humboldt, W. Von 29
Humphreys, G. W. 93
hunters-and-gatherers (societies) 56
hunting-and-gathering 57
hypothesis 205,215,218
hypothetical deduction 37
hypothetical reasoning 52
Hypothetico-Deductive Model 201

I
Ibsen, H. 224,237
iconic 99
idealization 4,64
idiomatic sense 85
idiom(s) 73,84
immediacy (tense/aspect) 159
immediate (tense/aspect) 156
impaired self 228
imperative (speech-act) 172
imperfective (aspect) 156,157,161,182
implicatures 7
importance 8
incrementation of knowledge 219
indefinite 103,131,132,133,144,145,153
induction 198,202,204,207,208
inductive inference 196,215
inductive testing 215,219
inductivism 198
inductivist(s) 195,200
inference 82
informational homogeneity 57
informational predictability 58
Inn, M. 254
innate essence(s) 23,41
intensional logic 7
intentional (deontic) states 111
intentionality 211
interpretant 26
interrogative (speech-acts) 105,172,173
intonation 95,188
intonational breaks 188

irrealis (assertion, modality) 129,130,150,151,
    161,162,164,169
irrelevance 107
islands of intimacy 61
isomorphism 247
Itkonen, E. 195

J
James, W. 225,237
Jespersen, O. 32,36,45
Johnson, M. 9,72,75,88
Just, M. 93

K
Kaas, J. 113
Kahneman, D. 53,223,254
Kant, I. 6,22,24,25,32,37,82,195,204
karma 241
Katz, J. 14,64
Kaufmann, W. 227,237
Kelly, J. P. 112
Keysar, B. 87
Kilpatrick, S. D. 238
Kintsch, W. 66,93,107,125,126,193
Klein, R. N. 229,230
Kuhn, T. 196,216,217,218
Kung Fu 251,252

L
Lakatos, I. 196,217,218
Lakoff, G. 9,64,72,75,76,88
L'Amour, L. 137,184
Landry, R. 233
Langacker, R. 92
Lao Tse 16,245,248,254
Lee, H. 252
Lees, R. B. 200
left-dislocation 180,185
Leibnitz 37
Leslie, A. 109,123
Levinson, S. 14,36,104
Lewis, D. 32,174,176
lexical phonology 100
lexicon 65,69,91,179
Li, C. N. 121
Lieberman, P. 95,100
limbic system 112
limbus 112
Linde, C. 70
linguistic relativity 30
literal usage 40
literal sense 84,85,86
live metaphor 85
Lo, P. 254
local coherence 146
Loftus, E. E. 66,69,107
logical categories 41

logical closure 217
logical consequences 215, 219
logical modalities 128
logical positivist(s) 9, 10, 23
logical presupposition 32
logical propositions 202
Longacre, R. 125
long-distance anaphoric devices 137
lower-certainty (subjunctive) 163
Lysaker, P. H. 229

M
Machiavellian intelligence 239
Machiavellian mind-reader 239
MacWhinney, B. 97
Malle, B. 108
manipulative speech-act(s) 105, 115, 162, 172
markedness 11, 139, 143, 157, 161, 192
martial arts 239, 254
Martin, J. H. 112
mass communication 61
Mayr, E. 9, 50, 51, 52, 59, 62, 88
McNeilly, M. 184
mean, doctrine of the 18
mega-modularity 110
Meltzoff, A. 108, 114, 235
Meno 41, 106
mental maps (generic) 65
mentalism 29
mental connectivity 134
mental models 92, 106, 107, 110, 113
mental operations 125, 144, 145
mental representation (of context) 100
Mesulam, M.-M. 93, 112, 113, 117, 118
metaphor(s) 8, 18, 40, 73, 81
metaphoric behavior 72, 77, 88
metaphoric language 65
metaphoric meaning 70, 72
metaphoric sense 85
Meyer, D. E. 69, 70
Milberg, W. 100
Milner, A. D. 254
mind-framing 232
Mishkin, M. 93, 115, 116
modal adverbs 162
modal auxiliaries 162, 187
modal logic 33
modality 149, 161, 172, 173, 181
mode(s) of inference 206, 207
mode(s) of processing 49
modesty 176
modularity 110
modus ponens 53
modus tolens 207, 216
motor performance 254
multiculturalism 64
multi-participant conversation 147

multi-propositional coherence 122
multi-propositional discourse 66, 67, 122
multiple self (theory) 224, 227
Montague, R. 33, 147, 149, 153
Morgan, J. 104
morphology 95
Morris, C. 13
mystics 15

N
narrator's voice 181, 194
natural categorization 51
natural communication 173
natural kinds 51
natural types 46, 47
necessary truth 150
Neeley, J. H. 70
NEG-assertion (modality) 129, 150, 151, 166, 167, 168, 174
negation 131, 174
neo-cortex 112
neo-cortical (motor-sensory 'shell') 112
network(s) 65, 69, 81, 125
neutralization 244, 245
Newton, I. 202
Nietsche, F. 237
node-activation 71
nominal predicate(s) 130
nominal referent(s) 142
non-contradiction (law of) 44
non-discrete (categories) 26
non-discreteness 12, 18
non-fact assertion 129
non-fact modality 128, 131
non-finite 192
non-human communication 115
non-human primates 109
non-literal meaning 70, 72, 75
non-referring 128, 130, 131, 153
non-topical 144, 145
non-truth (modality) 150, 151
novelty 87
nuclei of intimacy 61

O
objectivism 3, 30
obligation(s) 150
obsolete sense 86
old-brain 112
Oppenheim, P. 213
Ordinary Language Philosophy 27, 32
Ortonyi, A. 87
organized science 195
other minds 6, 91, 108, 110, 113, 120, 177, 193, 195, 216, 236
outlier (members) 39
over-generalization 53

P
Pa Kua 251
Palmer, F. 149
paradigm 216,218
paradox(es) 243,245,248,249,250,251,252,
   253
paragraph(s) 180
Park, R.E. 225,237
partial automation 100
participial (clauses) 182,192
particular statements 200
Paul, H. 29,31,36,92,203
Pawley, A. 174,176
Pearson, T.R. 174,175
Peer Gynt 224,237
Peirce, C.S. 6,11,13,15,26,27,195,199,206,
   207,208,215
Pepperberg, I. 95,120,121,123
perception 116
Percy, W. 73,88
perfect (aspect) 154,156,158,161
perfective 156,157,158,161,182
performance 14,79,198
perspective 1,194,232
perspective effects 54
perspective-shifting 97, 122
Petri, H.L. 115
philosophy of science 196,200
phonological continuity 189
phonological word(s) 120
pidgin communication 95,99,100,125
Plato 4,9,12,17,22,23,29,39,41,171,195,250
Platonic categories 28,41,42,45,47,48
Platonic essentialism 62
Platonism 56
pluperfect (aspect) 152
politeness 174,176
polysemy 71,85
Popper, K. 195,196,197,198,199,200,201,203,
   207,208,210,212,215,216,220
positivist(s) 202,214
Posner, M. 35,88,93,117,118,229,230,233,
   234,254
possible truth (modality) 150,151
possible worlds (semantics, pragmatics) 33,147
posterior-parietal cortex 117,230,231,233,234,
   236
Povinelli, D. 108,109,119
power (deontics) 173
Power, M. 58
pragmatic approach (metaphor) 73
pragmatic framing 234
pragmatic freedom 75
pragmatic inference 216
pragmatic judgement 216
pragmatic middle-ground 39,195
pragmatic reasoning 205

pragmatics 14,75,166,167,195,203,221,239
pre-adaptation(s) 110
pre-grammatical communication 95,100,122,
   125
pre-grammatical discourse 99
pre-grammatical pidgin 97
pre-human communication 122,125
Premack, D. 95,108,109,114,115,120,123
pre-initial clause(s) 179, 182
present-perfect (tense/aspect) 159
pre-Socratic (philosophers) 15,171
presumptive meaning 7
presupposition 7,32, 129,130,150,151,169
preterit (tense/aspect) 156,158
Preuss, T.M. 108,109,119
primitive representations 113
private meaning 30
private self 228
procedural memory 92,197
profiling 55
progressive (aspect) 154
pronoun(s) 104,136
propositional information 66,67
propositional modalities 128,147,177
propositional semantics 96
proposition(s) 149
prototype (high-frequency) 70
prototype-based categories 46,51
prototype node-clusters 111
prototype-like categories 47,236
prototype nodes 71
prototype(s) 35,39,46,84
proximate (deixis) 160
public self 228
purpose 11,204,247
purpose clauses 183

Q
quantum mechanics 6
Quattrone, G.A. 228
Quillian, M.R. 46,69
Quine, W.van O. 120,128,198

R
radial categories 64
Ramsay, V. 183
rationalism 23,199
rationalist(s) 22,23,196
realis (assertion) 150,151,161,169,174
realis (modality) 115
reasoning by feature association 52,59,91,103,
   111,212,223
reductionism 6,22,198
reductionist(s) 196
reference 126,128,129,130
referent (of consciousness) 113
referential coherence 97,125,135,144,145

referential continuity 135, 136, 188, 191
referential discontinuity 136, 189
referential intent 127, 128, 130
referring 128, 130, 131
Reh, M. 82
relativism 6
Relativity (Theory) 6
relevance 8, 147, 204, 219, 232, 239
remote (tense/aspect) 156, 159, 160, 161
representation systems 113
Research Programme 217
restrictive relative clause 104, 152, 153
rhythmic-hierarchic structure 48
rhythmics 95
Ricoeur, P. 31
Riddoch, J. M. 93
Ristau, C. 120
rituals of de-alienation 62
Rizzolatti, G. 114, 254
Rohrty, R. 220
Ross, J. R. 209
Rothbart, M. 50, 51, 55, 63
Rude, N. 192
Russell, B. 2, 5, 28, 32, 37, 118, 126, 128, 177, 200,
    201, 249
Russell's paradox 2, 36, 177

S
Sadalla, E. 237
saliency 11
Sanford, A. 102
Sapir, E. 30, 45, 202
Sapir-Whorf Hypothesis 30
Saussure, F. De 4
Savage-Rumbaugh, S. 95, 121, 122
scala naturae 10
Schneider, W. 93, 117, 231, 234, 254
Schuman, J. 95, 97
Schwaneveldt, R. W. 69, 70
science 195
Scollon, R. 122
Scott, D. 149, 153
Scriven, M. 209
search operations 143
Searle, J. 32, 104, 149
second-language pidgin 97
selective attention 35
selectivity (of mental models) 106
self 221, 222, 224, 226, 227, 236
self-consciousness 110, 117, 221
self-deception 227, 237
self-inclusion (paradoxes) 177
self-presentation 235
self-representation 235, 236, 237
Selinker, L. 95, 97
semantic bleaching 82
semantic change 88

semantic memory 66, 91, 92, 94, 100, 120, 197
semantic network(s) 65, 84
semantic priming 35, 69
semantics 75, 167
semiotic relation 12
semiotics 26
sensory-motor codes 69
sensory representation 113
sequential (tense/aspect) 157, 158
sequential order 95
Shallice, T. 93, 94
Shapiro, M. 13
Shaolin (boxing) 251
shared cultural perspective 62
shared current discourse 103
shared knowledge 235
shared speech-situation 102
Shiffrin, R. M. 66, 254
similarity 8, 9, 18, 72
Simon, H. 48
simultaneous (tense/aspect) 157, 158
situational inferences 99
situational (shared) knowledge 58
skilled performance 106
Slobin, D. 169
Smith, E. E. 45
social categories 51, 55
social cooperation 120, 235
social deontics 173
social pragmatics (science) 216
social primates 60
social restraint 236, 237
sociality 237
society of intimates 56, 60, 61, 63, 177, 223, 235,
    237
society of strangers 56, 60, 61
sociology of science 216
Socrates 17, 22, 23, 41, 106
somatic representation 113
soul 10, 20
spatio-temporal reference 122
speaker's attitude 149
speciation 62
speech act(s) 104, 105, 106, 171, 172, 181
Sperber, D. 13, 232
Spitzer, M. 69, 70
spreading activation 69
Squire, L. 66, 93, 115
status (deontics) 173
stereotyping 49, 51
Stiles, D. 58
Strawson, P. 32, 126
structuralism 214
structuralist(s) 23
sub-consciousness 252
subject pronoun(s) 139
subjective certainty 176

subjunctive (mood) 162, 163, 164, 165, 166
subordinate clause(s) 182
Sun Tsu 244, 246
Sweetzer, E. 82
Swinney, D. A. 70, 120
switch-reference 137, 181, 191
Syder, F. 174, 176
synolon 18
syntactic innovation 73
syntax 92

T

Tai Chi Chuan 239, 240, 242, 244, 243, 245, 248,
     249, 250, 251, 252, 253, 254
Tao 242, 243
Tao Teh Ching 16, 242, 243, 245, 247, 248, 249,
     254
Taoism 16
Taoist metaphysics 242
tautology 168, 202
taxonomic boundaries 10
taxonomies 59
taxonomy 9, 59
Taylor, M. 51, 52, 55, 63
teleology 11, 221
temporal deixis 154
temporal grounding 154
temporal links 182
temporal perspective 155
temporality 181, 210
tense 153, 154
terminated activation 137, 143
Terrace, H. 95
testability 219
text 125, 145
thalamus 117
thematic continuity 182
thematic orientation 154
theories 196
Theories of Mind 7, 109, 119, 120, 232
Theory of Mind 7, 109, 119, 120
Theory of Types 2, 28, 118, 249
Thompson, S. 183
Tomasello, M. 95, 109, 121, 122
Tomlin, R. 133, 146
topical 144, 145
topicality 130, 133, 147
topical entities 143
topical referent 141, 181
Trabasso, T. 125
traditional music 179
Transcendental Schema 25
transformations of referent 113
Traugott, E. 96, 115
Treisman, A. 93, 94, 107, 120
truth 126, 173, 175

truth-conditional logic 177
Tsuchihashi, M. 174
Tucker, D. 93, 112, 113, 117
Turner, M. 75
Tversky, A. 53, 223, 228

U
Ungerleider, L. 115
universal quantifier 128
universal statements 200
universe of discourse 127, 128, 147
usage frequency 84, 139, 193

V
vagueness 27
van Dijk, T. 66, 93, 107, 125, 126
verbal complements 152, 153
visceral representation 113
visual sketch-pad 94
vivid (aspect) 159, 160
vocabulary-cued processing 99

W
warrior 240
Way of the Warrior 240, 241
weak manipulation (subjunctive) 165
Wellman, H. 108
Whiten, A. 108, 109, 214
Whorf, B. L. 30
Wilson, D. 13, 232
Winograd, T. 34
Wisdom, J. 6, 7
Wittgenstein, L. 5, 6, 9, 24, 28, 30, 42, 43, 198,
     199, 202, 208, 210, 220
Wittgensteinean (categories) 42, 46, 48, 64
Woodruff, G. 108, 109, 114, 115, 120, 123
word association 70
working memory 92, 93, 94, 100, 106, 125, 134,
     145, 193
Wright, S. 131, 141
Wu-Wei 242, 243, 244, 245

X
Xenophon 123

Y
Yang Jen-Fu 254
Yang, L. 82
Yin-Yang 16, 249, 251
yoga 246
Young, P. 64, 223

Z
zero anaphora 136
Zipf, G. 12, 139
Zola-Morgan, S. 115